Judging Free Speech

Judging Free Speech

First Amendment Jurisprudence of US Supreme Court Justices

Edited by

Helen J. Knowles and
Steven B. Lichtman

palgrave
macmillan

JUDGING FREE SPEECH

First published in 2015 by PALGRAVE MACMILLAN® in the United States—a division of St. Martin's Press LLC, 175 Fifth Avenue, New York, NY 10010.

Where this book is distributed in the UK, Europe and the rest of the world, this is by Palgrave Macmillan, a division of Macmillan Publishers Limited, registered in England, company number 785998, of Houndmills, Basingstoke, Hampshire RG21 6XS.

Palgrave Macmillan is the global academic imprint of the above companies and has companies and representatives throughout the world.

HC ISBN: 978-1-137-43491-3
PBK ISBN: 978-1-137-43490-6

Library of Congress Cataloging-in-Publication Data

Judging free speech : First Amendment jurisprudence of US Supreme Court Justices / edited by Helen J. Knowles, Steven B. Lichtman.
pages cm
Includes bibliographical references and index.
ISBN 978-1-137-43491-3 (hardback)
1. Freedom of speech—United States. 2. United States. Constitution. 1st Amendment. 3. Judges—United States. 4. United States. Supreme Court—Officials and employees. I. Knowles, Helen J., 1973– editor. II. Lichtman, Steven B., editor.
KF9345.J83 2015
342.7308'53—dc23 2015009618

A catalogue record of the book is available from the British Library.

Design by SPi Global.

First edition: September 2015

10 9 8 7 6 5 4 3 2 1

Contents

Acknowledgments

This book was borne out of a 2012 unsolicited email, the type of email that a junior scholar is never disappointed to receive. "Are you working on anything that has the potential to be a book project which Palgrave Macmillan would be interested in publishing?" Or words to that effect. This was followed by a phone conversation with Scarlet Neath, during which Helen pitched the proposal that would become the book you are now reading. In short, the project was not a difficult sell. This is partly because during that conversation Helen confidently informed Scarlet that the project would have the benefit of two *co*-editors. "It is only a matter of asking the co-editor I have in mind; I 'know' he will never turn me down." Or words to that effect. After that phone call ended, a few minutes went by as an email was composed to that first choice, Helen's good friend and colleague Steven Lichtman. As you can see, he did not turn her down. In his typically inimitable and restrained manner, Steven responded by saying: "project sounds wicked cool . . . can I also write the chapter on Thomas?" Had Steven not sent that positive reply, this project would have been shelved; there was no second editorial choice.

Throughout the life of this project, the two of us have benefited from the assistance, input, and wisdom of numerous individuals. At Palgrave, we first worked with Scarlet and then with Brian O'Connor and Elaine Fan, all of whom did a masterful job helping two first-time book editors get their manuscript to and over the finish line. That goal would not have been achieved without the assistance of two very talented and hard-working individuals. After engaging us in extremely useful conversations about free speech jurisprudence—especially about the Roberts Court—Brandon Metroka worked tirelessly to proofread and citation-check the entire manuscript. In so doing, he built upon the work of Elena Veatch (Skidmore College, '16). During her two years as a member of the faculty at Skidmore, Helen had the privilege of teaching several courses in which Elena excelled as a student. Since July 2014, when she was hired as the principal research assistant for *Judging Free Speech*, Elena has been as much a part of this project as have the co-editors, who are both exceptionally grateful to her for the incredible amount of time and effort that she cheerfully devoted to the laborious research tasks assigned to her. Together, Brandon and Elena pointed out numerous important errors, sparing the co-editors some major embarrassment. Of course, Helen and Steven remain responsible for the inevitable occasions where they have gone astray.

The co-editors' expression of gratitude also extends to the Government Department at Skidmore for providing the funding to hire Elena. Beyond the Government Department, a debt of gratitude is also owed Skidmore for awarding Helen a Faculty Development Grant to hire Ginger Kimler, who did a Herculean job copyediting the final manuscript before it was submitted to Palgrave.

Of course, this project would not be what it is, nor would it have been a true labor of love upon which Steven and Helen never tired of working, were it not for the fantastic contributors, to whom a very special expression of thanks must go. Helen and Steven are also very grateful to the following people who, at various stages of the project, provided them with invaluable advice and/or engaged them in equally invaluable dialogues about expressive freedom: Bill Blazek, Christian Castaing, Christopher Ericson, Roy Ginsberg, Mark Graber, Andrew Lowy, Kirstin Mishkin, Steve Rosow, Ron Seyb, Mark Silverstein, Steve Wasby, and the individuals who served as the anonymous reviewers for the book proposal submitted to Palgrave.

Very special expressions of thanks are due the co-editors' colleagues and students at Skidmore College and Shippensburg University—this project benefited from their wisdom and spirit.

We also wish to thank our colleagues and friends who frequent the annual meeting of the New England Political Science Association. Over the years, NEPSA has been a joyously collegial source of inspiration and counsel for both of us, and it is our fervent hope that this project lives up to the standard of excellence that NEPSA sets.

A particular expression of gratitude goes to our cover artist, Arthur Lien, who responded to our cold-call inquiry about the availability of the cover image with magnanimity and grace.

Last, but by no means least, are the friends and family members to whom we wish to say a huge "thank you."

Helen extends her thanks to her mother, Rae, for her undying love and support, and to Toffee the cat and Doc the horse for making a concerted effort to prevent her from going insane. She is also very grateful to Craig, Linda, and Justin Warkentin, her Thanksgiving 2014 hosts, for giving her the time and space she needed to spend incalculable hours of the holiday working on the final throes of the manuscript.

Steven extends his gratitude to his parents, Joyce and Phil, for being there every step of the way and for showing him what real strength is; to Lynn, for turning the lights back on; and to Cosmo, for making a concerted effort to get cat hair all over his laptop.

HJK, Fayetteville, NY
SBL, Frederick, MD

Introduction: Oh What a Tangled Web They Weave

Helen J. Knowles and
Steven B. Lichtman

Appearances can be very deceptive. The Free Speech Clause of the First Amendment to the US Constitution is linguistically straightforward and, at first glance, there appears to be no room for multiple interpretations. As Justice Hugo L. Black famously declared in 1959, "I read 'no law abridging . . .' to mean *no law abridging*."[1] However, even Black, one of the Supreme Court's staunchest defenders of free speech, was not a true First Amendment absolutist, because on several occasions he supported governmental abridgment of that freedom. He was, one might say, a "qualified absolutist."[2] For example, in *United States v. O'Brien* (1968) Black joined six of his colleagues in holding that David Paul O'Brien had no constitutionally protected right to burn his draft card on the steps of the South Boston Courthouse to protest the Vietnam War. Similarly, in *Adderley v. Florida* (1966) he refused to view expressive *conduct* as constitutionally protected *speech*. Black wrote the majority opinion upholding the convictions of a group of individuals who violated a state trespass law by assembling in the driveway of a county jail and protesting that institution's incarceration policies (which included racial segregation).[3] Ultimately, Black was no different from any other justice; a jurist who frowned upon any and all governmental efforts to suppress speech has never graced the Supreme Court's bench.

This does not mean that there is disagreement about the sanctity of free expression and its crucial importance in a democracy. Indeed, "[c]onsensus about the connection between free speech and democracy may be the single unifying free speech theme throughout American history."[4] However, commentators and judges alike have offered myriad competing theories about how to define and best protect the speech-democracy "connection"; and, the application of those theories in cases has been subject to the ebb and flow of different coalitions of justices on the Court. The result is a veritable crazy quilt of First Amendment decisions that can present particularly pressing interpretive challenges.

TAKING OPINIONS SERIOUSLY, BECAUSE "VOTING IS ONE THING AND EXPRESSING VIEWS IN SUPPORT OF A VOTE QUITE ANOTHER"[5]

There are, of course, various ways to analyze Supreme Court decisions, including those addressing freedom of speech. Scholars working within the law and courts subfield of political science have taken many different methodological approaches to analyzing judicial behavior and created various models for explaining the set of processes that constitute judicial decision making. These bodies of literature, the strengths and weaknesses of which are well documented elsewhere, play important roles in informing our understanding of the different participants in the legal system and the forces that constrain and shape their interactions.[6]

In this book, however, we take our cue from the pioneering law and courts scholar C. Herman Pritchett, who once felt it necessary to admonish members of his profession to remember that while "[p]olitical scientists . . . have done so much to put the 'political' in 'political jurisprudence' [they] need to emphasize that it is still 'jurisprudence.'"[7] In other words, while there is much to be learned from studying how individual justices vote, this volume is dedicated to the idea that the opinions themselves matter, and they matter a great deal. Analysis of the opinions fills an important need, because it is in the justices' opinions that we find their public explanations and reasoning for their decisions—explanations and reasoning that lawyers and judges will draw upon in subsequent cases.

To be sure, there is often a divide between "political scientists" who emphasize votes and "legal researchers" who focus on the language of opinions.[8] But where many political scientists dismiss the opinions as little more than florid decoration of—or cover for—individual justices' ideological preferences or political predilections, the authors of the chapters in this volume share our methodological belief in the virtues of unpacking free speech jurisprudence using a qualitative approach.

There is another related idea at the core of this book. Even as we stress that opinions matter, we must also remember that opinions do not descend immaculately from a clear blue sky. Opinions are written by people, and those opinions will reflect the philosophical perspectives of the people who write them. There is much to be gained by studying the jurisprudence of free speech as more than just a procession of cases. Jurisprudence is the intellectual output of individual jurists who committed themselves to understanding the subject and to teaching the subject to the nation but who did so through the filter of their own constitutional principles. Moreover, they did so while contending with colleagues on the Court whose constitutional principles differed from their own.

Therefore, the opinions they produced were the end products of not only several rounds of editing but also several rounds of negotiating. A justice tasked with writing a free speech opinion had to do so in a way that would garner the support of colleagues, which in turn means that those colleagues had some capacity to nudge the author in a particular direction. But the reality that bargaining is part of the process of constructing an opinion does not mean that the opinion is only politics, nor does it mean that the language and ideas found in an opinion should be waved off as mere window-dressing. In fact, the opposite is true, for as Justice Felix Frankfurter once asserted, "voting is one thing and expressing views in support of a vote quite another."[9] Examining how individual justices craft their free speech opinions thus enables us to track and explain competing judicial philosophies across time.[10]

We are mindful, though, of Jerome Frank's astute observations that "few" of his fellow jurists "become masters of the writer's craft," and "[t]heir opinions are oases in a vast desert of dullness."[11] It is the rare judicial opinion that is well-written *and* facilitates identification of the forest, the trees, and the deadwood. The nine Supreme Court justices who are highlighted in this volume often produced such opinions, though as much can be learned from their stumbles as from their successes.

Our Starting Nine

The nine justices covered by this volume, listed in chronological order (with their chroniclers), are as follows:

Oliver Wendell Holmes Jr. (1902–1932) (Frederick Lewis)
When the Supreme Court first began to consider the meaning and scope of the First Amendment's Free Speech Clause—a process that did not begin in earnest until World War I—Oliver Wendell Holmes emerged as the leading voice on the subject. It was Holmes who announced the Court's first real

methodology for deciding free speech questions. And then, only months after that announcement, it was Holmes who declared that his colleagues were misapplying that methodology. Subsequently, as the Court consistently refused to invest the concept of free speech with any real vitality, Holmes and fellow Justice Louis D. Brandeis laid out a sweeping vision of the First Amendment. It is no exaggeration to suggest that the modern law of free expression in the United States was birthed in the opinions written by Holmes and Brandeis in the 1920s and 1930s, opinions that were mostly dissents and concurrences which were ultimately vindicated in later Supreme Court rulings. As Anthony Lewis observed, "[t]he Holmes-Brandeis views of free speech persuaded the country and, in time, the Court."[12]

George Sutherland (1922–1938) (Samuel Olken)
As one of the "Four Horsemen"—the bloc of laissez-faire conservatives who so bedeviled President Franklin D. Roosevelt in the early years of the New Deal—George Sutherland is not often thought of as playing a prominent role in civil liberties in general, or in freedom of speech cases in particular. However, while Sutherland's output on freedom of speech is limited, the philosophy that he presented in his handful of opinions serves as a contemporaneous counterpoint to the embryonic Holmes-Brandeis perspective, especially in its focus on the intersection of economic regulation and freedom of the press. Sutherland's opinions thus illustrate the alternative path the law could have taken and help illuminate the direction in which the law eventually traveled.

Hugo L. Black (1937–1971) (Kevin McMahon and Michael Paris)
Only four justices—William O. Douglas, Stephen Field, John Paul Stevens, and John Marshall—served longer on the Supreme Court than Hugo Black. And for the entirety of Black's tenure, the First Amendment was a paramount concern for the Court; this was an era in which foundational free speech principles were established and refined. Black's Supreme Court career began with the First Amendment in eclipse but ended with the First Amendment in ascendancy, and Black played a prominent role in that journey. Famed for his absolutist view of the Free Speech Clause, Black was eventually perceived to have moved away from that posture, though the depth of his shift may be overstated. While Black's absolutist view of the First Amendment may have limited his impact on his colleagues, he is one of the most consequential figures in the history of free expression.

John Marshall Harlan II (1955–1971) (Douglas Edlin)
The grandson of a legendary justice of the same name, the second Justice John Harlan was nominated by a president determined to alter what he saw as the Court's liberal orientation. Indeed, Harlan for the most part fulfilled President Dwight Eisenhower's expectations and carved out a distinguished record of eloquent jurisprudential conservatism in his Supreme Court career. But where in an earlier era deprioritization of individual freedom may have

been one of judicial conservatism's defining characteristics, in Harlan's skilled hands judicial conservatism made ample room for civil liberties. In many areas, Harlan served as a jurisprudential foil for the justices covered immediately before and after him in this volume, yet on freedom of speech he often found common cause with them.

William J. Brennan Jr. (1956–1990) (James Foster)
With a Supreme Court tenure nearly as long—and a passion for free speech equally as pronounced—as that of Hugo Black, William Brennan is central to the constitutional evolution of freedom of speech in the second half of the twentieth century. Throughout his career, Brennan was often both the philosophical conscience of the Court and a crafty builder of juridical alliances, and his work on free expression was emblematic of his dualist nature. Author of one of the most important free speech opinions in Supreme Court history, 1964's *New York Times v. Sullivan*,[13] Brennan crafted a free speech legacy in that landmark decision as well as in other cases that positioned him as arguably the most influential justice on the subject.

Potter Stewart (1958–1981) (Keith Bybee)
In seven pithy words, Potter Stewart seemed to cement a dubious First Amendment legacy. But the justice famous for saying about objectionable pornography that "I know it when I see it" had a much richer and more complex outlook on free expression, especially in the area of freedom of the press. A classic centrist, Stewart tacked toward moderation in most other areas, but on freedom of the press he staked out a doctrinaire posture that would prove critical in American constitutional and political history, especially once the news media in the 1960s took on a more investigatory orientation. As the institutional press reinvents itself in the Internet age, Stewart's philosophy on freedom of the press is once again resonant.

Anthony M. Kennedy (1988–present) (Helen Knowles)
Although typically described as the contemporary Court's "swing vote," by contrast in free speech cases Anthony Kennedy has often adopted a strident approach to expressive freedom that is best characterized as libertarian. This aspect of his jurisprudence is particularly evident in cases involving content-based regulations. In the early years of his Supreme Court tenure, Kennedy sometimes wrote opinions in which he toned down his hostility to governmental efforts to, as he perceives it, shape the nature of individuals' thought processes—telling people what to think and say. Yet, as time went by and the Court's personnel changed, he was confronted with opportunities (e.g., in *Citizens United v. FEC*)[14] to pen opinions mounting a full frontal attack on such laws.

Clarence Thomas (1991–present) (Steven Lichtman)
Appointed to the seat that had been occupied by Thurgood Marshall, Clarence Thomas has proven to be the heir to Hugo Black. For well over a decade,

Thomas's free speech jurisprudence was absolutist in nature. Even more so than his fellow conservative Antonin Scalia, Thomas advanced an uncompromising version of the First Amendment that operationalized libertarian principles and made little room for any type of limitation on speech. Willing and eager to position himself as the Court's resident free speech iconoclast, Thomas periodically took positions on expression that were unique, both among his contemporaries and the Supreme Court's history writ large. But like Hugo Black, Thomas eventually—and puzzlingly—tempered his absolutism.

Stephen G. Breyer (1994–present) (Mark Tushnet)
The First Amendment's preeminence in American law and politics is a direct function of the relationship between free speech and democracy, especially the idea that political information must flow freely so that citizens can make informed choices. Perhaps no current justice has explored this relationship as thoughtfully as Stephen Breyer, who predicated his view of free speech on the principle of "active liberty": the right of the people to participate in democratic decision making. Breyer is one of the most difficult justices to pin down, for in his two decades on the Court he sometimes opposed restrictions on expression but also sometimes tolerated them. Nevertheless, he consistently undergirded his decisions with a complicated emphasis on the centrality of political participation.

This book uses the work of these nine justices as the lens through which to view the long-term development of free speech jurisprudence. We stress that this is not merely a matter of chronology but also a matter of methodological diversity. We have included both proponents of using "tests" to resolve free speech cases and trenchant critics of that approach. For example, Holmes's metaphor of a wide-ranging marketplace of ideas was nevertheless cabined by the "clear and present danger test" he contributed to the nation's free speech lexicon.[15] By contrast, the writings of Kennedy and Thomas repeatedly emphasize that any juridical efficiency gained from the use of "tests" far too frequently comes at the expense of individuals' expressive freedom. And one might argue that over the long course of his career, Black wrote opinions that embodied both of these perspectives—embracing and rejecting jurisprudential rigidity. Inclusion of these diverse perspectives allows readers to formulate their own assessments of the wisdom of speech regulation: *if* it should be done, *when* it should be done, and/or *how* it should be done.

We also endeavored to select justices who are generally regarded as high-quality jurists. Although an authoritative model of judicial "greatness" or even "near greatness" is of course elusive (regardless of whether the analysts are law professors, political scientists, journalists, or judges), there is a rough consensus about the composition of the upper echelon of the men and women who have sat on the Supreme Court. Holmes is consistently seen as at, or near, the top of polls and studies ranking members of the Court; similarly, Black, Brennan, and Harlan II are invariably ranked as great or near great.[16] Admittedly, the reputations of Justices Sutherland and Stewart are more complicated, but Court scholars do not see either of them as jurisprudentially deficient. Only with the passage of more time will the historical rankings of Kennedy, Thomas, and Breyer become clear. Nevertheless, the inclusion of these three current members of the Court provides a useful means of illustrating that Court's relationship to contemporary trends in judicial politics.

The word "politics," however, must be read with scrupulous care, because the case law on freedom of speech involves votes and opinions that typically defy traditional ideological labels. All too often commentators are quick to describe the decisions of the US Supreme Court—especially sharply divided ones—as either "liberal" or "conservative." Such descriptions are rarely useful (except as media sound bites) and frequently inaccurate. This is particularly true in First Amendment cases in part because, as Burt Neuborne astutely observes, that section of the Bill of Rights "is not the preserve of a particular political enclave. It is not a liberal doctrine. It is not a conservative doctrine. It is an American doctrine."[17]

Take, for example, the 1989 decision in *Texas v. Johnson* striking down a state law that made it a crime to desecrate the American flag. The five-justice majority consisted of the three most "liberal" members of the Court (Justices Thurgood Marshall, Brennan, and Harry A. Blackmun), one justice at the ideological center of the Court (Kennedy), and one of the most "conservative" justices (Antonin Scalia).[18]

Even decisions in which the Court's "familiar ideological split" is on full display can nevertheless reinforce Neuborne's description of First Amendment jurisprudence. This was true in *Citizens United v. Federal Election Commission* (2010), in which the Court held that it was unconstitutional to place limits upon the use of corporate funds to finance independent "electioneering communications."[19] Justice Kennedy's opinion for the five-justice majority was joined by his four more "conservative" colleagues (Chief Justice John Roberts and Justices Antonin Scalia, Clarence Thomas, and Samuel Alito); dissenting were the four more moderate (or "liberal") members of the Court (Justices John Paul Stevens, Ruth Bader Ginsburg, Stephen Breyer, and Sonia Sotomayor). That split certainly seems to "have reinforced, warranted or not, the image the court finds most distasteful—that its decisions are political as well," an image which secured further reinforcement in the remarks made by President Barack Obama in his 2010 State of the Union Address and in the op-ed pages of the nation's newspapers.[20] However, as Kathleen Sullivan points out, *Citizens United* was a "victory for free speech rights [which] emanated from a majority of Justices conventionally viewed as conservative, over the dissent of four Justices conventionally viewed as liberal, with virtually all political criticism arising from the political left."[21] In other words, all too often the US Supreme Court's expressive freedom decisions are anything but easily categorizable statements of predictable jurisprudential ideology.

And yet, analysis of opinions remains an important vehicle for identifying the patterns that have occurred over time, precisely because decisions in court cases—both who wins and the stated reasons why they win—are shaped by the times and places in which they were conceived. Supreme Court opinions have been influenced by various sociopolitical and sociolegal factors, the existence and importance of which have been subject to considerable fluctuation. It is indeed true that "[t]he study of law can be disappointing at times, a matter of applying narrow rules and arcane procedure to an uncooperative reality."[22] And in its First Amendment free speech decisions the Court has, over time, concocted a bewildering compendium of rules (some narrow, some broad). However, by using the opinions in those cases to examine the historical trends that have shaped, and have in turn been shaped by the justices' decisions, the overall jurisprudential picture becomes clearer. Consequently, an historical approach to free speech jurisprudence, in the words of some of the greatest contemporary practitioners of that approach, "provides a sound framework for understanding crucial episodes in American constitutional politics."[23]

A Potted History of American Free Speech Jurisprudence before World War I

All too often, accounts of freedom of speech in the United States leave the impression that the nation's meaningful and important First Amendment "conversation" did not begin until March 3, 1919, when the Supreme Court announced its decision in *Schenck v. United States*.[24] This is as misleading as saying that the beginning of the Supreme Court's "real" work can be traced back only as far as the Marshall Court and its 1803 decision in *Marbury v. Madison*.[25] Free speech jurisprudence in America did not begin with *Schenck*, nor with any decision of the US Supreme Court. It did not even begin with the words of the First Amendment to the US Constitution. Its origins go back much further and, in fact, predate American independence.

The colonial era was brimming with discussions about the boundaries of expressive freedom, although those discussions usually led to resolutions that sound strange to twenty-first-century analysts. Consistent with principles of English common law, it was typical of colonial era legal commentators to argue that there existed *only one inviolate aspect of expressive freedom*—the freedom of the press to publish without fear of prior restraint. The government could not *prevent* the press from running a particular story, but it could seek to *punish* the press after publication.[26] Aspects of freedom of speech, some of which we today take for granted as near absolutes—such as the freedom to criticize the government—remained subject to comprehensive government restraints. The 1735 acquittal of New York printer John Peter Zenger, who had been charged with "seditious libel" for printing newspaper columns critical of New York's royal governor, was a brief and anomalous victory for the free trade in ideas.

During the framing of the US Constitution, many Federalists insisted that a Bill of Rights was unnecessary. As Alexander Hamilton asked rhetorically in *Federalist 84*, regarding freedom of speech, "[w]hy should it be said that the liberty of the press shall not be restrained when no power is given by which restrictions may be imposed?"[27] The Constitution created a federal government of distinctly limited powers—confined to those enumerated in the document's text—and those did not include the power to abridge free speech. The anti-Federalists were far more skeptical of the nature of the new national government, and their efforts to impede ratification succeeded in reviving the idea of a bill of rights, an idea that had died, without much discussion, during the constitutional convention. Today we accept that "[t]he very purpose of a Bill of Rights, was to withdraw certain subjects from the vicissitudes of political controversy, to place them beyond the reach of majorities and officials and establish them as legal principles to be applied by the courts," because "[o]ne's right to life, liberty, and property, to free speech, a free press, freedom of worship and assembly, and other fundamental rights may not be submitted to vote; they depend on the outcome of no elections."[28] However, within only seven years of the ratification of the Bill of Rights, the passage of the Alien and Sedition Acts demonstrated that as invaluable as the first provision of the final Bill of Rights was considered to be, it did not suddenly translate into sharp limits upon the ability of the federal government to suppress individuals' speech rights. The Sedition Act of 1798—"An act for the punishment of certain crimes against the United States"—included a provision making it a crime:

> [t]o write, print, utter or publish, or cause it to be done, or assist in it, any false, scandalous, and malicious writing against the government of the United States, or either House of Congress, or the President, with intent to defame, or bring either into contempt or disrepute, or to excite against either the hatred of the people of the United States, or to stir up sedition, or to excite unlawful combinations against the government, or to resist it, or to aid or encourage hostile designs of foreign nations.[29]

As Geoffrey Stone observes, this was evidence that the Federalists possessed "little faith in free and open debate" and that they feared "that the common man was easily manipulated and misled." Criminalizing sedition, the nascent First Amendment notwithstanding, was a suitable way of attempting to ensure that the "power and danger of public opinion" would not trigger in the young United States such events as those recently witnessed in France.[30]

Meaningful limits upon the ability of the federal government to suppress individuals' speech rights remained elusive in the nineteenth century. For example, one important free speech controversy arose in the 1830s as the nation struggled with the conflicts arising out of the existence and persistence of the "peculiar institution" of human enslavement. In 1835 and 1836, one of the products of the improved organization of abolitionists was a significant increase in the number of antislavery petitions submitted to Congress. The governmental response was swift and unrelenting. Members of Congress moved to shield the South from antislavery influences by prohibiting congressional submission or discussion of petitions on the subject of slavery and/or abolition. The South had to be protected from "fanatics [who] aimed to 'excite a servile insurrection.'"[31] Imposition of this gag rule followed governmental condoning, in 1835, of mail censorship. In direct contravention of federal law, Amos Kendall, President Andrew Jackson's postmaster general, turned a blind eye to the policies imposed by postmasters who sought to prohibit antislavery mails from reaching proslavery states. These instances of the suppression of speech were components of a campaign, by southerners, to construct a "legal Maginot Line" protecting their interests.[32]

Ultimately, one might argue, the gag rule was "[o]ne of the most serious tactical blunders southern politicians ever made . . ." because now "abolitionists could argue plausibly that the Slave Power would even subvert the Constitution to preserve their evil institution."[33] Indeed, the 1830s ended well for abolitionists because they "were able to disseminate their arguments to an ever wider and slightly more receptive audience" and because they "discovered the force and usefulness of *constitutional dialectic*."[34] When the subject of that dialectic was free speech, the message was unmistakable and clear—suppression of expressive freedom was yet another example of enslavement, and this time government was the master. In other words, "[i]n spite of their optimistic faith that truth would vanquish error, the abolitionists did not sit back and wait for the invisible hand to select the best from the marketplace of ideas."[35]

Historically, that marketplace has shrunk when the nation has gone to war. Free speech faces "perilous times" when governmental efforts at suppression are ramped up in the name of "national security." And this did not suddenly begin during World War I. Individuals seeking to criticize the government confronted similar obstacles two generations earlier during the Civil War.[36] "History is [indeed] replete with examples of governmental efforts to suppress speech on the grounds that emergency measures are necessary for survival that in retrospect appear panicky, disingenuous, or silly."[37]

During Reconstruction, the ratification of the Fourteenth Amendment in 1868 provided the potential for an expansion in free speech protection. The potential came from the language of the Due Process Clause of the Amendment—"nor shall any State deprive any person of life, liberty, or property, without due process of law." On its face, the language of the First Amendment offers *no* protection of speech from the suppressive actions of the local and state governments. It is only "Congress [that] shall make no law . . . abridging the freedom of speech, or of the press." The Supreme Court confirmed that the Bill of Rights was limited (to the federal government) in its application in *Barron v. Baltimore* (1833).[38]

Although that decision still stands, in subsequent cases (primarily during the twentieth century) the Court has used the Due Process Clause of the Fourteenth Amendment to apply provisions of the Bill of Rights to the actions of state governments (this is the process of "incorporating" the Bill of Rights). The Court first incorporated the Free Speech Clause of the First Amendment in *Gitlow v. New York* (1925). While this was a path-breaking theoretical expansion of free speech—since, by incorporating the First Amendment to the states, the Court had told the states that their power to impose restrictions on speech was constrained—in practice nothing much changed. Even as the Court announced that a New York law prohibiting criminal advocacy was subject to restraints imposed by the First Amendment, it still upheld the conviction of Benjamin Gitlow, who ran afoul of the law when he published the "Left Wing Manifesto." Gitlow's pamphlet did not advocate any criminal action (it only *urged* "abstract doctrine"), but the Court nevertheless chose to conclude that it contained "the language of direct incitement." Regulating that language was a legitimate use of a state's police powers because the words incited action that threatened the health, safety, and welfare of citizens.[39]

The decision and jurisprudential approach in *Gitlow* were generally consistent with the outcomes of most other free speech cases that came before the nation's courts between the end of the Civil War and the late 1930s.[40] As David Rabban astutely observes, "[t]his historical record poses a substantial challenge to current constitutional theorists who identify an independent judiciary as the best protection for individual rights in a democracy."[41]

To be sure, during the late nineteenth and early twentieth centuries there existed a radical, libertarian tradition that sought to offer speech greater protection by treating it as "one aspect of the personal liberty 'to be free in the enjoyment of all faculties.'"[42] However, this tradition offered little protection for dissenters like Charles Schenck and Ben Gitlow who encountered a progressive tradition that instead saw as valuable that speech which brought about "social harmony" rather than individual fulfillment.[43] Dissenting during a time of war and deigning to criticize democratic values were not forms of expression that the First Amendment required society to accept.

Eventually, though, the "broader patterns of social justification change," and as a result, "the structure of particular political arguments changes." As Mark Graber reminds us, when this intellectual transformation happens "[t]hinkers begin to ponder what was once inconceivable, advocates begin to assert what was once unsayable, and audiences begin to accept what was once unbelievable."[44] It is our hope that readers of this volume will be able to see these changes manifest themselves, across time, in the free speech jurisprudence of the various justices that our contributors analyze, and that those analyses will foster a recognition and appreciation of both the jurisprudence of the justices *and* their respective places in history. For, as Justice William O. Douglas observed in 1957, it is important to understand that "[t]he audience . . . that hissed yesterday may applaud today, even for the same performance."[45]

* * *

What time has thus far told us is that American free speech law is messy and that the justices who have contributed to it have woven a very tangled web of decisions. No doubt some readers of this volume will believe that their "favorite" First Amendment jurist is missing from this book's lineup. It is our hope that they will nevertheless agree that the "starting nine" does consist of members of the Court who have placed important strands within that web. Rather than reducing First Amendment law to the votes of "conservative" and/or "liberal" justices and rather than insisting that any particular member of the Court at any given time merely decides that they know an unconstitutional speech restriction when they see it, our goal in this book is to stimulate meaningful debates about the myriad ways in which members of the US Supreme Court have across time both drawn upon their predecessors' approaches and carved out new contributions to the collective endeavor of judging free speech.

Annotated Timeline of Important Free Speech Decisions[a]

Date	Case	Justice
1735	*THE ZENGER TRIAL* Criminal trial of publisher of newspapers that criticized New York's royal governor ends in acquittal when jury refuses to apply seditious libel law; landmark for freedom of the press.	n/a
1907	*PATTERSON v. COLORADO* Court suggests that First Amendment does not bind the states, and even if it does it would merely require the application of the common law "bad tendency" test to uphold contempt sanction against a newspaper that had criticized the state Supreme Court.	HOLMES
1917	*MASSES PUBLISHING CO. v. PATTEN* Federal District Judge Learned Hand rejects New York Postmaster's attempt to prevent a monthly revolutionary magazine from being sent through the mail, asserting that government can only restrict speech that incites illegal activity; Hand is reversed by Second Circuit Court of Appeals, and the US Supreme Court declines to hear the case.	HAND
1919	*SCHENCK v. UNITED STATES* Conviction of anticonscription pamphleteer during World War I upheld unanimously; announcement of "clear and present danger test."	HOLMES
1919	*ABRAMS v. UNITED STATES* Eight months after *Schenck*, Court (7-2) applies "clear and present danger test" to uphold conviction of protestor against US interference with Russian revolution; Holmes dissents (joined by Brandeis), arguing that the protestor was not a danger and describing free speech as a commitment to the marketplace of ideas.	CLARKE
1925	*GITLOW v. NEW YORK* Incorporation of First Amendment to the states; Socialist New York State legislator's conviction under state law for publishing "Left Wing Manifesto" upheld 7-2 (over dissent by Holmes, joined by Brandeis).	SANFORD

1927	*WHITNEY v. CALIFORNIA* Conviction of founder of Communist Labor Party upheld unanimously under California "Criminal Syndicalism Act"; Brandeis concurs only on technical grounds but presents thunderous and poetic expansion of freedom of speech.	SANFORD
1931	*NEAR v. MINNESOTA* "Public Nuisance Law" that allowed state officials to enjoin publication of "malicious, scandalous, and defamatory" periodicals struck down, 5-4, as an unconstitutional prior restraint on the press.	HUGHES
1942	*CHAPLINSKY v. NEW HAMPSHIRE* Unanimous Court sustains arrest of Jehovah's Witness who called a policeman a "goddamned racketeer" and a "damned Fascist"; Murphy deems this "fighting words" unprotected by the First Amendment, thereby introducing the Court's categorization approach to free speech.	MURPHY
1942	*VALENTINE v. CHRESTENSEN* Court unanimously announces that commercial speech is not protected by the First Amendment; case will be overruled in 1976's *Virginia Pharmacy Board* decision.	O. ROBERTS
1943	*MARTIN v. STRUTHERS* 5-4 Court holds that West Virginia cannot ban door-to-door leafleting.	BLACK
1943	*WEST VIRGINIA STATE BOARD OF EDUCATION v. BARNETTE* State law requiring students to start school day with a flag salute thrown out upon challenge by Jehovah's Witnesses whose religion bars worshiping earthly images; 6-3 decision overrules *Minersville School District v. Gobitis*, which had been decided only three years earlier.	JACKSON
1949	*TERMINIELLO v. CHICAGO* 5-4 Court invalidates Chicago "breach of the peace" ordinance; Jackson warns in dissent that the Court risks turning the Constitution into a "suicide pact."	DOUGLAS
1951	*DENNIS v. UNITED STATES* Plurality decision at the height of the second "Red Scare" upholds Smith Act convictions of leaders of the Communist Party for advocating violent overthrow of the United States.	VINSON

(*continued*)

(continued)

Date	Case	Justice
1952	*JOSEPH BURSTYN, INC. v. WILSON* Unanimous Court invalidates New York State's attempt to prevent movie theaters from showing *The Miracle*, which was deemed to be sacrilegious by a state licensing board; case marks the end of an era of expansive governmental power to censor films.	CLARK
1957	*YATES v. UNITED STATES* By 6-1, Court holds that the Smith Act only applies to defendants who actively take steps to overthrow the government; mere membership in the Communist Party is protected.	HARLAN "2"
1957	*ROTH v. UNITED STATES/ALBERTS v. CALIFORNIA* Court's first attempt to define obscenity; 6-3 decision allows restriction of material that the average person, applying community standards, would think appeals to "prurient interest."	BRENNAN
1958	*NAACP v. ALABAMA* Unanimous Court declares that civil rights group cannot be forced to reveal its membership lists; that information is protected by the right to freedom of association.	HARLAN "2"
1958	*SPEISER v. RANDALL* Decided the same day as *NAACP v. Alabama*; unanimous Court holds that California violated the First Amendment when it denied a World War II veteran tax exemption because he refused to sign a loyalty oath.	BRENNAN
1959	*SMITH v. CALIFORNIA* Invalidation of arrest of bookstore owner who was unaware that some of the books for sale in his store contained obscene material; in concurrence, Black announces his view that in the First Amendment, "'no law abridging' [can be read] to mean no law abridging."	BRENNAN

1964	*NEW YORK TIMES v. SULLIVAN* In arguably the most important First Amendment case in history, the Court unanimously throws out a multimillion-dollar libel verdict against the *New York Times* for running an advertisement critical of Alabama officials' actions against civil rights protestors; Brennan asserts that freedom of speech means "that debate on public issues should be uninhibited, robust, and wide-open" and establishes that governmental officials must prove "actual malice" to win a libel case.	BRENNAN
1964	*JACOBELLIS v. OHIO* Fragmented Court reverses conviction of an Ohio movie theater operator who exhibited a controversial French film; Stewart, in concurrence, suggests that while he cannot precisely define obscenity, "I know it when I see it."	BRENNAN
1967	*CURTIS PUBLISHING CO. v. BUTTS* ***Sullivan*** standard for libel applies to any public figure, not just governmental officials; divided Court nevertheless sustains libel judgment in favor of University of Georgia head football coach against the ***Saturday Evening Post***.	HARLAN "2"
1968	*UNITED STATES v. O'BRIEN* While upholding (by 8-1) the conviction of an antiwar protestor who had burned his draft card, the Court announces that "symbolic speech" can claim First Amendment protection; establishment of four-part test for constitutionality of regulations on symbolic speech.	WARREN
1969	*TINKER v. DES MOINES INDEPENDENT COMMUNITY SCHOOL DISTRICT* 7-2 decision invalidating the suspension of students who wore black armbands to school in protest of the Vietnam War; Fortas declares that neither students nor teachers "shed their constitutional rights to freedom of speech or expression at the schoolhouse gate."	FORTAS
1969	*STANLEY v. GEORGIA* Georgia law criminalizing possession of obscene materials in the privacy of one's home unanimously declared unconstitutional.	T. MARSHALL
1969	*BRANDENBURG v. OHIO* Conviction of Ku Klux Klan leader unanimously thrown out; Court announces new rule that government can only ban speech that both advocates "imminent lawless action" and is likely to produce such action, effectively melding the Holmes and Hand approaches into a very high standard for regulation of expression.	per curiam

(*continued*)

(continued)

Date	Case	Justice
1971	*COHEN v. CALIFORNIA* Divided Court throws out conviction of man who wore jacket emblazoned with "Fuck the Draft" in a Los Angeles courthouse; noting that "one man's vulgarity is another man's lyric," Harlan suggests that onlookers can avoid having their sensibilities disturbed by "averting their eyes."	HARLAN "2"
1971	*NEW YORK TIMES v. UNITED STATES* Injunction against publication of "Pentagon Papers" thrown out (6-3) as a prior restraint on the press; each justice contributes his own concurrence or dissent.	per curiam
1972	*BRANZBURG v. HAYES* 5-4 decision that journalists may be compelled to reveal their sources in a criminal investigation; freedom of the press does not provide automatic immunity from subpoena.	B. WHITE
1973	*MILLER v. CALIFORNIA* 5-4 Court refuses to abandon the notion that obscenity is unprotected by the First Amendment, but the *Roth* standard for obscenity is discarded in favor of new rule defining it as material lacking in "serious literary, artistic, political, or scientific merit" (a.k.a the "SLAPS" test).	BURGER
1974	*GERTZ v. ROBERT WELCH, INC.* Introduction of libel law distinction between public and private figures; while public figures must still prove "actual malice," private figures need only prove negligence to win a libel lawsuit (although they must prove actual malice to win punitive damages).	POWELL
1976	*BUCKLEY v. VALEO* 1974 Amendments to 1971's Federal Election Campaign Act upheld in part; sharply divided Court invalidates limits on campaign expenditures but upholds limits on campaign contributions in a landmark campaign finance law opinion.	per curiam
1976	*VIRGINIA STATE PHARMACY BD. v. VIRGINIA CITIZENS CONSUMERS COUNCIL* 7-1 decision reversing field on commercial speech and announcing that advertising does enjoy some level of First Amendment protection.	BLACKMUN

1977	*COLLIN v. SMITH* Supreme Court of Illinois refuses to enjoin planned march by American Nazi Party members into Skokie, Illinois, a town with a large population of Holocaust survivors; US Supreme Court declines to hear the case.	n/a
1978	*FCC v. PACIFICA FOUNDATION* Divided Court upholds fine against a radio station that broadcast George Carlin's "Filthy Words" monologue in daytime hours; FCC given broad discretion to bar radio stations from broadcasting indecent material when children may be listening. (The Carlin monologue is reproduced, verbatim, in the Appendix to the Court's opinion).	STEVENS
1980	*CENTRAL HUDSON GAS & ELECTRIC CORP. v. PUBLIC SERVICE COMMISSION* Announcement of four-part test to assess the constitutionality of a regulation on commercial speech; test applied in 8-1 ruling invalidating total ban on utility advertising in New York.	POWELL
1982	*NEW YORK v. FERBER* Unanimous Court announces that mere possession of child pornography may be criminalized without offending the First Amendment.	B. WHITE
1983	*CONNICK v. MYERS* 5-4 decision sustaining the dismissal of a public employee who had circulated a questionnaire about her boss; Court determined that the questionnaire was not a matter of public concern.	B. WHITE
1986	*AMERICAN BOOKSELLERS v. HUDNUT* Seventh Circuit Court of Appeals, in opinion by Judge Frank Easterbrook, invokes free speech to throw out Indianapolis antipornography ordinance that had designated pornography as an act of discrimination against women; US Supreme Court declines to review the decision.	EASTERBROOK
1988	*HUSTLER MAGAZINE, INC. v. FALWELL* Unanimous Court rules that outrageous satire of public figures is protected by the First Amendment; throws out libel verdict in favor of Reverend Jerry Falwell over *Hustler* fake advertisement that depicted him losing his virginity to his mother in an outhouse.	REHNQUIST

(*continued*)

(continued)

Date	Case	Justice
1989	*TEXAS v. JOHNSON* 5-4 Court holds that burning an American flag is constitutionally protected symbolic political speech; throws out conviction of protestor arrested outside 1984 Republican National Convention.	BRENNAN
1992	*R.A.V. v. CITY OF ST. PAUL* Court unanimously refuses to add "hate speech" to the list of categories of speech that are not protected by the First Amendment; invalidates conviction of Minnesota teenager who had burned a cross on the lawn of an African-American family.	SCALIA
1995	*HURLEY v. IRISH-AMERICAN GAY, LESBIAN, AND BISEXUAL GROUP OF BOSTON* Unanimous Court allows organizers of Boston's St. Patrick's Day Parade to refuse to allow gay group to march; even though the parade is in the public streets, organizers are a private organization that retains freedom of association rights.	SOUTER
2000	*BOY SCOUTS OF AMERICA v. DALE* 5-4 Court allows Boy Scouts to expel an Eagle Scout from his scoutmaster position after learning that he is gay, citing freedom of association; majority accepts Scouts' contention that Dale's mere presence in the group would compromise the group's mission of cultivating morally upstanding behavior.	REHNQUIST
2002	*ASHCROFT v. FREE SPEECH COALITION* 7-2 decision striking down two provisions of the Child Pornography Prevention Act of 1996, which covered computer-generated and online images; the provisions were deemed to be so overbroad that they would criminalize protected expression.	KENNEDY
2003	*McCONNELL v. FEC* Bipartisan Campaign Reform Act of 2002 upheld by divided Court; joint opinion preserves statutory finding that "soft money" contributions to political parties are *de facto* payments for access that may be regulated pursuant to campaign finance law's anticorruption rationale. Decision will be largely overruled in 2010 in *Citizens United v. FEC*.	O'CONNOR and STEVENS

2003	*VIRGINIA v. BLACK* Over the lone dissent of Clarence Thomas, the Court declares Virginia law banning cross burning to be unconstitutional; the law had defined all cross burnings as *prima facie* attempts to intimidate—even those done as part of a ceremonial ritual, as was the case here.	O'CONNOR
2007	*MORSE v. FREDERICK* 6-3 decision upholding punishment of student who displayed "BONG HiTS 4 JESUS" banner during school-sanctioned recess to watch Olympic torch relay; Court holds that schools may ban speech antithetical to their mission and accepts school's characterization of the banner as contradicting the school's antidrug policies.	J. ROBERTS
2010	*CITIZENS UNITED v. FEC* Bitterly divided Court holds that First Amendment bars government from limiting the independent political expenditures of corporations, undoing century-old regulations on corporations' political activity and gutting 2003 decision in *McConnell v. FEC.*	KENNEDY
2011	*SNYDER v. PHELPS* 8-1 decision invalidating tort claim against Westboro Baptist Church in favor of father of a fallen soldier whose funeral WBC had picketed; Court held that since the pickets were more than 1000 feet from the church and gravesite, it was protected political speech.	J. ROBERTS
2012	*UNITED STATES v. ALVAREZ* Divided Court declares the "Stolen Valor Act" unconstitutional; Congress may not criminalize making false statements about military service and honors.	KENNEDY
2014	*McCUTCHEON v. FEC* 5-4 Court invalidates biennial aggregate limit on amount of money individuals can donate to political candidates (limits on the size of individual gifts are unaffected); such limits had been upheld in *Buckley v. Valeo* but are now deemed unconstitutional.	J. ROBERTS

[a] All cases are US Supreme Court cases unless otherwise noted. "Justice" references the author of the Opinion of the Court. Significant concurrences and/or dissents are referenced in the annotation of each case.

NOTES

1. *Smith v. California*, 361 U.S. 147, 157 (1959) (Black, J., concurring) (emphasis added).
2. Rodney A. Smolla, *Free Speech in an Open Society* (New York: Alfred A. Knopf, 1992), 24.
3. *United States v. O'Brien*, 391 U.S. 367 (1968); *Adderley v. Florida*, 385 U.S. 39 (1966).
4. David M. Rabban, *Free Speech in Its Forgotten Years* (New York: Cambridge University Press, 1997), 13.
5. Justice Felix Frankfurter, quoted in David M. O'Brien, *Storm Center: The Supreme Court in American Politics*, 9th ed. (New York: W. W. Norton, 2011), 280.
6. Some of the seminal readings addressing and/or employing these different models are Jeffrey A. Segal and Harold J. Spaeth, *The Supreme Court and the Attitudinal Model Revisited* (Cambridge: Cambridge University Press, 2002); Lee Epstein and Jack Knight, *The Choices Justices Make* (Washington, DC: CQ Press, 1998); Cornell W. Clayton and Howard Gillman, eds., *Supreme Court Decision-Making: New Institutionalist Approaches* (Chicago, IL: University of Chicago Press, 1999); Nancy L. Maveety, ed., *The Pioneers of Judicial Behavior* (Ann Arbor, MI: University of Michigan Press, 2002).
7. C. Herman Pritchett, "The Development of Judicial Research," in *Frontiers of Judicial Research*, eds. Joel B. Grossman and Joseph Tanenhaus (New York: Wiley, 1969), 42.
8. Wayne V. McIntosh et al., "Textualism v. Active Liberty: Testing the Doctrinal Approaches of Justice Scalia and Breyer" (unpublished paper presented at the UK American Politics Group Annual Conference, Institute for the Study of the Americas, University of London, January 3–5, 2008).
9. Quoted in O'Brien, *Storm Center*, 280.
10. For a useful conceptualization of the opinions-votes distinction, see Pamela C. Corley, Amy Steigerwalt, and Artemus Ward, *The Puzzle of Unanimity: Consensus on the United States Supreme Court* (Palo Alto, CA: Stanford University Press, 2013).
11. Jerome N. Frank, "Some Reflections on Judge Learned Hand," *University of Chicago Law Review* 24 (1957): 672.
12. Anthony Lewis, *Make No Law: The Sullivan Case and the First Amendment* (New York: Random House, 1991), 89. It is hard to say that Brandeis is in truth the "real" giant of American free speech law. The reason we say this is somewhat surprising, but it also serves as a more satisfying answer to the question of why we selected Holmes over Brandeis for inclusion in this volume. While Brandeis's free speech jurisprudence is legendary for its quality, that quality comes from a very small number of the justice's opinions. Brandeis simply did not write many opinions on freedom of speech, and he never spoke for a majority of the Court in a speech-protective fashion. See Steven B. Lichtman, "The Disappearing

Jurisprudence of Louis Brandeis," *Brandeis University Law Journal* 3 (2013): 9–28.

13. *New York Times v. Sullivan*, 376 U.S. 254 (1964).
14. *Citizens United v. Federal Election Commission*, 558 U.S. 310 (2010).
15. See *Abrams v. United States*, 250 U.S. 616, 630 (1919) (Holmes, J., joined by Brandeis, J., dissenting) ("the best test of truth is the power of the thought to get itself accepted in the competition of the market"). David Richards has argued that Holmes's combination of the marketplace metaphor and the "clear and present danger" test meant that, "free speech protection would be extended only to the incredible fatuities of the lunatic fringe." David A. J. Richards, "Free Speech as Toleration," in *Free Expression: Essays in Law and Philosophy*, ed. W. J. Waluchow (Oxford: Clarendon Press, 1994), 33.
16. See Michael Comiskey, *Seeking Justices: The Judging of Supreme Court Nominees* (Lawrence, KS: University Press of Kansas, 2004); William G. Ross, "The Ratings Game: Ranking Supreme Court Justices," *Marquette Law Review* 79 (1996): 401–452.
17. Burt Neuborne, "First Amendment," *Touro Law Review* 6 (1989): 130. This is an important theme in Floyd Abrams, *Friend of the Court: On the Front Lines with the First Amendment* (New Haven, CT: Yale University Press, 2013).
18. *Texas v. Johnson*, 491 U.S. 397 (1989).
19. Robert Barnes, "High Court Shows It Might Be Willing to Act Boldly," *Washington Post*, January 22, 2010, A4; 558 U.S. 310 (2010).
20. Barnes, "High Court Shows"; Barack Obama, "Address Before a Joint Session of the Congress on the State of the Union," January 27, 2010. Online by Gerhard Peters and John T. Woolley, *The American Presidency Project*, http://www.presidency.ucsb.edu/ws/?pid=87433. For example, see Bradley A. Smith, "Newsflash: First Amendment Upheld," *Wall Street Journal*, January 22, 2010 (hailing the decision as "wonderful" for its "restor[ation of] political speech to the primacy it was intended to have under the First Amendment"); "The Court's Blow to Democracy," *New York Times*, January 22, 2010 (calling *Citizens United* a "blow to democracy"); and "Judicial Activism Inc.," *Washington Post*, January 22, 2010 (labeling the decision "Judicial Activism Inc.").
21. Kathleen M. Sullivan, "The Supreme Court, 2009 Term—Comment: Two Concepts of Freedom of Speech," *Harvard Law Review* 124 (2010): 143–144.
22. Howard Gillman, Mark A. Graber, and Keith E. Whittington, *American Constitutionalism: Volume II – Rights and Liberties* (New York: Oxford University Press, 2013), xxvii.
23. Ibid.
24. *Schenck v. United States*, 249 U.S. 47 (1919).
25. There was most definitely Supreme Court life before the Marshall Court and *Marbury*. For example, see Maeva Marcus, ed., *The Documentary*

History of the Supreme Court of the United States, 1789–1800, 8 vols. (New York: Columbia University Press, 1986–2007).

26. Preventing prior restraint remains to this day "the chief purpose" of the Free Press Clause. That clause serves as "a virtually insurmountable barrier between government and the print media so far as government tampering, in advance of publication, with news and editorial content is concerned." *Near v. Minnesota*, 283 U.S. 697, 713 (1931); *Miami Herald Publishing Co. v. Tornillo*, 418 U.S. 241, 259 (1974) (White, J., concurring).
27. J. R. Pole, ed., *Alexander Hamilton, James Madison, John Jay, The Federalist* (Indianapolis, IN: Hackett Publishing, 2005), 455.
28. *West Virginia v. Barnette*, 319 U.S. 624, 638 (1943).
29. Sedition Act of 1798, http://constitution.org/rf/sedition_1798.htm.
30. Geoffrey R. Stone, *Perilous Times: Free Speech in Wartime, From the Sedition Act of 1798 to the War on Terrorism* (New York: W. W. Norton, 2004), 33, 34.
31. Edward B. Rugemer, "Caribbean Slave Revolts and the Origins of the Gag Rule: A Contest between Abolitionism and Democracy, 1797–1835," in *Contesting Slavery: The Politics of Bondage and Freedom in the New American Nation*, eds. John Craig Hammond and Matthew Mason (Charlottesville, VA: University of Virginia Press, 2011), 94 (quoting South Carolina Congressman James Henry Hammond).
32. Michael Kent Curtis, *Free Speech, 'The People's Darling Privilege': Struggles for Freedom of Expression in American History* (Durham, NC: Duke University Press, 2000), 125.
33. Kenneth M. Stampp, "The Irrepressible Conflict," in *The Imperiled Union: Essays on the Background of the Civil War*, ed. Kenneth M. Stampp (New York: Oxford University Press, 1980), 236.
34. William M. Wiecek, *The Sources of Antislavery Constitutionalism in America, 1760–1848* (Ithaca, NY: Cornell University Press, 1977), 188 (emphasis added). Also see Helen J. Knowles, "The Constitution and Slavery: A Special Relationship," *Slavery and Abolition* 28 (2007): 309–328.
35. Curtis, '*The People's Darling Privilege*,' 419.
36. Stone, *Perilous Times*, Chapter 2.
37. Smolla, *Open Society*, 319.
38. *Barron v. Baltimore*, 32 U.S. 243 (1833).
39. *Gitlow v. New York*, 268 U.S. 652, 665 (1925).
40. One outlier was the 1917 decision, *Masses Publishing Co. v. Patten*, 244 F. 535 (S.D.N.Y., 1917). In that case, the New York Postmaster had attempted to prevent *The Masses*—a self-described "monthly journal of revolution"—from mailing its July 1917 issue to subscribers. Federal District Judge Learned Hand declared that the Postmaster's actions were a violation of the First Amendment, which, in his eyes, only allowed government to restrict speech that directly incited illegal acts (and *The Masses* contained no such speech). Although Hand was reversed by the Second

Circuit Court of Appeals, his views on free speech would still prove to be influential. Indeed, as several scholars have suggested, the shift Holmes made on free speech—which Frederick Lewis chronicles in Chapter 1—began after Holmes found himself seated next to Hand on a train and the two jurists spent the remainder of the journey engaged in a deep discussion about the contours of the First Amendment. See Thomas Healy, *The Great Dissent: How Oliver Wendell Holmes Changed His Mind—and Changed the History of Free Speech in America* (New York: Henry Holt, 2013); G. Edward White, *Justice Oliver Wendell Holmes: Law and the Inner Self* (Oxford: Oxford University Press, 1993).

41. Rabban, *Forgotten Years*, 131.
42. Mark A. Graber, *Transforming Free Speech: The Ambiguous Legacy of Civil Libertarianism* (Berkeley, CA: University of California Press, 1991), 8.
43. Rabban, *Forgotten Years*, 3.
44. Graber, *Transforming Free Speech*, 10.
45. *Kingsley Books, Inc. v. Brown*, 354 U.S. 436, 447 (1957) (Douglas, J., joined by Black, J., dissenting).

CHAPTER 1

OLIVER WENDELL HOLMES JR. AND THE "MARKETPLACE OF IDEAS": EXPERIENCE PROVES TO BE THE "LIFE OF THE LAW"

Frederick P. Lewis

Perhaps no Supreme Court justice is more associated with constitutional free speech doctrine than Oliver Wendell Holmes Jr. Many know the phrase "clear and present danger" or the metaphor about "falsely shouting fire in a theatre," both of which come from his 1919 Opinion of the Court in *Schenck v. United States.*[1] As the first instance in which the Supreme Court authoritatively interpreted the First Amendment's free speech guarantee to determine the constitutionality of a Congressional statute, authoring this opinion alone would constitute a significant contribution to speech jurisprudence.

But it is his *Abrams v. United States* dissent, written several months thereafter, in which he offered his exposition of what has come to be widely known as the "marketplace of ideas," that still impresses with its eloquence a century later.[2] *Abrams*, along with a series of dissenting libertarian speech opinions that followed and ultimately began to persuade the majority, led to Holmes's reputation as "the Great Dissenter" and constitutes another major contribution to speech doctrine. Furthermore, the marketplace of ideas concept that Holmes first articulated on the Court can now be seen as foreshadowing the ascendancy of libertarian speech doctrine that developed in Supreme Court decisions during the second half of the twentieth century and which continues to the present day. Holmes's approach to the law is often summed up in one of his most famous and oft-quoted phrases: "The life of the law has not been logic; it has been experience."[3] The ultimate ascendancy of libertarian speech doctrine in American constitutional jurisprudence uniquely exemplifies the truth of this, as so much of mid-twentieth-century speech doctrine was to be shaped by the tumultuous national experience of the 1960s and early 1970s. That doctrine now prevails all across the Court's ideological spectrum and thus, for good or ill, Holmes may be justly credited as the "intellectual father" of a US speech "marketplace" that is more open than anywhere else in the world.

In the Anglo-American tradition, a libertarian speech philosophy is seen as having its roots in the writings of John Milton and John Stuart Mill. Milton's *Areopagitica* is primarily a tract against prior restraint while Mill's *On Liberty* remains the classic philosophical explication of speech libertarianism. However, from a legal standpoint it was William Blackstone's *Commentaries* that had the greatest influence in early America. At that time, judicial protection for free speech and press was largely limited to "freedom from prior restraint." A government could not restrain speech or press in advance, but it could penalize expression that had "bad tendencies" likely to result in law violation after it occurred.[4]

In the years after the Revolution, the Alien and Sedition Acts of 1798 were passed by Congress under President John Adams and the Federalist Party, aimed at the opposition party then forming under the leadership of Thomas Jefferson and James Madison. Enforcement of the Sedition Act led to the arrest of several newspaper editors who published criticism of the administration amidst a climate of anxiety among many of the propertied, a climate that was produced by the radicalism of the French Revolution. Although the Supreme Court never evaluated the Act, Jefferson's victory in the presidential election of 1800 was seen as the repudiation of this legislation, and many reasonably assume that today's Supreme Court would find such Congressional restrictions on speech and press unconstitutional. Justice William Brennan said as much in the 1964 decision *New York Times v. Sullivan* in which he observed that "[a]lthough the Sedition Act was never tested in this Court, the attack upon its validity has carried the day in the court of history."[5] As James Foster points out in Chapter 5 herein, *Sullivan* was one of Brennan's most significant free speech opinions.

Despite the Alien and Sedition Acts, the early years of the republic actually present a mixed picture. These early decades were often characterized by freewheeling political speech in newspaper broadsides that went very far even by contemporary standards. But as the nineteenth century moved on, the sectional tension grew over the issue of slavery, and increasingly southern hostility to antislavery activity was manifested by suppression of antislavery speech in southern states. For many, this was symbolized by South Carolina Representative Preston Brooks's vicious walking cane attack upon Massachusetts Senator Charles Sumner on the floor of Congress in 1856. It was not for nothing that the Republican Party's early campaign slogan was "Free Men, Free Soil, Free Speech, Fremont."[6]

The Civil War that followed produced episodes where military commanders arrested individuals who spoke out or published material that severely criticized the war or the policies of Abraham Lincoln administration. However, these were typically short-lived, overturned by President Lincoln, or subsumed within larger controversies about the extent of the president's war powers.[7] Instead, during the nineteenth century most deprivations of free speech occurred at the state and local level.

During this period, no remedy from the Supreme Court or any other federal court was available to bring First Amendment challenges to those deprivations. This is because of the Supreme Court's 1833 decision in *Barron v. Baltimore*, which held that the provisions of the national Constitution's Bill of Rights, by themselves, bound only the national government to their requirements.[8] It was not until the twentieth century that the Court held that the Due Process Clause of the Fourteenth Amendment incorporated the First Amendment, thereby applying that Amendment's free speech provisions to state and local regulations.[9]

Although the extent of free speech rights may have varied at different times and places, solidly libertarian conceptions of free speech did not gain ascendancy in national constitutional doctrine until the middle of the twentieth century. Indeed, actions of the national government that implicated free speech issues did not produce any authoritative interpretation by the US Supreme Court until the outbreak of World War I.

As the United States entered that war, Congress enacted the Espionage Act of 1917, which criminalized wartime mailings, false reports, and false statements intended to interfere with the operation or success of the US armed forces or promote the success of its enemies, as well as "willful obstruction of the recruiting or enlistment service" of the United States. The Act also made it criminal to publish in wartime any information that the president declared to be "of such character that it is or might be useful to the enemy."[10] In addition, a 1918 amendment made it illegal to "utter, print, write, or publish any disloyal, profane, scurrilous, or abusive language about the form of government of the United States, or the Constitution of the United States, . . . or any language intended to bring the form of government . . . or the Constitution . . . or the military or naval forces . . . or the flag . . . of the United States into contempt, scorn, contumely or disrepute."[11]

The social circumstances that surrounded the prosecutions of those who objected to World War I significantly influenced the creation of a repressive climate. After the Civil War, an enormous influx of immigrants challenged existing social and cultural norms, resulting in considerable hostility between "old stock" pre–Civil War Americans who were mostly Protestants from northern and western Europe, and "new stock" Americans, mostly Catholic or Jewish immigrants from southern and eastern Europe. In the public's mind, radicalism in its many forms—and antiwar dissent in particular—was associated with new immigrant "aliens."[12]

In 1919, the Supreme Court decided three speech cases involving individuals prosecuted under the Espionage Act. It is as the author of these initial First Amendment opinions that Oliver Wendell Holmes Jr. made his first important contribution to free speech doctrine.

Holmes and Free Speech

Holmes was the son of a socially prominent Boston physician and writer whose humorous "Autocrat of the Breakfast-Table" essays achieved widespread popularity in the United States and in England.[13] After some indecision about a career path, the younger Holmes decided to study law and early on turned a critical eye to the law as he encountered it. Holmes found its formalism off-putting, and he became an exemplar of an analytic approach that became known as "legal realism," which he displayed in his most renowned writings, *The Common Law* and *The Path of the Law*, and in many of his judicial opinions. He also had a unique talent for formulating aphorisms and quotable phrases, and many of his most famous ones are still cited and repeated with great frequency today.

Holmes fought and was wounded in the American Civil War, attended and later taught at Harvard Law School, and served on the Massachusetts Supreme Judicial Court, becoming its chief justice in 1899. In 1902, President Theodore Roosevelt appointed him to the US Supreme Court, where he served for thirty years, retiring only a few months before Franklin D. Roosevelt was elected president.

Holmes was assigned to write the Opinion of the Court in all three of the speech cases that were issued by the Supreme Court in 1919, and all three were unanimous. The first was *Schenck v. United States.*[14] Charles Schenck was convicted under the Espionage Act because of a flyer he sent out to potential draftees during World War I. The flyer advocated support for the Socialist Party and urged that the draft violated the Thirteenth Amendment's prohibition against involuntary servitude. It argued that in the presidential election of 1916, the American people had not voted to authorize war. It also asked readers to vote for the Socialist Party and to write to their Congressmen asking that conscription be abolished. The flyer reminded readers of their right to petition for a redress of grievances and asked them to come to party headquarters to sign a petition; it asked readers not to submit to intimidation, but it did not call for violence.

Holmes based his analysis upholding Schenck's conviction around an analogy to shouting fire in a crowded theater: "The most stringent protection of free speech would not protect a man in falsely shouting fire in a theatre and causing a panic." He added that the words could be punished where they are "used in such circumstances and are of such a nature as to create a clear and present danger that they will bring about the substantive evils that Congress has a right to prevent. It is a question of proximity and degree."[15]

Holmes had begun his venture into speech jurisprudence in 1907 in *Patterson v. Colorado*,[16] a case in which the Court upheld a contempt sanction against a newspaper that had criticized state judges. Writing for the majority, Holmes suggested that the First Amendment was inapplicable. He also suggested that even if the First Amendment did apply, the protection it offered was minimal. In doing so, he relied on the common law tradition and on Blackstone's view that free speech only consisted of the absence of prior restraint.

Although he had abandoned that position by 1919, now in *Schenck* (as he would do in the two cases that followed it) he continued to take a position that gave little practical protection to wartime dissent, particularly when it came from political radicals. That the words of Schenck's pamphlet constituted a "clear and present danger" in any meaningful sense of that phrase seems doubtful; nor does mailing out the pamphlet—even to draft-age men—really seem analogous to falsely shouting fire in a crowded theatre.

Holmes followed his *Schenck* opinion with the Opinion of the Court in *Frohwerk v. United States.*[17] Frohwerk had published twelve editorials criticizing the war, and he and another individual were charged with conspiracy, in the preparation and publication of a newspaper, to violate the Espionage Act. While Holmes conceded that "[w]e do not lose our right to condemn either measures or men because the Country is at war," and "[i]t does not appear that there was any special effort to reach men who were subject to the draft," his opinion deferred to the jury's conclusions and upheld the conviction.[18]

The third case, *Debs v. United States*,[19] involved Eugene Debs, who was the frequent Socialist Party candidate for US president and a prominent labor leader at a time when labor organizing was both vigorously pursued and opposed. Here Holmes's opinion stressed that the members of the jury were carefully instructed that they could not find the defendant guilty for advocating any of his opinions "unless the words used had as their natural tendency and reasonably probable effect to obstruct the recruiting service" and "unless the defendant had the specific intent to do so in his mind."[20] Although Holmes mentioned the *Schenck* case in support of his opinion's result, he did not repeat his "clear and present danger" test, and Debs's conviction and jail sentence remained intact.

Thus, despite his later reputation as the "Great Dissenter" and "intellectual father" of libertarian speech doctrine, Holmes's early judicial opinions that touched upon speech issues were not particularly protective of expressive freedom. Only later did his opinions reflect a viewpoint that had evolved and changed.

HOLMES AND THE "MARKETPLACE OF IDEAS"

That evolution and change is generally viewed as first manifesting itself in Holmes's dissent in *Abrams v. United States*,[21] a case arising from another 1919 prosecution under the Espionage Act (this time for printing and distributing a pamphlet critical of the government and advocating resistance to the war effort). However, what precipitated that change remains the subject of extensive study and discussion. For example, Sheldon Novick minimizes the magnitude of the change. He observes that another case, *Baltzer v. United States*,[22] came to the Court in 1918 before *Schenck* was argued. Baltzer involved a defendant convicted of obstructing the draft for expressing his antiwar views by writing to public officials. Though the Court had voted to affirm the conviction, Holmes circulated a proposed dissent so vigorous[23] that it evidently prompted the Justice Department to withdraw the prosecution; consequently, the Court never issued a ruling in the case. However, Stephen M. Feldman concludes that despite *Baltzer*, "Holmes's vote to dissent in *Abrams* and his expressed rationale justifying his dissent appeared to suggest an unprecedented appreciation, on Holmes's part, for free expression and its contributions to society."[24]

The preponderant scholarly view is that Holmes's thinking evolved under the sustained influence of friends and colleagues who were committed to a more expansive view of speech protection. One was Learned Hand, then a judge on the US District Court for the Southern District of New York, who sought to bring Holmes to the more speech-protective view of free speech Hand expressed in his opinion in *Masses Publishing Co. v. Patten* in 1917. Hand stressed that speech should be punished only if it was an incitement—by which he meant, if its words directly urged listeners or readers to violate the law.[25] Another was the young Harold Laski (later a professor at the London School of Economics and chairman of the British Labour Party), whose stimulating intellectual company Holmes very much enjoyed and who sought to influence the justice's views on a number of subjects.[26] Additionally, scholars have given considerable weight to the influence of Zechariah Chafee, then a young Harvard Law professor.[27] Supreme Court Justice Louis D. Brandeis, who later joined several of Holmes's most famous dissents, was also seen as influential.

Thomas Healy, who has written extensively about this period of Holmes's life, sums up his conclusion about Holmes's free speech shift this way:

> In the nine months since he had written *Schenck*, *Frohwerk*, and *Debs*, Holmes had come under considerable pressure to rethink his answer to these questions. He had been attacked in the pages of the *New Republic* and the *Harvard Law Review*, challenged in correspondence with Hand, confronted over tea by Chafee. Laski had fed him one book after another espousing a liberal view of free speech, and [Felix] Frankfurter[28] had tried to arrange for him to write a piece on tolerance in the *Atlantic Monthly*.[29]

These "lobbying" efforts soon bore fruit in *Abrams*.

In his *Abrams* dissent, joined only by Brandeis, Holmes wrote some of the most notable passages in American constitutional law, eloquent statements of a libertarian approach to freedom of speech that, over the next sixty years, gradually achieved ascendency in the Supreme Court's free speech doctrine.

First, Holmes wrote:

> It is only the present danger of immediate evil or an intent to bring it about that warrants Congress in setting a limit to the expression of opinion where private rights are not concerned. Congress certainly cannot forbid all effort to

change the mind of the country. Now nobody can suppose that the surreptitious publishing of a silly leaflet by an unknown man, without more, would present any immediate danger that its opinions would hinder the success of the government arms or have any appreciable tendency to do so.[30]

He then began the rationale that is still often quoted:

Persecution for the expression of opinions seems to me perfectly logical. If you have no doubt of your premises or your power, and want a certain result with all your heart, you naturally express your wishes in law, and sweep away all opposition. To allow opposition by speech seems to indicate that you think the speech impotent, as when a man says that he has squared the circle, or that you do not care wholeheartedly for the result, or that you doubt either your power or your premises.

And then, most famously:

But when men have realized that time has upset many fighting faiths, they may come to believe even more than they believe the very foundations of their own conduct that the ultimate good desired is better reached by free trade in ideas—that the best test of truth is the power of the thought to get itself accepted in the competition of the market, and that truth is the only ground upon which their wishes safely can be carried out. That, at any rate, is the theory of our Constitution. It is an experiment, as all life is an experiment.[31]

With the *Abrams* marketplace of ideas dissent, Holmes began a series of influential dissenting opinions throughout the early 1920s in which he applied the "clear and present danger" test with more rigor than he had in *Schenck* (though still insisting that he had applied the test correctly in that case). He was usually joined in these opinions by Brandeis[32] in an association that came to be widely appreciated over time. Brandeis's own contribution to the development of First Amendment doctrine was significant for its emphasis on the Amendment's democratic purposes.[33]

Brandeis was appointed to the Supreme Court in 1916 by President Woodrow Wilson. His nomination had provoked strong opposition due to his Jewish religion[34] and his long record of advocacy of progressive causes. Progressive opinion before World War I was focused on social solidarity and reform and tended to see excessive emphasis on individualism and individual rights as destructive.[35] After the war, in response to the repression of radical and antiwar speech during the war and the immediate postwar period, progressives began to stress the importance to democracy itself of a broad protection of free speech. Building upon Holmes's *Abrams* dissent, Brandeis gave emphasis in his dissents to free speech's democratic function. That concept ultimately became part of the underpinning of the "preferred position" footnote[36] that encapsulated the Supreme Court's predominant approach to constitutional questions in the wake of the Court-packing crisis of 1937. Deference to democracy, while intervening in furtherance of the democratic process, offered a rationale for judicial restraint in the economic area coupled with judicial activism in pursuit of protection of civil liberties and civil rights.

In 1927, in *Whitney v. California*, the Court upheld the conviction of Anita Whitney under the California Criminal Syndicalism Act. The concurring opinion written by Brandeis has come to be viewed as the most lyrical expression of his approach to freedom of speech:

> Those who won our independence believed that the final end of the State was to make men free to develop their faculties, and that, in its government, the deliberative forces should prevail over the arbitrary. They valued liberty both as an end, and as a means. They believed liberty to be the secret of happiness, and courage to be the secret of liberty. They believed that freedom to think as you will and to speak as you think are means indispensable to the discovery and spread of political truth; that, without free speech and assembly, discussion would be futile; that, with them, discussion affords ordinarily adequate protection against the dissemination of noxious doctrine; that the greatest menace to freedom is an inert people; that public discussion is a political duty, and that this should be a fundamental principle of the American government.[37]

When Holmes did write during this period, he too was capable of employing language that stirred. For example, in *Gitlow v. New York* (1925) the Court upheld the conviction of Benjamin Gitlow for violating New York's criminal anarchy laws. Dissenting (joined by Brandeis), Holmes said:

> If what I think the correct test is applied, it is manifest that there was no present danger of an attempt to overthrow the government by force on the part of the admittedly small minority who shared the defendant's views. It is said that this manifesto was more than a theory, that it was an incitement. Every idea is an incitement. It offers itself for belief and if believed it is acted on unless some other belief outweighs it or some failure of energy stifles the movement at its birth. The only difference between the expression of an opinion and an incitement in the narrower sense is the speaker's enthusiasm for the result. Eloquence may set fire to reason. But whatever may be thought of the redundant discourse before us it had no chance of starting a present conflagration. If in the long run the beliefs expressed in proletarian dictatorship

are destined to be accepted by the dominant forces of the community, the only meaning of free speech is that they should be given their chance and have their way.[38]

Holmes and Brandeis wrote their free speech dissents in cases that were decided against the backdrop of the Red Scare period that immediately followed the end of World War I, a time during which a majority of the Court resolutely continued to uphold Congressional and state laws against First Amendment claims. Over time, however, the reaction to the upsurge in government repression gradually strengthened the hand of those who recognized the doctrinal inadequacies of the Court's speech jurisprudence.[39]

Holmes left the Court in 1932, but that year also brought President Franklin D. Roosevelt and his New Deal.[40] After the retirements or deaths of several justices in the period following his 1937 Court-packing effort, FDR's appointments to the Court reinforced the trend toward expanding constitutional protection for free speech. By the time Brandeis left the Court in 1939, the Court majority was regularly citing the "clear and present danger" test in cases where it upheld free speech rights, and it continued to do so into the 1940s.[41] Nevertheless, it is one thing to give the First Amendment some serious enforcement. It is another to bring doctrine to an exposition of full-fledged libertarianism. And before that happened, the momentum of expanding free speech protection experienced a setback.

The Libertarian Ascendency: Experience Proves To Be the Life of the Law

The beginning of the Cold War in the late 1940s, and the acquisition of nuclear weapons by the Soviet Union, meant that the United States found itself vulnerable to nuclear attack by long-range bombers. Additionally, revelations of espionage by Soviet spies gave support to American anxieties over subversion and the drawn-out undeclared war in Korea contributed to the development of a strong anti-Communist, speech-restrictive climate in the United States.

At the Supreme Court, this climate was evident in *Dennis v. United States* (1951), upholding the Smith Act, a 1940 statute criminalizing subversive activities.[42] The Supreme Court majority opinion turned to Holmes's "clear and present danger" test and asked:

What has been meant by the use of the phrase "clear and present danger" of the utterances bringing about the evil within the power of Congress to punish.

> Obviously, the words cannot mean that, before the Government may act, it must wait until the putsch is about to be executed, the plans have been laid and the signal is awaited. If Government is aware that a group aiming at its overthrow is attempting to indoctrinate its members and to commit them to a course whereby they will strike when the leaders feel the circumstances permit, action by the Government is required.[43]

As noted above, in the *Masses* case in 1917 Learned Hand, then a district court judge, wrote a speech-protective opinion that had an important influence on Holmes's thinking about expressive freedom. By the 1950s, Hand had risen to become the chief judge of the Second Circuit Court of Appeals, the intermediate appellate court that heard *Dennis.* In his opinion in that case, Hand adopted an approach that watered down the "clear and present danger" standard to what has since been described as a clear and probable danger standard: "whether the gravity of the 'evil,' discounted by its improbability, justifies such invasion of free speech as is necessary to avoid the danger."[44] The US Supreme Court majority adopted Hand's new approach.

Critics denounced the Smith Act convictions as based on little more than the defendants' ideological commitment to Marxist concepts of inevitable revolution coupled with otherwise legal political activity. The language of Justice William O. Douglas's *Dennis* dissent echoed the earlier dissents of Holmes and Brandeis:

> Petitioners, however, were not charged with a "conspiracy to overthrow" the Government. They were charged with a conspiracy to form a party and groups and assemblies of people who teach and advocate the overthrow of our Government by force or violence and with a conspiracy to advocate and teach its overthrow by force and violence. It may well be that indoctrination in the techniques of terror to destroy the Government would be indictable. . . . But the teaching which is condemned here is of a different character. So far as the present record is concerned, what petitioners did was to organize people to teach and themselves teach the Marxist-Leninist doctrine.[45]
>
> Full and free discussion has indeed been the first article of our faith. We have founded our political system on it. It has been the safeguard of every religious, political, philosophical, economic, and racial group amongst us. We have counted on it to keep us from embracing what is cheap and false; we have trusted the common sense of our people to choose the doctrine true to our genius and to reject the rest.[46]

As the 1950s progressed, and the nation's anti-Communist anxiety subsided, the Court began to announce decisions that emphasized that abstract advocacy of revolution could not be prosecuted and that

Congress's investigatory powers had limits.[47] It also clarified that prosecutors of Communist Party members could not rely on "mere membership" in the party to establish criminal liability but had to show that the accused had joined the party with the specific intent of joining a conspiracy to overthrow the government.[48] As a result of these decisions, the Holmesian libertarian speech concepts began to gain renewed traction, ultimately culminating in the 1969 decision in *Brandenburg v. Ohio*.[49] In that case, the Court finally announced a demanding standard for governmental restrictions on speech. Restrictions were constitutional only if the speech was attempting to incite imminent lawless action and was likely to produce such action.

This trend continued throughout the rest of the twentieth century and into the twenty-first century. The reasons for this ascendency are complex, but clearly a great part of the doctrinal development that expanded the constitutional free speech guarantee in the libertarian direction, foreshadowed by the Holmes *Abrams* dissent's marketplace of ideas rhetoric, took place within the context of the social, cultural, and political turmoil of the 1960s and early 1970s.

The US Supreme Court of the late 1800s had played a critical role in legitimizing the system of state-mandated racial segregation known as "Jim Crow" by interpreting away the meaning that was at the heart of the three amendments to the US Constitution enacted during the Reconstruction period that immediately followed the Civil War. With only limited exceptions, the cause of civil rights for the former slaves in the post–Civil War decades found little sympathy in the Court. In dramatic contrast, the Supreme Court of the 1960s, led by Chief Justice Earl Warren, operated as a virtual fairy godmother to the Civil Rights Movement's struggle to defeat segregation. And because that struggle involved protests, demonstrations, press and media appeals, and other expressive forms, the Warren Court's support for civil rights frequently required, as a practical matter, significantly broadening rights to free expression as the movement's struggles both dramatized the need for broad libertarian speech doctrine and provided the occasions for its expansion and development.

To a significant degree, the transformation of Holmes's marketplace of ideas concept from an aspiration to a doctrinal reality in the United States is a by-product of the Court's response to the protest movements of the 1960s and early 1970s (including the protests against the Vietnam War, which were not always peaceful or limited to speech). In this respect, Holmes's claim that experience is the life of the law proved prescient in that it does indeed seem that it was this experience that did so much to shape and develop the nation's free speech legal doctrine in so dramatic a fashion. This is evident in cases like *Edwards v. South Carolina*, *New York Times v. Sullivan*, *Brandenburg v. Ohio*, and *Cohen v. California*[50] (as set forth in detail in Chapters 4, 5, and 6 of this book).

Conservative Support for a Libertarian Speech Marketplace

Though much liberal opinion advocated basic libertarian concepts of speech toleration in the 1950s and early 1960s, the same cannot really be said of the preponderance of conservative opinion of that period.[51] However, as shown in Chapters 6, 7, and 8 herein, by the late 1960s and early 1970s, libertarian speech doctrine was beginning to gain support from justices whose outlooks ranged all across the political spectrum.[52]

Perhaps one reason why the conservative movement that came to power with the election of President Ronald Reagan in the 1980s had within it elements that possessed such a strong respect for libertarian speech concepts is that the conservative rise was preceded by a self-conscious effort to make conservatism a movement of ideas. A growing conservative intellectual establishment saw itself as having challenged the liberal intellectual establishment that dominated in previous decades and believed that conservatism won that battle because of the force of its ideas. Even if the claim that conservatism came to power in the United States primarily because of the strength of its ideas is unpersuasive to many, it cannot be disputed that conservatism's rise included an intellectual establishment of some size which had utilized free speech extensively and arguably had an interest in its preservation. And the very self-conscious attempt to make conservatism a movement of ideas is generally characterized by a respect for libertarian speech concepts and Holmes's marketplace of ideas approach.[53]

Conservative acceptance of libertarian constitutional speech rights has sometimes resulted in Court decisions where socially conservative views on homosexuality have been prioritized over the efforts of state and local governments to apply their laws prohibiting discrimination in public accommodations to gay people.[54] Indeed, in the near future the Court may be called upon to decide whether wedding photographers and the bakers of wedding cakes are engaged in artistic occupations whose First Amendment expressive rights trump state and local public accommodations laws when the photographers or bakers refuse to provide their services to those planning to marry in same-sex ceremonies. Nevertheless, it can be argued that with decisions such as *Lawrence v. Texas*[55] and *United States v. Windsor*,[56] the Supreme Court has not failed to advance the rights of gay people.

However, to many observers, it does seem that conservative support for libertarian speech doctrine has come at an unacceptably high price—a bar on government efforts to limit the impact of large aggregates of wealth and property upon the political process.[57] The narrow conservative majority on the contemporary Supreme Court has placed what increasing numbers of critics see as excessive limits on the ability of Congress and state legislatures to limit the amount of money that can be spent to influence the outcome of elections and referenda. In fact, it can be argued that the Supreme Court's use of the First Amendment to block these efforts is reminiscent of the Court's behavior in the early decades of the twentieth century and threatens to undermine democracy.

Lochner v. New York,[58] decided in 1905, is symbolic of a period in history when a very conservative Supreme Court frequently insisted that the Constitution was violated when state legislatures enacted reform legislation designed to ameliorate the harsher effects of the industrial revolution. The *Lochner* majority found unconstitutional a state law preventing bakers from working more than sixty hours a week. Progressives saw the Court as entrenching conservative economic theories in the Constitution to defeat populist and progressive reform efforts even when they succeeded in legislatures.

Personally skeptical of the wisdom of many of these reform efforts, Holmes wrote a dissent in *Lochner* in which he accused the majority of reading its free market ideology into the Constitution. "The Fourteenth Amendment does not enact Mr. Herbert Spencer's *Social Statics*," Holmes declared.[59] The *Lochner* decision came to symbolize an era in which the Court frequently struck down progressive state laws, as well as national laws, that regulated working conditions. In the eyes of many, today's Supreme Court, arguably the most conservative since the *Lochner* era, is using the First Amendment to enable wealthy interests to dominate the political system and frustrate contemporary reform efforts.

The first Supreme Court objection to limits on political money was the 1976 decision in *Buckley v. Valeo*, in which the Court held that limits on campaign expenditures unavoidably limited the quantity of available political speech and were thus unconstitutional.[60] Disseminating a political message does of course require that money be spent in many circumstances, and supporters of *Buckley* and its progeny argue strongly that the more free speech, the better. Liberal justices like

William Brennan supported the original *Buckley* holding alongside their more conservative counterparts, but over time this line of cases has come to be identified with the Court's conservatives, as the justices appointed by recent Republican presidents have aggressively expanded this approach.

Critics of this doctrinal development maintain that in a society that permits the accumulation of enormous wealth by individuals and corporations, substantial government regulation, coupled with public financing, is required to keep these large aggregates of special interest wealth from dominating elections. Yet in recent years, the Supreme Court under the leadership of Chief Justice John Roberts has emphatically rejected this notion. In *Citizens United v. Federal Election Commission*,[61] the Court removed long-standing restrictions on corporate spending. Then, in *McCutcheon v. Federal Election Commission*,[62] the Court likewise invalidated the two-year aggregate limit on the total amount of money an individual can donate to candidates for federal office. To many observers, Holmes's conception of a marketplace of ideas, while never without large imperfections, is warped to an extreme degree if great concentrations of wealth can "corner the market" and, over time, radically alter the shape of democratic discourse by literally drowning out other voices in a torrent of purchased messages.

THE FUTURE OF THE "MARKETPLACE OF IDEAS"

Other difficult issues have arisen recently outside of the context of campaign finance. Although *Brandenburg* is still the governing precedent, the events of September 11, 2001, have impacted free speech law. Concern about the potential for other terrorist attacks has induced the Supreme Court and other federal courts to sustain executive branch actions that may significantly erode or at least circumvent *Brandenburg*, to the concern of many analysts.

In *Holder v. Humanitarian Law Project*, dissenting Justice Stephen Breyer stated:

> [I] cannot agree with the Court's conclusion that the Constitution permits the Government to prosecute the plaintiffs criminally for engaging in coordinated teaching and advocacy furthering the designated [as terrorist] organizations' lawful political objectives. In my view, the Government has not met its burden of showing that an interpretation of the statute that would prohibit this speech- and association-related activity serves the Government's compelling interest in combating terrorism.[63]

Although the *Holder* majority suggested that independent advocacy was a different matter from the coordinated teaching and advocacy involved in that case, some critics see subsequent lower court cases as going further.[64]

Nevertheless, libertarian speech doctrine still remains formally ascendant. The claim throughout this chapter has been that the Holmes of the *Abrams* dissent can be plausibly described as the intellectual "father" of the libertarian marketplace of ideas approach that ultimately became ascendant in US Supreme Court speech doctrine and that, that ascendency was largely the result of the nation's experience, which Holmes claimed to be "the life of the law." Therefore it seems appropriate to conclude by asking the following question. If Holmes were alive today, what would he think of this development?

Of course, since much of the specific experience that has shaped, and is still shaping, speech doctrine was not part of Holmes's own life experience, there are many matters on which we have no real basis for intelligent speculation. But it seems reasonable to assume that Holmes would be pleased that twenty-first-century America has a very wide-open speech marketplace in many respects, with even broader participation now made possible through the Internet. At the same time, it is hard to imagine that the justice who held that "the Fourteenth Amendment does not enact Mr. Herbert Spencer's *Social Statics*" in *Lochner* would be enthusiastic about the line of cases that runs from *Buckley* to *Citizens United* and *McCutcheon*. Though personally conservative, he might well share the view that the Court majority was reading its ideology into the Constitution and that the decisions are a back-door *Lochner* that give billionaires and powerful corporate interests the ability to try to buy great influence for their points of view, warping the ability of the speech marketplace he so eloquently articulated to sift and weigh facts and ideas.

There are inevitably positives and negatives to our libertarian free speech marketplace, and the struggles surrounding it will surely continue. Many see the United States' tolerance of "hate speech" as excessive.[65] Continuing controversy can be anticipated about speech activities that the government connects to terrorism. And on the practical level, it can be plausibly argued that for many average citizens, free speech is not so much inhibited by the government as by their socio-economic circumstances.

Still, speech largely free from official restriction and punishment is essential to science, social progress, human rights, and democracy; it is surely an important ideal to aspire to even if imperfectly realized. And to a significant extent, we have Holmes to thank for setting our constitutional jurisprudence on that path toward its ultimate realization.

NOTES

1. *Schenck v. United States*, 249 U.S. 47 (1919).
2. *Abrams v. United States*, 250 U.S. 616 (1919).
3. Oliver Wendell Holmes Jr., *The Common Law* (1881; reprint Mineola, NY: Dover Publications, 1991), 1.
4. Leonard W. Levy, *Legacy of Suppression: Freedom of Speech and Press in Early American History* (Cambridge, MA: Harvard University Press, 1960).
5. *New York Times v. Sullivan*, 376 U.S. 254, 276 (1964).
6. John C. Frémont was the Republican Party's presidential candidate in 1856.
7. See Geoffrey R. Stone, *Perilous Times: Free Speech in Wartime from the Sedition Act of 1798 to the War on Terrorism* (New York: W. W. Norton, 2004), Chapter 2.
8. *Barron v. Baltimore*, 32 U.S. 243 (1833).
9. *Gitlow v. New York*, 268 U.S. 652 (1925). The due process theory does not claim that the rights protected are federal rights. It recognizes that the responsibility for securing them remains in the hands of the states, but it holds that the requirements of due process prevent the states themselves from violating them. Plenary federal authority over private action interfering with these rights is thus not conferred.

   The suppression of antislavery speech in the years before the Civil War was a very serious matter in many places and some commentators have suggested that as a result, key radical Republican drafters of the sweeping phrases of the Fourteenth Amendment's first section did indeed therein intend to nationalize civil liberties protections, including the First Amendment's free speech guarantee. Horace Flack, *The Adoption of the Fourteenth Amendment* (Baltimore, MD: Johns Hopkins Press, 1908); Jacobus tenBroek, *The Anti-Slavery Origins of the Fourteenth Amendment* (Oakland, CA: University of California Press, 1951).
10. Espionage Act (June 15, 1917), http://www.firstworldwar.com/source/espionageact.htm
11. Espionage Act (May 7, 1918), http://www.firstworldwar.com/source/espionageact1918.htm
12. Stone, *Perilous Times*, 182.
13. Though by some accounts the younger Holmes's relationship with his father was rather strained.
14. 249 U.S. 47 (1919).
15. Ibid., 52. According to Thomas Healy, the crowded theatre metaphor was first used by an attorney in the lower court proceeding in *Debs v. United States*, 249 U.S. 211 (1919). Thomas Healy, *The Great Dissent: How Oliver Wendell Holmes Changed His Mind—And Changed the History of Free Speech in America* (New York: Henry Holt, 2013), 97.
16. *Patterson v. Colorado*, 205 U.S. 454 (1907).
17. *Frohwerk v. United States*, 249 U.S. 204 (1919).
18. Ibid., 208.

19. *Debs v. United States*, 249 U.S. 211 (1919).
20. Ibid., 216.
21. 250 U.S. at 624–631 (Holmes, J., joined by Brandeis, J., dissenting).
22. *Baltzer v. United States*, 248 U.S. 593 (1918).
23. In 1918, Holmes also dissented in *Toledo Newspaper Co. v. United States*, 247 U.S. 402, 422–426 (1918) (Holmes, J., joined by Brandeis, J., dissenting), opposing the contempt conviction of a newspaper for articles critical of a federal judge.

    In *Baltzer*, Holmes wrote: "Real obstructions of the law, giving real aid and comfort to the enemy, I should have been glad to see punished more summarily and severely than they sometimes were. But I think that our intention to put out all our powers in aid of success in war should not hurry us into intolerance of opinions and speech that could not be imagined to do harm, although opposed to our own. It is better for those who have unquestioned and almost unlimited power in their hands to err on the side of freedom. We have enjoyed so much freedom for so long that perhaps we are in danger of forgetting that the bill of rights which cost so much blood to establish still is worth fighting for, and that no tittle of it should be abridged." Quoted in Sheldon M. Novick, "The Unrevised Holmes and Freedom of Expression," *Supreme Court Review* 303 (1991): 389.

    It does seem likely that because of *Baltzer*, Holmes was assigned to write the Opinion of the Court in the Espionage Act cases just discussed in order to achieve Court unanimity.
24. Stephen M. Feldman, "Free Speech, World War I, and Republican Democracy: The Internal and External Holmes," *First Amendment Law Review* 6 (2008): 237.
25. 244 F. 535 (1917). See Gerald M. Gunther, *Learned Hand: The Man and the Judge* (New York: Oxford University Press, 2010), 128.
26. The relationship is described at length and with extensive detail in Healy, *The Great Dissent.* See also Mark DeWolfe Howe, ed., *Holmes-Laski Letters: The Correspondence of Mr. Justice Holmes and Harold J. Laski 1916–1935* (Cambridge, MA: Harvard University Press, 1953).
27. Chafee authored the influential "Freedom of Speech in War Time," *Harvard Law Review* 32 (1919): 932–973 and *Freedom of Speech* (New York: Harcourt, Brace and Howe, 1920). Though Chafee was not at all a political radical, his initial publication of *Freedom of Speech* antagonized many and led to an effort to remove him from the Harvard Faculty. See Peter H. Irons, "'Fighting Fair': Zechariah Chafee Jr., the Department of Justice, and the 'Trial at the Harvard Club,'" *Harvard Law Review* 94 (1981): 1205–1236. His publication of a revised edition two decades later (Cambridge, MA: Harvard University Press, 1941) was well-received when the Bill of Rights was popularly viewed as a symbol of American freedom at a time when freedom was seriously threatened.
28. Felix Frankfurter became a professor at Harvard Law School and was appointed a Supreme Court justice in 1939 by President Franklin Roosevelt.

29. Healy, *The Great Dissent*, 201.
30. 250 U.S. at 628 (Holmes, J., joined by Brandeis, J., dissenting).
31. Ibid., at 630.
32. Holmes joined Brandeis in dissent in *Schaefer v. United States*, 251 U.S. 466 (1920) and *Pierce v. United States*, 252 U.S. 239 (1920), but not in *Gilbert v. Minnesota*, 254 U.S. 325 (1920). In the 1921 case of *United States ex rel. Milwaukee Social Democratic Publishing Co. v. Burleson, Postmaster General*, 255 U.S. 407 (1921), Brandeis wrote a lengthy dissent, and Holmes wrote a brief dissent of his own indicating that his mind had been changed by Brandeis's dissent.
33. It was actually Brandeis who held most consistently to protection of speech in a series of separate opinions he authored in the 1920s, usually, but not always, joined by Holmes. In this effort, Brandeis cited Holmes's "clear and present danger" test from the *Schenck* case, insisting that the words "clear and present danger" gave greater protection to speech than the old "bad tendency" test that said speech could be punished if it had a tendency to bring about violation of law. See Steven B. Lichtman, "The Disappearing Jurisprudence of Louis Brandeis," *Brandeis University Law Journal* 3 (2013): 9–28.
34. Brandeis was the first Jewish justice to serve on the Court.
35. Rabban points out that before the World War I cases there was a radical libertarian cultural view of free speech that opposed repression of speech including speech involving sexually-related expression that the Progressives tended to dismiss. David M. Rabban, *Free Speech in Its Forgotten Years, 1870–1920* (New York: Cambridge University Press, 1997), 5.
36. *United States v. Carolene Products*, 304 U.S. 144, 152, footnote no. 4 (1938).
37. *Whitney v. California*, 274 U.S. 357, 375 (1927) (Brandeis, J., joined by Holmes, J., concurring).
38. 268 U.S. at 673 (1925) (Holmes, J., joined by Brandeis, J., dissenting). Holmes's ability to coin a memorable phrase was also famously on display in 1929 when he dissented from the Court's refusal to allow a Quaker pacifist who refused to bear arms in defense of the United States to become a citizen saying "if there is any principle of the Constitution that more imperatively calls for attachment than any other it is the principle of free thought—not free thought for those who agree with us but freedom for the thought that we hate" and "I had not supposed hitherto that we regretted our inability to expel [Quakers] because they believe more than some of us do in the teachings of the Sermon on the Mount." *United States v. Schwimmer*, 279 U.S. 644, 654–655 (1929) (Holmes, J., joined by Brandeis, J., dissenting).
39. See, for example, *Fiske v. Kansas*, 274 U.S. 380 (1927), in which the Court that upheld the California Criminal Syndicalism conviction of Anita Whitney overturned a Kansas Criminal Syndicalism conviction. In the 1930s, the Court finally began to breathe life into the free speech guarantee, as the libertarian approach to free speech cases articulated in

Holmes's *Abrams* dissent and the Brandeis and Holmes dissents that followed began to be reflected in majority opinions striking down state and Congressional laws. In 1931, when faced with a state conviction of someone for displaying a red flag in *Stromberg v. California*, Chief Justice Hughes for the majority held that "[t]he maintenance of the opportunity for free political discussion to the end that government may be responsive to the will of the people and that changes may be obtained by lawful means, an opportunity essential to the security of the Republic, is a fundamental principle of our constitutional system. A statute which upon its face, and as authoritatively construed, is so vague and indefinite as to permit the punishment of the fair use of this opportunity is repugnant to the guaranty of liberty contained in the Fourteenth Amendment." 283 U.S. 359, 369 (1931). That year, the Court also struck down an injunction prohibiting publication of a "malicious" newspaper as a prior restraint in violation of the liberty of the press as incorporated through the Fourteenth Amendment in *Near v. Minnesota*, 283 U.S. 697 (1931). The Court struck down a separate sales tax on newspapers in *Grosjean v. American Press Company*, 297 U.S. 233 (1936). The following year, it rejected state conviction under a Criminal Syndicalism statute of a defendant for assisting in the conducting of a meeting under the auspices of the Communist Party in *De Jonge v. Oregon*, 299 U.S. 353 (1937); and in *Herndon v. Lowry*, it overturned the conviction of a Communist party organizer under a Georgia "insurrection" statute that Justice Owen Roberts for the Court described as "merely a dragnet which may enmesh anyone who agitates for a change of government." 301 U.S. 242, 263 (1937).

40. Reportedly, on the occasion of his ninety-second birthday Holmes was visited by the recently inaugurated President Franklin D. Roosevelt. When Holmes was later asked his opinion of the new president, he is supposed to have replied "a second-class intellect, but a first-class temperament." However, the story is deemed apocryphal by Richard A. Posner and held to actually represent Holmes's opinion of Theodore Roosevelt, not Franklin Roosevelt. See Posner's *The Essential Holmes* (Chicago, IL: University of Chicago Press, 1992), xvi.
41. See *Hague v. C.I.O.*, 307 U.S. 496 (1939); *Thornhill v. Alabama*, 310 U.S. 88 (1940); *Cantwell v. Connecticut*, 310 U.S. 296 (1940); *Bridges v. California*, 314 U.S. 252 (1941); *Thomas v. Collins*, 323 U.S. 516 (1945).
42. *Dennis v. United States*, 341 U.S. 494 (1951).
43. Ibid., 509.
44. *United States v. Dennis et al.*, 183 F.2d 201, 212 (2d Cir. 1950).
45. 341 U.S. at 581–582 (Douglas, J., dissenting).
46. Ibid., 584–585.
47. *Yates v. United States*, 354 U.S. 298 (1957); *Watkins v. United States*, 354 U.S. 178 (1957).

48. *Scales v. United States*, 367 U.S. 203 (1961); *Noto v. United States*, 367 U.S. 290 (1961).
49. *Brandenburg v. Ohio*, 395 U.S. 444 (1969).
50. *Edwards v. South Carolina*, 372 U.S. 229 (1963); 376 U.S. 254 (1964); 395 U.S. 444 (1969); *Cohen v. California*, 403 U.S. 15 (1971).
51. It is instructive here to consider the points that Douglas Edlin makes about conservatism in Chapter 4 herein.
52. It was conservative Justice John Marshall Harlan II who wrote the Opinion of the Court in *Cohen v. California*, where the Supreme Court overturned the conviction of a man who walked through a courthouse with "Fuck the Draft" written on the back of his jacket; Harlan held that "one man's vulgarity is another's lyric." 403 U.S. at 25.
53. The Supreme Court opinion that most clearly demonstrated what respect is, *Hustler Magazine v. Falwell*, 485 U.S. 46 (1988), was a unanimous decision written by conservative Chief Justice William Rehnquist rejecting on First Amendment grounds the claim for damages against *Hustler* magazine by prominent conservative religious figure Reverend Jerry Falwell for publishing a cartoon parody that portrayed Falwell as having sex with his mother in an outhouse.
54. *Hurley v. Irish-American Gay, Lesbian & Bisexual Group of Boston*, 515 U.S. 557 (1995) sustained the exclusion of a group from Boston's St. Patrick's Day Parade that sought to march in celebration of its members' identity as openly gay, lesbian, and bisexual Irish-Americans. Subsequently, the Court utilized the guarantee of free speech to overturn a New Jersey public accommodation discrimination ruling that supported the claim of a scoutmaster who had announced he was gay and was then dismissed from his position by the national Boy Scout organization. Again the Supreme Court majority rejected the state ruling and instead accepted the position of the Boy Scouts organization that allowing an openly gay scoutmaster would conflict with their expressive moral message found in the Boy Scout oath—a message that was protected by the U.S. Constitution's First Amendment free speech guarantee. *Boy Scouts of America et al. v. Dale*, 530 U.S. 640 (2000).
55. *Lawrence v. Texas*, 539 U.S. 558 (2003).
56. *United States v. Windsor*, 570 U.S. 12 (2013).
57. For a discussion of what is described as a New Deal for speech doctrine, see Cass R. Sunstein, *Democracy and the Problem of Free Speech* (New York: Free Press, 1993), particularly Chapters 2, 3, and 4.
58. *Lochner v. New York*, 198 U.S. 45 (1905).
59. Ibid., 75 (Holmes, J., dissenting). Spencer was a Social Darwinist whose writings claimed that society reflected nature in that natural selection and survival of the fittest meant that those on top of society were there because they had proved to be the strongest and thus belonged there.
60. *Buckley v. Valeo*, 424 U.S. 1 (1976).
61. *Citizens United v. Federal Election Commission*, 558 U.S. 310 (2010).

62. *McCutcheon v. Federal Election Commission*, 134 S. Ct. 1434 (2014).
63. *Holder v. Humanitarian Law Project*, 561 U.S. 1 (2012).
64. Writing in the *New York Times*, Andrew F. March described the conviction of one Tarek Mehanna as "based largely on things he said, wrote and translated. Yet that speech was not prosecuted according to the *Brandenburg* standard of incitement to 'imminent lawless action' but according to the much more troubling standard of having the intent to support a foreign terrorist organization." Andrew F. March, "A Dangerous Mind?" *New York Times*, April 21, 2012, SR1. See also *United States v. Tarek Mehanna*, 735 F.3d 32 (2013); *American University National Security Law Brief* 2, no. 2, Article 3, 2012, http://digitalcommons.wcl.american.edu/cgi/viewcontent.cgi?article=1035&context=nslb; Carol Rose, "It's Official. There Is a Muslim Exemption to the First Amendment," *Boston Globe*, April 12, 2012.
65. Ironically, much of America's uniquely libertarian approach to free speech doctrine—which effectively rejects legal restrictions on most "hate speech" directed to racial, religious, and other minorities—emerged from the Supreme Court's response to the long struggle to overcome the vestiges of slavery and achieve racial equality and civil rights that culminated in the Civil Rights Act of 1964 and the Voting Rights Act of 1965.

CHAPTER 2

GEORGE SUTHERLAND AND THE BUSINESS OF EXPRESSION

Samuel R. Olken

Although Justice George Sutherland was on the US Supreme Court from 1922 to 1938, he authored only two opinions pertaining to freedom of expression. Of those two opinions, one was a dissent in a 1937 case, *Associated Press v. NLRB*,[1] involving the application of the National Labor Relations Act to the editorial operation of a news agency. The year before, in *Grosjean v. American Press Co.*,[2] Sutherland delivered his lone majority opinion on freedom of the press in a case that arose from a Louisiana license tax imposed only upon periodicals for which circulation exceeded a certain threshold. Yet, notwithstanding the relative paucity of Sutherland's written analysis of the First Amendment, these opinions reveal an intriguing perspective about freedom of expression in a democratic republic and underscore the link between economic liberty and the value of the press. Like Justice Oliver Wendell Holmes Jr., with whom Sutherland served on the Supreme Court for a decade, Sutherland's contribution to the development of free speech jurisprudence emanated from a relatively sparse number of cases. Whereas Holmes's thirty-year tenure yielded a handful of seminal free speech opinions, Sutherland, whose Supreme Court career was almost half as long as Holmes's, produced only two free press opinions. Unlike Holmes, for whom the marketplace of ideas represented an abstract rationale for preserving freedom of expression in a democratic society, Sutherland instead sought to protect those involved in the business of expression—editors and publishers—from arbitrary and unreasonable economic regulations that fettered their freedom to produce and publish news stories.

Sutherland's emphasis on the business of expression in these cases differed considerably from the more abstract concept of the marketplace of ideas invoked two decades earlier by Holmes[3] and subsequently refined by Justices Louis Brandeis[4] and Benjamin Cardozo,[5] who as Sutherland's Court colleagues were far more solicitous toward the expression of ideas. In the vast majority of cases involving restrictions upon speech or the press that came before the Court during his tenure, Sutherland frequently voted to uphold governmental authority—both federal and local—to curb expression in verbal or written form deemed to pose a clear and present danger,[6] exhibit a dangerous tendency,[7] or constitute a nuisance.[8] He also believed the government could punish individuals, who for reasons of personal conscience refused to take loyalty oaths or otherwise publicly to swear their allegiance to the country during a time of war.[9] In a few instances, however, particularly when it appeared the threat posed by the expression was tenuous, Sutherland was more reluctant to uphold public restrictions.[10] Additionally, Sutherland accepted the notion that through the Due Process Clause of the Fourteenth Amendment the First Amendment protection afforded speech and the press applied as a limitation upon state governmental authority. However, Sutherland's was a far more restrictive approach toward freedom of expression than that adopted by more liberal members of the Court such as Holmes, Brandeis, Cardozo, or even Charles Evans Hughes.

Sutherland's significant contribution to the jurisprudence of free speech, of which freedom of the press is a correlative right, is that political factions, through the guise of economic regulations, could actually impede the manner in which the press disseminates speech or otherwise facilitates expression. Sutherland's aversion to political factions reflected his steadfast concern that factions could influence the political process in ways that advanced the interests of some groups to the detriment of others and thus subvert the democratic ideal of equal operation of the law. Sutherland's recognition of the connection between economic liberty and freedom of expression warrants attention because he analyzed the First Amendment issues in *Grosjean* and *Associated Press* through the prism of economic liberty, which was a fundamentally different approach than that employed by other members of the Court.

Conservative in his approach toward constitutional interpretation—indeed, Sutherland often sought to adhere to what he believed was the original meaning of the Constitution and decried the Supreme Court's increased willingness to adapt the Constitution to changing socio-economic conditions—Sutherland believed that the Constitution limited governmental authority in order to preserve individual liberty from the tyranny of democratic majorities. At the end of his tenure on a Supreme Court rift with disagreement over the constitutional limits of public regulation of private economic affairs, Sutherland analyzed the restrictions upon the press in *Grosjean* and *Associated Press* through the lens of his aversion to political factions and concluded that, as a practical matter, the cases involved both economic liberty *and* freedom of expression. Skeptical of governmental intervention into private economic enterprise, Sutherland realized that the economic regulations in these cases interfered with the business of the press, and, as such, impaired the public's right to receive pertinent information. One cannot isolate Sutherland's approach to freedom of expression from his jurisprudence of economic liberty. These are views that, in part, emanated from his personal experiences as a young westerner and his public life before he joined the Court in 1922.

Constitutional and Political Philosophy of George Sutherland

Raised on the Utah frontier in the aftermath of the Civil War, Sutherland developed a deep appreciation for individual liberty and self-reliance that would shape the contours of his constitutional and political philosophy. Throughout his public career, Sutherland often remarked that "individual initiative [and] self-reliance . . . were necessary to develop a real democracy."[11] Wary of legislation he thought unnecessarily interfered with personal freedom, Sutherland decried public regulation of private economic affairs that bore the influence of political factions. He regarded as illegitimate class legislation those laws procured from the government by political factions that bestowed advantages upon some favored groups to the detriment of other segments of society. From Sutherland's perspective, government delegitimized itself with laws that benefited some groups and burdened others if the exercise of public authority bore a remote relationship to the public welfare.[12] Conditioned from youth to regard government intervention in private enterprise as nettlesome and unnecessary in the absence of a compelling public imperative, Sutherland reposed more trust in the individual as an agent of social progress.

Yet despite Sutherland's strong commitment to sturdy individualism, which he believed strengthened the moral fiber of a democratic republic, he was neither a Social Darwinist nor even a staunch proponent of laissez-faire economics. Sutherland recognized the need, at times, for governmental action to redress gross social and economic inequality through means designed to promote the equal operation of the law.[13] Factional aversion and a fear of uncontrolled democratic majorities that threatened the security of personal rights and liberties were the lodestones of his legal and political philosophy. As Sutherland explained in a 1921 speech before the New York State Bar Association: "[A]ny law which arbitrarily separates men into classes to be punished or rewarded, not according to what they do but according to the class to which they are assigned is . . . despotic, no matter how large a majority may have approved it."[14] Accordingly, he considered class legislation the bane of democratic government and a threat to personal liberty. Caution rather than impulse guided his judgment about public matters, and the jurist regarded by some historians as reactionary and elitist was fairly progressive in his views about worker's compensation, suffrage for women, criminal procedure, and land use.[15]

At age twenty, Sutherland attended law school for a year at the University of Michigan, where he studied constitutional law under Thomas Cooley, a Michigan Supreme Court judge and one of the foremost legal theorists of the late nineteenth century. A Jacksonian Democrat, Cooley emphasized equal operation of the law and was wary of political factions that captured the legislative process and threatened the security of private rights through class, or partial, legislation inimical to the public welfare.[16] Through his lectures and his influential treatise, Cooley impressed upon Sutherland and other Gilded Age lawyers the need for constitutional limitations to protect private rights from the tyranny of ephemeral democratic majorities.[17] Cooley's insistence that jurists carefully scrutinize the substantive aspects of economic regulations and consider the operative effects of the law rather than merely look at the form of legislation anticipated the rise of substantive due process and, in retrospect, undoubtedly influenced the young law student from Utah who would eventually adopt his early mentor's views about constitutional law as an associate justice on the US Supreme Court.

After a year of formal legal education, Sutherland returned to Utah and embarked upon a lifelong career in law and politics. Active in the Republican Party, in 1902 Sutherland entered Congress, first as a member of the House of Representatives and later as a two-term senator. He distinguished himself as a proponent of a federal workmen's compensation law; was instrumental in the passage of the constitutional amendment giving women the right to vote; and was a staunch critic of protective tariffs he regarded as illegitimate class legislation that benefited certain groups at the expense of others because of their disparate treatment of agricultural products from certain parts of the country.[18] Similarly, he regarded proposals to restrict an independent judiciary through the recall of unpopular decisions as unwise and detrimental to social stability.[19] Though Sutherland tended to assess domestic legislative issues from the perspective of factional aversion, he was far more deferential to the federal government in matters of foreign policy, even going so far as to identify the president as "the sole organ."[20] In this regard, Sutherland followed the distinction between the internal and external powers of the federal government that Cooley himself had articulated in the latter half of the nineteenth century. In part, Sutherland's deference toward the federal government in matters of foreign policy and war explains his attitude toward restrictions upon speech and the press during his years on the Court when he joined in opinions that sustained the broad powers of government to limit the scope of expressive liberty for those persons and groups whose activities threatened national security.

Perhaps no episode from Sutherland's Senate career better demonstrates his distaste for political factions and foreshadows his approach toward the First Amendment than the support he leant to his Utah colleague Reed Smoot, who nearly lost his seat in the Senate amid allegations that since he was an apostle in the Mormon church, his religious beliefs compromised his duties as an elected public official. Accused of supporting polygamy and allowing church officials to influence his political judgment, Smoot faced censure by the Senate and possible expulsion. Sutherland himself was not a Mormon, even though his parents' brief membership in the Mormon Church facilitated their immigration to Utah from England in 1863, a year after his birth. Moreover, during his initial foray into Utah politics, the state Republican Party, which Sutherland joined, actively opposed Mormons and viewed their tolerance of polygamy as an impediment to Utah obtaining statehood in the late nineteenth century. However, as a US Senator, Sutherland realized how his colleague had been unfairly denigrated by political factions and their pernicious influence. In a passionate speech, Sutherland urged the Senate not to yield to the capricious whims of a democratic majority eager to persecute a member of a religious minority upon mere speculation and hearsay.[21] Ultimately, the Senate declined to punish Smoot, whose controversial affair revealed Sutherland's personal integrity, fairness, and devotion to principle.

In 1922, after a brief respite from public life following the conclusion of his second term in the Senate a few years before, President Warren Harding, a personal friend and former Senate colleague, appointed George Sutherland to the US Supreme Court. Over the next sixteen years, Sutherland would witness firsthand the Court's jurisprudential shift in matters of economic liberty from a rigid, heightened standard of review to a more flexible and deferential approach toward public regulation of private economic affairs. Moreover, throughout the 1920s and into the 1930s, the Court not only began to expand the broad concept of liberty beyond the scope of economic substantive due process but also struggled to apply the "clear and present danger" test. Sutherland, during the first several terms of his tenure, was part of the Taft Court's conservative majority, but after 1930, when the more moderate Charles Evans Hughes succeeded William Howard Taft as chief justice, Sutherland became one of the "Four Horsemen," a quartet of justices (along with Pierce Butler, Willis Van Devanter, and James McReynolds) infamous for having a tenacious hold upon classical notions of constitutional adjudication and rejecting the Court's willingness to adapt the Constitution to changing economic circumstances.[22] The jurisprudential shift within the Court, and Sutherland's refusal to accede to new standards of review in cases involving substantive due process and the Commerce Clause, is crucial for understanding his two late 1930s First Amendment opinions.

The Conservative Judicial Tradition

The constitutional jurisprudence of Justice George Sutherland reflected a conservative judicial tradition in which jurists primarily understood their role as guardians of private property and contract rights from the tyranny of ephemeral democratic majorities controlled by political factions. For Sutherland and other conservative jurists of the late nineteenth and early twentieth centuries, the Constitution embodied a set of fixed limitations intended by its framers to protect individual liberty from arbitrary and unreasonable governmental authority. Laws enacted at the behest of political factions to benefit some groups at the expense of others, in ways detrimental to the long-term public welfare, were regarded by Sutherland and other classical jurists as illegitimate class, or partial, legislation. Though often characterized as a proponent of laissez-faire economics, or even Social Darwinism in his constitutional philosophy, Justice Sutherland really believed in laissez-faire constitutionalism; he considered individual freedom to pursue a lawful occupation, to marry, to believe or not believe in a particular religion, or to hold controversial and unpopular abstract political beliefs the general rule and not the exception in our constitutional system. The Constitution, in Sutherland's view, limited the authority of government to interfere with personal liberty in the absence of essential circumstances. Like other conservative jurists of his generation, Sutherland perceived the judicial role as one that required judges to apply largely fixed rules to factual disputes and to avoid making policy. Classical jurists exalted individual liberty, especially that which concerned property and contract rights, which they regarded as the paradigm for other, noneconomic rights, such as the right to raise a family, to follow or not follow a religion, and those concerning education and freedom of expression.[23]

Conservative, classical jurists also adhered to a fairly strict distinction between the public and private sectors in their attempts to preserve private rights and liberties from incursion by political factions that captured the legislative process.[24] Largely through the advocacy of Sutherland's Michigan law professor, Thomas Cooley, and late nineteenth-century Supreme Court justices, such as Stephen Field[25] and Joseph Bradley,[26] the doctrine of substantive due process emerged as a potent constitutional limitation upon governmental authority. Interestingly, classical jurists, such as Sutherland, who professed to follow a close textual analysis of the Constitution employed a much broader interpretation of the constitutional phrase "due process" in their application of this open-ended provision of the Fourteenth (and in some cases, the Fifth) Amendment. An irony of the classical conservative judicial tradition to which Sutherland adhered is that he and other jurists, particularly solicitous of private property and contract rights, adopted a broad concept of liberty in their expansive use of the Due Process Clause as a constitutional limitation upon public power. Concerned with not only the form of the law but also its substance and, in particular, its operative effects, Sutherland and other conservative jurists regarded substantive due process as a means of curbing the excesses of political factions. They invoked it to protect private rights from partial, or class, legislation that did not bear a close and substantial, or even direct, relationship to the public welfare.[27]

Economic Rights and the Broad Concept of Liberty

Issues of economic liberty comprised the focal point of Sutherland's constitutional jurisprudence while on the Court. For Justice

Sutherland, like Justices Field and Bradley before him, as well as for conservative colleagues on the Court, such as Chief Justice Taft, and Sutherland's fellow dissenters in the 1930s, substantive due process encompassed liberty of contract. Sutherland, in accord with the conservative judicial tradition, essentially read this abstract concept into the constitutional meaning of due process and invoked it to broaden the scope of liberty protected by the Due Process Clause. A theoretical construct that presumed an inherent equality in the bargaining process between employers and their employees, liberty of contract involved both tangible and intangible interests of property arising from the pursuit of a lawful occupation. This doctrine appealed especially to Sutherland and other conservative jurists averse to political factions, skeptical of governmental intervention into private economic activity, and concerned with protecting personal liberty.

As a Supreme Court justice, Sutherland applied liberty of contract to void laws that interfered with the autonomy of private economic affairs[28] and public regulation of commercial enterprise that threatened to stifle competition.[29] For example, in *Adkins v. Children's Hospital*, Sutherland used liberty of contract as the rationale for invalidating a District of Columbia law, which imposed a minimum wage for women, that Sutherland thought had nothing to do with the quality of work performed and that he believed arbitrarily infringed upon the freedom of employers and employees alike to reach contractual agreements about compensation.[30] Similarly, he thought a federal law regulating the wages of coal miners violated substantive due process,[31] and he dissented from the Court's decision in 1937 to reverse course from *Adkins* and uphold a statute that prescribed a minimum wage for women.[32] Moreover, in *New State Ice Co. v. Liebmann*,[33] Sutherland found that an Oklahoma law regulating the manufacture, sale, and distribution of ice infringed upon the economic liberty of some businesses that had been deprived of access to local markets by a monopoly created by the legislature to benefit a few select companies. In cases where Sutherland considered the exercise of governmental authority reasonable, he believed the economic regulations at issue benefited the public as a whole, such as limitations upon the hours of women laborers,[34] workmen's compensation statutes,[35] or zoning ordinances that preserved land values while promoting the public welfare in neutral ways.[36] For Sutherland, factional aversion was the fulcrum upon which liberty of contract and substantive due process rested, and he used these concepts to implement a constitutional order that sought to protect private enterprise from unnecessary and illegitimate class legislation.

Sutherland served as an associate justice at a critical juncture in Supreme Court history, as the justices began to apply the broad concept of liberty beyond the realm of contract and property rights. In *Meyer v. Nebraska*,[37] the Court ruled that a state law that prohibited young students from learning foreign languages in public schools violated the substantive due process rights of teachers to expose their students to languages other than English and also interfered with the students' implied First Amendment right to acquire knowledge. Sutherland joined in Holmes's dissent, which considered the Nebraska law a reasonable national security measure in the aftermath of World War I.[38] In *Pierce v. Society of Sisters*,[39] the Court's decision invalidating an Oregon law that prohibited parents from sending their children to parochial schools rested in part upon a liberty of contract rationale and on parents' autonomy to make decisions about their children's educational and religious training, both of which are derived from the First Amendment. Sutherland, no doubt aware of the influential anti-Catholic political faction behind the Oregon law, joined in Justice McReynolds's majority opinion, which adopted a broad concept of liberty that encompassed both economic and First Amendment rights.[40]

Sutherland's constitutional conservatism was fundamentally different from the living constitutionalism advanced by the subject of the previous chapter, Oliver Wendell Holmes Jr. Often, in cases involving interpretation of the Contracts Clause[41] and the Commerce Clause,[42] Sutherland favored a near literal interpretation of the text of the Constitution and rejected a flexible application of constitutional principles to changing socio-economic circumstances. Yet notwithstanding his general convictions about the fixed meaning of the Constitution over time, Sutherland invoked a broad conception of liberty in his application of the Due Process Clause to protect private economic rights from incursion by democratic majorities. Fundamentally skeptical of political factions that influenced the democratic process, Sutherland regarded the Constitution as a negative set of limitations created to protect individual rights.

In contrast, Holmes was less skeptical about democratic majorities, as evidenced in his tolerance toward economic regulations with which he personally disagreed yet nevertheless thought within the power of government to implement.[43] His constitutional pragmatism cloaked a Social Darwinist bent through which Holmes viewed government efforts to regulate private economic affairs and informed his conviction that within a democracy the stronger, sounder views—whether they concerned economics or matters of public interest such as politics—would prevail.[44] Holmes's free speech metaphor, the marketplace of ideas (which Sutherland applied inconsistently in cases involving political expression) reflected his innate Social Darwinist tendencies. His articulation of what would become the rational basis standard of review in economic regulation cases also reflected his pragmatic view that judges should defer to legislative majorities and not impede local experimentation—an approach that was anathema to Sutherland, whose factional aversion rendered him unable to defer to legislative majorities and made him seem more ill at ease with the hustle and flow of democracy.

Often more pragmatic and progressive in his constitutionalism than Sutherland, Holmes realized by the end of his Court career that judicial intervention was necessary to maintain the marketplace of ideas from the prejudice and whims of the same democratic majorities he had no trouble deferring to in economic matters. Interestingly, in his *Grosjean* and *Associated Press* opinions, Sutherland may have actually moved closer to Holmes's recognition of the need for heightened judicial scrutiny of regulations of expression. Though for Sutherland, who viewed economic liberty as a paradigm for other constitutional rights, the fact that those cases specifically involved economic regulations of the business of expression rather than abstract expression of political speech may have been the reason he was more solicitous of the press in that particular context.

Sutherland's General Views of Freedom of Expression

During Sutherland's tenure as an associate justice, the Supreme Court also struggled to apply the "clear and present danger" test set forth by Justice Holmes in 1919,[45] as discussed in the previous chapter. In a series of cases arising from the prosecution of persons for criminal syndicalism and other offenses aimed at restricting expression of dissenting socio-political views, Sutherland joined Court decisions that upheld the convictions of those who dared to assemble in groups, those who otherwise expressed unpopular views about democracy or national security, or those who offered opinions about the merits of overthrowing the government. For example, Sutherland was part of the Court majority in *Gitlow v. New York*[46] that ruled the Due Process Clause of the Fourteenth Amendment incorporated the First Amendment Free Speech and Press Clauses yet sustained a New York law that curtailed the dissemination of speech presumed to have dangerous tendencies. Similarly, Sutherland joined Justice Butler's dissent in *Near v. Minnesota*,[47] agreeing that local government had the constitutional authority to punish as a public nuisance the publication of a periodical that in the past had published malicious and defamatory stories about public officials. Unlike Chief Justice Hughes, who considered the local ordinance an unconstitutional prior restraint,[48] Butler and, by implication, Sutherland reasoned that the law did not restrict expression so much as it curtailed a public nuisance.[49]

Perhaps Sutherland's reluctance to void these kinds of statutes, as well as those aimed at prohibiting criminal syndicalism, reflected his belief that government could restrict those forms of expression whose secondary effects, such as violence, harmed the public welfare. Moreover, Sutherland, who was very deferential toward the federal government in matters of foreign policy, war, and national security—what he and, before him, Cooley, had designated the external powers of the government[50]—appears to have extended such deference to public regulation of personal expression that threatened public safety and security. In this regard, his willingness to join Butler's *Near* dissent is plausible, as was his accord in cases where the Court curbed the expression of political radicals and would-be revolutionaries whose activity constituted more than mere abstract behavior.

Sutherland's deference to the federal government's external powers also probably explains his view that national security concerns trumped the liberty of conscientious objectors who refused to swear allegiance to the nation's military efforts. In *United States v. MacIntosh*,[51] Sutherland wrote a majority opinion that upheld the denial of citizenship to a Yale theologian who, in his citizenship petition, asserted he would not bear arms in defense of the country. In a few cases, however, such as *Stromberg v. California*[52] and *DeJonge v. Oregon*,[53] Sutherland joined Court opinions that struck down laws that arbitrarily restricted the unpopular political speech of persons or groups whose activities did not constitute a clear and present danger. In *Stromberg*, Sutherland agreed the California criminal syndicalism law infringed upon the First Amendment right of a woman who merely displayed a red flag in public. Notwithstanding these cases, however, it appears that on the whole Sutherland prior to 1936 had not demonstrated a robust support for freedom of speech or the press, and, in fact, was more tolerant of state and federal incursion upon expression that posed a threat in some way to the public welfare.

Moreover, unlike Justice Brandeis, who by the late 1920s had begun to question the utility of the "clear and present danger" test, noting the inherent vagueness of the terms "clear," "present," and "danger,"[54] Sutherland never appears to have harbored such doubts. Nor was Sutherland skeptical about Holmes's marketplace of ideas metaphor as an effective rationale for freedom of speech, an explanation that Holmes may have actually intended to appeal to conservative justices who regarded government regulation of private affairs with some disdain. Not until 1936 did Sutherland even appear to endorse the Brandeis view that democratic imperatives inform free speech jurisprudence.[55] What then compelled Sutherland to articulate at the end of his Supreme Court career a cogent defense of the press when previously he had remained in the background, often joining opinions that sustained restrictions upon expressive activities? The answer in large part involves context and Sutherland's palpable frustration with the shift in the Court's jurisprudence of economic liberty.

The Transformation of the Court's Constitutional Jurisprudence: Prologue to Sutherland's First Amendment Contribution

Throughout the 1930s, a schism developed within the Court over the limits of public regulation of private economic affairs. At the core of the disagreement was a debate over constitutional interpretation, as some members of the Court—specifically, Chief Justice Hughes and Associate Justices Brandeis, Cardozo, and Harlan Fiske Stone—demonstrated an increased willingness to adapt the Constitution to changing socio-economic circumstances to enable the government to meet public needs during the Depression. This approach was deferential toward governmental authority and revealed a more relaxed standard of judicial review than had existed at the height of the *Lochner* era when the Court followed the guardian approach in protecting private economic interests from the tides of democracy.[56] In contrast, Sutherland, the intellectual leader of the Four Horsemen, dissented from the Court's burgeoning constitutional adaptivity and urged his colleagues to apply the Constitution as intended by the framers regardless of the justices' personal views of changing conditions.[57] "[T]he meaning of the Constitution does not change with the ebb and flow of economic events," an exasperated Sutherland exclaimed in a 1937 dissent.[58] Increasingly discouraged by what he deemed the Court's abandonment of its constitutional duty, Sutherland decried the emergence of a two-tiered standard of review in which economic regulations required only a rational basis. Similarly, in Commerce Clause cases he refused to abandon the traditional direct-indirect standard for assessing the scope of federal power to regulate the effects of intrastate activities upon interstate commerce.[59] By 1936–1937, Sutherland and his fellow conservatives on the Court were aghast at the transformation in the Court's jurisprudence of economic liberty. Within this context, Sutherland considered the issues that arose in *Grosjean* and *Associated Press* and crafted opinions that linked economic liberty and freedom of expression.

Grosjean: Differential Taxation of the Press and Political Factions

In the twilight of his judicial career, Sutherland confronted constitutional issues at the intersection of economic liberty and freedom of expression. In *Grosjean* and *Associated Press*, he recognized that economic regulation of the business of the press could adversely affect the dissemination of news. Moreover, he perceived the symbiotic relationship between the business of the press and the content of its expressive activity. From his antifactional perspective, seemingly neutral laws of general application that adversely affected some segments of the press but not others were really no different than the types of illegitimate class legislation he decried in both liberty of contract cases and those involving progressive, or graduated, taxes imposed on some businesses but not others. For Sutherland, *Grosjean* and *Associated Press* involved both economic liberty *and* freedom of expression. Accordingly, his effort to meld these seemingly disparate concepts resulted in his recognition of the business of expression as a viable approach to assessing economic regulations of the press.

In *Grosjean*, a unanimous Supreme Court invalidated a Louisiana law that imposed a license tax upon the gross advertising receipts of only those periodicals within the state that had a weekly circulation of twenty thousand or more readers.[60] Dubbed by its proponents, Senator Huey P. Long and Governor Oscar Allen, as a "2% tax on lying"[61] the Louisiana law reflected a long-standing attempt by Long's political faction, which controlled the state legislature, to penalize his critics while raising revenue for a controversial public works program. The law was part of Long's scheme to tax the state's more profitable industries for the public benefit. Louisiana's largest newspapers, located in New Orleans and Shreveport and supportive of the state's largest industries, had published numerous editorials and stories that opposed Long's plan. His political faction controlled the statehouse, which responded with a license tax on 2 percent of the gross advertising revenue of the state's largest papers, all but one of which criticized (and at times mocked) Huey Long and his ideas.[62]

The affected periodicals, thirteen newspapers owned by nine different companies, asserted that the license tax violated the Fourteenth Amendment's Equal Protection Clause and the First Amendment's Free Press Clause. They realized that a tax upon their advertising revenue, which contributed far more to their operating costs than subscription fees, would restrict their ability to disseminate the news and thus indirectly but substantially affect their expressive activity. As James Thompson, of the *New Orleans Item and Tribune* (one of the large newspapers adversely affected by the license tax), noted, the tax was "a deliberate attempt to punish, muzzle and destroy newspapers . . . they can be taxed entirely out of business. They can be ruined or confiscated at pleasure by any political group temporarily dominating a legislature."[63] Conversely, the State justified the license tax as a neutral means of raising revenue and discounted any collateral First Amendment effects.

Initially, Sutherland and possibly five other justices viewed the Louisiana statute as illegitimate class legislation that violated the Equal Protection Clause of the Fourteenth Amendment. In fact, Sutherland drafted an opinion for the Court that would have ruled the license tax unconstitutional on this ground alone without any reference to the First Amendment.[64] Undoubtedly, Sutherland regarded the Louisiana license tax as comparable to the graduated, or progressive, chain store taxes he thought unconstitutional. In a series of previous cases, Sutherland expressed concern with these kinds of taxes because they imposed differential burdens upon companies in similar types of businesses on the basis of company size. Sutherland reasoned that a tax on chain stores penalized larger businesses and benefited independent ones engaged in the same enterprise and thus constituted illegitimate class, or partial, legislation that bore a remote relationship to the public welfare.[65] As such, these taxes violated the concept of equal protection and represented an unconstitutional infringement of economic liberty. At oral argument, Elisha Hanson, counsel for the American Newspaper Company, confirmed Sutherland's suspicion about the factional characteristics of the Louisiana license tax, when in response to an inquiry from Sutherland about whether the Louisiana law would diminish circulation, Hanson explained, "[y]es . . . [i]t would also turn the business of one newspaper group over to another."[66]

However, not all members of the Court agreed with Sutherland that local chain store taxes, or, as in this case, a license tax applicable only to some periodicals, represented illegitimate class legislation. Justices Cardozo, Brandeis, and Stone were more deferential toward local graduated taxes on chain stores and other large businesses, believing that such differential taxation was a reasonable way for states to foster economic competition.[67] These same justices, along with Hughes and Owen Roberts, by 1936 had also demonstrated a more flexible and pragmatic approach toward other aspects of public regulation of private economic affairs than had Sutherland and the other justices who had dissented in important economic liberty cases, such as *Home Building & Loan Association v. Blaisdell*,[68] *Nebbia v. New York*,[69] and *West Coast Hotel v. Parrish*.[70]

In fact, Cardozo informed Sutherland that he would not join in an opinion that struck down the Louisiana law on equal protection grounds and avoided the First Amendment issue. Cardozo also drafted a separate opinion that focused upon the freedom of the press and intimated that unless Sutherland changed the analytical emphasis of his opinion, Cardozo would file a concurrence in which Justices Brandeis and Stone would likely join.[71] Cardozo's draft did not address the economic liberty concerns of Sutherland but instead mentioned how the Louisiana tax adversely affected the dissemination of news and stressed the value of a free press in a democratic society.[72]

In response, Sutherland incorporated Cardozo's views about freedom of the press and produced a cogent analysis of how a differential tax upon the advertising revenues of newspapers impaired the freedom of the press to the detriment of democratic society. He expressly linked economic liberty and freedom of the press and presented a compelling defense of the business of expression from incursion by class legislation. Although Sutherland ultimately adopted Cardozo's First Amendment points, particularly his recognition that the Louisiana act threatened press autonomy in ways similar to the infamous eighteenth-century British taxes on knowledge and information,[73] Sutherland himself was not unaware of the First Amendment implications of such factional legislation. Nor was he ignorant of the connection between economic rights and those of expression. A year before he joined the Court, Sutherland told the New York State Bar Association that:

> The guaranties for safe-guarding life, liberty and property, freedom of speech and of religious worship, and all the other guaranties of the Constitution, would be of little value if their interpretation and enforcement depended upon arbitrary, shifting, temporary official edicts instead of the calm, judgment of the judiciary under the general law of the land.[74]

Given Sutherland's factional aversion, his recognition of a broad concept of liberty and his view, expressed in cases such as *New State Ice*

Company v. Liebmann,[75] that economic rights were a paradigm for other personal liberties, Sutherland's willingness to include Cardozo's points makes sense.

In *Grosjean*, Sutherland explicitly linked economic liberty and freedom of the press and suggested a new approach toward the First Amendment, one that recognized the business of expression. Beginning with the premise that constitutional limitations upon governmental authority exist to protect corporations as well as persons, a point Sutherland made in the chain tax cases, he reiterated that the Due Process Clause of the Fourteenth Amendment incorporated the Free Press Clause of the First Amendment.[76] For support, Sutherland cited two First Amendment cases, *Near v. Minnesota*[77] and *Gitlow v. New York*,[78] along with one about contractual liberty and due process, *Allgeyer v. Louisiana*,[79] an intriguing juxtaposition of precedent that signaled Sutherland's endorsement of a broad concept of liberty and his intent to link economic liberty and freedom of the press.

Sutherland then melded his views about political factions, economic liberty, and the First Amendment. Looking beyond the mere form of the tax, but also at its operative effects, a technique he often employed when assessing public regulation of private economic affairs, Sutherland revealed the essential fault of the license tax. The license tax was "itself suspicious"[80] because it targeted circulation volume rather than advertising receipts and had the "plain purpose of penalizing the [large] publishers and curtailing . . . a selected group of newspapers."[81] Noting the tax only applied to large newspapers, Sutherland found that it "operates as a restraint in a double sense. First, its effect is to curtail the amount of revenue realized from advertising, and, second, its direct tendency is to restrict circulation."[82] Taxing the advertising revenue of select newspapers was an indirect but significant way to restrict the newspaper's editorial and business operations. Since the business of publishing the news depended more upon advertising revenue than subscription fees, a punitive tax upon advertising profits could diminish the core expressive function of newspapers. Sutherland understood that because a newspaper's circulation involved both economic and expressive factors, regulation of one would necessarily affect the other.

Sutherland then applied Cardozo's historical insight that the Louisiana statute served a censorial function comparable to the eighteenth-century British knowledge and license taxes imposed upon the press: "to prevent or abridge the free expression of any opinion" critical of the government.[83] Differential taxation of the press signified a form of illegitimate class legislation that threatened the public welfare because it impeded the flow of ideas through its restrictions upon the lifeblood of newspapers—advertising revenue.[84] State control over newspaper revenue, therefore, meant it could control the dissemination of news and perhaps even its content. In modern terms, Sutherland perceived that the license tax actually functioned as a form of impermissible viewpoint discrimination in that it exempted newspapers favorable toward the Long political faction but punished those who were its critics. Sutherland also regarded the Louisiana tax as problematic because it had the potential to distort the marketplace of ideas. As with laws that restricted liberty of contract, the license tax interfered with the newspaper business. Implicitly aware of the analogy between liberty of contract and the autonomy of the press, Sutherland concluded that the tax was "bad not because it takes money from the . . . appellees" but because it was "a deliberate and calculated device to limit the circulation of information to which the public is entitled. . . . A free press stands as one of the great interpreters between the government and the people."[85] Through the guise of a seemingly neutral revenue regulation, Louisiana had infringed upon the business of expression.

Editorial Discretion and Economic Liberty

The following year, in his *Associated Press* dissent, Sutherland clarified the analogy between contractual liberty and freedom of expression. *Associated Press v. NLRB* was one of five cases decided on April 12, 1937, in which the Court upheld the application of the National Labor Relations Act to private businesses engaged in interstate commerce.[86] The case arose from an agency order that the private news organization reinstate an editorial employee terminated, in large part, for his union activities. In sustaining federal regulatory authority over local labor issues, the Court substituted a more pragmatic, flexible test that focused upon the close and substantial relationship between the intrastate activity and the stream of commerce for the stringent requirement preferred by Sutherland that local activities directly affect interstate commerce. This doctrinal shift complemented a similar change that occurred in the standard of review for public regulation of private economic affairs also decried by Sutherland in a series of notable dissents throughout the 1930s. Sutherland's *Associated Press* dissent reflected his frustration with the Court's jurisprudential transformation and the implication, made explicit the following year by Justice Stone in Footnote Four of *Carolene Products*,[87] that economic regulations would receive a less rigorous standard of review than noneconomic ones. Given his acute sensitivity toward political factions and recognition that a broad concept of liberty included both economic and noneconomic rights, Sutherland bristled at Roberts's apparent disregard of the First Amendment issue in this case.

Before the Court, the Associated Press (AP) argued that the NLRB edict that it rehire a discharged editor, Morris Watson, infringed upon its freedom of the press. AP, then as now, compiled raw news stories from its sources throughout the country, reformulated them in its New York office, and distributed them nationally. Though initially AP claimed it terminated Watson, a Newspaper Guild leader who helped unionize his fellow employees, for poor work performance, its invocation of editorial autonomy under the First Amendment suggested the company's primary concern, in the absence of any real evidence of Watson's malfeasance, was that Watson's union activities affected his editorial judgment in stories about labor issues.[88] AP also contested the constitutional authority of the federal government to regulate a private media entity whose editors produced stories before they entered the stream of commerce. The NLRB countered that AP's editorial operations had a close and substantial relationship with commerce and that the cease and desist order it issued to the AP pursuant to the National Labor Relations Act had only an ancillary effect upon the company's freedom of the press. Justice Roberts, for a 5-4 Court, agreed with the NLRB and sustained the agency's order and its underlying legal authorization as a seemingly neutral law of general application that had, at most, an incidental effect upon AP's First Amendment right to editorial autonomy.[89] Roberts construed the case as a Commerce Clause dispute and accused the AP of using the First Amendment as a pretext to justify the discharge of a union activist.[90] Having characterized the principal issue before the Court as an economic one, Roberts applied the new deferential standard and assumed the NLRB's action merely affected the editorial aspect of the AP peripherally, thus neglecting the possible interplay between the federal action and editorial discretion.

In stark contrast, Sutherland perceived that the application of the NLRA to a private news organization infringed its freedom to control its editorial operations. Though Sutherland questioned the power of the federal government to regulate the AP under the Commerce Clause, he focused instead on the First Amendment angle, which afforded him a fresh opportunity to criticize the Court's deference toward economic regulation while advancing the business of expression as a hybrid constitutional concept. Sutherland considered the NLRA unreasonable partial legislation enacted to benefit one class, union members, at the expense of others, such as employers and even those employees who did not want to join a union.[91] Inherently skeptical of this type of class legislation, Sutherland looked beyond the form of the law and scrutinized its operative effects, finding that the NLRA as applied to the AP interfered with its business of expression. Because he considered freedom of expression and liberty of contract as complementary facets of liberty protected by due process, he understood that the expressive and business functions of the AP intertwined.[92] Accordingly, he realized that government interference with how the AP made personnel decisions could affect the manner in which it edited stories and informed the public. Forcing the AP to employ an editor about whose labor bias it worried would compromise the editorial integrity of the private news entity and perhaps even distort the marketplace of ideas.[93] Freedom of the press in this context encompassed business judgment integral to the production of new stories and their dissemination to the public.[94] Consequently, Sutherland refrained, as had Roberts, from differentiating between the AP's economic liberty and its expressive activity. Moreover, he understood that a restriction upon the business discretion of the AP also implicated its right to determine its associates, a constitutional interest derived from both economic liberty and the First Amendment freedom of association.

From Sutherland's perspective, the NLRB order that the AP reinstate Watson was a form of compelled speech in contravention of the First Amendment. Freedom of the press signified "more than publication and circulation."[95] Thus, "the judgment of an administrative censor—cannot, under the constitution, be substituted for that of management in respect of the employment or discharge of employees engaged in editorial work."[96] Sutherland regarded the application of the NLRA in this context as unequal in that it benefited the union to the detriment of both the AP and its readers, since the federal agency order required the AP to retain an editor whose potential bias might affect the quality of the news the AP published.[97] While Sutherland acknowledged that Watson was free to engage in legally protected union activities,[98] he considered the First Amendment interests of his employer paramount.[99] Moreover, his aversion to factions convinced him that the NLRB order would sacrifice the editorial process to the benefit of some union members. By curtailing the editorial autonomy of the AP to make personnel decisions, the NLRB order, had, in effect, threatened to impair the private news organization's business of providing what it considered impartial news to the public.[100] Whom the AP assigned to edit its stories affected the content of these stories, and thus the NLRB edict also impeded the freedom of the press. Concerned that the Court's deferential analysis of the NLRA under the Commerce Clause had undervalued the adverse effects of the statute on the AP's expressive freedom, Sutherland worried that the Court's approach would invite further encroachment upon constitutional liberties through the guise of seemingly neutral economic regulations.[101] Whereas before Sutherland issued this warning in other cases involving only economic rights,[102] now, approaching the end of his tenure on a Court that had transformed its constitutional jurisprudence in ways with which he fundamentally disagreed, Sutherland felt compelled to admonish his colleagues not to abandon guardian review of the First Amendment.

CONCLUSION

As a tandem, Sutherland's opinions in *Grosjean* and *Associated Press* reveal the interplay of economic liberty and freedom of expression in the context of economic regulations of the press. Sutherland viewed freedom of the press through the prism of economic liberty. His was a conservative approach toward constitutional interpretation that reflected a deep-set aversion to political factions and a general skepticism of social experimentation at the expense of private rights, especially those involving property and contracts. Highly critical of the Supreme Court's increased willingness during the 1930s to adapt the Constitution to changing economic circumstances, as well as of the Court's growing deference to public regulation of private economic affairs, Sutherland adhered to a conservative judicial tradition that essentially regarded the Constitution as a set of largely fixed negative limitations of governmental authority set forth by its framers to protect private rights from the tyranny of democratic majorities. The Louisiana license tax and the application of the NLRA to the editorial department of a private news organization in these cases afforded Sutherland the opportunity to address the intersection of economic and expressive rights in a unique way.

While Sutherland himself never used the term "the business of expression," this phrase aptly describes the connection he perceived between these seemingly disparate issues of constitutional law. Though the modern Supreme Court has largely neglected to follow Sutherland's nuanced approach toward assessing the constitutional limits of press regulations that are economic in nature but have an adverse effect upon expressive activities,[103] the modern Court's use of intermediate scrutiny in cases involving content-neutral time, place, and manner regulations, as well as in commercial speech cases,[104] arguably suggests that some of Sutherland's insights continue to influence First Amendment jurisprudence. In particular, the requirements that these types of regulations be narrowly tailored and not discriminate on the basis of viewpoint address issues comparable to those Sutherland raised in his First Amendment opinions, albeit in a different context. Nevertheless, the modern Court has not closely examined the manner in which seemingly neutral economic regulations of the press can impede the expressive activities of the press. This is the lesson of the business of expression, a concept that marked the culmination of Justice Sutherland's constitutional jurisprudence.

Notes

1. *Associated Press v. NLRB*, 301 U.S. 103 (1937). For additional analysis and discussion of many of the points made in this chapter, the reader is encouraged to consult the following articles: Samuel R. Olken, "The Business of Expression: Economic Liberty, Political Factions and the Forgotten First Amendment Jurisprudence of Justice George Sutherland," *William and Mary Bill of Rights Journal* 10 (2002): 249–357 and Samuel R. Olken, "Justice George Sutherland and Economic Liberty: Constitutional Conservatism and the Problem of Factions," *William and Mary Bill of Rights Journal* 6 (1997): 1–88.
2. *Grosjean v. American Press Co.*, 297 U.S. 233 (1936).
3. See *Abrams v. United States*, 250 U.S. 616, 630 (1919) (Holmes, J., dissenting).
4. See *Whitney v. California*, 274 U.S. 357, 372 (1927) (Brandeis, J., concurring).
5. As discussed later in this chapter, Cardozo's draft concurring opinion in *Grosjean* emphasized the connection between free speech and democratic values.
6. See *Herndon v. Lowry*, 301 U.S. 242, 274–275 (1937) (Van Devanter, J., joined by McReynolds, Sutherland, and Butler, JJ., dissenting) (these dissenters would have upheld a criminal syndicalism conviction of a person who possessed Communist literature with the intent to distribute it to incite an unlawful insurrection).
7. See *Gitlow v. New York*, 268 U.S. 652 (1925).
8. See *Near v. Minnesota*, 283 U.S. 697, 735–738 (1931) (Butler, J., joined by Van Devanter, McReynolds, and Sutherland, JJ., dissenting) (this dissent argued that the government could restrict publications that created a nuisance).
9. See *United States v. Macintosh*, 283 U.S. 605 (1931).
10. See *De Jonge v. Oregon*, 299 U.S. 353 (1936) (Sutherland joined the Court's opinion invalidating the application of an Oregon criminal

syndicalism law to a person who organized and spoke about labor affairs at a nonviolent Communist Party meeting); *Stromberg v. California*, 283 U.S. 359 (1931) (Sutherland joined Hughes's opinion for the Court invalidating the criminal syndicalism conviction of a person who merely displayed a red flag in public). See also *Fiske v. Kansas*, 274 U.S. 380 (1927) (Sutherland joined the Court's decision overturning a criminal syndicalism conviction for insufficient evidence).

11. Letter from George Sutherland to Henry M. Bates, Dean, University of Michigan Law School (April 21, 1937) (transcript available in the Sutherland papers at the Library of Congress), quoted in Olken, "The Business of Expression," 259.
12. In an observation that reflected his factional aversion and penchant for individualism, Sutherland admonished that if government were "permitted to take from 'A' and give to 'B' . . . we shall have taken the first step . . . which leads from a republic where every man may rise in proportion to his energy and ability, to a commune where energy and sloth, ability and ignorance, occupy in common the same dead level of individual despair." George Sutherland, "Principle or Expedient? Address to the New York State Bar Ass'n," 18–19 (January 21, 1921).
13. See Olken, "Justice George Sutherland and Economic Liberty," 49–51 (discussing Sutherland's support for federal workmen's compensation).
14. Sutherland, "Principle or Expedient?" 19.
15. See Samuel R. Olken, "Justice Sutherland Reconsidered," *Vanderbilt Law Review* 62 (2009): 678–681.
16. See generally Alan Jones, "Thomas M. Cooley and 'Laissez-Faire Constitutionalism': A Reconsideration," *Journal of American History* 53 (1967): 751–771 (discussing Cooley's political and constitutional philosophy).
17. See generally Thomas Cooley, *A Treatise on the Constitutional Limitations Which Rest Upon the Legislative Power of the States of the American Union* (Boston, MA: Little, Brown & Co., 1883) (discussing the perils of class legislation).
18. See Joel Francis Paschal, *Mr. Justice Sutherland: A Man against the State* (Princeton, NJ: Princeton University Press, 1951) (chronicling Sutherland's pre-Court life).
19. See Olken, "Justice George Sutherland and Economic Liberty," 42–43.
20. See *United States v. Curtiss-Wright Export Corp.*, 299 U.S. 304, 319 (1936).
21. See Olken, "The Business of Expression," 263.
22. See generally Samuel R. Olken, "The Decline of Legal Classicism and the Evolution of New Deal Constitutionalism," *Notre Dame Law Review* 89 (2014): 2051–2092.
23. See *Pierce v. Society of Sisters*, 268 U.S. 510 (1925); *Meyer v. Nebraska*, 262 U.S. 390 (1923).
24. See, for example, *Charles Wolff Packing Co. v. Court of Industrial Relations*, 262 U.S. 522 (1923) (Chief Justice Taft finding insufficient public interest warranted industrial regulation of a private meatpacking plant).

25. See, for example, *Munn v. Illinois*, 94 U.S. 113, 141 (1877) (Field, J., dissenting) (invoking liberty of contract).
26. See, for example, *The Slaughter-House Cases*, 83 U.S. 36, 122 (1873) (Bradley, J., dissenting) (discussing liberty of contract as a limit upon state police powers).
27. See Olken "The Decline of Legal Classicism," 2062–2064; Olken, "Justice Sutherland Reconsidered," 655–660.
28. See, for example, *Tyson & Bro. v. Banton*, 273 U.S. 418 (1927) (invalidating a law that prescribed resale ticket prices).
29. See, for example, *Williams v. Standard Oil*, 278 U.S. 235 (1929) (invalidating a law that fixed gas prices).
30. *Adkins v. Children's Hospital*, 261 U.S. 525, 555–558 (1923).
31. *Carter v. Carter Coal Co.*, 298 U.S. 238 (1936).
32. *West Coast Hotel Co. v. Parrish*, 300 U.S. 379, 400–414 (1937) (Sutherland, J., joined by Van Devanter, McReynolds, and Butler, JJ., dissenting).
33. *New State Ice Co. v. Liebmann*, 285 U.S. 262 (1932).
34. See *Radice v. New York*, 264 U.S. 292 (1924).
35. See, for example, *Bountiful Brick Co. v. Giles*, 276 U.S. 154 (1928).
36. See, for example, *Euclid v. Ambler Realty Co.*, 272 U.S. 365 (1926).
37. 262 U.S. 390 (1923).
38. See *Bartels v. Iowa*, 262 U.S. 404, 412 (Holmes, J., joined by Sutherland, J., dissenting in both *Meyer* and *Bartels*).
39. 268 U.S. 510 (1925).
40. Ibid., 534–536.
41. See *Home Building & Loan Ass'n v. Blaisdell*, 290 U.S. 398, 449–452, 483 (1934) (Sutherland, J., joined by Van Devanter, McReynolds, and Butler, JJ., dissenting). Sutherland explained the "Constitution does not mean one thing at one time and an entirely different thing at another time." Ibid., 449. See also 300 U.S. at 403 (Sutherland, J., joined by Van Devanter, McReynolds, and Butler, JJ., dissenting).
42. 298 U.S. at 303–304, 307–309 (Sutherland distinguishing between commerce and industrial relations).
43. See *Lochner v. New York*, 198 U.S. 45, 74–77 (1905) (Holmes, J., dissenting).
44. In his *Lochner* dissent, Holmes remarked: "I strongly believe that my approval or disagreement has nothing to do with the right of a majority to embody their opinions in law." Ibid., 75. See also 250 U.S. at 630, wherein Holmes observed that "the ultimate good derived is better reached by free trade in ideas—that the best test of truth is the power of the thought to get itself accepted in the competition of the market."
45. *Schenck v. United States*, 249 U.S. 47, 52 (1919).
46. 268 U.S. 652 (1925).
47. 283 U.S. at 723 (1931) (Butler, J., joined by Van Devanter, McReynolds, and Sutherland, JJ., dissenting).
48. 283 U.S. at 697.

49. 283 U.S. at 731–738 (Butler, J., joined by Van Devanter, McReynolds, and Sutherland, JJ., dissenting).
50. See 299 U.S. at 315.
51. *United States v. MacIntosh*, 283 U.S. 605 (1931) (this decision was overruled by *Girourard v. United States*, 328 U.S. 61 (1946)).
52. 283 U.S. 359 (1931).
53. 299 U.S. 353 (1937).
54. *Whitney v. California*, 274 U.S. 357, 375–378 (1927) (Brandeis, J., concurring).
55. Ibid., 375 (Brandeis commenting that "freedom to think as you will and to speak as you think are means indispensable to the discovery and spread of political truth").
56. See Olken, "The Decline of Legal Classicism," at 2051–2052, 2071–2074, 2081–2087.
57. See 300 U.S. at 401–403 (Sutherland, J., joined by Van Devanter, McReynolds, and Butler, JJ., dissenting); 290 U.S. at 448–453, 483 (Sutherland, J., joined by Van Devanter, McReynolds, and Butler, JJ., dissenting).
58. 300 U.S. at 402 (Sutherland, J., joined by Van Devanter, McReynolds, and Butler, JJ., dissenting).
59. See 298 U.S. at 238.
60. 297 U.S. at 233.
61. Appellee's Brief at 9, *Grosjean*, 297 U.S. at 233 (quoting pamphlet published by US Senator Huey Long and Louisiana Governor Oscar Allen) (1934).
62. For an excellent discussion of the case, including its political background, see Richard C. Cortner, *The Kingfish and the Constitution: Huey Long, the First Amendment, and the Emergence of Modern Press Freedom in America* (Westport, CT: Praeger, 1996).
63. Ibid., 80 (quoting *New Orleans Item & Tribune* at 1, July 4, 1934).
64. Olken, "The Business of Expression," 293.
65. See, for example, *Great Atlantic & Pacific Tea Co. v. Grosjean*, 301 U.S. 412, 430–434 (1937) (Sutherland, J., joined by McReynolds and Butler, JJ., dissenting); *Colgate v. Harvey*, 296 U.S. 404, 422 (1935).
66. Cortner, *The Kingfish and the Constitution*, 163 (quoting New Orleans *Times-Picayune* at 28, January 14, 1936).
67. See, for example, 301 U.S. at 424–426; *Fox v. Standard Oil Co.*, 294 U.S. 87, 100 (1935); 283 U.S. 527 (1931). See also *Liggett Co. v. Lee*, 288 U.S. 517, 544–545, 547, 569–577 (1933) (Brandeis, J., joined by Stone, J., dissenting in part); 288 U.S. at 584–586 (Cardozo, J., joined by Stone, J., dissenting in part).
68. 290 U.S. 398 (1934) (upholding the Minnesota Mortgage Moratorium Act as a reasonable exercise of state police powers).
69. *Nebbia v. New York*, 291 U.S. 502 (1934) (sustaining New York's price-fixing regulation).
70. 300 U.S. 379 (1937) (upholding Washington's minimum wage law).

71. See Olken, "The Business of Expression," 298–299.
72. Ibid. See also Andrew L. Kaufman, *Cardozo* (Cambridge, MA: Harvard University Press, 1998), 539–541.
73. See Olken, "The Business of Expression," 298–299.
74. Sutherland, "Principle or Expedient?" 11.
75. 285 U.S. at 280.
76. 297 U.S. at 244.
77. 283 U.S. 697 (1931).
78. 268 U.S. 652 (1925).
79. *Allgeyer v. Louisiana*, 165 U.S. 578 (1897).
80. 297 U.S. at 251.
81. Ibid.
82. Ibid., 244–245.
83. Ibid., 245.
84. See Olken, "The Business of Expression," 300–305.
85. 297 U.S. at 250.
86. *NLRB v. Jones & Laughlin Steel Corp.*, 301 U.S. 1 (1937); *NLRB v. Fruehauf Trailer Co.*, 301 U.S. 49 (1937); *NLRB v. Friedman-Marks Clothing Co.*, 301 U.S. 58 (1937); *Washington, Va. & Md. Coach Co. v. NLRB*, 301 U.S. 142 (1937). Sutherland dissented in all but the last case.
87. *United States v. Carolene Products Co.*, 304 U.S. 144, 152–153, footnote no. 4 (1938).
88. See Olken, "The Business of Expression," 314.
89. 301 U.S. at 128–133.
90. Ibid., 131–132.
91. 301 U.S. at 140–141 (Sutherland, J., joined by Van Devanter, McReynolds, and Butler, JJ., dissenting).
92. Ibid., 136–137.
93. Ibid., 137–140.
94. Ibid.
95. Ibid., 137.
96. Ibid.
97. Ibid., 136–140.
98. Ibid., 139, 141.
99. Ibid., 137–140.
100. Ibid., 136–141.
101. Ibid., 141.
102. 300 U.S. at 401–404 (Sutherland, J., joined by Van Devanter, McReynolds, and Butler, JJ., dissenting).
103. See Olken, "The Business of Expression," 330–357.
104. See *44 Liquormart Corp. v. Rhode Island*, 517 U.S. 484, 498–505 (1996) (invalidating a complete ban on off-site retail liquor price advertising as an overly broad restriction of otherwise protected commercial speech). Commercial speech regulations must directly advance a substantial government interest. See *Central Hudson Gas & Electric Corp. v. Public Serv. Comm'n*, 444 U.S. 557, 564–566 (1980).

Chapter 3

Absolutism and Democracy: Hugo L. Black's Free Speech Jurisprudence

Michael Paris and Kevin J. McMahon

The speech struck some of America's legal cognoscenti as quaintly naïve, at best. The date was February 17, 1960. The speaker was US Supreme Court Justice Hugo Lafayette Black Jr., and the occasion was New York University School of Law's James Madison Lecture. There were, Justice Black proclaimed to a packed hall, "absolutes" in the Bill of Rights, "put there by men who knew what words meant, and [who] meant their prohibitions to be absolutes." This was especially the case, Black emphatically insisted, with the First Amendment. Its words were "plain" and "easily understood." No law means no law.[1]

Black's "literalism" and "absolutism" met some scathing critiques. For example, Yale Law School Professor Alexander Bickel argued that there was a danger in insisting, contrary to both historical experience and logic, that "whatever else must be true, there is a core of absolute literal meaning in the text, which it is the duty of the judge to render and apply literally."[2] If judges came to believe that they were drawing judgments from "a text incapable of yielding them," then the result would be judicial arrogance, a "happy judicial activism." Bickel concluded that "[s]uch a government is incompatible on principle with democratic institutions."[3]

By pitching his critique at the level of democratic theory, Bickel inadvertently touched upon one of the keys to understanding Black's position, especially as it relates to freedom of speech. Black's First Amendment expressive freedom jurisprudence flowed from a broad, coherent theory of democracy, reflecting both the man and his times. In adhering to a textualist approach, Black sought the creation and acceptance of propositions about freedom of speech, which would promote a vision of a well-functioning democratic polity, and what it means to be an equal citizen in that polity. This, in turn, *required* that courts enforce an absolute understanding of the right to free speech in an "activist" manner.

THE APPOINTMENT OF THE FIRST NEW DEAL JUSTICE

It is not clear how President Franklin Roosevelt arrived at the idea of appointing Hugo Black to the Supreme Court, but it is clear that he intended to upset the status quo in doing so. Roosevelt announced Black's nomination one month after the Senate defeated his Court-packing proposal. In selecting a nominee so soon after this bitter disappointment, the president sought to strike back at his Senate opponents and send a clear signal of his eagerness to transform the Court on his terms. However, Roosevelt faced a dilemma: how could he use the nomination to send a message to his antagonists, yet also secure Senate confirmation for his choice? He found his solution in the senior senator from Alabama, believing that the Senate would not refuse to confirm one of its own for the vacancy.

One of Roosevelt's primary criteria for any potential nominee was that nominee's position on his proposed Court-packing plan. As historian Robert Harrison has written, "anyone who had deserted [him] on that issue was eliminated from contention."[4] Unlike most southern senators, Black was an early and eager supporter of the plan to expand the Court's size to fifteen. In fact, seemingly unaware of the president's proposal, a week before its release Black had sent Roosevelt a letter suggesting a smaller expansion.[5]

And two weeks after the plan's unveiling, Black delivered a national radio address urging listeners to support it. In that broadcast, Black criticized the Court for usurping legislative powers and operating in a fashion inconsistent with the founding vision of the nation. "Most of the framers believed in popular government by the people themselves. Like Jefferson, they were not willing to trust lifetime judges with omnipotent powers over governmental policies . . . they knew that the people's liberty was safest with the people themselves or their properly elected representatives." Seeking to further delegitimize the justices' authority, Black said he believed the current Court was controlled by a "dominant five-judge philosophy [that was] the exact philosophy of the political group that could obtain only 8 electoral votes in the last Presidential election." For Black, the president's proposal would help solve the nation's problems by restoring democracy. "Our democracy can work out its own problems within our Constitution if the rights of human beings as human beings are given first importance and if our Constitution is not so misinterpreted and altered as to shackle the democratic processes themselves."[6]

According to Harrison, Roosevelt also endeavored to find jurists "who had come up the hard way, who had worked to improve the economic conditions of 'the little man,' and who had deplored the predatory practices and lack of public accountability of financiers, bankers, industrialists, and corporate leaders." Harrison adds, that "[t]he cardinal sin of the justices of the Old Court had been to distort the Constitution by reading their 'predilections' into the words of the text (while pretending not to), when their duty was to give effect to the plain meaning and obvious purpose of the Great Charter's greatest provisions."[7] Throughout his thirty-four years on the Court, Black would often remind his fellow justices of this sin.

For Roosevelt, the beauty of the Black nomination was that it upset so many of his opponents—particularly southern senators—who had sought to undermine his progressive agenda and derail his Court-packing proposal.[8] As Washington journalists Joseph Alsop and Turner Catledge noted, at the time of his appointment Black was "probably the most radical man in the Senate." Another report called his nomination a presidential "trick to ram the furthest Left-winger available down the Senate's throat." Still another concluded, "Mr. Roosevelt could not have made a worse appointment if he had named [labor leader] John L. Lewis."[9] However, the Senate's conservative southerners did not try to stop the nomination, thereby confirming Roosevelt's assumption that the Senate would not dare deviate from its institutional traditions no matter how angry the nomination made some of its members. Five days after he was nominated, Black was confirmed by a vote of 63-16.

Soon thereafter, however, the security of Black's seat on the Court was threatened by controversy stemming from the widespread rumors that he had once been a member of the Ku Klux Klan. Black's membership in the "Invisible Empire" was an open secret in Alabama, and journalists were easily able to confirm and even produce credible documentation of it. Roosevelt denied knowing that his new justice had once been a Klansman but also strongly implied that Black would need to clarify his involvement. On October 1, 1937, Black again went on nationwide radio, admitting that he had once been a member of the Klan but rejecting the notion that he possessed any racial or religious intolerance or prejudice. He pointed to his Senate record, which showed he was part of a "group of liberal senators who have consistently fought for the civil, economic and religious rights of all Americans, without regard to race or creed."[10]

According to Black biographer Tony A. Freyer, Black's decision to join the Klan in 1923 was most likely driven by his ambitions to succeed in politics and in the courtroom: "Lacking the support of the elite and the bosses, his election to statewide office was unlikely without Klan affiliation . . . Black's success as a trial lawyer also hinged on the Klan."[11] Nevertheless, for someone who often bucked the status quo, Black's decision to join the Klan represents a moment in his life when ambition prevailed over a willingness to stand alone in the face of powerful forces. Whatever his reasons for joining the Klan, Black's admitted membership stunned much of the nation and threatened his seat on the Court. While his radio address tempered the furor sufficiently to allow him to take his seat, the doubts remained.

From this dubious beginning, few would have suspected that Black would become one of the twentieth century's great defenders of civil rights and liberties. Black's commitment to advancing civil rights and liberties can be interpreted as part of an effort to make a clear break with his Klan membership. By contrast, the positions he took in free speech cases—particularly his distinction between conduct and speech—can be seen as evidence of his understanding of the ability of groups like the Klan to suppress democracy through their actions. But more than that, Black articulated a constitutional vision on the Court that had its origins in the conflicts of the 1930s and was in line with the fundamental principles of the New Deal democratic regime.[12]

SPEECH AND DEMOCRACY: FOUR PROPOSITIONS

Indeed, Black considered it essential to remain true to the principles that had brought him to the Court: defending the democratic process and committing to its results. Insofar as free speech was concerned, while he felt that it should flourish, he also understood—perhaps with his Klan history in mind—how politically charged conduct might easily erode the peace necessary for a functioning democracy and ultimately threaten the rights of the least advantaged. This tension between protecting speech necessary for full democratic participation and restraining potentially antidemocratic conduct is at the center of Black's approach to the First Amendment.

That approach is reminiscent of the arguments that Alexander Meiklejohn laid out in his seminal 1948 work *Free Speech and Its Relation to Self-Government*. If ideas are ruled out of bounds among "a group of free and equal [persons]" because they "are thought to be false or dangerous," or "unwise, unfair, un-American," Meiklejohn wrote, then "everything worth saying" about "the common good" may not be said.[13] There could be no deference to a democratic process that made judgments about who could speak or what ideas were dangerous ideas. The absolute protection of ideas was a condition of a legitimate process.

At the same time, however, the honorable quest for rational deliberation and decision making among equals cannot mean an absence of control. The "speech abridging activities of the [New England] town meeting," Meiklejohn argued, "indicate what the First Amendment does not forbid. When self-governing [persons] demand freedom of speech they are not saying that every individual has an unalienable right to speak, whenever, wherever, and however he [or she] chooses."[14] Consequently, official regulation of the content of what is said denies basic equality and rejects the foundational faith that each individual gets to hear and to decide for themselves what is true and what is false. This does not mean that the process cannot be unregulated or disordered but simply that the action or behavior of speaking must be appropriate to the setting.

The similarities between Meiklejohn's view of freedom of speech as a vital means to the end of self-government and Black's jurisprudence are clear (although, Black soon went beyond Meiklejohn to extend protection to forms of speech—such as obscenity and libel—that Meiklejohn had regarded as "private" and entitled to less protection). There is, however, also a strong affinity between Meiklejohn and Black on the vital importance of civility, order, and reason, and the need for government to secure these conditions of freedom of speech, understood as a means to democracy.[15]

Understanding how and why Black drew lines between "speech" and "conduct" helps us to understand the relationship, in Black's free speech jurisprudence, between democracy and individual expression. If Black categorized the targeted expression/activity as the content of speech, and not as conduct, then there was to be no "balancing."[16] If Black categorized the targeted activity as "conduct," then he could endorse some sort of balancing. From the distinctions that Black drew in myriad cases, four basic propositions emerge:

(1) Black typically subjected regulations that were vague, overbroad, or possibly discriminatory in either application or impact, to very strict scrutiny. Black sought to impose on government a strong requirement that it have clear rules for, and nondiscriminatory applications of, regulations of conduct that burdened speech. Official discretion was a threat to both content-neutrality and the widest possible dissemination of ideas.[17]
(2) In the balancing process, matters of government convenience (such as a concern with littering or noise) should not trump the robust protection of speech.[18]
(3) Medium bans (such as a restriction on sound trucks, or a prohibition of door-to-door canvassing or proselytizing) had to be strictly scrutinized in order to prevent government from taking away the means of communication used by ordinary (nonwealthy, relatively powerless) citizens.[19]

For the most part, Black's pursuit of these first three propositions produced speech-protective conclusions.

(4) However, if Black viewed the regulation as impacting "conduct," pure and simple, then he often afforded government significant leeway to regulate, provided that it did so in an even-handed way. Government might, if it so chose, deny the use of its public parks or the centers of its highways to all speakers, just as one presiding at a town meeting might forcibly silence a cacophony of speakers in the back of the hall while someone else legitimately had the floor. In situations in which speech was enmeshed with public action, if Black thought that persuasion was giving way to coercion or a threat of mob behavior, then he could come down in favor of government regulation.[20]

The essence of these propositions—as manifested in Black's absolutism—was evident early in his career, as was his sense of government power to maintain order in a nondiscriminatory way. As he stressed in his 1941 opinion for a five-justice majority in *Bridges v. California*:

> What finally emerges from the "clear and present danger" cases is a working principle that the substantive evil must be extremely serious and the degree of imminence extremely high before utterances can be punished. . . . For the First Amendment does not speak equivocally. It prohibits any law "abridging the freedom of speech, or of the press." It must be taken as a command of the broadest scope that explicit language, read in the context of a liberty-loving society, will allow.[21]

Several other 1940s cases—primarily those involving labor picketing—further allow us to observe Black's early thinking about the nature of the line between speech and conduct, and the role that civility and public order played in orienting his thinking about this boundary.

Milk Wagon Drivers Union v. Meadowmoor Dairies involved a state court injunction against picketing in an environment of pervasive violence.[22] Certain retail stores used nonunion vendors and lower prices to undercut union shops and union labor. Over many years, the conflict produced much violence against property and persons, but the specific picketing at issue here was peaceful. In a 6-3 decision, the Court upheld the injunction against the picketing and rejected the union's freedom of speech challenge. Justice Felix Frankfurter held that the picketing here was intertwined "with contemporaneously violent conduct,"[23] and the importance of federalism and deference to state courts counseled restraint.

Black dissented, opening his opinion with a sweeping declaration of principles:

> I view the guaranties of the First Amendment as the foundation upon which our governmental scheme rests and without which it could not continue to endure as conceived and planned. Freedom to speak and write about public questions is as important to the life of our government as is the heart to the human body. In fact, this privilege is the heart of our government. If that heart be weakened, the result is debilitation; if it be stilled, the result is death.[24]

Black then delved deeply into the record to show that the many acts of violence were remote, in both time and place, from the peaceful picketing. More importantly, he emphasized, the wording of the injunction—which banned "six thousand" union members from "discouraging or diverting" persons away from the stores in question, "including the use of said signs, banners or placards"—could be read as aimed not at violence but at the communicative content of the union's message.[25]

The following year, in *Carpenters & Joiners Union v. Ritter's Café*, Frankfurter once again wrote the Court's decision upholding an anti-picketing injunction; once again, Black dissented.[26] In that case, a union picketed a café because the owner had retained a contractor to erect a new building on land he owned about a mile away, using non-union labor. After the union stationed pickets at the café to publicize its dispute with the owner, the restaurant workers then struck the café, and other union workers refused to make deliveries to it. After his business declined by 60 percent, Ritter obtained a state court injunction banning the "off-site" picketing because it violated the state antitrust law. Frankfurter noted at the outset that the "claims on behalf of free speech are met with claims on behalf of the authority of the state to impose reasonable regulations for the protection of the community as a whole."[27] In his dissent, Black countered that people had a right to hear what the union had to say about Ritter and his behavior toward organized labor, and they had a right to hear it at his café. This peaceful picketing was not a "private quarrel" but rather a "national issue," and Black saw "no reason why members of the public should be deprived of any opportunity to get information which might enable them to use their influence to tip the scales in favor of the side they think is right."[28] The impact on Ritter's business was the result of persuasion, not coercion, and hence the target of the injunction was, for Black, the message, not the conduct.

Giboney v. Empire Storage and Ice Co., decided by the Court in 1949, strongly resembled *Ritter's Café*, but with one significant difference—the outcome of the case.[29] In *Giboney*, a union representing retail ice peddlers picketed a wholesaler, attempting to induce it to stop selling ice to nonunion peddlers. Empire Storage's truck drivers belonged to other unions, and they decided to go on strike; Empire Storage's business plummeted by 85 percent. Had the company acceded to the union's demand not to sell to nonunion peddlers, it would have been guilty of violating the state's antitrust law.

Logically, Black should have followed his speech-protective analysis in *Ritter's Café*, since the harm visited on Empire Storage did not stem from violence or coercion at the hands of the picketers, who were entirely peaceful. Sure enough, in the conference discussion and initial vote in *Giboney*, Black took this speech-protective position and commanded a slim 5-4 majority. But as Black did the initial drafting, he found that the opinion "would not write." He then changed his vote, and when the entire Court went along with him, *Giboney* ended up as a 9-0 decision in favor of upholding the state court injunction.[30]

Why did Black do this? He certainly did not have to change his mind in order to follow precedent; the "precedent" on labor picketing to that point provided substantial support for a decision either way. It seems that Black first reached a conclusion about a fair resolution of the controversy and only then searched for a rationale. For Black, it mattered that the union had first failed to "persuade" nonunion peddlers to join it and had next failed to "persuade" Empire Storage to refuse to do business with independent nonunion labor. All of the other distributors in the area had caved in; Empire Storage was the only holdout. Other union members, Black noted, would be risking expulsion from their unions if they crossed the lines at Empire

Storage. This meant that persuasion was veering over into coercion; Empire Storage, wrote Black, was being "compelled" to do something that state law rightly precluded.[31] No doctrinal logic could save Black from inconsistency with his dissenting opinion in *Ritter's Café*. On these facts, order, civility, and reason had given way to force, or at least so it seemed to Black. He was happy to draw a line, even if to others that line seemed rather blurry.

Black's views on speech, conduct, civility, and order are further illustrated by his dissent in *Feiner v. New York*, in which a speaker had been arrested for breach of peace after inciting a violent reaction from a crowd of listeners.[32] In his opinion for the Court, Chief Justice Fred Vinson simply asserted that the police were entitled to keep order and that Feiner was arrested not because of what he was saying but because violence was imminent. As he had done in *Meadowmoor Dairies*, Black went deeper into the record, down to actual testimony, in order to show that Feiner was likely targeted and punished for his actual views. Feiner stood alone, and did nothing but speak. His conviction therefore made "a mockery of the free speech guarantees in the First and Fourteenth Amendments," and amounted to "a long step toward totalitarian authority."[33]

In two other cases decided in the 1940s, Justice Black subjected facially neutral regulations of conduct to exceedingly strict scrutiny because they were likely unfairly to burden those without equal power or means to speak effectively. In *Martin v. City of Struthers*, an Ohio municipality sought to enforce an ordinance against Jehovah's Witnesses making it unlawful for persons to call at residences for purposes of "distributing handbills, circulars or other advertisements."[34] The case illustrates Black's thought process in drawing the line between speech and conduct. When the justices met in conference to discuss the case, Black viewed the behavior at issue as conduct that could be even-handedly regulated to serve the state's legitimate interest in protecting peoples' peace and repose in the privacy of their own homes. However, once Black read Justice Stone's dissenting opinion, he switched his vote, and then Stone graciously assigned the opinion to him.[35] The language of Black's opinion for the Court evoked a sturdy and engaged citizenry, and it emphasized the right of people to hear, as well as to speak. The channels of communication must be kept open, Black wrote, "if vigorous enlightenment was to triumph over slothful ignorance." This was especially so here, given the reliance on door-to-door campaigning and distribution by "the poorly financed causes of little people."[36] The balancing process came out in favor of the protection of speech.

The same spirit of fair play and protection for "the little people" animated Black's dissent in *Kovacs v. Cooper*, a 1949 case in which the Court upheld a flat ban on sound trucks.[37] The previous year, in *Saia v. New York*, the Court had struck down a ban on sound equipment because it allowed for certain exemptions at the discretion of the town's chief of police.[38] Here, however, the Court was satisfied that the ban was content-neutral and nondiscriminatory. After pointing out several difficulties in discerning the precise meaning of the ordinance at issue, Black objected to the absolute ban on all amplification equipment:

> The basic premise of the First Amendment is that all present instruments of communication, as well as others that inventive genius may bring into being, shall be free from government censorship or prohibition. Laws which hamper the free use of some instruments of communication thereby favor competing channels. Thus, unless constitutionally prohibited, laws like this Trenton ordinance can give an overpowering influence to views of owners of legally favored instruments of communication. . . . There are many who have ideas that they wish to disseminate but who do not have enough money to own or control publishing plants.[39]

The "right to freedom of expression," Black concluded, "should be protected from absolute censorship for persons without, as for persons with, wealth and power."[40]

As the 1950s approached, Black stood firm for the proposition that government should not leverage its power as an employer, as a regulator, as a granter of benefits, or as a licensor in order to restrict the freedom of speech. Beliefs and ideas about matters of public importance deserved vigorous protection from the courts, as Black emphasized in *United Public Workers v. Mitchell*, which involved Section 9(a) of the Hatch Act of 1940.[41] Section 9(a) prohibited almost all federal employees from taking "any active part in political management or in political campaigns." Employees retained only the right to vote and to express their opinions; they could not actively engage in any partisan political activities.[42] A closely divided Court upheld the restrictions, but Black dissented; he was the only justice to conclude that the challenged provision was unconstitutional on its face.[43] The purpose of the Hatch Act—the prevention of pernicious political activities—may have been laudable, but Congress's methods were far too crude. Black insisted that it did not matter that employees were left with the right to vote and freedom to express their opinion because:

> Popular government, to be effective, must permit and encourage much wider political activity by all the people. . . . Legislation which muzzles several million citizens threatens popular government, not only because it injures the individuals muzzled, but also because of its harmful effect on the body politic in depriving it of the political participation and interest of such a large segment of our citizens.[44]

Black concluded by noting that "other groups may later be compelled to sacrifice their right to participate in political activities for the protection of the purity of government," and that "Our political system . . . rests on the foundation of a belief in rule by the people—not some, but all the people."[45]

Mitchell clearly demonstrates the existence of two contrasting visions of democracy—the one held by the Court, and the one held by Hugo Black. The majority counseled that deference to the democratic process enabled the polity to make informed and wise judgments about the balance between liberty and other important values. Black retorted that the absolute protection of ideas and their expression is foundational and prior to the validity of democratic processes and outcomes. If courts fail to act aggressively to protect ideas, the cause of democracy is lost.

BLACK'S FINEST HOUR

Black's vision of democracy was sorely tested in the 1950s, during the second "Red Scare." From 1950 through 1961, he argued time and again for the absolute protection of political beliefs and their vigorous advocacy, even if the speakers were Communists and even if the advocacy proclaimed the desirability of overthrowing the US government by violent revolution. This was no small feat, for Black was taking this stand against what Geoffrey Stone has characterized as "a frenzy of anti-Red hysteria."[46] This was a "frenzy" to which *lower* federal courts responded with uniform hostility to legal challenges to constitutionally suspect measures backed by the other two branches. The only hope for the vindication of rights sacrificed on the altar of widespread fear was the US Supreme Court. And it was an issue that the Court decided to confront energetically. As Stone notes, "[a]s a consequence of World War I, the Court handed down six decisions involving the First Amendment. As a result of the Cold War, it handed down *sixty* such decisions. For roughly a decade, this was the dominant issue on the Court's docket."[47]

This decade was, arguably, Black's finest hour, for he was holding fast against challenging political circumstances and an acquiescent core of colleagues. Although the Court, up until this point, had often invoked the Holmes-Brandeis approach to the advocacy of unlawful conduct or other forms of expression producing harms, there was no guarantee that this approach would govern in this newly repressive environment. Moreover, while the Court had in the past opined that beliefs were absolutely protected from persecution, now many measures made belief in Communism and its tenets the staging ground for criminal punishment and civil disability.

A majority of the justices embraced an ad hoc balancing formula for judging freedom of speech challenges to anti-Communist provisions. Content-based speech regulations would be upheld if they were "reasonable," and the Court almost always found that they were. Justice Black set his face against that dominant view.

A crucial example of this divide among the justices was *American Communications Association v. Douds* (1950), in which the Court upheld the "non-Communist affidavit" provision of the Taft-Hartley Act.[48] That provision required, as a condition of protection under the Labor Act, that each officer of a labor union file an affidavit with the National Labor Relations Board, certifying nonmembership in the Communist Party or a lack of "affiliation" with "such party." It also required one to swear that one did "not believe in" or belong to "any organization that believes in or teaches, the overthrow of the United States Government by force or by any illegal or unconstitutional methods."[49]

Vinson's opinion for the Court began by addressing Congress's purpose, which was to eliminate "political strikes"—that is, strikes in which "Communist leaders of labor unions" subordinated "legitimate trade union objectives to obstructive strikes when dictated by Party leaders, often in support of the policies of a foreign government."[50] Could Congress "exert . . . pressures upon labor unions to deny positions of leadership to certain persons who are identified by particular beliefs and political affiliations"?[51] Vinson concluded that it could. The "clear and present danger" test was inapplicable, because the harm did not follow from speech but rather from whom the speakers were and what they were likely to do. The Court had never held that First Amendment freedoms were absolute, Vinson continued, and it would not do so now. The provision infringed on freedom of thought and speech, conceded Vinson, but it regulated the expression of views by relatively few people; it was not a "criminal" sanction, and the public interest advanced in support of it was substantial.[52] The provision was upheld in all respects.

"Freedom to think is absolute." This was the way in which Black opened his dissent in *Douds.* While history might indeed show that the "test oath" was highly effective at neutralizing "obnoxious minorities," the price that society paid for that effectiveness was constitutionally far too high. "[L]aws aimed at one political or religious group, however rational these laws may be in their beginnings, generate hatreds and prejudices which rapidly spread beyond control." Nothing was "more reckless or contagious" than fear. Restrictions were not "static."[53] They would deepen in intensity against the targeted group and quickly spread beyond that group to others. The Court had minimized the reach and harm of the affidavit requirements; they applied only to officers of unions, and the sanctions were not criminal. However, the Court's reasoning would logically cover "statutes barring Communists and their suspected sympathizers from election to political office, mere membership in unions, and in fact from getting or holding any jobs whereby they could earn a living."[54] And, time and again, history demonstrated that the test oath produced situations in which "spies and informers found rewards more tempting than truth." It was a basic "postulate of the First Amendment" that "our free institutions can be maintained without proscribing or penalizing political belief, speech, press, assembly, or party affiliation. . . . It is the heart of the system on which our freedom depends."[55]

As Thomas I. Emerson has observed, *Douds* was a watershed case because it established the general pattern that governed Red Scare cases for at least the next seven years. The majority took account of the content of beliefs and their expression and weighed them in the balance. Once this sort of balancing, often of "imponderables," was permitted, deference to the reasonable judgments of coequal branches of government quickly followed. Justice Black, by contrast, championed "absolute" protection for all ideas and their advocacy. Content-based regulation of thought and advocacy was antithetical to our constitutional democracy and the First Amendment.[56]

The fears that Black outlined in *Douds* quickly came to fruition in 1951. Four years earlier, President Harry Truman had issued an executive order authorizing loyalty investigations by the attorney general. Truman's order did not define "disloyalty" but rather authorized the attorney general to construct a list of subversive organizations he considered "totalitarian, fascist, communist, or subversive." The list was to be disseminated to all agencies for use in their loyalty investigations, and the organizations on the list were not entitled to a hearing to challenge the designation. Each federal agency was to conduct investigations of each employee based on public records (e.g., personnel files, FBI files). If a preliminary review of files yielded any "derogatory" information, then the FBI would conduct a field investigation. If after that there were "reasonable grounds" to doubt the person's loyalty, the agency would convene a hearing. The impugned employee could appear with counsel and present evidence, but there was no right to confront and cross-examine witnesses or even to learn the identity of the witnesses or nature of the other evidence against him or her. If "reasonable grounds" then existed for believing someone to be disloyal to the United States, that person would be denied the job or fired.[57]

In *Joint Anti-Fascist Refugee Committee v. McGrath*,[58] the Court heard the complaints of several organizations designated by the attorney general as "subversive." By the time the Court heard the case in 1951, JAFRC's entire board had been jailed for refusing to turn over lists of contributors and recipients of funds. The Court found the listing "arbitrary" in that it exceeded the authority given to the attorney general by the president's executive order. It held that organizations were constitutionally entitled to notice and some sort of hearing before being listed.[59] The justices were, however, badly fractured to the point that Justice Harold Burton's opinion for the Court gathered only one other signature, and even his co-signer Justice William O. Douglas offered a separate concurrence. The other three votes in favor of JAFRC—Black, Frankfurter, and Robert H. Jackson—provided their own solo concurrences.

Black's opinion in *JAFRC* speaks volumes about the absolutism he had come to embrace. Not even Douglas had dared to argue that the government had no business investigating and listing subversive organizations in an effort to guard against a "Fifth Column" threatening national security. Only Black took that position. Even with notice and a fair hearing, the president's order was aimed at beliefs and ideas, and it was therefore unconstitutional, Black concluded. The order "smacks of the most evil type of censorship" and had "almost every quality of bills of attainder." What was at work here was "prejudice, hate and fear" producing "irresponsible smears and persecution." The "cause of internal security would be fostered, not hurt, by faithful adherence to our constitutional guarantees of individual liberty."[60]

Two months later, the Court handed down its decision in the landmark case of *Dennis v. United States*,[61] in which twelve leaders of the Communist Party of the United States were convicted of violating the Smith Act of 1940. The defendants had been charged "not with attempting to overthrow the government, not with conspiring to overthrow the government, not with advocating the overthrow of the government, but with *conspiring to advocate* the overthrow of the government."[62] A nine-month trial established that the defendants were Communists, that they believed in the inevitability and necessity of the overthrow of the US government by force and violence, and that they met and talked about it a lot. The trial judge instructed the jury that the Smith Act did not prohibit advocacy of the "abstract doctrine" stating that it was moral to overthrow the government by force, but it did ban "advocacy of action for that purpose as speedily as circumstances would permit."[63]

The problem here was that the Court had spent much of the past decade paying homage to the Holmes-Brandeis formulation, which required a substantial risk of imminent harm. When *Dennis* came on appeal to the Second Circuit Court of Appeals, Judge Learned Hand refashioned the test to give more weight to the "gravity of the evil" and then balanced in favor of repression.[64] By a 6-2 vote (Justice Tom Clark did not participate), the Court upheld Judge Hand and adopted much of his reasoning. Writing for himself and three others (Burton, Stanley Reed, and Sherman Minton), Vinson's opinion basically argued that the "clear and present danger" formulation was simply inapplicable when it came to the Communist Party in the present "context of world crisis after crisis."[65] Justices Frankfurter and Jackson each wrote long concurring opinions in which they canvassed prior law and sought carefully to balance competing values and interests. Frankfurter was characteristically deferential to legislative judgments and determined to let everyone know just how mindful he was about the damage that that deference might do to freedom of thought and speech.[66] Only Justices Douglas and Black dissented.

In his exceedingly short and pointed dissent, Black insisted that the "clear and present danger" test stated a minimum, not a maximum, level of protection. "Public opinion being what it now is," he wrote, "few will protest the conviction of these Communist petitioners. There is hope, however, that, in calmer times, when present pressures, passions and fears subside, this or some later Court will restore the First Amendment liberties to the high preferred place where they belong in a free society."[67] Those calmer times were not on the immediate horizon. "*Dennis* provided the green light to Red hunters." Within three months, the FBI had arrested an additional forty-one party leaders, and between 1951 and 1957, 145 leaders and members faced criminal prosecutions.[68] Admittedly, these numbers are not large. However, "criminalization" of a group, whether for beliefs, advocacy, or "conduct" tied to beliefs and identity, does more than visit criminal sanctions on the unlucky members of that group targeted for prosecution. It invites and at the same time legitimizes the imposition of numerous other types of penalties on others in the group, and, in this instance, many more who merely associated with them. From the standpoint of the persecuted, once the criminalization battle is lost, most other battles are also lost.

Over the next few years, the Court heard numerous challenges to an array of federal and state measures aimed at Communists. Black never wavered from his absolutist position, regardless of whether the full Court rejected the challenges or (as it was increasingly inclined to do) provided relief to individual claimants on technical grounds while leaving the questionable laws in place.[69] By mid-1957, anti-Communist fervor had waned, Senator Joseph McCarthy had died, and William Brennan had replaced Sherman Minton on the Court. A majority of the justices were now willing to assert themselves against Congress and the states, albeit still not in the sweeping constitutional terms typically advanced by Black and Douglas.

That willingness came to the fore on June 17, 1957, when the Court announced its decision in *Yates v. United States*,[70] yet another Smith Act case. From *Dennis* until this point, the Court had consistently rejected challenges to Smith Act convictions, but in *Yates* the Court reversed course. Justice Harlan's opinion for the Court handled the case under the guise of statutory interpretation. The question, he said, was "whether the Smith Act prohibits advocacy and teaching of forcible overthrow as an abstract principle, divorced from any effort to instigate action to that end, so long as such advocacy or teaching is engaged in with evil intent." His answer was no. The Act proscribed only incitement. Those to whom the advocacy is addressed "must be urged to *do* something now or in the future, rather than merely to *believe* in something."[71] What it would mean to "incite" action at a remote time was left somewhat unclear.

By contrast, the focus of Black's concurring opinion in *Yates* was his rejection of the "clear and present danger" test. "Under the Court's approach," he wrote, "defendants could still be convicted simply for agreeing to talk as distinguished from agreeing to act. I believe that the First Amendment forbids Congress to punish people for talking about public affairs, whether or not such discussion incites to action, legal or illegal." Quoting Thomas Jefferson, Black emphasized that it would be "'time enough for the rightful purposes of civil government, for its officers to interfere when principles break out into overt acts against peace and good order.'"[72]

The Court's reversal of direction in *Yates* produced a serious backlash in Congress. Southern segregationists seething over *Brown v. Board of Education*[73] now found that they could make common cause against the Court with northern anti-Communist hawks. Over the next two years, Congress considered various Court-curbing measures, none more serious than Indiana Republican Senator William Jenner's jurisdiction-stripping proposal.[74] A much-modified version of Jenner's bill narrowly went down to defeat in 1958, but Congress's menacing message was clear, and a majority of the justices heard it—a majority from whom Black would continue to dissent.

Barenblatt v. United States (1959) provided the next occasion for Black to project his absolutist position.[75] Lloyd Barenblatt was an instructor at Vassar College when, in 1954, he received a subpoena to appear before the House Un-American Activities Committee (HUAC). Barenblatt had done his graduate work at the University of Michigan, and HUAC was interested in Communist infiltration there. Barenblatt read Meiklejohn's work just before appearing before the Committee and determined that he would refuse to answer the Committee's questions about affiliations and beliefs by invoking his First Amendment free speech rights, rather than his Fifth Amendment privilege against self-incrimination. A contempt citation and years of litigation followed, resulting in a conviction and a sentence of six months in jail.[76] By a vote of 5-4, the Court upheld Barenblatt's conviction. On his First Amendment claim, Justice Harlan's opinion for the Court endorsed "balancing" of the "competing private and public interests at stake in the particular circumstances shown." The Court, Harlan stated, had "consistently refused to view the Communist Party as an ordinary political party."[77]

Black's dissent attacked both HUAC and the Court's balancing logic. HUAC denied freedom of speech "through exposure, obloquy and public scorn."[78] In the clearest statement he had offered to date of his free speech formulation, Black conceded that balancing had indeed been used in the past, and was in fact appropriate, but only if regulations "indirectly affect ideas." Laws "directly aimed at curtailing speech and political persuasion" should not be subject to balancing. The Court was in effect reading "the First Amendment to say 'Congress shall pass no law abridging freedom of speech . . ., unless Congress and the Supreme Court reach the joint conclusion that on balance the interest of the Government in stifling these freedoms is greater than the interest of the people in having them exercised.'"[79] Even assuming that balancing was appropriate, the majority had misconceived the factors to be balanced. Barenblatt's interests were no different from "the interest of the people as a whole" who wanted to be "able to join organizations, advocate causes and make political 'mistakes' without later being subjected to governmental penalties for having dared to think for themselves." As Black explained, "no number of laws against communism can have as much effect as the personal conviction which comes from having heard its arguments and rejected them, or from having once accepted its tenets and later recognized their worthlessness."[80]

Conclusion

In conclusion, it is important to acknowledge that this chapter has not said a word about Black's absolutist approach to obscenity and libel. Famously, Black (along with Douglas) refused to participate in the viewing of pornographic films during the Court's consideration of whether those materials constituted obscenity. In his mind, there was no need since they were protected by the Constitution. Like his positioning on other speech issues, Black's absolutist stance here can be explained by his view about how the government must treat citizens when it comes to ideas, even arguably noxious or harmful ones.[81] His positioning in the libel cases was no less stark, given his total rejection of all libel law.[82] However, the space constraints of a single chapter in an edited volume foreclose the possibility of saying anything more about these two areas of the law.

So this chapter concludes where it started: Black's distinction between speech and conduct. Conventional wisdom holds that toward the end of his career Justice Hugo Black modulated his absolutism.[83] This perception is grounded in several important civil rights protest cases of the mid-1960s, in which (in either dissents or concurrences) Black outlined an interpretation of the Constitution that conflicted with that of the most liberal justices, including his long-time ally, Justice Douglas.[84] For example, in *Bell v. Maryland*,[85] Black wrote in dissent that Maryland's prosecution of "sit-in" protesters was well within the bounds of the Constitution and, indeed, a reasonable means to ensure peaceful democratic discussion:

> A great purpose of freedom of speech and press is to provide a forum for settlement of acrimonious disputes peaceably, without resort to intimidation, force, or violence. The experience of ages points to the inexorable fact that people are frequently stirred to violence when property which the law recognizes as theirs is forcibly invaded or occupied by others. Trespass laws are born of this experience.[86]

The conventional wisdom is also sourced in Black's dissent in *Tinker v. Des Moines Independent Community School District* (1969).[87] When siblings John and Mary Beth Tinker wore black armbands to school in silent but symbolic protest of the Vietnam War, the school authorities summarily suspended them. In his opinion for the Court, Justice Abe Fortas famously denied that students "shed their constitutional rights to freedom of speech or expression at the schoolhouse gate."[88] To Black, by contrast, the school was well within its authority to suspend the Tinkers for what he saw as their disruptive conduct. As he wrote, "Uncontrolled and uncontrollable liberty is an enemy to domestic peace."[89]

Black's dissents in these two cases have struck many analysts as out of character with his previous free speech opinions.[90] However, when viewed alongside the other opinions analyzed in this chapter, one can see that in these late-career dissents Black did not deviate very much from his younger self. In *Bell* and *Tinker*, Black saw protestors engaged in uncivil behavior that ***undermined*** the democratic process.[91] Black had absolute faith in the First Amendment, but his "constitutional faith" in the nation's demos was not unqualified. A particular, and essentially contested, vision of democracy guided Hugo Black throughout his long and volatile career.[92]

NOTES

1. Justice Black's lecture was later published in the NYU Law Review. See Hugo L. Black, "The Bill of Rights," *New York University Law Review* 35 (1960): 865–881.
2. Alexander M. Bickel, *The Least Dangerous Branch: The Supreme Court at the Bar of Politics* (Indianapolis, IN: Bobbs-Merrill Company, 1962), 86. Bickel clerked for Justice Felix Frankfurter between 1952 and 1953 and, as *The Least Dangerous Branch* demonstrated, he held greater sympathy for Frankfurter's jurisprudence than for Black's contrasting (and generally more "activist") approach to judging. On the differences between the judicial philosophies of Black and Frankfurter, see Mark Silverstein, *Constitutional Faiths: Felix Frankfurter, Hugo Black and the Process of Judicial Decision Making* (Ithaca, NY: Cornell University Press, 1984).
3. Bickel, *The Least Dangerous Branch*, 93, 96–97.
4. Robert Harrison, "The Breakup of the Roosevelt Court: The Contribution of History and Biography" (PhD diss., Columbia University, 1987), 18.
5. Ibid., 93.
6. Hugo L. Black, "Reorganization of the Federal Judiciary," radio address delivered February 23, 1937, *Vital Speeches of the Day* (September 1937), 675–676.

7. Harrison, "The Breakup," 296.
8. Kevin J. McMahon, *Reconsidering Roosevelt on Race: How the Presidency Paved the Road to Brown* (Chicago, IL: University of Chicago Press, 2004), Chapters 2–4.
9. Joseph Alsop and Turner Catledge, *The 168 Days* (New York: Doubleday, Doran & Co., 1938), 301; *Time* quoted in Howard Ball, *Hugo L. Black: Cold Steel Warrior* (New York: Oxford University Press, 1996), 93; David Lawrence of the *Chicago Tribune* quoted in William E. Leuchtenburg, *The Supreme Court Reborn: The Constitutional Revolution in the Age of Roosevelt* (New York: Oxford University Press, 1995), 186.
10. Hugo L. Black, "I Did Join the Klan," radio address delivered October 15, 1937, *Vital Speeches of the Day* (October 1937), 21.
11. Tony A. Freyer, *Hugo L. Black and the Dilemma of American Liberalism*, 2nd ed. (New York: Pearson Longman, 2008), 43.
12. Indeed, we would argue that certain and specific "regime principles" informed and shaped Justice Black's understanding of freedom of speech and its role in a democracy. As Mark Graber has written, regime politics scholars suggest that Supreme Court decision making is "politically constructed." They do not assert that it is politically determined. This still leaves a great deal of room for the justices to shape the contours of constitutional doctrine. Mark A. Graber, "Constructing Judicial Review," *Annual Review of Political Science* 8 (2005): 427. As one of us, focusing on presidential influences in the shape of Supreme Courts, has written elsewhere: "Even if successful . . . a president's policy toward the judiciary will not dictate the detail and timing of judicial action. The justices will work out these matters. Instead, it will help forge the institutional mission of the Court." McMahon, *Reconsidering Roosevelt on Race*, 19.
13. Alexander Meiklejohn, *Free Speech and Its Relation to Self-Government* (1948; reprint New York: Lawbook Exchange, 2011), 23, 26, 25.
14. Ibid., 23–24.
15. On Meiklejohn's claim that "private" speech is entitled to less protection, see Gerald Gunther and Kathleen M. Sullivan, *Constitutional Law, 13th Edition* (Westbury, NY: The Foundation Press, 1997), 1027.
16. Crucially, Black embraced this basic position at a time when clear majorities of the Court, often led by Felix Frankfurter or Robert Jackson, began with the alternative proposition that "reasonable" restrictions on the content of speech could be allowed if, in context, the speech would have plainly harmful consequences of some sort.
17. See, for example, Justice Black's comments in a letter to Justice Roberts regarding *Hague v. CIO*, 307 U.S. 496 (1939) (striking down a parade permit regulation because it granted officials too much discretion), quoted in Tinsley E. Yarbrough, *Mr. Justice Black and His Critics* (Durham, NC: Duke University Press, 1988), 177.

18. See, for example, *Martin v. City of Struthers*, 319 U.S. 141 (1943) (ban on door-to-door solicitations struck down), discussed later in the chapter.
19. See, for example, *Kovacs v. Cooper*, 336 U.S. 77 (1949) (Black, J., joined by Douglas and Rutledge, JJ., dissenting) (dissenting from upholding of restrictions use of amplification equipment). This is discussed later in the chapter.
20. See Yarbrough's discussion of Black's role in *Hague v. CIO* and Black's opinion for a unanimous Court in *Giboney v. Empire Storage & Ice Co.*, 336 U.S. 490 (1949), discussed later in the chapter.
21. *Bridges v. California*, 314 U.S. 252, 263 (1941).
22. *Milk Wagon Drivers Union of Chicago, Local 753 v. Meadowmoor Dairies Inc., No. 1*, 312 U.S. 287 (1941).
23. Ibid., 293.
24. Ibid., 301–302 (Black, J., joined by Douglas, J., dissenting).
25. Ibid., 308.
26. *Carpenters & Joiners v. Ritter's Café*, 315 U.S. 722 (1942).
27. Ibid., 725–726.
28. 315 U.S. at 730–731 (Black, J., joined by Douglas and Murphy, JJ., dissenting).
29. 336 U.S. 490 (1949).
30. Roger K. Newman, *Hugo Black: A Biography* (New York: Pantheon Books, 1994), 370–371. Black discussed this case in *A Constitutional Faith* (New York: Alfred A. Knopf, 1968), 56.
31. 336 U.S. at 503.
32. *Feiner v. New York*, 340 U.S. 315 (1951).
33. 340 U.S. at 323 (Black, J., dissenting).
34. 319 U.S. at 142.
35. Newman, *Hugo Black*, 296.
36. Ibid., 146.
37. 336 U.S. 77 (1949).
38. *Saia v. New York*, 334 U.S. 558 (1948).
39. 336 U.S. at 102 (Black, J., joined by Douglas and Rutledge, JJ., dissenting).
40. Ibid., 104.
41. *United Public Workers v. Mitchell*, 330 U.S. 75 (1947).
42. Ibid., 78.
43. The Court's decision was 4-3, with Jackson and Murphy not participating. Justice Frankfurter dissented because he argued that the Court lacked jurisdiction. Justice Douglas dissented in part because he thought that the First Amendment required more nuanced distinctions among types of government employees. Only Justice Black argued that a ban on political participation violated the First Amendment because statutes could be drawn to outlaw the objectionable conduct with which Congress could be properly concerned.

44. 330 U.S. at 110–111 (Black, J., dissenting).
45. Ibid., 113–114.
46. Geoffrey R. Stone, *Perilous Times: Free Speech in Wartime from the Sedition Act of 1798 to the War on Terrorism* (New York: W. W. Norton, 2004), 334.
47. Ibid., 395.
48. *American Communications Association v. Douds*, 339 U.S. 382 (1950).
49. Ibid., 385–386.
50. Ibid., 388.
51. Ibid., 390.
52. Ibid., 399–402.
53. 339 U.S. at 448–449 (Black, J., dissenting).
54. Ibid., 449.
55. Ibid., 447, 452.
56. Thomas I. Emerson, *The System of Freedom of Expression* (New York: Random House, 1970), 164–165.
57. Stone, *Perilous Times*, 343.
58. *Joint Anti-Fascist Refugee Committee v. McGrath*, 341 U.S. 123 (1951).
59. Ibid., 125–126.
60. 341 U.S. at 143 (evil type of censorship), 144 (bill of attainder), 145 (internal security fostered) (Black, J., concurring).
61. *Dennis v. United States*, 341 U.S. 494 (1951).
62. Stone, *Perilous Times*, 396.
63. Ibid., 398.
64. See the discussion by Frederick Lewis in Chapter 1 herein.
65. 341 U.S. at 510.
66. 341 U.S. at 517–561 (Frankfurter, J., concurring in affirmance of the judgment); 561–580 (Jackson, J., concurring).
67. 341 U.S. at 579–581 (Black, J., dissenting).
68. Stone, *Perilous Times*, 411.
69. See Lucas A. Powe Jr., *The Warren Court and American Politics* (Cambridge, MA: Harvard University Press, 2000), 76–93.
70. *Yates v. United States*, 354 U.S. 298 (1957).
71. Ibid., 318, 325.
72. 354 U.S. at 340 (Black, J., joined by Douglas, J., concurring in part and dissenting in part). *Yates* was one of four decisions handed down on what became known as "Red Monday." The other three cases were: *Sweezy v. New Hampshire*, 354 U.S. 234 (1957); *Watkins v. United States*, 354 U.S. 178 (1957); and *Service v. Dulles*, 354 U.S. 363 (1957). In all of these cases, although coming to rest on technical grounds, the Court made it plain that it was construing laws and practices in light of constitutional norms.
73. *Brown v. Board of Education*, 347 U.S. 483 (1954).
74. Powe, *The Warren Court*, 127–133.
75. *Barenblatt v. United States*, 360 U.S. 109 (1959).

76. For a brief account of the case, and Barenblatt's own statement about it, see Peter H. Irons, *The Courage of Their Convictions* (New York: Free Press, 1988), 81–104.
77. 360 U.S. at 126, 128.
78. 360 U.S. at 141 (Black, J., joined by Warren, CJ., and Douglas, J., dissenting).
79. Ibid., 143.
80. Ibid., 142–143 (balancing inappropriate); 144 (Barenblatt's real interests); 153–162 (attack on HUAC; bill of attainder; expose and punish).
81. See, for example, *Roth v. United States*, 354 U.S. 476 (1957); *Kingsley Pictures Corp. v. Regents*, 360 U.S. 684 (1959); *Smith v. California*, 361 U.S. 147 (1959); and *Ginzburg v. United States*, 383 U.S. 463 (1966).
82. See *Beauharnais v. Illinois*, 343 U.S. 250 (1952) and *New York Times v. Sullivan*, 376 U.S. 254 (1964).
83. Black retired from the Court on September 17, 1971, and died a week later. Yarbrough, *Mr. Justice Black*, 159–185, discusses the claims of scholars that Black was inconsistent over the course of his career, going from an absolutist position to a more restrictive one in the 1960s. See also, Andrew Martin and Kevin Quinn, "Dynamic Ideal Point Estimation via Markov Chain Monte Carlo for the U.S. Supreme Court, 1953–1999," *Political Analysis* 10 (2002): 134–153.
84. Although, it is important to note that in *Adderley v. Florida*, 385 U.S. 39 (1966), Black wrote for a unanimous Court upholding Florida's trespassing prosecution of protesters who had blocked a nonpublic jail driveway.
85. *Bell v. Maryland*, 378 U.S. 226 (1964).
86. Ibid., 346 (Black, J., joined by Harlan and White, JJ., dissenting).
87. *Tinker v. Des Moines Independent Community School District*, 393 U.S. 503 (1969).
88. Ibid., 506.
89. 393 U.S. at 524 (Black, J., dissenting). We find it interesting that Justice Black refused to join Justice Jackson's opinion for the Court in *West Virginia Board of Education v. Barnette*, 319 U.S. 624 (1943), the second flag salute case, choosing, instead, to base his argument on the Free Exercise Clause. Perhaps Black was reluctant to endorse Jackson's claim that the freedom of speech protected students in the public school setting.
90. See Yarbrough, *Mr. Justice Black*, 159–185 and Sylvia Snowiss, "The Legacy of Justice Black," *Supreme Court Review* 1973 (1973): 237.
91. Indeed, in *Tinker* Black reverted to his habit from previous cases of going straight to the evidentiary record. Where the majority simply presumed that the mere wearing of armbands was not disruptive, Black noted that "detailed testimony" showed otherwise. 393 U.S. at 517 (Black, J., dissenting).
92. Black, *A Constitutional Faith*.

Chapter 4

"Another's Lyric": John Marshall Harlan II, Judicial Conservatism, and Free Speech

Douglas E. Edlin

Justice John Marshall Harlan II was the grandson and namesake of a famous Supreme Court justice. His grandfather, the first Justice Harlan, is best remembered for dissenting alone from two of the Court's most morally retrograde and socially reactionary decisions.[1] The second Justice Harlan is often remembered for dissenting from decisions of the Warren Court, which is widely perceived as the most socially progressive Court in US history. Since he dissented from decisions of a liberal Court, and since he was nominated by President Dwight Eisenhower, a Republican, many conclude that the second Justice Harlan was a political and judicial conservative. Those conclusions are not contested in this chapter. But political conservatism and judicial conservatism are not the same thing. A study of the second Justice Harlan's decisions concerning the right to freedom of speech and expression, when placed in the context of his broader approach to judging, can help us to appreciate the difference between judicial conservatism and political conservatism.

It has become common in contemporary US politics to equate and conflate judicial and political conservatism. This conflation sometimes leads people to criticize conservative judges for decisions that are perceived to conflict with politically conservative values or goals. For example, the responses of political conservatives to Chief Justice John

Roberts's opinion upholding the Affordable Care Act[2] ranged from "I don't want to drink a beer with him today"[3] to "I feel like I just lost two great friends: America and John Roberts."[4] More generally, this also leads some political conservatives to categorize judges as "not real conservatives" if they reach decisions that do not seem consistent with politically conservative values and goals. Justices Sandra Day O'Connor and Anthony M. Kennedy are sometimes portrayed this way,[5] and Harlan has been as well.[6]

Of course, as with any political ideology, the political values and goals of conservatism have changed over time with respect to issues such as environmental policy, domestic surveillance, and foreign nation-building. It can, therefore, prove problematic to evaluate the "real conservatism" of a judge whose own outlook may remain consistent in the face of shifting political terrain. Moreover, and more importantly for purposes of this chapter, values of judicial conservatism may sometimes drive a judge to reach judicial decisions that conflict with the goals of his or her political ideology. We need to be careful to define what we mean by judicial conservatism and to distinguish it from what may commonly be understood as political conservatism at a given point in time.

Here, judicial conservatism is exemplified by a commitment to three values:

(1) respect for *stare decisis*, the legal doctrine that requires judges to follow precedent, which is demonstrated by a willingness to follow precedents with which the judge disagrees,[7]
(2) deference to democratically elected branches of government, which includes declining to overturn legislation whenever possible,[8] and
(3) deciding cases on the narrowest possible legal basis, which involves avoiding constitutional or controversial questions whenever possible.[9]

This understanding of judicial conservatism helps to explain why the terms activism and restraint are not used in this chapter to describe a judge or his rulings.

First, too frequently now, these terms are simply used as shorthand for "decision I disagree with" (in the case of activism) or "decision I agree with" (in the case of restraint).[10] Second, it is tempting to assume that judicial restraint is the only value judges ought to pursue in their judging, which could lead us to lose sight of a core purpose of judicial independence: "to guard the constitution and the rights of individuals from the effects of those ill humours which the arts of designing men, or the influence of particular conjunctures, sometimes disseminate among the people themselves."[11] In other words, restraint is not always a good thing. Sometimes protecting constitutional rights means that judges are supposed to reach "activist" decisions.[12] Sometimes our Constitution and our courts are meant to ensure that an individual's right to equal protection or to free speech is deemed more important than the desire of others to make her sit only in segregated railroad cars or classrooms, or not to hear what she has to say. As we will see, the second Justice Harlan recognized the importance of the courts' role in this regard just as much as his grandfather did. Whatever the value of vigorously pursuing politically conservative goals may be for political conservatism, that pursuit should not automatically be imputed as a goal of judicial conservatism—not, at least, if we are going to continue to claim judicial independence as a value of the judicial institution.

JOHN HARLAN AS A JUSTICE

Born at the close of the nineteenth century to a family that arrived in the United States from England in the seventeenth century, John Marshall Harlan II came from a long line of prominent lawyers and politicians. His grandfather was named for Chief Justice John Marshall, and Justice Harlan was named for his grandfather. After distinguishing himself academically at Princeton and at Oxford as a Rhodes Scholar, Harlan began his legal career with a prominent New York law firm. At the urging of one of the firm's partners, Harlan worked at the firm part of the day and attended law school in the afternoons. After excelling in legal practice, Harlan was appointed as a federal prosecutor and then a judge on the US Court of Appeals for the Second Circuit. He was nominated, confirmed, and appointed to the Supreme Court in 1955.[13]

Like all federal judges, Supreme Court justices are nominated by the president and confirmed by the Senate.[14] Politics has always influenced the nomination process, and political reaction to and commentary on the Court's opinions is nothing new. But the constant evaluation of an individual justice's decisions, and the justice himself, according to a rigid political yardstick is a fairly recent development.[15] When Harlan served on the Court, conservative justices often articulated positions that did not necessarily follow an ideological algorithm.[16] Justice Byron White, for example, could be a liberal on racial issues (or, even more precisely, on certain racial issues[17]) but not with respect to gay rights.[18] More recently, justices who do not decide cases in accordance with a political perspective or party affiliation are often derided as lacking ideological commitment or consistency. When Harlan sat on the Court, he could more easily maintain a meaningful distinction between judicial and political conservatism and he often demonstrated his commitment to the principles of judicial conservatism—respect for precedent,[19] deference to political branches of government,[20] and avoidance of constitutional or contentious issues—wherever possible.[21] And statistical analysis of Harlan's voting record on the Court demonstrates that political ideology did not dictate his judicial rulings.[22]

Respecting Government and Protecting Speech: Harlan's Balancing Analysis

Harlan's understanding of the right to freedom of speech was nuanced and context-dependent. He questioned whether the rights protected under the First Amendment could be claimed directly against the states (as opposed to the federal government).[23] He did not believe that the right necessarily encompassed a right not to speak, and he wrote two opinions allowing penalties to be imposed upon individuals who declined to answer questions regarding their possible membership in the Communist Party.[24] At the same time, however, he authored two opinions that significantly limited the power of the government to prosecute people for holding and expressing certain political views.[25] Harlan's interpretation of the right to freedom of expression balanced his judicial deference to government against the right of individuals to criticize the government.

These and other opinions demonstrate Harlan's belief that the government could sometimes subject the right of free speech to certain regulations, provided the government could demonstrate the need for those regulations. That is to say, Harlan did not believe that the right of free speech under the First Amendment was "absolute" and entirely immune from any possible legislative restriction.[26]

First, Harlan accepted that certain forms of expression contain elements of speech and conduct that are not speech. In these circumstances, the government can sometimes regulate acts that might contain an element of expression, provided that the regulation is not primarily directed at the suppression of speech itself. For example, in *United States v. O'Brien*, the Supreme Court upheld a federal statute that criminalized the burning of draft cards during the Vietnam War.[27] Even in these cases, however, the burden imposed on the government when attempting to justify the regulation is significant:

> We cannot accept the view that an apparently limitless variety of conduct can be labeled "speech" whenever the person engaging in the conduct intends thereby to express an idea . . . This Court has held that when "speech" and "nonspeech" elements are combined in the same course of conduct, a sufficiently important governmental interest in regulating the nonspeech element can justify incidental limitations on First Amendment freedoms . . . [W]e think it clear that a government regulation is sufficiently justified if it is within the constitutional power of the Government; if it furthers an important or substantial governmental interest; if the governmental interest is unrelated to the suppression of free expression; and if the incidental restriction on alleged First Amendment freedoms is no greater than is essential to the furtherance of that interest.[28]

Although Harlan agreed with the majority of the Court that the statute at issue in *O'Brien* was constitutional, he wrote a brief concurrence to underscore his opinion that, even where the government's interest in regulating expression is substantial and the restriction on expression is incidental, a claim of a First Amendment violation may still exist if the regulation would effectively prevent a speaker from reaching an audience with whom he could not communicate in any other way.[29] Harlan did not think this concern was raised in this case because burning a draft card was not the only effective way for O'Brien to express his opposition to the war in Vietnam.

Second, even where speech (not conduct) is involved, Harlan recognized that the Supreme Court had traditionally identified two broad categories of regulation that are not precluded by the First Amendment: (1) restrictions on certain forms of expression, such as obscenity[30] or speech that creates a "clear and present danger,"[31] which are not constitutionally protected,[32] and (2) regulations addressed to the manner or forum of the speech rather than to its content.[33]

Harlan's position that the government could regulate speech, provided the government established the need for the regulation, led him to the view that the right of free speech must sometimes be balanced against the government's interest in restricting certain speech.[34] If the regulation at issue was truly necessary for the government to protect itself or for the government to protect individuals from imminent physical harm, then Harlan would balance these concerns against the right of an individual to express herself. The government may not, however, merely attempt to protect itself from criticism[35] or to protect citizens from dissenting or unpopular views.[36]

The two justices, Hugo Black[37] and William O. Douglas,[38] who read the First Amendment as an absolute bar against any government restriction on the freedom of expression, were sharply critical of

Harlan's balancing approach. In his dissent from one of Harlan's opinions that upheld penalties for declining to answer questions regarding membership in the Communist Party, Black expressed his concerns with Harlan's approach in this way:

> The recognition that California has subjected "speech and association to the deterrence of subsequent disclosure" is, under the First Amendment, sufficient in itself to render the action of the State unconstitutional unless one subscribes to the doctrine that permits constitutionally protected rights to be "balanced" away whenever a majority of this Court thinks that a State might have interest sufficient to justify abridgment of those freedoms. As I have indicated many times before, I do not subscribe to that doctrine for I believe that the First Amendment's unequivocal command that there shall be no abridgment of the rights of free speech and assembly shows that the men who drafted our Bill of Rights did all the "balancing" that was to be done in this field.[39]

Black and Douglas's absolutist stance is appealing in its complete commitment to the value of free expression. Unfortunately, it is extremely difficult to apply in practice. So much so, in fact, that Black and Douglas sometimes deviated from it.[40] In any event, their position has never attracted a majority of the Supreme Court[41] and Harlan's balancing analysis, while still subject to criticism, better represents the Court's approach when determining the protection of speech under the First Amendment. It also represents Harlan's view of the judicial role and responsibility to consider carefully, in each case, the different factual circumstances and legal rights at stake and to fashion a judgment that treats the parties fairly under the law and establishes a legal standard that can guide courts and citizens in the future.[42]

In his final term on the Court, in perhaps his most famous First Amendment opinion, Harlan had the opportunity to work through his method of balancing the competing concerns of social order and individual expression.

COHEN V. CALIFORNIA

On April 26, 1968, Paul Robert Cohen was at the Los Angeles County Courthouse. He was there to appear as a witness at a trial, and he was walking down a corridor wearing a jacket with the words "Fuck the Draft" written on the back. His jacket also displayed peace symbols and the words "Stop the War."[43] He was arrested and convicted for violating this California statute:

> Every person who maliciously and willfully disturbs the peace or quiet of any neighborhood or person, by loud or unusual noise, or by tumultuous or offensive conduct, or threatening, traducing, quarreling, challenging to fight, or fighting, or who . . . use[s] any vulgar, profane, or indecent language within the presence or hearing of women or children, in a loud and boisterous manner, is guilty of a misdemeanor.[44]

Although Cohen could not be found guilty of using profane or indecent language "in a loud and boisterous manner," the California Court of Appeal upheld his conviction under the statute for maliciously disturbing the peace by engaging in offensive conduct.[45] Cohen's conviction was upheld despite the fact that he "did not engage in, nor threaten to engage in, nor did anyone as the result of his conduct in fact commit or threaten to commit any act of violence. The defendant did not make any loud or unusual noise, nor was there any evidence that he uttered any sound prior to his arrest."[46]

At his trial, Cohen testified that, "he wore the jacket knowing that the words were on the jacket as a means of informing the public of the depth of his feelings against the Vietnam War and the draft."[47] Harlan began his analysis by emphasizing that this case was about the words on Cohen's jacket. This was not a case about conduct; it was a case about speech.[48]

Harlan then reaffirmed his position that the First Amendment does not create an absolute right for "every individual to speak whenever or wherever he pleases, or to use any form of address in any circumstances that he chooses."[49] Harlan went on to determine whether Cohen's message fell within any of the categories of speech that the Court deemed unprotected or less fully protected by the First Amendment. First, Harlan noted that Cohen's message did not urge anyone to disobey or disrupt the draft. So this was not a case about advocating illegal action.[50] Second, Harlan pointed out that the California statute at issue applied generally throughout the state. This was not an attempt to create a defined time, place, or manner restriction "to preserve an appropriately decorous atmosphere in the courthouse."[51] Third, Cohen's speech could not be classified as obscenity.[52] Fourth, the case did not involve "fighting words" because Cohen's message was not directed toward any individual or individuals who could reasonably have seen his jacket as a personal insult or epithet that might be "likely to provoke a violent reaction."[53] Fifth, Cohen's language also could not be seen as intentionally targeted at a particular group or audience that might be expected to react with hostility to his message.[54] Cohen removed his jacket when he entered the courtroom, and there was no evidence that anyone (other than a police officer in the courtroom who later arrested Cohen) was especially upset by Cohen's jacket. In fact, the judge in the courtroom declined the police officer's request to hold Cohen in contempt of court.[55] Sixth, Harlan concluded that this was not an instance in which Cohen was forcing an unwilling or captive audience to confront his speech.[56]

After systematically explaining what this case was not about—not conduct; not illegal advocacy; not a time, place, or manner restriction; not obscenity; not "fighting words"; not hostile audiences; not captive audiences—Harlan then explained what this case was about. In his view, the issue presented in *Cohen* was this: "whether California can excise, as 'offensive conduct,' one particular scurrilous epithet from the public discourse, either upon the theory of the court below that its use is inherently likely to cause violent reaction or upon a more general assertion that the States, acting as guardians of public morality, may properly remove this offensive word from the public vocabulary."[57]

The answer, according to Harlan and the Court, was "no." The reasons for this decision rest primarily on the constitutional and social values that the First Amendment reflects and protects, one of which is that the freedom to choose how we express ourselves belongs to each of us rather than to the government. The underlying premise here is that genuine self-government requires uninhibited self-expression.[58] Harlan saw in this reciprocal relationship "the hope that use of such freedom will ultimately produce a more capable citizenry and more perfect polity and in the belief that no other approach would comport with the premise of individual dignity and choice upon which our political system rests."[59] This faith that a freer citizenry will lead to a better nation captures an Aristotelian belief in the mutual enrichment of citizens and the State.[60] A State that provides more freedom to its citizens will result in citizens who are better able to govern themselves.

A correlative concern that undergirds the First Amendment is the worry that government encroachment upon free self-expression of individuals is a constant threat to the values of autonomous self-government because any decision by the government to restrict certain forms of expression places the power to define the scope and content of public discourse in the hands of a few politicians or the majority of citizens.[61] In either case, government restriction of self-expression will result in the silencing of a minority and the stifling of dissent. However, the First Amendment is grounded in the conviction that permitting the free expression of dissenting and minority perspectives will allow all those who are governed by the State to see their government as respectful of and responsive to their views. Allowing the free expression of dissent and criticism of the government will sometimes contribute to change and progress for our society.[62] For this reason, Harlan said in *Cohen*, the Constitution prevents the government from specifying for us the opinions that we may express and instead places "the decision as to what views shall be voiced largely into the hands of each of us."[63]

Three Words (Two, Really)

When considering Harlan's reasoning in *Cohen*, it is helpful to consider the words themselves in more detail. With this in mind, some people tend to focus on the first word, and some people tend to focus on the last word. Two aspects of Harlan's approach are important here. In determining that the language on Cohen's jacket could not reasonably be regarded as obscene, Harlan noted that, in one way or another, obscenity is about sexual arousal. And as Harlan wryly observed in *Cohen*, "[i]t cannot plausibly be maintained that this vulgar allusion to the Selective Service System would conjure up such psychic stimulation in anyone."[64] Put differently, Harlan is saying that no one is going to get turned on by reading the word "fuck" on Cohen's jacket.

Harlan acknowledged and emphasized the importance of allowing speakers to express their emotions along with their ideas through their speech.[65] The fact that an audience might find certain speech emotionally disturbing does not inhibit its protection under the Constitution because merely finding a speaker's words or ideas offensive does not protect an audience from hearing them.[66] Although the First Amendment has been applied to protect speakers and audiences,[67] as Harlan explained in *Cohen*, if members of an audience find themselves offended by what they read, it is ordinarily their obligation to shelter "their sensibilities simply by averting their eyes."[68]

This brings us to the last word on Cohen's jacket. In terms of legal doctrine, the analysis of the last word moves us to the concepts of "hostile audiences" or "fighting words." In its brief to the Supreme Court, the State of California asked the Court to consider the consequences of holding that the First Amendment protects the speech on Cohen's jacket. What will follow, the State said, is the public display of signs such as these:

> "Fuck Catholics"; "Fuck Negroes"; "Fuck Whites"; "Fuck Jews";—signs carried in protest of these "groups"; against public institutions (a "Fuck the United States Congress" sign in protest over enactments of the National

Legislature); or against public officials (a "Fuck Nixon" sign carried by an opponent of the war policies of the President of the United States; a "Fuck the Justices of the United States Supreme Court" sign displayed in protest of decisions rendered by this Honorable Court).[69]

The Court was not persuaded by this argument, and the reasons are instructive in thinking about the scope of protection afforded by the First Amendment. As Harlan indicated in *Cohen*, the first four hypothetical signs mentioned in the State's brief describe identifiable groups of people who might reasonably take offense (and perhaps respond with anger) at those messages. If the message on Cohen's jacket were directed at a specific group then the State might have been able to restrict his expression to prevent members of that group from responding aggressively. But as Harlan pointed out in *Cohen*, this was not "an instance of the exercise of the State's police power to prevent a speaker from intentionally provoking a given group to hostile reaction."[70] Similarly, Cohen's jacket was not directed at any specific individuals, so the case did not involve what the Court has sometimes called "fighting words." In certain instances, the Court has held that a State may restrict the public use of "personally abusive epithets which, when addressed to the ordinary citizen, are, as a matter of common knowledge, inherently likely to provoke violent reaction."[71]

In Harlan's view, Cohen was permitted to express himself as he did because the message on his jacket "was clearly not 'directed to the person of the hearer.' No individual actually or likely to be present could reasonably have regarded the words on appellant's jacket as a direct personal insult."[72] And even if Cohen's message had been directed at certain individuals identified in the State's brief, such as the president, members of Congress, or justices of the Supreme Court, it seems very likely that his speech would still be protected by the First Amendment because of "a profound national commitment to the principle that debate on public issues should be uninhibited, robust, and wide-open, and that it may well include vehement, caustic, and sometimes unpleasantly sharp attacks on government and public officials."[73]

Speech and Conduct

Cohen was about "the *words* Cohen used to convey his message."[74] At the very start of his legal discussion, Harlan immediately categorizes this as a speech case rather than a conduct case. In this respect, it is useful to compare *Cohen* with *O'Brien*. Harlan concurred with the

O'Brien majority that a federal statute penalizing the burning of draft cards did not violate the First Amendment because the government had a "legitimate and substantial purpose" in preventing the destruction of draft cards to ensure the proper administration of the military.[75] So what differentiates O'Brien's criticism of the draft and the Vietnam War from Cohen's? For Harlan, the answer lies in the balance of rights and interests at stake. The only conduct for which California punished Cohen was wearing a jacket with words on it. There was no conduct in which Cohen was engaged that could be regulated without either broadly prohibiting legal conduct (wearing a jacket) or impeding Cohen's expression of his views (criticizing the draft).[76] So Harlan concluded that the case was about speech itself. And the State of California did not have a legitimate and substantial purpose in preventing Cohen from using certain words in public out of a general and unsubstantiated concern with potential violence or public morality.[77]

Unlike *Cohen*, however, *O'Brien* involved speech and conduct. The Court did not deny that burning a draft card expressed opposition to the war in Vietnam. But burning a draft card was not exclusively a form of expression; it was also conduct that interfered with the government's ability to manage the armed forces. So the Court concluded that *O'Brien* involved expression that contained "speech and nonspeech elements . . . combined in the same course of conduct."[78] Unlike *Cohen*, the Court determined in *O'Brien* that the government had a legitimate and substantial purpose in preventing the burning of draft cards that was separate from simply preventing O'Brien from expressing his opposition to the war.

The balancing of interests at stake in *O'Brien* and *Cohen* demonstrates well Harlan's approach to First Amendment cases. The speakers' interest in expressing their opposition to the Vietnam War was fundamentally the same in each case, but the government interest in *O'Brien* was substantial and the government interest in *Cohen* was negligible. As a result, Cohen's right to express himself in the form he chose was upheld while O'Brien's chosen form of expression was restricted due to the government interest in that case.

Comparing Harlan's analysis of speech and conduct in *Cohen* and *O'Brien* reveals an interesting point about Harlan's understanding of his role and responsibilities as a judge. In *O'Brien*, where Harlan perceived a legitimate government purpose in preserving draft cards apart from restricting speech and where he found many alternative avenues for O'Brien to express his opposition to the Vietnam War, Harlan concluded that the First Amendment would tolerate the restriction and that his role as a judge was to defer to Congress's judgment.

Conversely, in *Cohen*, where California had no discernible interest merely in removing the word "fuck" from all forms of public expression, and where Cohen's speech fell under no recognized category of unprotected or less-protected speech, Harlan concluded that the First Amendment protected Cohen's expression and that his role as a judge was to enforce Cohen's right to express himself.

Justice Harlan's First Amendment and Judicial Conservatism

One year after the Court decided *O'Brien*, Harlan wrote the majority opinion in a case that involved the burning not of a draft card but of an American flag. In *Street v. New York*,[79] the Court reviewed the conviction of Sidney Street, a black man who had, in response to the shooting of James Meredith,[80] taken his American flag to a street corner in Brooklyn, set it on fire, and said (among other things): "If they let that happen to Meredith we don't need an American flag."[81]

Street was convicted of violating a New York statute that made it a misdemeanor "publicly [to] mutilate, deface, defile, or defy, trample upon, or cast contempt upon either by words or act [any flag of the United States]."[82] Street was tried by a judge sitting without a jury. He was convicted and given a suspended sentence. On appeal, Street argued that the New York statute was unconstitutional for three reasons: (1) the statute criminalizes speech that is protected by the First Amendment, (2) the statute "does not clearly define the conduct which it forbids," and (3) the statute criminalizes damaging or destroying an American flag, which is a form of expression protected by the First Amendment.[83]

Harlan's decision in *Street* exhibits the practical application of his judicial conservatism and his principled commitment to the values of the First Amendment. In his opinion for the majority, Harlan determined that the Court need not address Street's second and third arguments because the case could be decided on the first argument alone. Harlan noted that the trial judge issued a general verdict against Street that did not specify whether Street was convicted for the words he spoke against the flag, the burning of the flag, or both. Consequently, relying on precedents from 1931 and 1942, Harlan decided that Street's conviction could be overturned if it was possible that his conviction was based solely or partly upon the words that he spoke.[84]

The Court ruled that Street's speech was constitutionally protected and he could not be punished by New York for his words, and since his conviction may have been based, at least in part, on his speech, his conviction must be overturned.[85] In reaching this decision, Harlan very deliberately and carefully declined to decide whether flag-burning was speech protected by the First Amendment.[86] In doing so, Harlan acted consistently with two of the core principles of judicial conservatism: respect for precedent and avoidance of constitutional questions wherever possible. At the same time, Harlan acted consistently with his judicial responsibility to enforce an individual's constitutional rights (even against the wishes of a majority) and his personal concern for the First Amendment's protection of political speech.

The benefits of Harlan's approach can be seen in the case in which the Supreme Court determined whether flag-burning is constitutionally protected as a form of expression. In *Texas v. Johnson*,[87] which was decided twenty years after *Street*,[88] the Court was again asked to determine whether flag-burning is expression protected by the First Amendment. Writing for the Court, William Brennan referred specifically to Harlan's decision in *Street* and applied his reasoning in *Johnson*. In responding to the State's argument that it could prohibit flag-burning out of an interest in "preserving the flag as a symbol of nationhood and national unity,"[89] Brennan quoted and relied upon language from Harlan's decision in *Street*:

> Rejecting the argument that the conviction could be sustained on the ground that Street had "failed to show the respect for our national symbol which may properly be demanded of every citizen," we concluded that "the constitutionally guaranteed freedom to be intellectually . . . diverse or even contrary, and the right to differ as to things that touch the heart of the existing order, encompass the freedom to express publicly one's opinions about our flag, including those opinions which are defiant or contemptuous."[90]

The Court went on to hold in *Johnson* that flag-burning is a form of expression that is protected by the First Amendment and cannot be prohibited by the State.[91]

Consistent with his judicial conservatism, Harlan declined in *Street* to decide whether flag-burning was expression protected by the Constitution. Instead, he decided the case on a more limited basis. He thereby afforded the Court the benefit of his reasoning in *Street*, along with many additional precedents from the intervening two decades, which assisted the Court in coming to its final conclusion when the question was squarely and finally presented in *Johnson*.

Consistent with Harlan's approach to the First Amendment, the language the Court quoted from *Street* in *Johnson* emphasizes the constitutional protection of an individual's right to be intellectually diverse, to differ, and to express opinions that are defiant. For Harlan, this was the core of the freedom guaranteed by the First Amendment—the freedom of adult individuals to express in public their own political views[92]—especially when those views challenge the government or the majority. The right to freedom of expression, in Harlan's view, must protect the ability to disagree and to dissent. This conception of free expression links Harlan's opinion in *Street* with his opinion in *Cohen*. Just as Harlan emphasized in *Street* that the Constitution guarantees "the freedom to express publicly . . . opinions which are defiant,"[93] he emphasized in *Cohen* that our constitutional values prohibit any "governmental power to force persons who wish to ventilate their dissident views into avoiding particular forms of expression."[94] Each of us must be free to speak his mind so that all of us are free to live in a nation in which we can recognize ourselves in our society and so that this exchange of differing views within our public discourse can, in turn, improve the ability of our government to treat everyone with respect and dignity, to reach closer to the aspirations of our Constitution.

CONCLUSION

Public debate in the United States today is characterized more by combat than by communication. We all could benefit from another aspect of Harlan's judicial conservatism not yet discussed in this chapter. Harlan saw a connection between the constitutional protection of an individual's dissenting beliefs and that individual's personal dignity.[95] This led him to realize that we should always keep our minds open and remain willing to listen to those with whom we disagree, particularly when we find ourselves in the majority and when we find their views unpleasant or unpopular.[96] We can find this willingness in the most famous line Harlan wrote in *Cohen*: "while the particular four-letter word being litigated here is perhaps more distasteful than most others of its genre, it is nevertheless often true that one man's vulgarity is another's lyric."[97] This willingness to listen with an open mind requires some humility because we must constantly accept the possibility that we are mistaken. The humility in Harlan's judicial conservatism was evident throughout his career and was sometimes explicit in his candid acknowledgment of errors he had made in prior opinions.[98]

Political conservatism and judicial conservatism seem to be going in different directions. Or maybe to be more precise, there is increasing public pressure for judicial conservatism to follow political conservatism.

Nevertheless, freedom of speech remains one of the seemingly rare constitutional principles on which conservatives and liberals can still agree. The libertarian component of conservatism intersects with liberalism's concern with tolerance of minority and individual viewpoints, and both perspectives converge at the same point: the government should not prevent individuals from speaking their minds. And we can see this convergence in the votes of conservative and liberal justices in some important free speech cases.[99]

Like any writer who is worth reading, Harlan's views cannot be fully understood by a simple attempt to place him in a single category. For this reason, among others, Harlan is regarded by many judges and lawyers of all political ideologies—Justice Ruth Bader Ginsburg,[100] Justice David H. Souter,[101] and Justice Samuel A. Alito,[102] for instance—as an example to aspire to. In his respect for precedent, his deference to the representative branches of government, and his willingness to avoid constitutional or contentious questions where he could, Harlan demonstrated his judicial conservatism, his belief in the institutions and processes of government, and his respect for the Court's role in government and his responsibilities as a judge.

At the same time, Harlan also believed in the unique importance of freedom of expression for deliberative democracy. Free speech is often understood as a prerequisite for a democratic system of government to function and for the people governed by that system to flourish.[103] We can understand these mutual benefits in terms of the government's ability to adapt to changing social views and needs, the citizens' broader understanding of the plural society in which they live, or an individual's assurance that he can speak his mind even if no one else is persuaded. A willingness to listen is meaningless without affording others the opportunity to speak. For Harlan, protecting free speech *was* protecting the democratic process.

Just as Harlan believed in the value of judicial dissent for legal development, he believed in the value of political dissent for political development.[104] His understanding of the United States as a constitutional democracy led him to dissent frequently from Supreme Court decisions with which he disagreed, and it led him to protect the right of individuals to dissent from government actions with which they disagreed. In both types of case, his motivation reflected his belief that we can improve our understanding of our world only if we continue to discuss freely the issues that concern us and that the First Amendment was intended, beyond all else, to ensure that the conversation will continue.

NOTES

1. See *Civil Rights Cases*, 109 U.S. 3 (1883); *Plessy v. Ferguson*, 163 U.S. 537 (1896).
2. See *Nat'l Fed'n of Indep. Bus. v. Sebelius*, 132 S. Ct. 2566 (2012).
3. Rep. Phil Gingrey (R-GA), quoted in Meghan Kiesel, "Supreme Court Health Care Ruling Inspires Creative Vitriol," *ABC News*, June 29, 2012, http://abcnews.go.com/Politics/OTUS/supreme-court-health-care-ruling-inspires-creative-vitriol/story?id=16678659
4. Rep. Jack Kingston (R-GA), @JackKingston, Twitter, June 28, 2012, 8:05 AM EST, https://twitter.com/JackKingston/status/218359574539943937
5. See, for example, Charles Krauthammer, "Philosophy for a Judge," *Washington Post*, July 8, 2005, A23 ("Unlike a principled conservative such as Antonin Scalia, . . . O'Connor had no stable ideas about constitutional interpretation"); Bruce Fein, "A Court of Mediocrity: Supreme Court Commentary," *American Bar Association Journal* 77 (October 1991): 78 ("Justice Kennedy offers no principled clue as to where private action ends and state action begins . . . Kennedy's contrived reasoning suggests that judges should blink at the Constitution to escape politically or socially unpalatable results") (discussing *Edmondson v. Leesville Concrete Co.*, 500 U.S. 614 (1991)).
6. See Jeffrey Toobin, *The Nine: Inside the Secret World of the Supreme Court* (New York: Random House, 2007), 21 ("Both [Justice Scalia and Judge Bork] were real conservatives, not 'squishes,' as young Federalist Society lawyers referred to Harlan, Stewart, and the other moderate conservatives").
7. To accentuate my differentiation of judicial and political conservatism, I should emphasize that politically liberal judges often demonstrate their commitment to this aspect of judicial conservatism. See, for example, *Baze v. Rees*, 553 U.S. 35, 87 (2008) (Stevens, J., concurring in the judgment) ("[t]he conclusion that I have reached with regard to the constitutionality of the death penalty itself makes my decision in this case particularly difficult. It does not, however, justify a refusal to respect precedents that remain a part of our law").
8. Again, as a way of considering the various interactions and distinctions between judicial and political conservatism, notice that Chief Justice Roberts's decision to uphold the Affordable Care Act by construing the legislation under Congress's power to levy taxes, rather than under Congress's power to regulate interstate commerce, is consistent with this element of judicial conservatism. See 132 S. Ct. at 2593–2596.
9. See *Ashwander v. Tennessee Valley Authority*, 297 U.S. 288, 346–348 (1936) (Brandeis, J., joined by Stone, Roberts, and Cardozo, JJ., concurring). The motivating idea here is that judges should make "an effort to minimize the judicial presence in American public life." Cass R. Sunstein, *One Case at a Time: Judicial Minimalism on the Supreme Court* (Cambridge, MA: Harvard University Press, 1999), 39.

10. Compare Representative Michele Bachmann (R-MN), "This was an activist court that you saw today" (CNN television broadcast, June 28, 2012) (referring to the Supreme Court decision in *Sebelius*) with Senator Al Franken (D-MN), "Citizens United was an incredible act of judicial activism," quoted in "Franken Bill Seeks to Limit Corporations' Influence on Elections," *St. Cloud Times*, April 29, 2010 (referring to the Supreme Court decision in *Citizens United v. Fed. Election Comm.*, 558 U.S. 310 (2010)).
11. Alexander Hamilton, "Federalist No. 78," in Alexander Hamilton, John Jay, and James Madison, *The Federalist* (Indianapolis, IN: Liberty Fund, 2001), 405.
12. See, for example, Richard A. Posner, *The Federal Courts: Challenge and Reform* (Cambridge, MA: Harvard University Press, 1985), 322 ("[t]he framers of the Constitution gave the federal judges extraordinary guarantees of independence in part so that they would be fearless in protecting individual rights against encroachment by the other branches of government").
13. See Tinsley E. Yarbrough, *John Marshall Harlan: Great Dissenter of the Warren Court* (New York: Oxford University Press, 1992), Chapters 1–3. The brief summary in the text is largely drawn from Yarbrough's biography.
14. See U.S. Const., Art. II, Sec. 2.
15. But not unprecedented. See William S. Carpenter, *Judicial Tenure in the United States with Especial Reference to the Tenure of Federal Judges* (New Haven, CT: Yale University Press, 1918), 119–123.
16. See Lewis F. Powell Jr., "What Really Goes On at the Supreme Court?" in David M. O'Brien, ed., *Judges on Judging: Views from the Bench*, 4th ed. (Washington, DC: CQ Press, 2013), 129–130.
17. See, for example, *UJO of Williamsburgh v. Carey*, 430 U.S. 144, 161 (1977) (upholding the constitutionality of § 5 of the Voting Rights Act); *Shaw v. Reno*, 509 U.S. 630, 668–670 (1993) (White, J., joined by Blackmun and Stevens, JJ., dissenting) (arguing that the creation of a majority-minority voting district did not violate the Fourteenth or Fifteenth Amendment); *Regents of University of California v. Bakke*, 438 U.S. 265, 326–327 (1978) (author of separate opinion, but joining Brennan, Marshall, and Blackmun in concluding that a quota-based affirmative action admissions program did not violate principles of equal protection).
18. See *Bowers v. Hardwick*, 478 U.S. 186 (1986) (ruling that a State could criminalize the consensual sexual activities of gay adults).
19. See, for example, *Orozco v. Texas*, 394 U.S. 324, 327–328 (1969) ("[D]espite my strong inclination to join in the dissent . . . I can find no acceptable avenue of escape from *Miranda* in judging this case. . . . Therefore, and purely out of respect for *stare decisis*, I reluctantly feel compelled to acquiesce in today's decision of the Court") (Harlan, J., concurring) (citations omitted).
20. See, for example, *New York Times Co. v. United States*, 403 U.S. 713, 756 (1971) (Harlan, J., joined by Burger, CJ., and Blackmun, J., dissenting)

("It is plain to me that the scope of the judicial function in passing upon the activities of the Executive Branch of the Government in the field of foreign affairs is very narrowly restricted"); *A Book Named "John Cleland's Memoirs of a Woman of Pleasure" v. Att'y Gen. of Mass.*, 383 U.S. 413, 459 (1966) (Harlan, J., dissenting).

21. See, for example, *Desist v. United States*, 394 U.S. 244, 258 (1969) (Harlan, J., dissenting) ("This Court is entitled to decide constitutional issues only when the facts of a particular case *require* their resolution for a just adjudication on the merits") (citation omitted) (emphasis in original); *United States v. Vuitch*, 402 U.S. 62, 91–95 (1971) (Harlan, J., joined by Brennan, Marshall, and Blackmun, JJ., dissenting) (arguing that the Court lacked jurisdiction to review the dismissal of an indictment against a doctor for performing abortions in violation of a DC criminal statute).
22. See Lee Epstein and William M. Landes, "Was There Ever Such a Thing as Judicial Self-Restraint?" *California Law Review* 100 (2012): 571–576.
23. See, for example, *Griffin v. California*, 380 U.S. 609, 615–616 (1965) (Harlan, J., concurring); *Pointer v. Texas*, 380 U.S. 400, 408–409 (1965) (Harlan, J., concurring in the result).
24. See *Konigsberg v. State Bar of California*, 366 U.S. 36, 46–47 (1961); *Barenblatt v. United States*, 360 U.S. 109, 126–128 (1959). It is not entirely clear whether Harlan's view in these cases was motivated by his own perception that the Communist Party posed unique threats to US national security or whether he was simply following precedent that assumed this assessment. See 360 U.S. at 128. The biographical evidence suggests the latter. Harlan privately expressed concerns about prosecuting or penalizing people for their political support of communism. See Yarbrough, *John Marshall Harlan*, 190–194.
25. See *Yates v. United States*, 354 U.S. 298, 311–312, 319–322, 324–327 (1957); *Scales v. United States*, 367 U.S. 203, 232–234 (1961). Particularly in light of the Cold War political climate in which the Court was operating at the time, Justice Harlan's opinion in *Yates* has been called "a brilliant example of legal craftsmanship and judicial statesmanship on the side of the angels." Harry Kalven Jr., *A Worthy Tradition: Freedom of Speech in America* (New York: Harper & Row, 1989), 222.
26. See 366 U.S. at 49. See also *Kovacs v. Cooper*, 336 U.S. 77, 85 (1949) ("Of course, even the fundamental rights of the Bill of Rights are not absolute"); *Whitney v. California*, 274 U.S. 357, 373 (1927) ("[A]lthough the rights of free speech and assembly are fundamental, they are not in their nature absolute. Their exercise is subject to restriction") (Brandeis, J., concurring); *Frohwerk v. United States*, 249 U.S. 204, 206 (1919) ("[T]he First Amendment while prohibiting legislation against free speech as such cannot have been, and obviously was not, intended to give immunity for every possible use of language") (citation omitted).
27. See *United States v. O'Brien*, 391 U.S. 367 (1968).
28. Ibid., 376–377.

29. Ibid., 388–389.
30. In his *Konigsberg* opinion, Harlan cites *Roth v. United States*, 354 U.S. 476 (1957), as excluding obscenity from protected speech under the First Amendment. See *Konigsberg*, 366 U.S. at 50. Harlan's dissent in *Roth* was motivated by his concern that "Congress has no substantive power over sexual morality" and, accordingly, "the federal interest in protecting the Nation against pornography [is] attenuated, but the dangers of federal censorship in this field are far greater than anything the States may do. . . . Different States will have different attitudes toward the same work of literature. The same book which is freely read in one State might be classed as obscene in another." 354 U.S. at 504, 505–506 (1957) (Harlan, J., dissenting). Harlan's view that a single national standard is inappropriate when attempting to make case-specific determinations about obscenity was adopted by the Supreme Court in *Miller v. California*, 413 U.S. 15, 32, 37 (1973) ("It is neither realistic nor constitutionally sound to read the First Amendment as requiring that the people of Maine or Mississippi accept public depiction of conduct found tolerable in Las Vegas, or New York City . . . [O]bscenity is to be determined by applying 'contemporary community standards,' not 'national standards'") (citations omitted).
31. See *Schenck v. United States*, 249 U.S. 47, 52 (1919).
32. See *Chaplinsky v. New Hampshire*, 315 U.S. 568, 571–572 (1942).
33. To establish this point just with respect to a couple of the cases Justice Harlan cites in *Konigsberg*, see *Cox v. New Hampshire*, 312 U.S. 569, 574–576 (1941); and *Kovacs*, 336 U.S. at 87.
34. See generally Justice Harlan's balancing analysis in *NAACP v. Alabama*, 357 U.S. 449, 460–466 (1958).
35. See, for example, *Elrod v. Burns*, 427 U.S. 347, 374, footnote no. 29 (1976) ("[T]he purpose of the First Amendment includes the need . . . to enable every citizen at any time to bring the government and any person in authority to the bar of public opinion by any just criticism upon their conduct in the exercise of the authority which the people have conferred upon them") (citations omitted and internal quotation marks deleted).
36. See *Terminiello v. Chicago*, 337 U.S. 1, 4–5 (1949) ("[A] function of free speech under our system of government is to invite dispute. It may indeed best serve its high purpose when it induces a condition of unrest, creates dissatisfaction with conditions as they are, or even stirs people to anger. Speech is often provocative and challenging. It may strike at prejudices and preconceptions and have profound unsettling effects as it presses for acceptance of an idea. . . . There is no room under our Constitution for a more restrictive view. For the alternative would lead to standardization of ideas either by legislatures, courts, or dominant political or community groups").
37. See, for example, *Smith v. California*, 361 U.S. 147, 157 (1959) ("I read 'no law . . . abridging' to mean *no law abridging*") (Black, J., concurring) (emphasis in original).

38. See, for example, *CBS, Inc. v. Democratic Nat'l Cmte.*, 412 U.S. 94, 156 (1973) ("The ban of 'no' law that abridges freedom of the press is in my view total and complete") (Douglas, J., concurring in the judgment).
39. 366 U.S. at 60–61 (Black, J., joined by Warren, CJ., and Douglas, J., dissenting). See also 360 U.S. at 143 (Black, J., joined by Warren, CJ., and Douglas, J., dissenting) ("Congress shall pass no law abridging freedom of speech, press, assembly and petition, unless Congress and the Supreme Court reach the joint conclusion that on balance the interest of the Government in stifling these freedoms is greater than the interest of the people in having them exercised").
40. See, for example, *Adderley v. Florida*, 385 U.S. 39, 46–47 (1966) (Black authoring the Court's opinion upholding the criminal trespass conviction of students protesting outside a jail where a classmate was held); *Brandenburg v. Ohio*, 395 U.S. 444, 455–456 (1969) (Douglas, J., concurring) ("Picketing, as we have said on numerous occasions, is 'free speech plus.' . . . It can be regulated as to the number of pickets and the place and hours, because traffic and other community problems would otherwise suffer") (citations omitted).
41. For another example of a justice's approach to deciding speech cases that has not attracted other members of the Court, see Helen Knowles's discussion in this volume of Justice Kennedy's attempt to discontinue the use of strict scrutiny analysis when evaluating content-based regulations of expression in Chapter 7 herein.
42. See, for example, Gerald Gunther, "In Search of Judicial Quality on a Changing Court: The Case of Justice Powell," *Stanford Law Review* 24 (1972): 1013–1014 (describing Harlan as a judge who "viewed balancing not as an escape from judicial responsibility, but as a mandate to perceive every free speech interest in a situation and to scrutinize every justification for a restriction of individual liberty. . . . The Harlan legacy . . . is rich in sensitive, candid, and articulate perceptions of competing concerns, and in overarching approaches which retain their capacity to instruct").
43. See William Cohen, "A Look Back at *Cohen v. California*," *UCLA Law Review* 34 (1987): 1596.
44. *Cohen v. California*, 403 U.S. 15, 16, footnote no. 1 (1971) (quoting Cal. Penal Code § 415).
45. The Court of Appeal determined that Cohen acted maliciously because "he must have been aware that his behavior would vex and annoy a substantial portion of his unwilling 'audience.'" *People v. Cohen*, 1 Cal. App. 3d 94, 99, 81 Cal. Rptr. 503, 506 (1969). The Court of Appeal ruled that Cohen's conduct disturbed the peace because his "acts constituted the type of offensive conduct prohibited by section 415 in that it had a tendency to incite others to violent behavior or to disturb the peace." *Cohen*, 1 Cal. App. 3d at 100, 81 Cal. Rptr. at 506.
46. See 403 U.S. at 16–17.
47. 1 Cal. App. 3d at 97–98, 81 Cal. Rptr. at 505, quoted in 403 U.S. at 16.
48. 403 U.S. at 18.

49. Ibid., 19.
50. Ibid., 18.
51. Ibid., 19.
52. Ibid., 20.
53. Ibid.
54. Ibid.
55. Ibid., 19, foonote no. 3.
56. Ibid., 21–22.
57. Ibid., 22–23.
58. See *Garrison v. Louisiana*, 379 U.S. 64, 74–75 (1964).
59. 403 U.S. at 24 (citation omitted).
60. See Aristotle, *Politics* (C. D. C. Reeve, trans.) (Indianapolis, IN: Hackett Publishing Company, 1998), 1279a–b, 77–78. Of course, Aristotle did not define citizens or regard democracy exactly as we do today.
61. See 274 U.S. at 375–376 (Brandeis, J., concurring); *Edwards v. South Carolina*, 372 U.S. 229, 237 (1963).
62. See *De Jonge v. Oregon*, 299 U.S. 353, 364–365 (1937).
63. 403 U.S. at 24.
64. Ibid., 20.
65. Ibid., 26 (language "conveys not only ideas capable of relatively precise, detached explication, but otherwise inexpressible emotions as well. In fact, words are often chosen as much for their emotive as their cognitive force. We cannot sanction the view that the Constitution, while solicitous of the cognitive content of individual speech, has little or no regard for that emotive function which, practically speaking, may often be the more important element of the overall message sought to be communicated").
66. See *Street v. New York*, 394 U.S. 576, 592 (1969).
67. See, e.g., *Martin v. City of Struthers*, 319 U.S. 141, 143 (1943).
68. 403 U.S. at 21.
69. Respondent *Cohen* brief, 20–21 (internal punctuation deleted).
70. 403 U.S. at 20 (citations omitted). Even here, though, if an audience is likely to be upset by a speaker's message, it is usually the obligation of the audience to avoid the speaker, not the speaker's obligation to remain silent. Compare *Collin v. Smith*, 578 F.2d 1197, 1207 (7th Cir. 1978), *cert. denied*, 439 U.S. 916 (1978) (noting that the mainly Jewish residents of Skokie, Illinois, should "simply avoid the Village Hall for thirty minutes on a Sunday afternoon" if they wished to refrain from observing a neo-Nazi march through their town). However, where the purpose of speech is to target specific individuals or members of a group solely for the purpose of intimidation, the speech may be restricted. See *Virginia v. Black*, 538 U.S. 343, 363 (2003) ("[t]he First Amendment permits Virginia to outlaw cross burnings done with the intent to intimidate because burning a cross is a particularly virulent form of intimidation . . . Virginia may choose to regulate this subset of intimidating messages in light of cross burning's long and pernicious history as a signal of impending violence") (dicta).

71. 403 U.S. at 20 (citation omitted).
72. Ibid.
73. *New York Times Co. v. Sullivan*, 376 U.S. 254, 270 (1964) (citations omitted). The Court conceded in *Sullivan* that these caustic attacks on public officials might occasionally lead to "vilification" and "excesses and abuses"; nevertheless, these are "in the long view, essential to enlightened opinion and right conduct on the part of the citizens of a democracy." Ibid., 271.
74. 403 U.S. at 18 (emphasis in original).
75. See 391 U.S. at 377–380.
76. See 403 U.S. at 18.
77. Ibid., 22–23.
78. 391 U.S. at 376.
79. 394 U.S. 576 (1969).
80. James Meredith was the first black person to attend the University of Mississippi. Three years after he graduated, Meredith attempted to walk from Memphis, Tennessee, to Jackson, Mississippi. He began his March against Fear on June 6, 1966. Shortly after beginning his March on June 6, Meredith was shot by a sniper. For a comprehensive account of Meredith's March, see Aram Goudsouzian, *Down to the Crossroads: Civil Rights, Black Power, and the Meredith March Against Fear* (New York: Farrar, Straus & Giroux, 2014).
81. 394 U.S. at 579.
82. N.Y. Penal Law § 1425, subd. 16, par. d (1909), superseded by N.Y. Laws 1965, c. 1031, § 52, quoted in 394 U.S. at 578. The language under which Street was convicted remained unchanged in the updated legislation.
83. See 394 U.S. at 580–581.
84. Ibid., 585–586, 587 (discussing *Stromberg v. California*, 283 U.S. 359, 367–368 (1931) and *Williams v. North Carolina*, 317 U.S. 287, 292 (1942)).
85. See 394 U.S. at 590–593.
86. Ibid., 594.
87. *Texas v. Johnson*, 491 U.S. 397 (1989).
88. After *Street*, and before *Johnson*, the Court declined opportunities (as it often does with contentious issues) to address whether flag-burning was protected expression. See *Kime v. United States*, 459 U.S. 949 (1982) (denying certiorari). In his dissent from the denial of certiorari in *Kime*, Justice Brennan offered a preview of his opinion seven years later in *Johnson*. See 459 U.S. at 950–951 (Brennan, J., dissenting from the denial of certiorari).
89. 491 U.S. at 413.
90. Ibid., 414 (quoting 394 U.S. at 593) (other citation omitted and internal quotation marks deleted).
91. Ibid., 417–418.

92. Harlan saw things somewhat differently, and maybe a bit paternalistically, when the speakers were younger. For example, in *Tinker v. Des Moines Ind. Comm. Sch. Dist.*, 393 U.S. 503 (1969), he dissented from a decision upholding the right of students to wear black armbands to school as an expression of protest against the Vietnam War. In contrast to his decisions in *Street* and *Cohen*, in which adults expressed their political opinions in public places, when students expressed their political views in school Harlan concluded that "school officials should be accorded the widest authority in maintaining discipline and good order in their institutions" and the burden should fall on the speakers to demonstrate that "a particular school measure was motivated by other than legitimate school concerns." Ibid., 526 (Harlan, J., dissenting).
93. 394 U.S. at 593.
94. 403 U.S. at 23. See also 274 U.S. at 374 ("[A] State is, ordinarily, denied the power to prohibit dissemination of social, economic and political doctrine which a vast majority of its citizens believes to be false and fraught with evil consequence") (Brandeis, J., concurring).
95. Conservatives and liberals alike have perceived this connection between the protection of a person's right to express her own views and respect for her personal dignity. See James Foster's discussion of Justice Brennan's view of free expression and human dignity in the next chapter.
96. Compare Yarbrough, *John Marshall Harlan*, 342–343.
97. 403 U.S. at 25.
98. See, for example, *Lewis v. Manufacturers Nat'l Bank of Detroit*, 364 U.S. 603 (1961). As a postscript to Justice Douglas's opinion for a unanimous Court, Justice Harlan renounced an opinion he had written while serving on the Second Circuit. See ibid., 610 ("As the judge who wrote for the Court of Appeals in *Constance v. Harvey*, 215 F.2d 571, I think it appropriate to say that I have long since come to the view that the second opinion in *Constance* was ill-considered. I welcome this opportunity to join in setting the matter right") (citation omitted).
99. For a recent example, see *Snyder v. Phelps*, 131 S. Ct. 1207 (2011).
100. US Senate, Committee on the Judiciary, *Hearings on the nomination of Ruth Bader Ginsburg to be Associate Justice of the Supreme Court of the United States*, 103rd Cong., 1st sess., July 20, 21, 22, and 23, 1993, 172.
101. US Senate, Committee on the Judiciary, *Hearings on the nomination David H. Souter to be Associate Justice of the Supreme Court of the United States*, 101st Cong., 2nd sess., September 13, 14, 17, 18, and 19, 1990, 54, 140, 143, 196, 202, 232, 276.
102. US Senate, Committee on the Judiciary, *Hearings on the nomination of Samuel A. Alito, Jr. to be Associate Justice of the Supreme Court of the United States*, 109th Cong., 2nd sess., January 9, 10, 11, 12, 13, 2006, 129 (statement of Senator Charles Schumer reiterating Alito's view).

103. See Thomas I. Emerson, *The System of Freedom of Expression* (New York: Random House, 1970), 6–9.
104. And Justice Harlan's dissenting opinions did influence the development of the law. See, for example, *Planned Parenthood v. Casey*, 505 U.S. 833, 848–849 (1992); *Teague v. Lane*, 489 U.S. 288, 303–310 (1989); *Griffith v. Kentucky*, 479 U.S. 314, 322–323 (1987); *Moore v. City of East Cleveland*, 431 U.S. 494, 500–506 (1977). See also Martha A. Field, "Justice Harlan's Legal Process," *New York Law School Law Review* 36 (1991): 162.

Chapter 5

Justice Civility: William J. Brennan Jr.'s Free Speech Jurisprudence

James C. Foster

The analyses in this book make abundantly clear that First Amendment speech and press guarantees did not spring fully grown—Athena-like—from the collective brow of the Founding generation.[1] On the contrary, despite the foremost placement and categorical language of those fourteen little words—"Congress shall make no law . . . abridging the freedom of speech, or of the press"—the Founders, along with their political allies and their political enemies, often opted to punish instead of protect oppositional speech. During the raucous, freewheeling early decades of the American Republic, the First Amendment was disregarded and irrelevant.[2] It was not until well after the Civil War, the abandonment of Reconstruction, and almost two decades into the twentieth century, that the US Supreme Court turned its attention to free speech concerns. During the First Red Scare (1917–1920), when the justices eventually addressed the range, scope, and content of First Amendment speech and press safeguards, they initially narrowed these paired provisions almost to the vanishing point.[3] In effect, constitutionally protected civic discourse was reduced to toothless discourse.

Justice William J. Brennan Jr. devoted his thirty-three years on the US Supreme Court (October 15, 1956–July 20, 1990) to reversing this trend. Brennan's free speech jurisprudence represents a marked shift in the Court's attitude toward First Amendment protections. As he observed in his inaugural foray into First Amendment jurisprudence, in *Roth v. United States*, "[t]he protection given speech and press was fashioned to assure unfettered interchange of ideas for the bringing about of political and social changes desired by the people."[4] Unfettered, but not unlimited. As Brennan also noted in his *Roth* majority opinion: "the unconditional phrasing of the First Amendment was not intended to protect every utterance."[5] Nevertheless, on an imaginary continuum, on which restricted speech sits at one end and unrestricted speech sits at the other end, Brennan's career trajectory saw him move resolutely toward embracing a spacious view of First Amendment safeguards. Differently stated, on a second continuum imagine a (libertarian) "night watchman" concept of the state at one end, and a (paternalistic) "nanny state" concept at the other. Throughout his career, particularly when it came to "obscenity" and the First Amendment, Brennan unfalteringly migrated away from the latter view of government and toward the former.

Brennan's free speech jurisprudence resulted from interactions between his personal biography and the social circumstances and controversies roiling during the tumultuous era he served on the US Supreme Court. He was both his own person and a man shaped by the historical period in which he lived. As noted in the Introduction to this book, opinions like those Brennan authored afford insight into his judicial philosophy while also providing a window—a "lens"[6]—into his life and times. Brennan rejected formulaic incantations in lieu of a contextual approach to free speech. Civil discourse—the leitmotif of how Brennan understood free speech and press—guided his nuanced interpretation of the First Amendment. This leitmotif is on display from Brennan's first term freshman opinion in *Roth*, to his valedictory First Amendment opinion in *United States v. Eichman*, written during his final term on the Court.[7]

Born April 25, 1906, into a large, gregarious Irish Catholic family, Brennan, the second of eight children, came by his progressive conviviality predictably. Then, as now, his birthplace, Newark, New Jersey, was a cauldron of class and race politics. He watched his father charm and jostle his way, initially into, then up the Newark political establishment. William Brennan Sr. began as an immigrant with scant education. He initially parlayed blue-collar jobs laying streetcar track, shoveling coal, and, eventually, working in a brewery, into labor organizing; ultimately, he was elected Newark City Commissioner in charge of overseeing Public Safety. Like father, like son, one might say. Not entirely. Brennan Jr. graduated from the University of Pennsylvania's Wharton School of Finance and Commerce, then

Harvard Law School. After graduating from Harvard Law in 1931, until World War II broke out Brennan practiced labor law with the firm then called Pitney Hardin & Skinner (Brennan became a name partner in 1945). During the war, Brennan facilitated labor-management relations in essential war industries, rising to the rank of Colonel.

After his military service, Brennan's reform political activism, coupled with his expressed desire to leave the intrusive demands of private practice, led Republican New Jersey Governor Alfred E. Driscoll to appoint Brennan to the New Jersey Superior Court as a trial judge in 1949. Despite Brennan's Democratic Party affiliation, in 1951 Governor Driscoll elevated the widely admired and respected Brennan to the Supreme Court of New Jersey. Brennan was filling this seat when, amidst the 1956 presidential election, Dwight D. Eisenhower was looking for a US Supreme Court nominee to replace Sherman Minton, who had retired on October 15 due to poor health. Brennan had caught the attention of Herbert Brownell, President Eisenhower's Attorney General and trusted advisor, when Brownell heard Brennan speak at a May 1956 conference addressing court congestion and delay. Appointing Brennan appealed to Eisenhower for several tactical reasons. First, Brennan was a Democrat, while the President had previously appointed two Republicans—Earl Warren and John Marshall Harlan II—to the Court. Second, in addition to appearing bipartisan, appointing the Catholic New Jerseyan Brennan would shore up Eisenhower's standing with important religious and regional constituencies. Third, Brennan's status as a sitting state judge would make him the first such jurist to be appointed to the US Supreme Court since Benjamin Cardozo in 1932.

Eisenhower named Brennan to the Court via a recess appointment, on October 15, 1956. He was confirmed formally by a Senate voice vote on March 19, 1957. In a delightful twist of history, presaging clashes to come, the only voice raised against Brennan's nomination was Senator Joseph McCarthy's. The Wisconsin Solon objected to Brennan's characterization of the hearings and investigations that took McCarthy's name as "witch-hunts."

Setting the stage for the discussion that follows, three landmark US Supreme Court decisions serve to frame Brennan's First Amendment jurisprudence. All three judgments were handed down before Brennan joined the Court. Two of the three are what might be called aspirational, in the sense that they provided ambitious objectives that guided Brennan's reading of the First Amendment. The third might be described as a good bad example of the sort of approach to the First Amendment speech and press clauses that Brennan rejected.

First, Footnote Four to *United States v. Carolene Products Co.* casts the Court in the role of defender of procedural democracy.[8] As Justice Harlan Fiske Stone put it, "legislation which restricts those political processes which can ordinarily be expected to bring about repeal of undesirable legislation is to be subjected to more exacting judicial scrutiny."[9] Speaking, writing, and publishing are essential democratic practices. Limit these participatory modes and one hamstrings the civil discourse without which democracy cannot exist. Footnote Four thus articulates one core foundational aspect of Brennan's view of First Amendment jurisprudence. Second, *Brown v. Board of Education* stands for the proposition that contemporary American society must be an inclusive society. As Chief Justice Earl Warren put it, "does segregation of children in public schools solely on the basis of race, even though the physical facilities and other 'tangible' factors may be equal, deprive the children of the minority group of equal educational opportunities? We believe that it does."[10] True to the *Brown* Court's encompassing vision, Brennan, Eisenhower's Catholic justice,[11] embraced a catholic understanding of the First Amendment. That is, Brennan professed a universalist view of speakers, writers, and publishers, thus affirming openness—openness that is the very essence of a just society. In this regard, Brennan's First Amendment jurisprudence was an all-comers approach.

Third, Brennan was deeply suspicious of the "low value speech"[12] framework that the Court created in *Chaplinsky v. State of New Hampshire.* That framework categorically rules out whole sorts of expression as beyond the pale of constitutional protection: "There are certain well defined and narrowly limited classes of speech," the *Chaplinsky* Court held unanimously, "the prevention and punishment of which have never been thought to raise any Constitutional problem. These include the lewd and obscene, the profane, the libelous, and the insulting or 'fighting' words."[13] Precluding consideration of any speech act merely on the basis of its presumed "slight social value"[14] is anathema to Brennan's First Amendment jurisprudence. The consequence of adopting the *Chaplinsky* shortcut is that "classifying replaces thinking."[15]

While rejecting the mindless[16] *Chaplinsky* framework, Brennan's First Amendment jurisprudence sought to nurture the democratic political processes specified in Footnote Four via civil discourse and aspired to advance the inclusive social vision of *Brown* by being open to a wide variety of speakers under diverse circumstances. Throughout his career, Brennan deviated further and further from the *Chaplinsky* paradigm.[17] Over the course of his thirty-four-year tenure on the

Court, Brennan departed from categorically unprotected "fighting words," eventually sheltering even flag burning.

A Warrior on First Amendment Front Lines

Building on Justice Oliver Wendell Holmes's eventual embrace of free speech protections, discussed in Chapter 1 herein, Brennan is the primary architect of contemporary speech and press doctrine.[18] He fashioned path-breaking First Amendment protections out of the controversies that found their way to the Supreme Court during an extraordinarily tumultuous, divisive time in American history.[19] He recast free speech doctrine in *Chaplinsky*'s shadow.[20] Still, Brennan's initial First Amendment outing is notable for its un-Brennan-like substance. His "First Amendment Odyssey" got "off to a limping start"[21] with his majority opinion in *Roth v. United States*, which falls squarely within the *Chaplinsky* ambit. Recall that the *Chaplinsky* Court embraced a rigid two-tiered framework, siloing speech intrinsically worthy of First Amendment protection from another silo isolating speech inherently outside the First Amendment. The key words in the previous sentence are "intrinsically" and "inherently." The *Chaplinsky* paradigm results from the justices deeming certain classes of expression essentially ineligible for protection—by their very nature. Says whom? Said Justice Frank Murphy, author of the unanimous *Chaplinsky* opinion. The Constitution offers no shelter to "utterances [that] are no essential part of any exposition of ideas, and are of such slight social value as a step to truth that any benefit that may be derived from them is clearly outweighed by the social interest in order and morality";[22] utterances like obscenity.

The Court's treatment of speech it considers obscene might itself be characterized as "obscene" in the sense that its *Chaplinsky* approach offends principled decision making. In decisions like *Roth*, the six justices in the majority read the radically open-textured language of the First Amendment ("Congress shall make no law") in a way that arbitrarily forecloses protection based solely upon a subjective judgment of taste.[23] Samuel Roth's case illustrates how treating obscenity as low-value speech is both futile and faulty. Roth was indicted and convicted by a New York jury of violating the federal Comstock Act, an 1873 law named after its champion, Anthony Comstock, whose zealous opposition to "vice" and crusades against "smut-peddlers" made him both influential and a laughing stock.[24] Roth's crime was mailing circulars that advertised books with such lascivious titles as *Wanton by Night* and *Wild Passion*, along with a quarterly publication, *American Aphrodite*, all found obscene by a federal jury. "The dispositive question," Brennan wrote, "is whether obscenity is utterance within the area of protected speech and press." Brennan continued: "[E]xpressions found in numerous opinions indicate that this Court has always assumed that obscenity is not protected by the freedoms of speech and press. . . . [I]t is apparent that the unconditional phrasing of the First Amendment was not intended to protect every utterance."[25] Not every "utterance"—there is that word, again. In the context of the *Chaplinsky*-flavored *Roth*, "utterance" becomes a pejorative; in other words, an obscene "utterance" is a categorically unprotected "utterance" that "appeals to prurient interest."[26] "Brennan's clerks were not sure what he meant when he suggested using the term 'prurient interest.' Brennan told his clerks to check the dictionary. When they reported back finding the definition [Latin, present participle of *prūrīre*] 'to itch,' Brennan smiled mischievously and said, 'That's precisely right. If you had an itch you had to scratch it and that was prurient interest.'"[27] One might conclude that, under Brennan's *Roth* reading, itch-provoking speech is unprotected by the First Amendment.

After sixteen years of attempting to square a circle by creating a defensible constitutional standard for obscene speech, Brennan abandoned the quixotic quest. It was a less deferential, perhaps less condemnatory Brennan who dissented in 1973 in *Paris Adult Theatre I v. Slaton*.[28] Brennan changed his mind amidst an era when Americans were torn by deeply hypocritical attitudes toward sexuality and sexual expression; devouring "pious pornography"[29] and condemning hardcore imagery—while awash in both. It was during this time period that Americans became profoundly divided over issues raised by the Second Wave of Feminism and the Gay Rights Movement. Sex had become conflicted, and hotly contested.[30] Brennan concluded that it was time for a "significant departure"[31] from the "approach initiated 16 years ago in *Roth v. United States*."[32] Dissenting from a 5-4 decision upholding the Georgia conviction of the owners and managers of the Paris Adult Theatre for showing "Magic Mirror" and "It All Comes Out in the End," Brennan wrote:

> I am reluctantly forced to the conclusion that none of the available formulas . . . can reduce the vagueness to a tolerable level while at the same time striking an acceptable balance between the protections of the First and Fourteenth Amendments, on the one hand, and, on the other, the asserted state interest in regulating the dissemination of certain sexually oriented materials. Any effort to draw a constitutionally acceptable boundary on state power must resort to such indefinite concepts as "prurient interest," "patent offensiveness," "serious literary value," and the like. . . .

> [T]he concept of "obscenity" cannot be defined with sufficient specificity and clarity to provide fair notice to persons who create and distribute sexually oriented materials, to prevent substantial erosion of protected speech as a byproduct of the attempt to suppress unprotected speech, and to avoid very costly institutional harms. Given these inevitable side effects of state efforts to suppress what is assumed to be *unprotected* speech, we must scrutinize with care the state interest that is asserted to justify the suppression. For, in the absence of some very substantial interest in suppressing such speech, we can hardly condone the ill effects that seem to flow inevitably from the effort. . . .
>
> I would hold . . . that, at least in the absence of distribution to juveniles or obtrusive exposure to unconsenting adults, the First and Fourteenth Amendments prohibit the State and Federal Governments from attempting wholly to suppress sexually oriented materials on the basis of their allegedly "obscene" contents.[33]

Brennan's *Paris Adult Theatre I* dissent exhibits key aspects of his free speech jurisprudence. First, he was not hidebound. After wandering for sixteen years in a doctrinal desert that he himself had created in *Roth*, Brennan abandoned the entire two-tiered *Chaplinsky* approach, rejecting the presumption that so-called obscene speech has "slight social value." Second, as a corollary to the first, Brennan embraced a generous understanding of the value of diverse sorts of speech. Standing the *Chaplinsky* assumption on its head, Brennan presumed that broad modes, manners, and forms of expression have value for purposes of the First Amendment. Third, when sexually explicit expression was involved, Brennan was skeptical of alleged state interests in proscribing it. Regarding sexual imagery, and despised speech generally, he was a First Amendment Doubting Thomas, requiring that government actors seeking to restrict, ban, criminalize, or otherwise exclude "deviant" materials from protection carry the burden of showing a narrowly tailored, compelling state interest.[34] Fourth, Brennan's aversion to formulaic doctrine is on display. In *Miller v. California*, the companion case to *Paris Adult Theatre I*, Chief Justice Warren Burger, working squarely within the *Roth* framework, sought to reduce "obscenity" to yet another repackaged test.[35] From Brennan's point of view, any attempt to create and to apply constitutional guidelines composed of buzzwords such as "contemporary community standards," "patently offensive," and the old standby, "prurient interest," is fraught with First Amendment jeopardy.

Finally, and perhaps most fundamentally, Brennan sought to stimulate, not stymie, the free flow of all sorts of expression. Although he was no First Amendment "absolutist," like the younger Hugo Black or the iconoclastic William O. Douglas, Brennan's basic impulse was to understand the First Amendment as intended to facilitate dissemination of ideas. Thus understood, the First Amendment existed to further human development. "Bluntly stated," writes political scientist David E. Marion, "expression for Brennan deserves special protection against being 'cabin'd, cribb'd, and confin'd,' to paraphrase William Shakespeare's Macbeth, for the reason that it serves the purpose of control over one's destiny."[36] For Brennan, aspiring toward that end was synonymous with civility.

Ultimately, more detailed attention will be devoted to the organic relation Brennan perceived and nurtured between free speech, civility, and human dignity.[37] For now, the focus remains primarily on some of Brennan's landmark opinions that furthered civility. The Second Red Scare (1945–1954) and the Civil Rights Movement (1954–1965) provided the contexts and the raw materials for Brennan's journey from *Chaplinsky*'s shadows into the sunlight of his path-breaking free speech jurisprudence.

His passage began the year after his "highly formalistic, originalist, and wooden"[38] *Roth* opinion. "Brennan loved to boast that the only senator who voted against his confirmation was Joseph McCarthy himself. . . . Ironically, in his own perverse way, Joseph McCarthy may have been the only member of the Senate who saw clearly into the heart and mind of William Brennan, for once Brennan joined the Court, he was an implacable foe of the witch hunts."[39] Justice Brennan's opposition to loyalty oaths, a central feature of McCarthyism, is on display in *Speiser v. Randall*, which, notably, pertained to a California law requiring speech rather than proscribing it.[40] Lawrence Speiser was an honorably discharged World War II veteran. Speiser also was a prominent American Civil Liberties Union attorney.[41] He applied for a veteran's property tax exemption provided by California law. Speiser struck the mandatory oath language from his 1954–1955 application for the exemption, arguing that the oath violated the US Constitution. Consequently, his application was denied and Speiser sued. "Before Brennan's confirmation, the Court had consistently upheld almost every effort of the government to prosecute, expose, harass, humiliate, blacklist, and persecute members of the Communist Party and their 'fellow travelers.'"[42] The year 1957 was a turning point, and the newly appointed Brennan's voice was pivotal.[43]

The very first line of his constitutional analysis in *Speiser* is: "It cannot be gainsaid that a discriminatory denial of a tax exemption for engaging in speech is a limitation on free speech."[44] The fatal flaw of the California loyalty oath was twofold. First, Brennan rejected the State's distinction between rights and privileges, a distinction that made the veteran's property tax exemption contingent upon swearing loyalty. California argued that conditions attached to a "'privilege' or 'bounty'"[45] cannot be deemed infringements. Brennan saw this argument as exactly wrong, and replied: "To deny an exemption to claimants who engage in certain forms of speech is, in effect, to penalize them for such speech. Its deterrent effect is the same as if the State were to fine them for this speech."[46] Second, the process by which California administered its loyalty oath was constitutionally flawed. Brennan comes to this conclusion, in a manner conjuring *Carolene Products*, by scrutinizing strictly California's denial of tax exemptions. "When we deal with the complex of strands in the web of freedoms which make up free speech," he wrote, "the operation and effect of the method by which speech is sought to be restrained must be subjected to close analysis and critical judgment in the light of the particular circumstances to which it is applied."[47] In this case, his "close analysis and critical judgment" led Brennan to conclude, first, that the California tax exemption procedure unconstitutionally placed the burden of proof on the claimant to show that (s)he had not engaged in the forbidden speech, thereby requiring Speiser and others similarly situated to prove a negative. Second, by assigning this onerous burden to the claimant, the California procedure chills speech because, "[i]n practical operation . . . this procedural device . . . can only result in a deterrence of speech which the Constitution makes free."[48]

Brennan's *Speiser* opinion breaks with previous First Amendment doctrine and pioneers a more speech protective jurisprudence in striking ways. Initially, he was willing to scrutinize strictly a loyalty oath requirement implicated in the ongoing mid-twentieth-century national obsession with internal security. Consequently, his inquiry led him to reject the right/privilege distinction, on which California had relied to justify its denial, as an impediment to free speech. Finally, Brennan read the California tax exemption procedure as imposing an impossible, speech-chilling, burden on those claiming the benefit. "[T]his idea came to be known as a doctrine of unconstitutional conditions."[49]

Five years after *Speiser*, Brennan again exercised his judicial imagination to complement protecting speakers from the excesses of the campaign against internal subversion with protecting activists from Jim Crow oppression. "Law—combined with violence and economic coercion—had long served as the South's bulwark for maintaining the institution of segregation."[50] *National Association for the Advancement of Colored People v. Button*[51] arose out of Virginia's fiendishly ingenious use of law to stigmatize, to isolate, and to destroy the NAACP, which, in the face of massive southern resistance, was employing litigation to enforce the mandate of *Brown v. Board of Education* to eliminate dual (segregated) schools "with all deliberate speed."[52] In a series of facially neutral pieces of legislation, Virginia effectively targeted not only the NAACP but also NAACP lawyers. Specifically, Virginia adopted statutes prohibiting lawyers from engaging in three practices[53] that may be conveniently summarized as soliciting business. These laws also required organizations employing lawyers who solicited business—read: pursued civil rights litigation—to produce its financial reports and membership lists.

Early in his opinion for the six justices in the *Button* majority, Brennan articulates the Court's conclusion: "We hold that the activities of the NAACP, its affiliates and legal staff shown on this record are modes of expression and association protected by the First and Fourteenth Amendments which Virginia may not prohibit, under its power to regulate the legal profession, as improper solicitation of legal business."[54] As a practical matter, the Court's ruling was profoundly consequential. Had the NAACP lost it likely would have been out of the litigating business, its life-blood.

That said, *NAACP v. Button* is every bit as important for the content of Brennan's analysis. "Our concern," he wrote, "is with the impact of enforcement of [the Virginia law] upon First Amendment freedoms."[55] Brennan's opinion is virtually a catalog of First Amendment concepts that he would deploy throughout his career to advance freedom of speech:

- *vagueness and overbreadth*—"[T]he objectionable quality of vagueness and overbreadth . . . depend[s] upon . . . the danger of tolerating, in the area of First Amendment freedoms, the existence of a penal statute susceptible of sweeping and improper application."[56]
- *breathing space and narrow specificity*—"Because First Amendment freedoms need breathing space to survive, government may regulate in the area only with narrow specificity."[57]
- *chilling effect*—"These freedoms are delicate and vulnerable, as well as supremely precious in our society. The threat of sanctions may deter their exercise almost as potently as the actual application of sanctions."[58]

NAACP v. Button thus illustrates how Brennan's free speech jurisprudence is at once socially momentous and doctrinally innovative. In one fell swoop, he neutralized one of the most potent tools in the arsenal of states resisting the changes ratified in *Brown* while breaking new ground by expanding the range of tools available to defenders of free speech. But Brennan was just getting warmed up. The year after *Button*, he authored the majority opinion in a watershed civil rights/ First Amendment case.

Arguably, *New York Times v. Sullivan* is the culmination of the Brennan First Amendment odyssey.[59] Brennan's opinion certainly is a defining landmark during his journey. It stands as a pillar of free speech jurisprudence. For that reason, and at the same time, *Sullivan* played a key role in "Disarming the South."[60] The echoes of *Brown* and *Carolene Products* reverberate throughout the controversy at the heart of *Sullivan*. The litigation arose amidst sit-ins by Alabama State College students to protest Jim Crow–segregated public lunchrooms. The sit-in participants were inspired by other students taking direct action throughout the South, seeking to enforce and extend the *Brown* mandate and to enfranchise blacks discriminated against by laws "prejudice[d] against discrete and insular minorities." The lawsuit was brought by L. B. Sullivan, Commissioner of Public Affairs for Montgomery, Alabama. Sullivan sued four black Alabama clergy[61] and the *New York Times* Company for libeling him in a full-page fund-raising advertisement titled "Heed Their Rising Voices," published in the newspaper on March 29, 1960. The ad was endorsed by sixty-four notables and signed at the bottom by the Committee to Defend Martin Luther King and the Struggle for Freedom in the South.

Commissioner Sullivan had the facts and the law on his side. The advertisement contained several inaccurate statements pertaining to events surrounding the Montgomery sit-ins, to arrests of Dr. King, and to assaults on Dr. King and his family. "Although [none] of these statements [mentioned Sullivan] by name . . . he argued, the [ad] would be read as accusing the Montgomery police, and hence him, of answering Dr. King's protests . . . [with a] 'wave of terror.'"[62] Sullivan demanded a retraction. The *Times* did not publish one, and Sullivan sued, claiming the ad had defamed him. The trial judge instructed the jury that, under Alabama law, the statements in the advertisement were "'libelous *per se*,' [intrinsically libelous] and . . . because the statements were libelous *per se*, 'the law . . . implies legal injury from the bare fact of publication itself,' 'falsity and malice are presumed.'"[63] The jury awarded Sullivan $500,000 (roughly $3,760,400.00 in current dollars). Underscoring the high stakes at risk in this litigation, and the politically charged environment within which it played out, immediately following Sullivan's damages award the Alabama Governor, two other Montgomery Commissioners and Montgomery's Mayor all filed suit. The potential monetary damages were astronomical.

Writing for a unanimous Court, Brennan demolished both the Alabama trial judge's application of the long-standing libel *per se* rule to Sullivan's suit and the Supreme Court of Alabama's upholding of the trial court's instructions.[64] In the process of doing so, Brennan reshaped libel law, he reinvented free speech doctrine, and he reinforced the Civil Rights Movement.

First, reshaping libel law. Justice Brennan wrote:

> Under Alabama law, . . . once "libel *per se*" has been established, the defendant has no defense as to stated facts unless he can persuade the jury that they were true in all their particulars. . . . Unless he can discharge the burden of proving truth, general damages are presumed, and may be awarded without proof of pecuniary injury. . . . The question before us is whether this rule of liability, as applied to an action brought by a public official against critics of his official conduct, abridges the freedom of speech and of the press that is guaranteed by the First and Fourteenth Amendments. . . .
>
> In deciding the question now, we are compelled by neither precedent nor policy to give any more weight to the epithet "libel" than we have to other "mere labels" of state law. [quoting *NAACP v. Button*]. . . . [E]rroneous statement is inevitable in free debate, and . . . it must be protected if the freedoms of expression are to have the "breathing space" that they "need . . . to survive," [quoting *NAACP v. Button*]. . . . What a State may not constitutionally bring about by means of a criminal statute is likewise beyond the reach of its civil law of libel. The fear of damage awards under a rule such as that invoked by the Alabama courts here may be markedly more inhibiting [chilling] than the fear of prosecution under a criminal statute. . . . The [Alabama] rule thus dampens the vigor and limits the variety of public debate. . . .
>
> The constitutional guarantees require, we think, a federal rule that prohibits a public official from recovering damages for a defamatory falsehood relating to his official conduct unless he proves that the statement was made with "actual malice"—that is, with knowledge that it was false or with reckless disregard of whether it was false or not.[65]

Second, reinventing free speech doctrine. Justice Brennan wrote:

> The general proposition that freedom of expression upon public questions is secured by the First Amendment has long been settled by our decisions. . . . The First Amendment, said Judge Learned Hand, "presupposes that right conclusions are more likely to be gathered out of a multitude of tongues than through any kind of authoritative selection. To many, this is, and always will be, folly, but we have staked upon it our all." *United States v. Associated Press*, 52 F.Supp. 362, 372 (D.C.S.D.N.Y.1943). . . .

> Thus, we consider this case against the background of a profound national commitment to the principle that debate on public issues should be uninhibited, robust, and wide-open, and that it may well include vehement, caustic, and sometimes unpleasantly sharp attacks on government and public officials. The present advertisement, as an expression of grievance and protest on one of the major public issues of our time, would seem clearly to qualify for the constitutional protection.[66]

Third, reinforcing the Civil Rights Movement. Covering the decision, *New York Times* reporter Anthony Lewis wrote:

> The case could have immediate impact on press coverage of race relations in the South. The Times argued that the purpose and effect of these [libel] suits was to discourage coverage of the racial situation. . . . Justice Brennan said, "[T]he pall of fear and timidity imposed [by such libel suits] upon those who would give voice to public criticism is an atmosphere in which the First Amendment Freedoms cannot survive."[67]

With his opinion in *Sullivan*, Brennan defanged libel law as a weapon in ways that kept the nation's attention riveted to ongoing struggles for racial justice. Thanks to Brennan's seminal opinion, the Civil Rights Movement continued to play out on the front pages of newspapers and in the living rooms of Americans.

Given the momentousness of *Sullivan*,[68] it is perhaps curious that Brennan's most controversial free speech opinion overshadows his earlier watershed work. In *Texas v. Johnson*, a five-vote majority overturned Gregory Lee "Joey" Johnson's conviction for "desecrating a venerated object" when Johnson burned an American flag during a protest at the 1984 Republican Party convention in Dallas, Texas.[69] Brennan's opinion for the *Johnson* majority represented a climactic emotional chapter in a two-decade long shouting match between members of Congress and state legislators, and the Supreme Court. The combatants disputed whether "patriotism" required protecting the Flag, or protecting protesters who "misuse" it. Even Brennan's dissenting colleagues were outraged. Chief Justice William Rehnquist fulminated: "The American flag . . . does not represent the views of any particular political party, and it does not represent any particular political philosophy. The flag is not simply another 'idea' or 'point of view' competing for recognition in the marketplace of ideas. Millions and millions of Americans regard it with an almost mystical reverence."[70] Among those millions were congressional majorities that adopted the Flag Protection Act of 1989—overturned by the

US Supreme Court in *United States v. Eichman*[71]—as well as four failed efforts to amend the First Amendment to criminalize flag burning. This was "[t]he first time in the nation's history that altering the Bill of Rights was seriously contemplated."[72]

While separated by a quarter century, *Sullivan* and *Johnson* are both informed by Brennan's democratizing impulse. Articulating the same principles as *Sullivan*, in his *Johnson* opinion protecting flag burning Brennan said:

> If there is a bedrock principle underlying the First Amendment, it is that the government may not prohibit the expression of an idea simply because society finds the idea itself offensive or disagreeable. . . . To say that the government has an interest in encouraging proper treatment of the flag . . . is not to say that it may criminally punish a person for burning a flag as a means of political protest. . . . The way to preserve the flag's special role is not to punish those who feel differently about these matters. It is to persuade them that they are wrong.[73]

These bedrock First Amendment principles exist because Brennan carved them out of constitutional materials. Free speech is at the core of American life because Brennan, shaping the stuff of the First Amendment, protected expression. Brennan was the sculptor.

Legacy of Civility

Although Brennan was a practicing Catholic, he was a born *mensch*.[74] Bill Brennan's free speech jurisprudence was of a piece with Bill Brennan as a person. Brennan lived a civil life. Civility played out in Brennan's life in three innately connected ways. As a human being, Brennan was a considerate person; as a member of a collegial judicial body, Brennan was an accommodating coalition builder; as a political thinker he "is a Framer."[75] "E. M. Forster regularly exhorted his friends and readers, if they were to be fulfilled as human beings, to 'only connect.' Justice Brennan surely connected."[76] Brennan connected congenially with almost every person in his life. He connected effectively with his Supreme Court colleagues, and he connected enduringly with civility as the wellspring of human regard.

What does it mean to say that civility is the hallmark of Brennan's interpersonal relationships, his judicial role, and his legacy? The answer to that question is both deep-seated and depends upon context.[77] Basically, Brennan embraced human dignity as the lodestone of his life and work. Just how his philosophical conception of dignity played out in practical terms was shaped by specific circumstances. Two brief vignettes illustrate the point: call them The Too-Clever-by-Half Student and The Imperfect Feminist.

The student in question is Matthew N. Fraser. He managed his buddy Jeff Kuhlman's 1983 campaign for Student Body V.P. at Bethel High School (BHS) in Washington State. Clever—and adolescent—Fraser laced his speech nominating Kuhlman during an all school assembly with sexual double-entendres. When Fraser's appeal of his three-day suspension and his removal from the graduate speaker selection list eventually arrived at the Supreme Court, seven justices, including Brennan, voted to uphold the school's discipline. What at first glance seems an anomalous vote becomes, upon further examination, a useful window into Brennan's subtle understanding of civility.

First, in a manner reminiscent of Justice Brandeis in *Whitney v. California*, Brennan wrote a concurring opinion clearly designed to confine the "breadth"[78] of Chief Justice Burger's endorsement of school administrators' discretion to sanction student speech. Second, Brennan's pragmatism is on display. He modulates the level of First Amendment protection to the situation where Fraser spoke. During a school assembly, sexual innuendo may be reasonably deemed uncivil speech. Third, Brennan strikes a "delicate accommodation"[79] between Fraser's speech rights and BHS administrators' authority. Finally, Brennan demonstrates his Janus-like wisdom, understanding "that the Constitution looks in two directions at once by granting power to government and limiting that power."[80]

All these characteristics are demonstrated in this passage from Brennan's concurrence in *Bethel School District No. 403 v. Fraser*:

> To my mind, the most that can be said about respondent's speech—and all that need be said—is that, in light of the discretion school officials have to teach high school students how to conduct civil and effective public discourse, and to prevent disruption of school educational activities, it was not unconstitutional for school officials to conclude, under the circumstances of this case, that respondent's remarks exceeded permissible limits.[81]

In other words, civil speech is protected speech—and civility is not absolute.

The flawed feminist is Brennan himself. The man who had refined the free speech realm, expanding its reach and its protections—not to mention the person who had pioneered the equal protection of women[82]—could only belatedly bring himself to hire a woman as a clerk. The justice who penned the words "[t]here can be no doubt that our Nation has had a long and unfortunate history of sex discrimination[;]" and that . . . "such discrimination was rationalized by an attitude of 'romantic paternalism' which . . . put women not on a pedestal, but in a cage,"[83] was, ironically, a patriarchal romantic. It was not until 1974—eighteen years into his tenure on the Court—that Brennan reluctantly swallowed his "generational chivalry,"[84] and hired Marsha Berzon, his first female clerk. Before then, Brennan considered the idea of a female clerk an uncivil oxymoron. "Brennan simply felt more comfortable around men. . . . He did not feel he could have the same sort of relaxed rapport with a female clerk or colleague. . . . 'It's a strange kind of sexism,' his friend Abner Mikva . . . observed. 'He had [women] on such a pedestal he couldn't have their ears sullied by four-letter words.'"[85] A strange, and a paradoxical, sexism shaped by Brennan's archaic courtly understanding of civility; an understanding steeped in his embrace of public/private separate spheres,[86] where the personal is not political. It is a measure of Brennan's humanity that, simultaneously, he could be such a quick study—"When it comes to sex discrimination [doctrine] . . . he gets it"[87]—and so completely blind.[88]

Brennan recognized that a functional society is a conversation. He understood the wisdom expressed in that observation and he grasped the essence of civility as facilitating conversation. Brennan was the Supreme Court's "judicial midwife"[89] of conversing. Conversing is the core of civility and, in this regard, Brennan was a modern-day Alexis de Tocqueville.[90] He excelled in the "High Politics" of the First Amendment.[91] It is ironic that, given his breach with Felix Frankfurter, his former Harvard Law professor and fellow justice, Brennan came to personify Frankfurter's conception of the judicial role, becoming the First Amendment "legal philosopher" par excellence.[92] Brennan's legacy is the recognition and recovery of what the late Hannah Arendt referred to as the "lost treasure of The Revolution."[93]

Arendt describes this "lost treasure" as a puzzle, a puzzle constituted by the fateful tension between beginnings and foundations:

> [I]f foundation was the aim and the end of revolution, then the revolutionary spirit was not merely the spirit of beginning something new but of starting something permanent and enduring; a lasting institution, embodying this spirit and encouraging it to new achievements, would be self-defeating. From which it unfortunately seems to follow that nothing threatens the very achievements of revolution more dangerously and more acutely than the spirit which has brought them about.[94]

For Arendt, logically this puzzle "seemed unsolvable."[95] While it would be absurd to claim that Brennan solved the insolvable, it is beyond argument that he pragmatically went about untangling the riddle. Key to Brennan's accomplishment is his understanding that, by expressing freely, people are freed to reconstitute their political life.[96] Speaking is acting and acting, as Arendt so singularly knew, is the defining political characteristic of being human. Brennan's free speech jurisprudence also stands within the tradition of John Locke's view of the role of language in human understanding. With Locke, Brennan fathomed that the civil use of language is generative.[97] He knew that "the right of every individual to form and to express political judgments"[98] is fundamentally constitutive. Brennan devoted his career on the US Supreme Court to keeping Americans' diverse and, at times, unsettling conversations going.[99]

NOTES

1. The author thanks Editors Helen Knowles and Steven Lichtman for their conscientious, helpful revisions. He thanks his partner, Mindy Soules, for her intelligent, encouraging suggestions. Thank you, too, Matt Shinderman, for reporting that "read[ing] this work . . . exercise[d] my brain."
2. Leonard W. Levy, *Legacy of Suppression: Freedom of Speech and Press in Early American History* (Cambridge, MA: Harvard University Press, 1960).
3. See *Schenck v. United States*, 249 U.S. 47 (1919); *Abrams v. United States*, 250 U.S. 616 (1919); and *Gitlow v. New York*, 268 U.S. 252 (1925). Although the US Supreme Court upheld Benjamin Gitlow's conviction of violating the 1902 New York Criminal Anarchy Law, the *Gitlow* decision usually is cited as the opinion that applied the federal speech and press guarantees to the States. See Geoffrey R. Stone, *Perilous Times: Free Speech in Wartime from The Sedition Act of 1798 to The War on Terrorism* (New York: W. W. Norton, 2004). Also see the Introduction, Chapter 1 and Chapter 9 herein, 219 of *Judging Free Speech*.
4. *Roth v. United States*, 354 U.S. 476, 484 (1957).
5. Ibid., 483.
6. *Judging Free Speech*, "Introduction," 6.
7. *United States v. Eichman*, 496 U.S. 310 (1990).
8. *United States v. Carolene Products Co.*, 304 U.S. 144, 152–153, footnote no. 4 (1938). See John Hart Ely, *Democracy and Distrust: A Theory of Judicial Review* (Cambridge, MA: Harvard University Press, 1980).
9. 304 U.S. at 152–153, footnote no. 4.
10. *Brown v. Board of Education*, 347 U.S. 483, 493 (1954).
11. Seth Stern and Stephen Wermiel, *Justice Brennan: Liberal Champion* (Lawrence, KS: University Press of Kansas, 2010), Chapter 3.

12. Geoffrey R. Stone, "Free Speech in the Twenty-First Century: Ten Lessons Learned from the Twentieth Century," *Pepperdine Law Review* 36 (2009): 283–286.
13. *Chaplinsky v. New Hampshire*, 315 U.S. 568, 571–572 (1942).
14. Ibid., 572.
15. John F. Wirenius, "The Road Not Taken: The Curse of *Chaplinsky*," *Capital University Law Review* 24 (1995): 333. Compare Burton Caine, "The Trouble with 'Fighting Words': *Chaplinsky v. New Hampshire* Is a Threat to First Amendment Values and Should Be Overruled," *Marquette Law Review* 88 (2004): 441–562.
16. Compare Hannah Arendt, "Thinking and Moral Considerations: A Lecture," *Social Research* 38 (Autumn 1971): 417–446.
17. No doubt, Justice Brennan also was inspired by the free speech philosophy underlying Justice Louis Brandeis's eloquent concurring opinion in *Whitney v. California*. Brennan can be described as a latter-day Brandeis, albeit not as lyrical. In *Whitney* Brandeis wrote: "Those who won our independence believed that the final end of the State was to make men free to develop their faculties, and that, in its government, the deliberative forces should prevail over the arbitrary. . . . They recognized the risks to which all human institutions are subject. But they knew that order cannot be secured merely through fear of punishment for its infraction; that it is hazardous to discourage thought, hope and imagination; that fear breeds repression; that repression breeds hate; that hate menaces stable government; that the path of safety lies in the opportunity to discuss freely supposed grievances and proposed remedies, and that the fitting remedy for evil counsels is good ones," 274 U.S. 375, 375 (1927) (Brandeis, J. concurring); see Vincent Blasi, "The First Amendment and the Ideal of Civic Courage: The Brandeis Opinion in *Whitney v. California*," *William & Mary Law Review* 29 (1988): 653–697; and Morton J. Horwitz, "In Memoriam: William J. Brennan, Jr.," *Harvard Law Review* 111 (1997): 23–28. Compare the unsigned *per curiam* opinion Justice Brennan wrote for the Court in *Brandenburg v. Ohio*, 395 U.S. 444 (1969).
18. Geoffrey R. Stone, "Justice Brennan and the Freedom of Speech: A First Amendment Odyssey," *University of Pennsylvania Law Review* 139 (1991): 1333–1355. Discussion in this section draws on Stone's article, and on David E. Marion, *The Jurisprudence of Justice William Brennan, Jr.: The Law and Politics of "Libertarian Dignity"* (Lanham, MD: Rowman & Littlefield, 1997), esp. Chapter 3. For detailed analysis of Justice Brennan's voting record, 1956–1986, see Edward V. Heck, "Justice Brennan and the Heyday of Warren Court Liberalism," *Santa Clara Law Review* 20 (1980): 841–887; and Edward V. Heck, "Justice Brennan and Freedom of Expression Doctrine in the Burger Court," *San Diego Law Review* 20 (1987): 1153–1183.
19. See, for instance, Rick Perlstein, *Nixonland: The Rise of a President and the Fracturing of America* (New York: Scribner, 2009).

20. "When Justice Brennan joined the Court in 1956, the Court had never found that a federal law violated free speech." Laurence H. Tribe, "In Memoriam: William J. Brennan, Jr.," *Harvard Law Review* 111 (1997): 42.
21. Stone, "A First Amendment Odyssey," 1336.
22. 315 U.S. at 572.
23. The Court's qualifying—hence narrowing—of the unconditional black-letter First Amendment language did not commence with either *Chaplinsky* or *Roth*. See, for instance, Justice Oliver Wendell Holmes Jr.'s statement in *Patterson v. Colorado*: "the main purpose of such constitutional provisions is 'to prevent all such previous restraints upon publications as had been practiced by other governments,' and they do not prevent the subsequent punishment of such as may be deemed contrary to the public welfare," 205 U.S. 454, 462 (1907), citing *Commonwealth v. Blanding*, 3 Pick. 304, 313–314 (1825); *Respublica v. Oswald*, 1 Dall. 319, 1 U.S. 325 (1788). Also see Justice Holmes's more well-known *Schenck* statement: "The question in every case is whether the words used are used in such circumstances and are of such a nature as to create a clear and present danger that they will bring about the substantive evils that Congress has a right to prevent. It is a question of proximity and degree." 249 U.S. at 52. Compare *Judging Free Speech*, Chapter 1 herein, 30–36.
24. 18 U.S.C. § 1461. A December 12, 1895 *New York Times* editorial reported Comstock's influence while parodying his prudish views as "Comstockery." See Anna Bates, *Weeder in the Garden of the Lord: Anthony Comstock's Life and Career* (Lanham, MD: University Press of America, 1995); and Leigh Ann Wheeler, *Against Obscenity: Reform and the Politics of Womanhood in America, 1873–1935* (Baltimore, MD: Johns Hopkins University Press, 2004).
25. 354 U.S. at 481, 483. Compare *Beauharnais v. Illinois*, 343 U.S. 250 (1952).
26. 354 U.S. at 489.
27. Stern and Wermiel, *Justice Brennan*, 124. The *reductio ad absurdum* example of subjectivity in the realm of "obscenity," of course, is Justice Potter Stewart's observation: "[T]he [*Roth*] Court . . . was faced with the task of trying to define what may be indefinable. . . . I shall not today attempt further to define the kinds of material I understand to be embraced within [the] shorthand description [hard core pornography], and perhaps I could never succeed in intelligibly doing so. But I know it when I see it." *Jacobellis v. Ohio*, 378 U.S. 184, 197 (1964) (Stewart, J., concurring). For a humorous, and revealing, description of "movie days" when some of the justices would convene at the Court to view movies that were exhibits in obscenity cases, see Bob Woodward and Scott Armstrong, *The Brethren: Inside the Supreme Court* (New York: Simon & Schuster, 1979), 198–200.
28. *Paris Adult Theatre I v. Slaton*, 413 U.S. 49 (1973).

29. Nancy M. Tischler, "Pious Pornography," in Christianity Today, Inc., ed., *The Christian Ministry in a World of Crisis* (Washington, DC: Christianity Today, 1972).
30. In America, sex has never been morally uncontroversial. See James A. Morone, *Hellfire Nation: The Politics of Sin in American History* (New Haven, CT: Yale University Press, 2004).
31. 413 U.S. at 75 (Brennan, J., joined by Stewart and Marshall, JJ., dissenting).
32. Ibid., 73.
33. Ibid., 84, 103, 113. Compare *Miller v. California*, 413 U.S. 15 (1973) (the companion case to *Paris Adult Theatre I*). Also see Stern and Wermiel, *Justice Brennan*, 365–368.
34. Compare Brennan's majority opinion in *Ginsberg v. New York*, 390 U.S 629 (1968) with his concurring opinion in *New York v. Ferber*, 458 U.S. 747 (1982) (Brennan, J., joined by Marshall, J., concurring in the judgment).
35. "The basic guidelines for the trier of fact must be: (a) whether 'the average person, applying contemporary community standards' would find that the work, taken as a whole, appeals to the prurient interest, . . . (b) whether the work depicts or describes, in a patently offensive way, sexual conduct specifically defined by the applicable state law; and (c) whether the work, taken as a whole, lacks serious literary, artistic, political, or scientific value." 413 U.S. at 24.
36. Marion, *The Jurisprudence of Justice William J. Brennan, Jr.*, 60.
37. Compare *Judging Free Speech*, Chapter 4 herein, 106–107, 112.
38. Stone, "A First Amendment Odyssey," 1336.
39. Geoffrey R. Stone, "Free Speech in the Age of McCarthy: A Cautionary Tale," *California Law Review* 93 (2005): 1405–1406.
40. *Speiser v. Randall*, 357 U.S. 513, 515 (1958). California law required all persons applying for the veterans property tax exemption to swear: "I do not advocate the overthrow of the Government of the United States or of the State of California by force or violence or other unlawful means, nor advocate the support of a foreign Government against the United States in event of hostilities."
41. "Obituary, Lawrence Speiser, 68, a Civil Liberties Lawyer," *The New York Times*, September 1, 1991.
42. Stone, "Free Speech in the Age of McCarthy," 1406. See, for instance, *American Communications Association v. Douds*, 339 U.S. 382 (1950); *Dennis v. United States*, 341 U.S. 494 (1951); *Adler v. Board of Education*, 342 U.S. 485 (1952); and *Barsky v. Board of Regents*, 347 U.S. 442 (1954).
43. Compare the decisions specified in note 42 with *Yates v. United States*, 354 U.S. 298 (1957); *Watkins v. United States*, 354 U.S. 178 (1957); *Sweezy v. New Hampshire*, 354 U.S. 234 (1957); *Scales v. United States*, 367 U.S. 203 (1961); *Elfbrandt v. Russell*, 384 U.S. 11 (1966); and *Keyishian v. Board of Regents*, 385 U.S. 589 (1967).

44. 357 U.S. at 518.
45. Ibid.
46. Ibid.
47. Ibid., 520.
48. Ibid., 526.
49. Stern and Wermiel, *Justice Brennan*, 137.
50. Ibid., 213.
51. *National Association for the Advancement of Colored People v. Button*, 371 U.S. 415 (1963).
52. *Brown v. Board of Education (II)*, 349 U.S. 294, 301 (1955).
53. Barratry, champerty, and maintenance. See Del Dickson, *The Supreme Court in Conference, 1940–1985: The Private Discussions Behind Nearly 300 Supreme Court Decisions* (New York: Oxford University Press, 2001).
54. 371 U.S. at 428–429.
55. Ibid., 431. See Renee Newman Knake, "Why the Law Needs Music: Revisiting *NAACP v. Button* through the Songs of Bob Dylan," *Fordham Urban Law Journal* 38 (2011): 1303–1321.
56. 371 U.S. at 432–433.
57. Ibid., 433.
58. Ibid., 432–433. Compare Heck, "Justice Brennan and Freedom of Expression Doctrine in the Burger Court," 1168.
59. *New York Times v. Sullivan*, 376 U.S. 254 (1964).
60. Stern and Wermiel, *Justice Brennan*, Chapter 9. "[P]erhaps no justice deserves more credit for advancing the cause of the civil rights movement during the first half of the 1960s than Brennan. His opinions helped protect the NAACP and sit-in demonstrators, curbed the use of libel suits as a method of intimidating the press, and provided protestors greater access to appeals in the federal courts. . . . [T]aken together, Brennan's opinions sent a clear signal to lower courts that the law could no longer be employed as a bludgeon against the civil rights movement." Ibid., 211.
61. Ralph David Abernathy, S. S. Seay Sr., Fred L. Shuttlesworth, and J. E. Lowery. See Garrett Epps, "The Civil Rights Heroes the Court Ignored in *New York Times v. Sullivan*," *The New York Times*, March 20, 2014.
62. 376 U.S. at 258.
63. Ibid., 262.
64. The Alabama Supreme Court held that "'where the words published tend to injure a person libeled by them in his reputation, profession, trade or business, or charge him with an indictable offense, or tend to bring the individual into public contempt,' they are 'libelous *per se*'; that 'the matter complained of is, under the above doctrine, libelous *per se*, if it was published of and concerning the plaintiff,' and that it was actionable without 'proof of pecuniary injury . . . such injury being implied.'" Quoted in 376 U.S. at 263.
65. Ibid., 267, 268, 269, 272, 277, 279–280.
66. Ibid., 269, 270, 270–271.

67. Anthony Lewis, "High Court Curbs Public Officials in Libel Actions," *The New York Times*, March 10, 1964, 1. See Anthony Lewis, *Make No Law: The Sullivan Case and the First Amendment* (New York: Random House, 1991). Compare *Judging Free Speech*, Chapter 1 herein, 38–39.
68. Harry Kalven wrote that Justice Brennan's *Sullivan* opinion "may prove to be the best and most important [the Court] has ever produced in the realm of freedom of speech." Harry Kalven Jr., "*The New York Times* Case: A Note on the Central Meaning of the First Amendment," *Supreme Court Review* 1964 (1964): 193–194.
69. *Texas v. Johnson*, 491 U.S. 397 (1989).
70. 491 U.S. at 429 (Rehnquist, CJ., joined by White and O'Connor, JJ., dissenting).
71. 496 U.S. 310 (1990).
72. Stern and Wermiel, *Justice Brennan*, 527. On other reactions to Brennan's opinion in *Johnson*, see ibid., 526–527; Robert Justin Goldstein, *"Saving Old Glory": The History of the American Flag Desecration Controversy* (Boulder, CO: Westview Press, 1995); and Kim Isaac Eisler, *A Justice for All: William J. Brennan, Jr., and the Decisions That Transformed America* (New York: Simon & Schuster, 1993), 273–278. Compare *Judging Free Speech*, Chapter 7 herein, 171–174.
73. 491 U.S. at 414, 418, 419. Compare *Judging Free Speech*, Chapter 4 herein, 110–112.
74. "A caring, decent person—man or woman—who can be trusted. [Mensch] refers in a much larger sense to acting in an honorable and proper way. The term is bestowed as a compliment on someone who has done the right thing without asking for thanks or credit." Joyce Eisenberg and Ellen Scolnic, *The JPS Dictionary of Jewish Words* (Philadelphia, PA: Jewish Publication Society, 2001), 100.
75. Frank I. Michelman, "Super Liberal: Romance, Community, and Tradition in William J. Brennan, Jr.'s Constitutional Thought," *Virginia Law Review* 77 (1991): 1332.
76. Norman Dorsen, "A Tribute to Justice William J. Brennan, Jr.," *Harvard Law Review* 104 (1990): 22. E. M. Forster (1879–1970) was an influential English novelist who grappled with the human perils of social divisions rooted in class, station, and status. He authored *A Room with a View*, *A Passage to India*, and *Howards End*. "Only connect" is the epigraph to *Howards End*.
77. Compare Justice Clarence Thomas's (now apparently abandoned) "First Amendment Absolutism," analyzed in Chapter 8.
78. *Bethel School District No. 403 v. Fraser*, 478 U.S. 675, 688 (1986) (Brennan, J., concurring in the judgment).
79. *Clements v. Fashing*, 457 U.S. 957, 977 (1982). But see Clay Calvert, "Mixed Messages, Muddled Meanings, Drunk Dicks, and Boobies Bracelets: Sexually Suggestive Student Speech and the Need to Overrule or Radically Refashion *Fraser*," *Denver University Law Review* 90 (2012): 131–173.

80. Heck, "Justice Brennan and Freedom of Expression Doctrine in the Burger Court," 1172. Compare James Madison (as Publius), *Federalist 51, The Federalist Papers* (New York: Mentor Books, 1961), introduction by Clinton Rossiter.
81. 478 U.S. at 687–688 (Brennan, J., concurring in the judgment). As a complement to his *Fraser* concurrence, it is instructive to compare Brennan's dissent in *Hazelwood School District v. Kuhlmeier*, 484 U.S. 260 (1988).
82. See *Frontiero v. Richardson*, 411 U.S. 677 (1973) (plurality opinion).
83. Ibid., 684.
84. Marsha Berzon quoted in Stern and Wermiel, *Justice Brennan*, 401. Compare David J. Garrow, "Justice Brennan, a Liberal Lion Who Wouldn't Hire Women," *Washington Post*, October 17, 2010; and Michael O'Donnell, "Without Artifice: On William Brennan," *The Nation*, November 17, 2010.
85. Stern and Wermiel, *Justice Brennan*, 388.
86. Jean Bethke Elshtain, *Public Man, Private Woman*, 2nd ed. (Princeton, NJ: Princeton University Press, 1993); Susan Moller Okin, *Women in Western Political Thought* (Princeton, NJ: Princeton University Press, 1979); and Susan Moller Okin, *Justice, Gender and the Family* (New York: Basic Books, 1989).
87. Nina Totenberg quoted in Stern and Wermiel, *Justice Brennan*, 386.
88. Brennan's contradictory humanity is reminiscent of Walt Whitman's:

    "Do I contradict myself?
    Very well then I contradict myself,
    (I am large, I contain multitudes.)"

    Leaves of Grass, Book III, Song of Myself, section 51, lines 1324–1326, http://whitmanarchive.org/published/LG/1891/poems/27, accessed April 23, 2014. It would be surprising if Justice Brennan's understanding of "human dignity" was not gendered—to some extent. It also would be surprising if there were no seepage between Brennan's universalist jurisprudence and his parochial personal views. What matters is that, in the end, "[h]is was an equal opportunity dignity." Stephen J. Wermiel, "Law and Human Dignity: The Judicial Soul of Justice Brennan," *William & Mary Bill of Rights Journal* 7 (1998): 224. In Brennan's own words: "[R]ecognition of full equality for women—equal protection of the laws—ensures that gender has no bearing on claims to human dignity." Brennan, Transcript of Speech Given at the Text and Teaching Symposium, Georgetown University, October 12, 1985.
89. Marion, *The Jurisprudence of Justice William J. Brennan, Jr.*, 5–11. Compare Hannah Arendt on Socrates's three similes: the gadfly, the midwife, and the sting ray from "The Life of the Mind (Volume 1)," Peter Baehr, ed., *The Portable Hannah Arendt* (New York: Penguin Classics, 2003), 402–403. Also see Arendt, "Thinking and Moral Considerations: A Lecture."

90. "[C]ivility [is] constructive engagement with others through argument, deliberation, and discourse." Susan Herbst, *Rude Democracy: Civility and Incivility in American Politics* (Philadelphia, PA: Temple University Press, 2010), 19, 12–22.
91. Marion, *The Jurisprudence of Justice William J. Brennan, Jr.*, Chapter 1. Compare Mark Tushnet, "Members of the Warren Court in Judicial Biography: Themes in Warren Court Biographies," *New York University Law Review* 79 (1995): 763–767.
92. Felix Frankfurter, "The Supreme Court in the Mirror of Justices," *University of Pennsylvania Law Review* 105 (1957): 795. While Brennan always respected Felix Frankfurter's intellect, and the Brennan and Frankfurter families remained friends, behind the scenes of the Court the two justices jousted testily. Frankfurter resented bitterly and took personally Brennan's apostasy, as the latter drifted from the former's orbit of influence. As for Brennan, he "knew better than to treat colleagues with the kind of disdain Frankfurter displayed. [H]e learned one final lesson from his professor: the danger of coming on too strong, particularly with new colleagues." Stern and Wermiel, *Justice Brennan*, 192.
93. Hannah Arendt, *On Revolution* (New York: Viking Press, 1963), Chapter 6.
94. Ibid., 235.
95. Ibid.
96. About such reconstituting, law professor Robert C. Post observes: "First amendment doctrine attempts to protect an *arena* for . . . [this] process of critical interaction. . . . It thus creates '*a cleared and safe space*' within which can occur precisely that 'uninhibited, robust, and wide-open' debate on public issues that one would expect to emerge when dominant cultural traditions are denied access to the force of law to silence the clash of divergent perspectives. Contemporary constitutional doctrine looks to this debate to constitute that 'universe of discourse' within which public opinion, and hence democratic policy, may be formed" (italics added). Robert C. Post, "The Constitutional Concept of Public Discourse: Outrageous Opinion, Democratic Deliberation, and *Hustler Magazine v. Falwell*," *Harvard Law Review* 104 (1990): 637–638. Compare Michelman, "Super Liberal"; and Geoffrey R. Stone, "What You Can't Say Will Hurt You," *The New York Times*, August 15, 2005.
97. "[B]y [the words] *civil* use, I mean such a communication of thoughts and ideas by words as may serve for the upholding common conversation and converse, about the ordinary affairs and conveniences of civil life, in the societies of men, one amongst the other." John Locke, *An Essay Concerning Human Understanding*, ed. A. Woozley (London: Fontana [first published 1689], 1973), 299–300.
98. Brennan, Transcript of Speech, October 12, 1985.
99. Compare *Judging Free Speech*, Chapter 4 herein, 112–113.

Chapter 6

Potter Stewart Meets the Press

Keith J. Bybee

Although there are nearly fifty words in the First Amendment, a few Supreme Court justices have developed distinctive approaches to free expression by boiling the Amendment down to a single phrase.[1] Justice Hugo Black, for example, thought the essential meaning of "Congress shall make no law . . . abridging the freedom of speech, or of the press" could be found in just three words: "I read 'no law . . . abridging' to mean *no law abridging*."[2]

Justice Potter Stewart, whose service on the Court (1958–1981) overlapped with Justice Black's for thirteen years, also found special significance in a small segment of the First Amendment. Taking up the same passage that attracted Black's attention ("Congress shall make no law . . . abridging the freedom of speech, or of the press"), Stewart zeroed-in on the words "or of the press."[3]

Stewart's selection is in many ways a curious one. For one thing, his preferred term does not have anything like the intuitive appeal or immediate force of Black's favored text. It is difficult to imagine Stewart successfully explaining his emphasis on the press simply by thundering, "I read 'or of the press' to mean *or of the press*!"

It is also by no means clear that Stewart identified the most significant or worthy protection in the First Amendment. Scholars have argued that the Press Clause adds little value beyond that already secured by the Amendment's freedom of speech guarantee.[4] In his own time on the high bench, Stewart did not persuade a majority of his fellow Supreme Court justices to adopt his special focus on the press. And in the years after Stewart left the Court a number of justices have written that journalists do not possess any unique constitutional privileges beyond those held by other speakers.[5]

Indeed, some justices have gone further and suggested that reporters, far from being elevated above other speakers, may actually be located somewhat beneath them.[6] Chief Justice Warren Burger resolutely opposed all broadcast news coverage of the Court and prohibited any television coverage of his otherwise public speeches. Burger was furious when CBS News broadcast selections from audiotapes of the Court's oral arguments (the fact that the tapes were ten years old did nothing to cool Burger's rage, and he demanded that the FBI investigate how CBS News obtained the recordings).[7] Chief Justice William Rehnquist, Burger's successor, maintained the barriers to media coverage instituted by his predecessor. Rehnquist also once told a gathering of Court reporters, "the difference between us and the other branches of government is that we don't need you people of the press." Justice Samuel Alito, Justice Ruth Bader Ginsburg, Justice Anthony Kennedy, and Justice Antonin Scalia have all publicly criticized journalists. Justice Clarence Thomas has called members of the media "smart-aleck commentators," "snot-nosed brats," "talking heads who shout at each other," and "snotty-nosed smirks."[8]

Stewart's valorization of press freedom not only seems to be out of step with the views of other justices but also seems to be in tension with his own reputation as a jurist more interested in moderation and narrow reasoning than in bold statements.[9] Over time and across issues, Stewart voted both for and against the liberal decisions that defined the Court under Chief Justice Earl Warren. As the Court grew more conservative under Burger, Stewart continued along a centrist path, endorsing different positions along the ideological spectrum from case to case. By all accounts, Stewart thought of himself as a careful lawyer advancing his arguments only so far as the issue at hand required. Stewart was willing to follow this method of highly specific analysis and narrow decision making whether it led to the left, to the right, or to the ground between the contending voting blocs on the high bench. Thus the twin hallmarks of Stewart's overall jurisprudence were "the skill of precision" and "the penchant for compromise and moderation."[10] On the whole, "his opinions did not embody a judicial philosophy but rather were specific responses to legal problems that came before him in concrete cases."[11] This is hardly the sort of judge that one would expect to fashion a novel reading of how the Constitution protects the press.

Finally, to the extent that Stewart is generally known for making any noteworthy claim connected to the First Amendment, his renown is entirely unrelated to his view of press freedom. In a mid-1960s case about free expression and obscenity, Stewart wrote that when it comes to identifying hardcore pornography, "I know it when I see it."[12] Stewart's comment has been very widely quoted, so much so that it has been deemed "one of the most famous phrases in the entire history of Supreme Court opinions."[13] "I know it when I see it" has attracted so much attention because it stands as an example of intuitive, gut-level judgment—a kind of judgment that is quite unusual in the context of highly detailed and carefully reasoned judicial opinions. One can criticize Stewart for voicing a gut feeling or one can celebrate the space that he created for nonrational judgment in a hyper-rational forum.[14] Whether Stewart emerges from such a debate as a villain or a hero, we are left none the wiser about why he thought the Press Clause was so important.

Why did Stewart think freedom of the press deserved particular attention? How did the singular stress he placed on the press shape his understanding of free speech and inform his decisions on the Court? What was the value of Stewart's original vision? And with the press and the news media as a whole now undergoing significant change, what can Justice Stewart's press-freedom jurisprudence mean today?

FAST TRACK TO THE SUPREME COURT

Potter Stewart was born into a prominent and well-connected family in 1915.[15] His mother, Harriet Loomis Potter, came from a family that controlled the oldest bank in Michigan. His father, James Garfield Stewart, was a native Ohioan and staunch Republican who followed a very successful career as a lawyer with a very successful career in public life, first as a member of the Cincinnati City Council, then as Cincinnati mayor, and ultimately as a justice on the Ohio Supreme Court.

Stewart's youth was one of material comfort and privilege. His boyhood home was a custom-built manse with a living room forty-six feet in length (for reference, forty-six feet is about five feet longer than a standard seventy-eight passenger school bus[16]). The house was so large that Stewart's father got lost in it when the family first moved in. Stewart attended private school in Cincinnati and then boarding school at Hotchkiss in Connecticut. He majored in English at Yale University, and he was a member of the honor society Phi Beta Kappa and the elite secret society Skull and Bones. After graduating in 1936, Stewart spent a year on fellowship at Cambridge University and subsequently enrolled in Yale Law School, where future president of the United States Gerald Ford and future Supreme Court justice Byron White were among his classmates.[17]

Stewart's first job after law school was at the prestigious Wall Street law firm Debevoise, Stevenson, Plimpton & Page. Like many Americans of his generation, Stewart was swept up by World War II, and he ended up spending three years on active duty as a navigator in the Atlantic Fleet. Stewart returned to Debevoise after the war only to leave the firm and move back to Cincinnati with his young family in 1947. Stewart joined an established Cincinnati law firm and, like his father before him, became very active in the Republican Party and city politics. He was soon elected to the Cincinnati City Council and appeared to be on his way to becoming mayor. But Stewart instead found himself headed for the bench. As fate would have it, the death of eighty-year-old Judge Xenophon Hicks left a vacancy on the Sixth Circuit of Appeals. The two men initially considered for Hicks's position were rejected, the first because of his advanced age and the second because his temperament seemed unsuited for judicial work. Stewart was then recommended to the Eisenhower Administration by Ohio Senator Robert Taft with the somewhat less-than-enthusiastic (and possibly apocryphal) endorsement, "I have finally found someone who is neither too old nor unqualified." Stewart was summarily nominated and confirmed. He was thirty-nine years old.

Stewart had been on the Sixth Circuit for only four years when Supreme Court Justice Harold Burton announced he would retire because of his declining health. Stewart was tapped for the open seat, in part because he was well-known to the Republican establishment and trusted by the Eisenhower Administration to side with the more conservative bloc on the Court (Justices Felix Frankfurter, Tom Clark, John Harlan, and Charles Whittaker) against the liberals (Chief Justice Warren and Justices Black, William Douglas, and William Brennan).[18] It also probably did not hurt that during the search for Burton's replacement Stewart had a chance to schmooze with the Eisenhower Administration's new Attorney General, William P. Rogers, at a Yale Law School alumni event.

Stewart's appointment came in the fall of 1958 just as the Court's term had begun. Since Congress was not in session, Stewart was sworn in and began to serve on the Court without Senate confirmation. The formal confirmation process followed his recess appointment six months later. During the Senate hearings, Stewart drew some opposition from southern Democrats angered by his unwillingness to denounce the landmark desegregation decision, *Brown v. Board of Education*.[19] Stewart otherwise attracted broad bipartisan support, and his confirmation passed the Senate by a large margin. Thus, at age forty-three, Stewart became the second-youngest person to join the

Court since the Civil War; only William O. Douglas, who was forty when he took his seat, was younger.[20]

Taken as a whole, Stewart's life leading up to his Supreme Court appointment presents a record of unbroken professional success as well as a textbook illustration of the old boy network in action. If we look a bit more closely at these years, we can also find some indications of Stewart's special interest in the press.

Stewart had an impressive career as a student reporter, and he ultimately became editor of the *Yale Daily News*.[21] During his time on the paper, he demonstrated a commitment to independent journalism by authoring articles in favor of New Deal programs that cut against the Republican sentiments of the Yale student body. Later in life, as a party activist and as an elected official, Stewart undoubtedly gained an appreciation of the role played by the press in the conduct of politics. And in his final months as a circuit court judge, Stewart began to show how his regard for the press could be translated into constitutional law.

The case was *Garland v. Torre*.[22] Marie Torre, an entertainment reporter for the *New York Herald Tribune*, wrote a story about the difficulties besetting the production of a television special featuring the actress and singer Judy Garland.[23] A CBS executive told Torre that Garland had a "highly developed inferiority complex" generated by the fact that Garland thought of herself as "terribly fat." Torre quoted the executive in her story without providing the executive's name. After the story was published, Garland sued CBS for (among other things) making false and defamatory comments about her. In preparation for trial, Garland's lawyer demanded that Torre name her source and Torre refused, citing (among other things) the First Amendment's guarantee of a free press. A federal district court judge ordered Torre to give up her source, Torre continued to refuse, and the judge sentenced Torre to ten days in jail for criminal contempt. Torre appealed the district court's decision, and Stewart found himself with a high-profile freedom of the press controversy on his hands.[24]

Stewart upheld the district court ruling, but he did so in a way that recognized important safeguards for reporters. He began with the assumption that the First Amendment gives journalists some protection against divulging their confidential sources: "we accept at the outset the hypothesis that compulsory disclosure of a journalist's confidential sources of information entails an abridgement of press freedom by imposing some limitation on the availability of news."[25] Stewart then argued that the essential task of the court was to balance this freedom of the press against the demands of the judicial process.

"Freedom of the press, hard-won over the centuries by men of courage, is basic to a free society. But basic too are courts of justice, armed with the power to discover truth. The concept that it is the duty of a witness to testify in a court of law has roots fully as deep in our history as does the guarantee of a free press."[26] Stewart ruled that in the case at hand the interest in "fair administration of justice" trumped press freedom.[27] But he left open the possibility that the balance might come out the other way if the courts were being used "to force a wholesale disclosure of a newspaper's confidential sources of news" or where "the identity of the source was of doubtful relevance" to the case being litigated.[28]

Stewart's agreement with the lower court was clearly a loss for an individual reporter. It meant that Torre would go to jail for ten days. At the same time, Stewart's rationale was also an important victory for freedom of the press, signaling that other reporters might prevail in the future as courts considered the shielding of sources on a case-by-case basis. In ringing terms, Stewart had ruled that the Constitution provided some special protection to journalists' newsgathering. This was a historic claim, and it brought Stewart national attention for the first time in his career.[29] As we shall see, Stewart would substantially develop and deepen his commitment to press freedom during his tenure on the Supreme Court.

A New Constitutional Structure: The Organized Press

Why did press freedom deserve special emphasis in constitutional law? In *Garland v. Torre*, Stewart answered that question by referring to the centuries-long struggle against censorship. As Stewart developed his free-press reading of the First Amendment while on the Supreme Court, he relied less on the long history of struggle and more on other sources. The first place he turned to was the plain text of the Constitution.

According to Stewart, the fact that press freedom is explicitly mentioned alongside free speech in the First Amendment must mean something. "If the Free Press guarantee meant no more than freedom of expression, it would be a constitutional redundancy."[30] Many state constitutions contemporaneous with the drafting of the US Constitution mentioned freedom of the press without recognizing a general right to free speech; since one freedom could be recognized without the other, Stewart reasoned that the Founders must have understood themselves to be communicating two separate ideas when they listed both freedom of speech and freedom of the press in the First Amendment.[31]

Stewart argued that the plain text of the Constitution also underscored the importance of press freedom in yet another way. The terms of the Constitution failed to extend protection directly to any private business other than the press.[32] As a "matter of abstract policy," we might think that the business of publishing a newspaper is no more worthy of protection than, say, the business of banking or the practice of medicine. "But we are here to uphold a Constitution. And our Constitution does not explicitly protect the practice of medicine or the business of banking from all abridgement by government. It does explicitly protect the freedom of the press."[33] Thus, freedom of the press was not only constitutionally distinct from freedom of speech—the press was also constitutionally distinct from all other private enterprise.

In Stewart's view, the plain text of the Constitution also suggested that critical to the press was its status as a formally ordered establishment. Stewart noted that the roster of rights in the Constitution was addressed almost exclusively to individuals. "Most of the other provisions in the Bill of Rights protect specific liberties or specific rights of individuals: freedom of speech, freedom of worship, the right to counsel, the privilege against compulsory self-incrimination, to name a few."[34] In contrast to all these individual guarantees, "the Free Press Clause extends protection to an institution."[35] As a result, the press freedom cannot be understood as simply one more individual liberty. Instead, the Free Press Clause must be understood as being, "in essence, a *structural* provision of the Constitution."[36] Reporters do not receive protection as individuals but as representatives of "the organized press," an institution that Stewart defined as consisting of "daily newspapers and other established news media."[37]

Stewart's interpretation is not the only way to read the basic terms of the Press Clause. Many have argued, for example, that the word "press" refers to the technological means of mass dissemination rather than to a specific institution or business.[38] If one accepted Stewart's interpretation, however, then his appeal to the words of the Constitution gave him important rhetorical leverage. He could concede that the news media has not always behaved well. "Newspapers, television networks, and magazines have sometimes been outrageously abusive, untruthful, arrogant and hypocritical," Stewart acknowledged.[39] The scorn that many people (including a number of Supreme Court justices) heaped on individual journalists was often well-deserved. Yet, in spite of the well-earned criticism, Stewart could argue that the protection of the press as an institution must be maintained because it is clearly mandated by the plain language of the Constitution. In this same vein, Stewart could use the words of the Constitution against his colleagues on the Supreme Court. As we shall see, Stewart often advanced his understanding of the press freedom in dissent, with a majority of the Court disagreeing with his position. By grounding his views in the explicit words of the Constitution, Stewart endeavored to side-step judicial precedent that suggested freedom of the press extended no further than the individual right to freedom of speech.[40] In doing so, he could portray himself as an unwavering adherent to the letter of the nation's supreme law rather than as a justice who happened to have a personal affinity for journalists.

As advantageous as the plain text of the Constitution could be for a press-centered view of the First Amendment, it also had an important limitation. The words of the Constitution conferred a special status on the press without ever explaining what such a status was for. Was the purpose of press freedom to "insure that a newspaper will serve as a neutral forum for debate, a 'market place for ideas,' a kind of Hyde Park corner for the community"?[41] Or was the purpose of press freedom the more specifically political one of guaranteeing "a neutral conduit of information between the people and their elected leaders"?[42] If the goal was to secure a forum in which any idea could be expressed, then constitutionally required press freedom was consistent with the government regulating the media to make sure that it is "genuinely fair and open" to all points of view.[43] On the other hand, if the goal was simply to establish clear lines of communication between the government and the governed, then press freedom was consistent with regulations limiting the media to being an unbiased carrier of political messages. And what if the purpose of press freedom was something else altogether? What would be the appropriate reach of government regulation then?

In an innovative move, Stewart argued that the "primary purpose" of the Free Press Clause was to "create a fourth institution outside of the Government as an additional check on the three official branches."[44] Stewart supported his claim with a wide variety of sources.[45] He pointed to the British experience centuries before the American Revolution when the British Crown came to understand that a free press meant "expert, organized scrutiny of government." He also referred to the American Founders, who thought of the press as an essential restraint on government excess, and to the nineteenth-century British thinker Thomas Carlyle, who considered the press to be the "Fourth Estate," far more important than any of the parties that held elected office.

Most significantly, Stewart drew upon the modern American experience with "investigative reporting and an adversary press" that had exposed corruption at the highest levels of the federal government and had catalyzed the resignation of President Richard Nixon. Stewart celebrated the adversarial press and its dedication to discovering truth. He had great personal respect for Bob Woodward and Carl Bernstein, the *Washington Post* reporters who had doggedly investigated the Watergate burglary and cover-up.[46] In fact, after Watergate, Stewart encouraged Woodward to write an investigative exposé of the Supreme Court itself. Stewart wanted to use the press to check judicial excesses; he was especially interested in publicly revealing Burger's mismanagement of the Court and removing Burger from the bench. Woodward, along with his fellow *Washington Post* colleague Scott Armstrong, took up Stewart's suggestion and in 1979 published *The Brethren*, a scorching behind-the-scenes critique of the Court that relied on Stewart as the primary source.[47]

For Stewart, then, history (both American and British) and contemporary experience together demonstrated that the function of the organized press was to be part of the checks-and-balances system. Committed to its own independent investigation and verification of events and facts, the press was locked in an endless competition with the legislative, executive, and judicial branches, working as an ever-vigilant guardian to keep government accountable and the people free.

Unlike other views of a free press's purpose that would allow regulation to ensure openness or neutrality, Stewart's checks-and-balances understanding put a premium on press autonomy and the protections that would grant the news media the wherewithal to confront government directly.[48] Thus, when the Supreme Court ruled that it should be difficult to sue newspapers for libel in order to ensure that the public discussion remained "uninhibited, robust, and wide-open" replete with "vehement, caustic, and sometimes unpleasantly sharp attacks on government and public officials," Stewart voted with his fellow justices.[49] When Stewart felt that the standard of proving libel had later shifted, making it more difficult for the news media to defend itself against lawsuits, he dissented and urged his colleagues to return to a standard that would save the press from potentially ruinous litigation.[50]

Stewart again dissented when a majority of the justices expressed varying degrees of sympathy for the view that reporters could be required to disclose confidential sources and information to grand juries.[51] Stewart argued that the protection of confidentiality followed from a commonsense set of propositions. To serve their constitutional purpose of exposing governmental malfeasance, newspapers must be able to publish. To publish, reporters must be able to gather news.

And to gather news, reporters must be able to form confidential relationships with informants. "If it is to perform its constitutional mission, the press must do far more than merely print public statements or publish prepared handouts. Familiarity with the people and circumstances involved in the myriad background activities that result in the final product called 'news' is vital to complete and responsible journalism, unless the press is to be a captive mouthpiece of 'newsmakers.'"[52] According to Stewart, giving grand juries unrestricted subpoena power over journalists would deter informants from talking to the press and in turn would ensure that reporters would no longer be able to investigate and check abuses of power independently (for an indication of how the issue of shielding confidential sources should have been handled, Stewart helpfully directed his fellow Supreme Court justices to his old circuit court decision *Garland v. Torre*).[53] In short, Stewart insisted that the sources and methods of the press must be shielded against government interference. In cases where the Court considered whether media could be compelled to follow governmental rules about what to publish, Stewart agreed with his colleagues when they supported press autonomy.[54] He vigorously dissented when he saw press autonomy sacrificed to government control.[55]

This is not to say that Stewart always sided with journalists whenever they landed in court. For Stewart, the ultimate goal was to preserve a competitive system of checks-and-balances between the judiciary, the legislature, the executive, and the press. The system would not be meaningfully competitive if one player was given a permanent advantage. "The press is free to do battle against secrecy and deception in government," Stewart wrote. "But the press cannot expect from the Constitution any guarantee that it will succeed. . . . [The Constitution] establishes the contest, not its resolution."[56]

Stewart believed it was appropriate for the government to recognize that reporters occasionally needed some practical accommodations (e.g., space to use sound equipment and cameras) that members of the public did not.[57] But, as a matter of principle, Stewart thought the Constitution did not require that members of the press be given access to information and institutions beyond that given to the public. In several cases where journalists sued to open corrections facilities to greater coverage, Stewart not only voted against the press but also wrote the opinion of the Court denying the press's demand for special access.[58] And when the Court ruled, in the famous *Pentagon Papers* case, that newspapers could publish an illegally leaked, classified history of the Vietnam War, Stewart explained that his agreement with the Court's decision did not mean that the newspapers could not ultimately be punished by Congress for what they had printed.[59] In the battle of checks-and-balances, every institution must learn to hold its own. Whether the press was to gain or lose the information it seeks in any given instance, Stewart thought "we must rely, as so often in our system we must, on the tug and pull of the political forces in American society."[60]

What can be made of Stewart's press-centric reading of the First Amendment? As a piece of constitutional theorizing, his reading was inventive and provocative. He made a novel case for separating freedom of the press from freedom of speech and then he creatively incorporated the organized press into the Constitution's fundamental separation-of-powers architecture. As James Madison wrote over two centuries ago, in order to avoid the twin evils of anarchy and tyranny one "must first enable the government to control the governed; and in the next place oblige it to control itself."[61] Madison believed that the constitutionally established rivalry between the legislative, judicial, and executive branches would achieve the goal of a self-controlled government by pitting ambitious officials against one another, arranging "the several offices in such a manner as that each may be a check on the other" and ensuring that "the private interest of every individual may be a sentinel over the public rights."[62] Stewart argued, in effect, that the press was as much a part of the Madisonian scheme as any department of the federal government. In making this argument, Stewart could claim to have developed a fresh way of understanding the First Amendment that placed the institutional media—an entity that he called "a conspiracy of intellect, with the courage of numbers"—at the very core of American constitutionalism.[63]

One difficulty with Stewart's argument is that he placed the press in the somewhat ambiguous position of playing official and nonofficial roles at the same time. On the one hand, Stewart was committed to media autonomy and to making sure that news could be gathered largely without governmental interference. On the other hand, Stewart assigned the press a governing position as a constitutionally denominated participant in the checks-and-balances system. News journalists were simultaneously outside of government and a constituent element of government. Stewart did not fully explain how this double role could be managed by the press or by the other branches of government. Nor did he explain why this arrangement would be accepted as legitimate by the people in a system where membership in the federal government typically required election or appointment. If journalists were to be a part of the government, why should they be exempt from formal processes of ratification?

Another difficulty with Stewart's approach is that he did not persuade a majority of his colleagues on the Supreme Court to embrace his view.[64] As a consequence, the Court's treatment of press freedom in some ways ended up being quite the opposite of what Stewart had hoped. Consider, again, the task of ensuring a competitive checks-and-balances system that included the organized press. Stewart's default preference was to allow the give-and-take of the political system to calibrate the positions of competing institutions. And, in fact, for much of American history the press established and defended its prerogatives in one political battle after another. Beginning in the mid-twentieth century, however, cases involving the powers and freedom of the established press began to surface on the Supreme Court's docket.[65] At this point, the Court became a player *and* the referee in the extended checks-and-balances game. One could rightly note that the Court frequently plays both roles, and by the time the Court began hearing press cases it already had amassed a good deal of experience being both participant and rules keeper in earlier separation-of-powers disputes between the Court, Congress, and the President.[66] But in other separation-of-powers cases, all members of the Court recognized that the judiciary, legislative, and executive branches are the central, constitutionally sanctioned players. This was not the case when it came to the organized press.

Stewart deemed the news media to be engaged in adversarial competition along with the three branches of government, but other Supreme Court justices did not see the constitutionally designated system of checks-and-balances at stake in the press cases they heard. Thus, in adjudicating press freedom disputes, the other justices came to think of the news media as just another claimant rather than as a co-equal institution playing its constitutionally mandated structural role. It is this framing of the news media that prevailed in the Court's First Amendment jurisprudence. As Chief Justice John Roberts told an audience of reporters and journalism students several decades after Stewart left the Court, "Do not think for a moment that [the First Amendment's] words alone will protect you. Without an independent judiciary to give life and substance to the constitutional text as law, the words are nothing but empty promises."[67] Roberts's assertion that the media owes the Court a primary debt of gratitude is a long step away from Stewart's belief that every American should thank the press.[68]

One way back to Stewart's press-centered understanding of the First Amendment might be for the Supreme Court to disengage itself from press freedom disputes and, as Stewart suggested, to allow the "tug and pull" of politics to determine the boundaries of the separation-of-powers system.[69] It seems unlikely that Stewart himself would have ever been able to engineer such a retreat because his generally preferred style of case-by-case judging—where he advanced arguments only so far as the question at hand required—was ill-suited to the task of creating large-scale change. Much like Harlan and his judicially conservative methods of decision making described in Chapter 4 herein, Stewart often charted a path that avoided contentious issues where possible and sought moderate outcomes. This kind of incremental, centrist judging can convey important lessons about the importance of listening to all sides and the value of balancing contending interests. Yet these very virtues also make it difficult to shift the status quo and to turn the law in a substantially different direction.

Even if judicial disengagement were to occur and formal legal doctrine no longer actively rejected the idea of special press freedom, there remains the issue of change in the press itself. Stewart anchored his view of the First Amendment in a specific understanding of journalism that in many ways no longer describes the media landscape. Regardless of the Supreme Court's current disposition toward the news media, we must ask whether it is still possible to situate the press within the checks-and-balances structure.

WATCHDOGS AND VERIFICATION TODAY

When Stewart looked at the organized press of his day, he saw a set of print and broadcast entities that were dedicated to ideals of verification and watchdog journalism.[70]

The news media verified the accuracy of the information they gathered by accessing and comparing a wide variety of sources and by filtering their reporting through a series of editors before publication or broadcast. These consensus rules and procedures of good journalism were designed to produce an objectively valid rendering of events. Although objectivity might not be achieved in any given news story, the pursuit of it was broadly accepted as a professional goal. Continuous scrutiny of government was another widely shared goal. News journalists not only strived to be a credible source of objective information but also worked to monitor and critique those in power. The aim was to investigate the doings of officials, to uncover wrongdoing, and to present the results for discussion and judgment—all with an eye toward furnishing citizens with the information they needed to be self-governing.

The objective, watchdog news media that Stewart knew was of relatively recent vintage. The quest for objectivity did not emerge as a regulative ideal in American journalism until well after World War I.[71] The press's thoroughgoing commitment to government criticism came even later. It is true that the American practice of investigative journalism began in the early twentieth century with muckraking, a brand of reform-oriented reporting designed to expose corruption and to provoke change.[72] Even so, muckraking was an exceptional form of journalism until the 1960s, when fallout from the Vietnam War led journalists to adopt a broadly adversarial relationship to government and to dedicate themselves to scrutinizing the uses of official power.[73]

Stewart understood that over time the news media had not always adhered to the same practices or ascribed to the same values.[74] Yet he did not appear to consider whether journalism would continue to change and how change might affect the press's constitutional role. As it turns out, some of the changes that have occurred in the decades since Stewart's retirement from the bench are broadly consistent with Stewart's original vision. Consider the rise of journalism written from an explicitly partisan point of view. The established press of Stewart's time universally favored a studiously impartial voice for the reportage of news, with journalists' opinions reserved only for editorials. This consensus has fallen apart. Although outlets like MSNBC and Fox News share the same institutional structure as other news media, they present all their coverage from a clearly political perspective. Journalists who continue to stress impartiality in their reporting have argued that such "activist" news media seriously undermine the ideals of verification and watchdog monitoring: politically committed journalists not only portray facts as they would like them to be (rather than as they are) but also limit scrutiny to the public officials from opposing parties.[75] There is some truth to this criticism, but it should not be overstated. Unlike the partisan newspapers of early American history,[76] many of the crusading journalists of today still accept the ideal of objective verification and argue that the frank statement of personal values makes their reporting more accurate and reliable. As Glenn Greenwald argues, "rigorous adherence to the facts" is best promoted "by being honest about one's perspective and subjective assumptions rather than donning a voice-of-god, view-from-nowhere tone that falsely implies that journalists reside above normal viewpoints and faction-loyalties that plague the nonjournalist and the dreaded 'activist.'"[77] The disagreement between proponents of nonpartisan and partisan journalism is not over whether or not news reporting can objectively verify facts but how such verification is best achieved. As for holding officials accountable, it is no doubt true that ideologically committed journalists are more likely to monitor their opponents more closely than their allies. But so long as there are a multitude of such journalists writing from a wide range of perspectives, the news media as a whole can still play an important watchdog role no matter which party happens to be in power.[78]

While the proliferation of openly partisan journalism threatens Stewart's conception of the press as an essential constitutional structure, the rapid decline of the news media's business model—especially among newspapers—represents a much greater threat. Revenue generation has long played a critical role in the development of the American press into a powerful institution. As the great newspaper publisher Joseph Pulitzer explained, the relationship between profit and a robustly autonomous press is quite direct: "Circulation means advertising, and advertisements mean money, and money means independence."[79] Today, money pays for journalists to gather the news, for editors to supervise the journalists, for fact-checkers to confirm claims, for graphic designers to convey information visually, for technical staff to build and use databases, and for lawyers to defend the press against lawsuits.[80] Unfortunately, the money is drying up quickly. In 2013, newspaper print advertising revenue fell to its lowest level (in constant dollars) since the Newspaper Association of America began tracking revenue in 1950.[81] The revenue decline began in 2000 as advertising dollars fled from newspapers to other platforms. And the decline has only accelerated, with print advertising revenues decreasing more than 50 percent since 2008.[82] Newspapers have reported some new advertising revenues from digital ventures. But the new revenue streams are not nearly large enough to compensate for the drop in print advertisements.[83] As a consequence, the capacity of newspapers to engage in the sort of newsgathering and adversarial investigation that Stewart prized has significantly diminished.

In view of this decline, it is tempting to argue that the blogosphere is capable of taking over the role played by the organized press.[84] One might think of the blogosphere as a watchdog with many sets of eyes turned toward public affairs. The interests and opinions of individual bloggers are highly varied; and just as the politically committed news media in aggregate may check the government, so too the blogosphere as a whole may ensure that every official act is monitored from a wide range of perspectives. One might also think of the blogosphere as enacting a decentralized form of verification.[85] There is a developing set of blogging norms—norms that call for bloggers to link to original sources, to post self-corrections, and to encourage critical feedback from commenters—and these norms engage the blogosphere in a collective process of error correction. The result is a kind of networked, peer-produced review that replaces the one-way transmission of news from press to readers with the multidirectional sharing of information among participants.

The blogosphere nonetheless falls quite short of replacing the Fourth Estate. As even some blogging boosters concede, the blogosphere is highly dependent on the reporting produced by the established press.[86] The collective error-correction practices of the blogosphere may help ensure that news reports are accurately disseminated across the Internet. These practices might also help verify the accuracy of the news reports themselves as bloggers scrutinize a journalist's sources and reasoning. Yet this dissemination and checking of the news is not the same as—or a substitute for—independent, professional newsgathering.[87] As the established press shrinks and fewer news stories are produced, there is less grist to be run through the blogosphere mill.

Of course, it is true that blogs allow for an unprecedented number of people to publish information about what is happening immediately around them. It is also true that disclosures by figures like Edward Snowden and Bradley Manning (neither of whom are traditional news journalists) injected huge troves of information into the blogosphere and, in turn, produced heated discussion, sharp criticism, and sustained pressure for government accountability.[88]

From Stewart's perspective, however, neither an increase in local reportage nor the courageous actions of whistle blowers will suffice. Stewart envisioned the competition between the press and the branches of government taking place at the national level, where the power is the greatest and the risks of tyrannical action are the most serious. More coverage of local affairs does advance the idea of an open press, a free marketplace for ideas that has space for every opinion and point of view. Yet, for Stewart, the crucial fact is that a marketplace for ideas does not directly address the Madisonian challenge of bringing a strong national government under control. Indeed, as we have seen, Stewart firmly rejected the notion that the aim of the First Amendment's Press Clause was to create an open venue for all expression. He insisted instead that the primary purpose of press freedom was to fashion "a fourth institution outside of the Government as an additional check on the three official branches."[89] As we have also seen, Stewart's use of the word "institution" was intentional and important. Toe-to-toe confrontation with federal powers requires institutional organization to ensure that engagement in the checks-and-balances system is vigorous, consistent, and sustained. Lone acts of whistle blowing may inspire debate and lead to policy change, but such acts are costly and unlikely to be regularly repeated. The long prison term being served by Manning and the life in exile being faced by Snowden illustrate the high price individuals can be compelled to pay when they attempt to hold the government accountable on their own. By contrast, the institutional press spares its informants from enormous personal sacrifice by shielding their identities. Stewart understood that this practice was essential for newsgathering and for effectively checking government (that is why he believed the anonymity of sources deserved constitutional protection). He saw checks-and-balances as an endless, grinding contest waged by formally established rivals. Private individuals who jump in without organizational support run the risk of being crushed.

CAN WE LIVE WITHOUT AN INSTITUTIONAL PRESS?

Stewart's reading of the First Amendment is an unusual one. Drawing upon history, the plain text of the Constitution, contemporary American experience, and his own biography, Stewart interpreted the Press Clause as a structural provision inserting the organized news media into the Constitution's checks-and-balances system alongside the judicial, legislative, and executive branches of the federal government. He believed that if the established press's autonomy was preserved, then reporters would directly help realize the grand purposes of the Constitution's separation-of-powers design, ensuring that the ambitions of officials are pitted against one another and that the powers of government serve the public interest.

There were some internal tensions in his arguments and Stewart had limited success persuading his colleagues on the Supreme Court to accept his vision. Over time, an even greater difficulty for Stewart's view emerged. The established press around which he constructed his arguments greatly declined. There is more and more speech today, with a huge diversity of ideas and opinions continually expressed in the blogosphere. But there is also less and less adversarial, investigative journalism backed by independent, formally organized media institutions. It is this kind of news journalism that is demanded in the ceaseless checks-and-balances contest. Without it, we are a nation with an overflowing free marketplace for ideas—but no free press.

Stewart actually contemplated a United States with only free speech and concluded that it was "possible to conceive of the survival of our Republic without an autonomous press."[90] "For openness and honesty in government, for an adequate flow of information between the people and their representatives, for a sufficient check on autocracy and despotism, the traditional competition between three branches of government might be enough."[91] It might work. But Stewart did not think this was the system we have had, nor did he believe that it was one we should want.

Notes

1. The author thanks Nicole Elsasser Watson for truly excellent research assistance. In addition to her tireless research and careful copyediting, Nicole helpfully highlighted the tensions inherent in Stewart's treatment of the media as both an official and unofficial actor.
2. *Smith v. California*, 361 U.S. 147, 157 (1959) (Black, J., concurring) (emphasis original).
3. Potter Stewart, "Or of the Press," *Hastings Law Journal* 26 (1974–1975): 631–637.
4. Vikram David Amar, "From Watergate to Ken Starr: Potter Stewart's 'Or of the Press' a Quarter Century Later," *Hastings Law Journal* 50 (1999): 711–715; Margaret A. Blanchard, "The Institutional Press and Its First Amendment Privileges," *Supreme Court Review* 1978 (1978): 225–296.
5. See *Citizens United v. Fed. Election Comm'n*, 558 U.S. 310, 352 (2010); *Dun & Bradstreet, Inc. v. Greenmoss Builders, Inc.*, 472 U.S. 749, 783–784 (1985) (Brennan, J., joined by Marshall, Blackmun, and Stevens, JJ., dissenting).
6. Except where indicated, the information and quotations in the remainder of this paragraph are drawn from RonNell Andersen Jones, "U.S. Supreme Court Justices and Press Access," *Brigham Young University Law Review* 2012 (2012): 1791–1817.
7. Keith J. Bybee, "Open Secret: Why the Supreme Court Has Nothing to Fear from the Internet," *Chicago-Kent Law Review* 88 (2013): 309–323.
8. Jones, "Justices and Press Access," 1806, footnote no. 96.
9. Leon Friedman, "Potter Stewart," in *The Justices of the United States Supreme Court: Their Lives and Major Opinions*, eds. Leon Friedman and Fred L. Israel (New York: Chelsea House Publishers, 1997), 1546–1573; Gayle Binion, "Potter Stewart," in *Biographical Encyclopedia of the Supreme Court: The Lives and Legal Philosophies of the Justices*, ed. Melvin I. Urofsky (Washington, DC: CQ Press, 2006), 486–492.
10. Binion, "Potter Stewart," 489.
11. Friedman, "Potter Stewart," 1547. The merits of Stewart's case-by-case approach are considered later in this chapter.
12. *Jacobellis v. Ohio*, 378 U.S. 184, 197 (1964) (Stewart, J., concurring).
13. Paul Gewirtz, "On 'I Know When I See It,'" *Yale Law Journal* 105 (1996): 1023.
14. Ibid.
15. Except where indicated, this biographical section of the chapter draws upon Joel Jacobsen, "Remembered Justice: The Background, Early Career, and Judicial Appointments of Justice Potter Stewart," *Akron Law Review* 35 (2002): 227–250.
16. See "Blue Bird Vision," Blue Bird Corporation, accessed June 2, 2014, http://www.blue-bird.com/uploadedFiles/Downloads/bb-vision.pdf
17. Stewart is also said to have attended Yale with future president of the United States George H. W. Bush (see Friedman, "Potter Stewart," 1558–1559). This appears not to have been the case (Jacobsen,

"Remembered Justice," 232). The mistake is understandable given the elite circles in which Stewart traveled and given the fact that Stewart and Bush were later to become friends.

18. Friedman, "Potter Stewart," 1550. Given the record of moderation that Stewart compiled on the Court (described at the outset of this chapter), anyone who expected him to side only with the conservatives was bound to be disappointed.
19. *Brown v. Board of Education*, 347 U.S. 483 (1954). Although there were liberals and conservatives on the high bench, *Brown* was decided unanimously.
20. When confirmed in 1991, Justice Clarence Thomas took over the spot of second youngest individual to join the modern Court by being a few months younger than Stewart. The youngest person to join the Court was Justice Joseph Story, who was thirty-two when President James Madison appointed him in 1811.
21. Friedman, "Potter Stewart," 1549; Rowena Scott Comegys, "Potter Stewart: An Analysis of His Views on the Press as Fourth Estate," *Chicago-Kent Law Review* 59 (1982): 157–208.
22. *Garland v. Torre*, 259 F.2d 545 (1958). This case was argued in the Second Circuit Court of Appeals. Stewart, a judge on the Sixth Circuit, was sitting by designation in the Second Circuit. For an overview of the designation process, see Dan Baker-Jones, "Sitting by Designation," *Nota Bene* (blog), April 25, 2012, accessed June 2, 2014, http://notabeneuh.blogspot.com/2012/04/sitting-by-designation.html
23. The background information of the case is drawn from Jacobsen, "Remembered Justice."
24. *Garland* was decided by a three-judge panel. Stewart wrote the opinion and was joined by Second Circuit Chief Judge Charles Edward Clark and Second Circuit Judge Caroll C. Hincks. As luck would have it, both Clark and Hincks were, like Stewart, Yale men. See "Biographical Directory of Federal Judges: Clark, Charles Edward," Federal Judicial Center, accessed June 2, 2014, http://www.fjc.gov/servlet/nGetInfo?jid=439&cid=999&ctype=na&instate=na; "Biographical Directory of Federal Judges: Hincks, Carroll Clark," Federal Judicial Center, accessed June 2, 2014, http://www.fjc.gov/servlet/nGetInfo?jid=1052&cid=999&ctype=na&instate=na
25. 259 F.2d at 548.
26. Ibid.
27. Ibid., 549.
28. Ibid., 549–550.
29. Jacobsen, "Remembered Justice," 246–247.
30. Stewart, "Or of the Press," 633.
31. Ibid., 633–634.
32. Ibid., 633. As Samuel R. Olken notes in Chapter 2 herein, Justice Sutherland also attached significance to the press's status as a business. Sutherland saw the press as a site where economic liberty and free speech intersected and, as a result, Sutherland thought the press deserved

protection in order to preserve the business of expression. By contrast, Stewart did not link the business aspect of the press to economic freedoms. For him, the relevant context for the Press Clause was not free enterprise but was instead (as we shall see) the Constitution's separation-of-powers system.

33. *Zurcher v. Stanford Daily*, 436 U.S. 547, 576 (1978) (Stewart, J., joined by Marshall, J., dissenting).
34. Stewart, "Or of the Press," 633.
35. Ibid.
36. Ibid (emphasis original).
37. Ibid., 631.
38. See Eugene Volokh, "Freedom for the Press as an Industry, or for the Press as a Technology? From the Framing to Today," *University of Pennsylvania Law Review* 160 (2012): 459–540.
39. Stewart, "Or of the Press," 636.
40. For a list of such precedents, see Blanchard, "Institutional Press."
41. Stewart, "Or of the Press," 634.
42. Ibid.
43. Ibid., 635.
44. Ibid., 634.
45. Ibid., 631–632, 634, 637. For a brief review of the term "Fourth Estate," see Comegys, "Potter Stewart," 162–163.
46. Richard Davis, *Justices and Journalists: The U.S. Supreme Court and the Media* (New York: Cambridge University Press, 2011), 137–138.
47. Bob Woodward and Scott Armstrong, *The Brethren: Inside the Supreme Court* (New York: Simon and Schuster, 1979).
48. Stewart did not think that effective press scrutiny of different parts of government required identical levels of press freedom. Given the different way in which the judiciary functions, for example, greater restrictions on access and disclosure may be appropriate for coverage of the courts. See Comegys, "Potter Stewart," 179–180.
49. *New York Times Co. v. Sullivan*, 376 U.S. 254, 279 (1964).
50. *Herbert v. Lando*, 441 U.S. 153, 199–203 (1979) (Stewart, J., dissenting).
51. *Branzburg v. Hayes*, 408 U.S. 665, 725–752 (1972) (Stewart, J., joined by Brennan and Marshall, JJ., dissenting).
52. Ibid., 729.
53. Ibid., 743, footnote no. 33.
54. *Columbia Broad. Sys., Inc. v. Democratic Nat'l Comm.*, 412 U.S. 94, 132–146 (1973) (Stewart, J., concurring); *Miami Herald Publ'g Co. v. Tornillo*, 418 U.S. 241 (1974).
55. *Pittsburgh Press Co. v. Pittsburgh Comm'n on Human Relations*, 413 U.S. 376, 400–404 (1973) (Stewart, J., joined by Douglas, J., dissenting).
56. Stewart, "Or of the Press," 636.
57. *Houchins v. KQED, Inc.*, 438 U.S. 1, 16–19 (1978) (Stewart, J., concurring in the judgment).

58. *Pell v. Procunier*, 417 U.S. 817 (1974); *Saxbe v. Washington Post Co.*, 417 U.S. 843 (1974).
59. *N.Y. Times Co. v. United States*, 403 U.S. 713, 727–731 (1971) (Stewart, J., joined by White, J., concurring).
60. Stewart, "Or of the Press," 636.
61. James Madison, *Federalist Paper*, No. 51.
62. Ibid.
63. Stewart, "Or of the Press," 634.
64. For a contrarian, more Stewart-friendly characterization of modern First Amendment law, see Sonja R. West, "The Stealth Press Clause," *Georgia Law Review* 48 (2014): 729–756, arguing that a majority of Supreme Court justices should implicitly acknowledge the idea that the press is constitutionally unique and that beneath the surface of judicial opinions a "Stealth Press Clause" is at work.
65. The date is from Stewart, "Or of the Press," 632. Blanchard traces the first institutional press cases to the late 1930s and early 1940s. Blanchard, "Institutional Press," 228.
66. One of the earliest and more striking examples of the Court's double role in the separation-of-powers context can be found in *Marbury v. Madison*, 5 U.S. 137 (1803).
67. Carol L. Boll, "Newhouse III Dedication: A Day to Remember," *Newhouse Network*, Fall 2007, 3. Although the Supreme Court's doctrine is not particularly favorable to the press, scholars have noted that the lower courts have in practice recognized some special accommodations for reporters. See, for example, David A. Anderson, "Freedom of the Press," *Texas Law Review* 80 (2002): 429–530. For the argument that the Obama Administration has similarly pursued a somewhat contradictory policy of alternately refusing and endorsing special press protection, see Adam Liptak, "Supreme Court Rejects Appeal from Reporter Over Identity of Source," *New York Times*, June 2, 2014, accessed June 2, 2014, http://www.nytimes.com/2014/06/03/us/james-risen-faces-jail-time-for-refusing-to-identify-a-confidential-source.html
68. Stewart, "Or of the Press," 637.
69. Ibid., 636.
70. The description of the news media in this paragraph is drawn from Michael Schudson, *Discovering the News: A Social History of American Newspapers* (New York: Basic Books, 1978). For an extended discussion of journalistic ideals, see Bill Kovach and Tom Rosenstiel, *The Elements of Journalism: What Newspeople Should Know and the Public Should Expect* (New York: Crown Publishers, 2001).
71. Schudson, *Discovering the News*, 121–159.
72. Louis Filler, *Crusaders for American Liberalism* (Yellow Springs: Antioch Press, 1961); Thomas C. Leonard, *The Power of the Press: The Birth of American Political Reporting* (New York: Oxford University Press, 1986).
73. Schudson, *Discovering the News*, 160–194.
74. Stewart, "Or of the Press," 631.

75. Bill Keller, "Is Glenn Greenwald the Future of News?," *New York Times*, October 27, 2013, accessed June 2, 2014, http://www.nytimes.com/2013/10/28/opinion/a-conversation-in-lieu-of-a-column.html?module=Search&mabReward=relbias%3Ar
76. Schudson, *Discovering the News*, 12–60.
77. Keller, "Glenn Greenwald."
78. For the argument that watchdog journalism has long had a political bias, see Ricardo Puglisi and James M. Snyder Jr., "Newspaper Coverage of Political Scandals," *Journal of Politics* 73 (2011): 931–950.
79. Quoted in George Brock, *Out of Print: Newspapers, Journalism, and the Business of News in the Digital Age* (London: Kogan Page, 2013), 56.
80. Keller, "Glenn Greenwald."
81. Mark J. Perry, "Creative Destruction: Newspaper Ad Revenue Continued Its Precipitous Free Fall in 2013, and It's Probably Not Over Yet," *American Enterprise Institute: Carpe Diem* (blog), April 25, 2014, accessed June 2, 2014, http://www.aei-ideas.org/2014/04/creative-destruction-2013-newspaper-ad-revenue-continued-its-precipitous-free-fall-and-its-probably-not-over-yet/
82. Ibid.
83. Jordan Weissmann, "The Decline of Newspapers Hits a Stunning Milestone," *Slate: Moneybox* (blog), April 28, 2014, accessed June 2, 2014, http://www.slate.com/blogs/moneybox/2014/04/28/decline_of_newspapers_hits_a_milestone_print_revenue_is_lowest_since_1950.html
84. Steven Johnson and Paul Starr, "Are We on Track for a Golden Age of Serious Journalism?," *Prospect*, May 4, 2009, accessed June 2, 2014, http://www.prospectmagazine.co.uk/magazine/areweontrackforagoldenageofseriousjournalism/
85. Paul Horwitz, *First Amendment Institutions* (Cambridge: Harvard University Press, 2013), 166–173.
86. Ibid., 171.
87. Johnson and Starr, "Golden Age."
88. A word of explanation about this chapter's reference to "Bradley" Manning is appropriate. Subsequent to sentencing, Pfc. Manning announced that she is transitioning from male to female and prefers to go by the name "Chelsea Manning" (see, Emmarie Huetteman, "'I Am a Female,' Manning Announces, Asking Army for Hormone Therapy," *New York Times*, August 23, 2013). However, since this chapter's reference occurs in the context of when Pfc. Manning provided WikiLeaks with confidential governmental files—a time during which Pfc. Manning was still publicly identifying himself as Bradley—the decision was made to refer to him as Bradley here.
89. Stewart, "Or of the Press," 634.
90. Ibid., 636.
91. Ibid.

CHAPTER 7

ANTHONY M. KENNEDY: "SPEECH IS THE BEGINNING OF THOUGHT"

Helen J. Knowles

Born in Sacramento in 1936, Anthony M. Kennedy was raised "in the same white colonial-style house . . . behind a camelia [*sic*] bush and a neat row of gardenias" in which he would live (with the exception of a few years) before moving to Washington, DC, in 1988, the year he was appointed to the Supreme Court by President Ronald Reagan.[1] "It was a wonderful town and a wonderful time. What's the movie with Jimmy Stewart? *It's a Wonderful Life*." This is how Justice Kennedy recalls the at-the-time economically booming capital of California.[2] These fond memories of his upbringing are emblematic of the air of pomposity, the elitist morality, and the unrealistically sunny disposition that Kennedy has been accused of bringing to his work at the US Supreme Court.[3]

Criticism or praise of Kennedy aside, it cannot be denied that his jurisprudence has been significantly shaped by his "approach to life [that] suggests a small-town innocence."[4] However, there is also much truth to the argument that Dahlia Lithwick made in an incisive 2012 *Slate* article, that "of all the current Supreme Court justices, he [Kennedy] is in fact most representative of that elusive Every American":

> [He] almost perfectly fits the profile of the mysterious and alluring swing-voter, that vanishing Independent whose vote is truly in play. He is quite conservative, but he exhibits brief moments of progressivism on issues that raise questions of basic justice and dignity—from gay rights to prisoner abuse.

> Like most Americans, he's not as conservative as the other four conservatives on the court. Nor, like most Americans, is he as liberal as the four liberals. He tries . . . to be open-minded in ways that many of us are not. He doesn't hate government, although he doesn't care for it much either. He can be moved by personal narrative. He cares what the rest of the world thinks of this country. And because he is, in a sense, the last of the true swing voters, everyone is always furious at him when he acts in a way that they don't expect.[5]

In freedom of speech cases, Kennedy's opinions cannot be described as either the product of an uncertain swing voter, or generally embodying a "small-town innocence." Lawyers might believe that it is important to pen so-called "Kennedy briefs," "fall[ing] over themselves to court Kennedy's favor by repeatedly citing the opinions of Justice Kennedy" because of the perception that on the Court Kennedy is "that vanishing Independent whose vote is truly in play." And commentators might characterize Kennedy as the consummate judicial "agonizer."[6] However, it is the rare First Amendment freedom of speech case in which Kennedy exhibits any degree of jurisprudential uncertainty.

Quite simply, Kennedy has a "'a thing' about the First Amendment," and that "thing" is underpinned by libertarian values.[7] Since joining the Court, he has generally been considered a conservative justice, but he is better described as adopting a libertarian approach when deciding cases involving expressive freedom. He has voted against the government in approximately three quarters of those cases, rejecting most government attempts to discriminate between different viewpoints, because these attempts represent a fundamental interference with individual sovereignty.[8]

There is one particular type of governmental restriction of free speech that especially incurs Kennedy's judicial wrath for its intrusion upon that sovereignty—any regulation that singles out speech based on its content. Kennedy has made it clear that he is unwilling to tolerate decisions that provide the government with opportunities to engage in content-based restrictions of speech unless the expression in question falls into a very small number of "historic and traditional categories long familiar to the bar."[9] He has sought to move the Court away from its traditional usage of strict judicial scrutiny—the test that asks whether the regulation (1) furthers a compelling government interest, (2) is narrowly tailored to meet that interest, and (3) is the least restrictive means of achieving the government's goal—for content-based laws. This hostility to content-based restrictions on speech has been a consistent, core component of Kennedy's free speech jurisprudence throughout his time on the Court.

TEXAS V. JOHNSON: "WE MUST MAKE DECISIONS WE DO NOT LIKE"[10]

In 1989, in one of his earliest Supreme Court opinions, Kennedy provided a strong indication of his hostility to governmental attempts to regulate the content of speech. This indication came in his concurrence in *Texas v. Johnson* and must have left little doubt in the minds of his colleagues about the direction his free speech jurisprudence would take.

During a political demonstration outside the 1984 Republican National Convention in Dallas, Texas, Gregory Lee "Joey" Johnson set fire to an American flag. Nobody was injured, but several onlookers later testified that they were "seriously offended" by the incident. One person returned to the site to collect the remains of the flag; he took them home and buried them in his backyard. The offense that Johnson's actions generated was sufficient to convict him under a Texas statute that made it a crime to "intentionally or knowingly desecrate . . . a state or national flag." This is because the State defined "desecrate" as to "deface, damage, or otherwise physically mistreat in a way that the actor knows will seriously offend one or more persons likely to observe or discover his action."[11] The five-justice majority that voted to strike down this law on First Amendment grounds was composed of Justice William J. Brennan (who wrote the opinion), and Justices Thurgood Marshall, Harry Blackmun, Antonin Scalia, and Kennedy.[12]

The Court concluded that Johnson's flag burning was a form of expression because it was conduct undertaken with "'[a]n intent to convey a particularized message . . . and the likelihood was great that the message would be understood by those who viewed it.'"[13] The conduct fell into a category of expression known as symbolic speech (nonverbal speech) that receives First Amendment protection because there is no clear line between speech and conduct. Those who wave (or burn) American flags are viewed as expressing themselves, or attempting to communicate a particular message, just as much as those who read speeches about Old Glory. The First Amendment protects both methods of expression. This does not mean, however, that governmental efforts to regulate speech that is harmful are evaluated under the same standard as efforts to regulate harmful conduct. The government has greater latitude to regulate the latter, even if it is conduct that is held to be expressive.

Since 1968, the standard of judicial review for government efforts to regulate expressive conduct has depended upon whether the regulation is related to the suppression of expression. If it is, then strict scrutiny is applied; if not, then the Court applies the *O'Brien* test. The Court conceived this test in 1968 in *United States v. O'Brien.*[14] This case was the result of David Paul O'Brien's decision, in 1966, to burn his draft card on the steps of the South Boston Courthouse. O'Brien was arrested and subsequently convicted of violating a federal law which, as amended in 1965, made it a crime to "forge, alter, knowingly destroy, knowingly mutilate, or in any manner change" a draft card.[15] The Court upheld the law by crafting and applying a test that led it to conclude that the purpose served by the law was to prevent the destruction of draft cards, an action unrelated to free expression. The *O'Brien* test begins with the Court asking whether the government has a constitutional power to regulate in the manner it has chosen (the government usually satisfies this requirement). Next, the question becomes whether the regulation furthers an "important or substantial interest" and is "unrelated to the suppression of free expression." Even if the regulation conforms to both of these components of the test, it can still be held unconstitutional if the restriction it imposes on First Amendment freedoms is "greater than is essential to the furtherance of that interest."[16]

In *Johnson*, Texas defended its flag desecration law by arguing that it served two purposes—(1) preventing the breaches of the peace that would result when witnesses to flag burning were offended by that action and (2) maintaining national unity. The Court summarily rejected the first argument; the facts of the case did not suggest that any such social disturbances had occurred. The second goal, of maintaining national unity (and the related aim of preserving the symbolic integrity of the flag), had to be viewed as directly related to the suppression of free expression. Texas, wrote Justice Brennan, was worried that flag burning would "lead people to believe either that the flag does not stand for nationhood and national unity, but instead reflects other, less positive concepts, or that the concepts reflected in the flag do not in fact exist, that is, that we do not enjoy unity as a Nation." These concerns, said Brennan, "blossom only when a person's treatment of the flag communicates some message." Strict judicial scrutiny was the required standard of review because the *O'Brien* test was clearly inapplicable. Ultimately, Brennan concluded that the Texas law could not withstand strict scrutiny, because "[i]f there is a bedrock principle underlying the First Amendment, it is that the government may not prohibit the expression of an idea simply because society finds the idea itself offensive or disagreeable."[17]

As James Foster shows in Chapter 5 herein, *Johnson* was a very controversial decision—both on and off the Court. Brennan's opinion generated passionate dissents authored by Chief Justice William H. Rehnquist and Justice John Paul Stevens. Both World War II veterans, the two men produced opinions that detailed the patriotic history and special symbolic value of the American Flag. It "was not," wrote Rehnquist, an item that merely conveyed "another 'idea' or 'point of view'" that was "competing for recognition in the marketplace of ideas." Rather, it is something that many "Americans regard . . . with an almost mystical reverence."[18] And as such, it should be treated in a special way; it is the flag, rather than Johnson's burning of it, that needs and deserves governmental protection, concluded Rehnquist.

Justice Kennedy's Concurrence: "Judicial Hand-Wringing"

Although he joined Brennan's opinion "without reservation," Kennedy chose to pen a two-page concurrence in *Johnson*. In six short paragraphs, Kennedy explained why he felt compelled to write separately and offer his own, personal defense of the Court's protection of the First Amendment, which he described as "a pure command of the Constitution."[19] Kennedy has since (somewhat apologetically) described his opinion as "judicial hand-wringing," perhaps because in it he said: "The hard fact is sometimes we must make decisions we do not like. We make them because they are right, right in the sense that the law and the Constitution, as we see them, compel the result."[20] Whatever misgivings he may have had about the decision to write in *Johnson*, there is no doubt that collectively his words were a powerful statement of his First Amendment views.

The first draft of Kennedy's concurrence contained passages that expressed his disdain for Johnson's actions. However, the language of the second and final version was noticeably toned down, perhaps not only in response to comments from Blackmun (whose marginalia on the first draft included objections to certain phrases that did not appear in the final opinion) but also out of recognition of essential First Amendment principles of tolerance and viewpoint diversity. For example, Kennedy wrote: "the flag is constant in expressing beliefs Americans share, beliefs in law and peace and that freedom which sustains the human spirit." Originally, he referred to beliefs "*all* Americans share." That the "all" was gone from his final opinion marked his awareness that the beliefs to which he was referring were not and should not be interpreted as the beliefs held by everyone, or even a majority. Indeed, in the final opinion Kennedy took pains to emphasize that this was not a case in which the justices could allow their decision to be affected by their "distaste for the result." Doing so would result in "undermining a valued principle that dictates the decision." He respected the passionate, heart-felt dissenting objections of his colleagues but felt compelled to say: "I do not believe the Constitution gives us the right to rule" in this way, "however painful this judgment is to announce."[21] Kennedy initially described Johnson's views as given with "vengeful insolence," but in the final draft of his concurrence they were simply noted as acts that constituted "speech, in both the technical and the fundamental meaning of the Constitution."[22] The concurrence was not "the first public sign that Kennedy might feel some conflicts about the court's conservative agenda."[23] Rather, *Johnson* was the first sign from the Supreme Court that a key animating principle of Kennedy's free speech jurisprudence is the toleration of all views.

Simon & Schuster: The Accidental Test

There is little doubt that Kennedy has a libertarian vision of the First Amendment's protection of freedom of speech. This can be seen in his decision to write a separate concurrence in *Texas v. Johnson*. However, the *doctrinal* impact of this vision did not become apparent until two years later with his opinion concurring in the judgment in *Simon & Schuster v. Crime Victims Board* (1991).[24] The Rehnquist Court (1986–2005) frequently mustered majorities willing to protect individuals' expressive freedom rights. Kennedy could often be found, however, writing separate opinions. With twenty-first century changes in personnel, as the Rehnquist Court gave way to the Roberts Court, Kennedy found himself needing to write fewer separate opinions in free speech cases. During the early years of his Supreme Court tenure, however, he frequently chose to take positions in opinions that provided individuals with even greater protection from government efforts to limit their speech because of disagreement with the viewpoints offered. *Simon & Schuster* was a good example of this endeavor.

The Court did not have difficulty deciding this case. It unanimously concluded that New York's "Son of Sam" law was unconstitutional. As its name suggests, the State enacted this law in the wake of the 1977 serial killings by David Berkowitz (popularly known as the "Son of Sam"). The law was designed to prevent criminals from profiting from their crimes through the publication of descriptions of their illegal activities. If an individual accused or convicted of a crime entered into a contract for any depiction of that crime, he or she was required to provide the New York Crime Victims Board with a copy of the contract and any income earned from the communication of the information. The money would be placed in escrow and would, for a five-year period, be made available to any victim of the crime who was awarded monetary damages in a related civil action. The coverage of the law extended to individuals who were neither accused nor convicted of a crime but who admitted to such activity in a work (such as a book). Simon & Schuster brought a First Amendment challenge to the law after it published a book containing the admissions of such an individual—the organized crime figure Henry Hill.

The Court did not hesitate to strike the law down. It was clearly a content-based regulation of speech because it only penalized those who engaged in expression on a particular subject (the commission of criminal activities). In her opinion for the Court, Justice Sandra Day O'Connor sharply criticized New York for enacting a law that "establishes a financial disincentive to create or publish works with a particular content."[25] Having established that the regulation was content-based, O'Connor proceeded to apply the strict judicial scrutiny test, which required the State to prove that passage of the law furthered a compelling state interest, was narrowly tailored to further that goal, and was the least speech-intrusive option. O'Connor concluded that such an interest—compensating crime victims—did exist but that it could be achieved in a way that resulted in less intrusion upon First Amendment speech rights. As she noted, during oral argument even the attorney for the Crime Victims Board had conceded that, as it stood, the law was "significantly over-inclusive" because of the breadth of its coverage. A law is held to be over-inclusive when not all of the speech that it restricts is related to the governmental interest. In *Simon & Schuster*, as O'Connor explained, "the statute applies to works on any subject, provided that they express the author's thoughts or recollections about his crime, ***however tangentially or incidentally.***"[26] Such a law could not be described as narrowly tailored.

Although there were no dissenters from the judgment in *Simon & Schuster*, O'Connor's opinion only spoke for herself and five other justices. In a short, three-sentence concurrence in the judgment, Blackmun suggested that the Court should have gone further. Many other states had in place similar laws, and Blackmun believed that it behooved the Court to draw attention to the constitutionally redeeming features of these statutes. The Court had an opportunity to provide "guidance" to a state, like New York, that might wish to enact a revised version of a constitutionally flawed law. Additionally, Blackmun concluded that the "Son of Sam" law was under-inclusive as well as over-inclusive, meaning that it was important to explain that there were many other types of speech that, if restricted, would similarly meet the goal of compensating victims. This became an important part of Blackmun's judgment that the New York law was unconstitutional—this statutory flaw was additional evidence that the State was making a content-based decision about targeting speech.[27]

Justice Kennedy's Concurrence: This Is "Raw Censorship"[28]

On December 1, 1991, eight days before the announcement of the Court's decision in *Simon & Schuster*, Jeff Meyer penned a memo to Blackmun, for whom he was clerking. Blackmun had not yet decided whether to write separately in the case, and Meyer wrote to inform him that he had "heard from AMK's [Kennedy's] chambers that he might be writing separately to address the underinclusiveness issue." Four days later, when Kennedy circulated the first draft of his concurrence, he did not focus on this flaw of the New York statute.[29] Like Blackmun, he refused to join O'Connor's opinion, but Kennedy did not believe that he needed to focus on anything very complex. His passionate opposition to the law was clear from the outset. The regulation, wrote Kennedy, "imposes severe restrictions on authors and publishers, using as its sole criterion the content of what is written." This should have terminated *any* discussion or use of strict judicial scrutiny because this "content has the full protection of the First Amendment." Given the egregious nature of the violation of freedom of expression that was the New York law, it was "unnecessary" and indeed "incorrect" to ask whether it addressed any compelling state interests.[30] Just as he had done at his confirmation hearing, Kennedy explained that the origins of the test lie not in First Amendment jurisprudence but rather in the Court's body of decisions about equal protection of the law. Kennedy then proceeded to make clear his views about the limited role that the test should play in First Amendment cases. It "has no real or legitimate place," he wrote, "when the Court considers the straightforward question whether the State may enact a burdensome restriction of speech based on content only." Indeed, concluded Kennedy, using the test in this case was dangerous to individual liberty because it "might be read as a concession that States may censor speech whenever *they* believe there is a compelling justification for doing so."[31]

As any student of the Supreme Court's free speech jurisprudence learns very early on, there are certain categories of content-based speech that fall beyond the protection of the First Amendment. In *Simon & Schuster*, Kennedy adopted the position that a restriction upon speech may be permissibly content-based when the expression in question falls into one of a very small number of "historic and traditional categories long familiar to the bar."[32] In *United States v. Alvarez*, discussed below, he identified these categories as speech intentionally advocating and likely to produce "imminent lawless action" (the standard established in *Brandenburg v. Ohio*[33]), obscenity, defamation, "speech integral to criminal conduct," the "fighting words" category from *Chaplinsky v. New Hampshire*,[34] child pornography, fraud, true threats, or "speech presenting some grave and imminent danger the government has the power to prevent."[35] It could not "be said with certainty that the foregoing types of expression are or will remain the only ones that are without First Amendment protection," but adherence to these categories grounded in "the Court's free speech tradition" was "preferable" to the type of "ad hoc balancing" that he feared in *Simon & Schuster*.[36] Placing categorical restrictions upon governmental power served to ensure that "[t]he vast realm of free speech and thought always protected in our tradition can still thrive, and even be furthered."[37]

UNITED STATES V. ALVAREZ: "LYING WAS HIS HABIT"[38]

This has not meant, however, that Kennedy has refused to employ this standard of review in cases questioning the constitutionality of content-based restrictions upon speech. In *Simon & Schuster*, Kennedy was writing alone and had no need to hold together a fragile coalition of justices by using a "standard" First Amendment test. The constraints upon any justice are very different, however, when he or she is the author of the majority opinion in a case—when he or she is "compos[ing] with tied hands."[39] Even though he believes that strict scrutiny has no proper place in First Amendment jurisprudence, Kennedy has on occasion found it institutionally necessary to subject a content-based statute to that standard of review when authoring a majority opinion. A good example of this occurred in 2012 when he wrote for the Court in *United States v. Alvarez*.

This case began with a lie; it was a lie that the respondent, Xavier Alvarez, would later argue was protected by the First Amendment. Alvarez won that argument when a majority of the Supreme Court agreed that the Stolen Valor Act of 2005, under which he had been indicted for making the false claim that he had received the Congressional Medal of Honor, was unconstitutional. The law "enhance[d] protections relating to the reputation and meaning of the Medal of Honor and other military decorations and awards."[40]

Alvarez knowingly made the false claim that he was a recipient of the medal while speaking at a public meeting of the Three Valley Water District Board in Claremont, California. Introducing himself at his first meeting as a newly elected member of the Board, he made the completely false statement that he was "'a retired marine of 25 years. I retired in the year 2001. Back in 1987, I was awarded the Congressional Medal of Honor. I got wounded many times by the same guy.'"[41] These lies were of no material benefit to Alvarez and therein lay the key to the case and the foundation for the Court's judgment that the Stolen Valor Act abridged the First Amendment's protection of expressive freedom.

In his plurality opinion Kennedy distinguished *Alvarez* from prior cases in which the Court had upheld prohibitions of false statements. Those cases, he emphasized, all involved "defamation, fraud, or some other legally *cognizable harm associated* with a false statement." By contrast, the Stolen Valor Act punished speech that was *merely* false, and it did so with what Kennedy described as a "sweeping, quite unprecedented reach."[42] Echoing the audibly indignant tone of the comments he made during the oral argument, Kennedy took a hard line in response to the government's attempts to defend the creation of "false statements" as a category of unprotected speech. A statute criminalizing these false statements, "whether shouted from the rooftops or made in a barely audible whisper"; whether made up by "a grandfather . . . to persuade a grandchild to join the military"; or whether, in the case of Alvarez, spoken in "a pathetic attempt to gain respect that eluded him," was, in Kennedy's mind, the product of a government seeking to impose an Orwellian degree of thought-control upon its citizens.[43]

Kennedy's plurality opinion in *Alvarez* provided (rather than offered) a civics lesson on the constitutional perils of permitting the government to regulate the content of speech. "The ordinary course in a free society," wrote Kennedy, is to remedy the ills of false speech by countering them with true speech. "The response to the unreasoned is the rational; to the uninformed, the enlightened; to the straight-out lie, the simple truth." This was, he observed, merely reiterating what so many of his predecessors on the Court had said.[44] From Justice Louis D. Brandeis's famous concurrence in *Whitney v. California* came the following words: "'If there be time to expose through discussion the falsehood and fallacies, to avert the evil by the processes of education, the remedy to be applied is more speech, not enforced silence'"; and from Justice Oliver Wendell Holmes Jr.'s equally famous dissent in *Abrams v. United States* (discussed by

Frederick Lewis in Chapter 1 herein) came these words of wisdom: "'the best test of truth is the power of the thought to get itself accepted in the competition of the market.'"[45]

Kennedy has a noticeable habit of bringing his opinions to a close with a paragraph free of legalese and citations. This is consistent with his larger judicial tendency to use uncluttered, layman's language in order to educate the citizenry about the key values of America's constitutional democracy. This was certainly the case in *Alvarez*. Below an ellipsis separating them from the rest of the opinion appeared the following concluding thoughts:

> The Nation well knows that one of the costs of the First Amendment is that it protects the speech we detest as well as the speech we embrace. Though few might find respondent's statements anything but contemptible, his right to make those statements is protected by the Constitution's guarantee of freedom of speech and expression. The Stolen Valor Act infringes upon speech protected by the First Amendment.[46]

Epitomized by this paragraph, the plurality opinion in *Alvarez* is reminiscent of all of the previous opinions penned by Kennedy in opposition to content-based speech restrictions.

Strict Scrutiny: The Lesser of Two Evils

There is, however, one important way in which *Alvarez* diverges from many of Kennedy's prior opinions—it does not contain a statement opposing the use of strict judicial scrutiny. In fact, his plurality opinion openly embraced that test. Kennedy explained that the Stolen Valor Act failed at least one prong of that standard of review. The federal government defended the 2005 law by contending that it "protect[ed] the reputation and integrity of its military honor system" and that the enhanced penalty provision protected the specific integrity of the Medal of Honor. Solicitor General Donald Verrilli made this very clear from the outset of the oral argument, indicating that the federal government firmly believed such an interest could survive even the strictest judicial scrutiny.[47] *All the justices agreed that this interest existed and that it was compelling*; their opinions are replete with copious examples of the bravery, heroism, and courage of Medal of Honor recipients throughout American history. For the Kennedy-led plurality, however, the constitutional flaw of the Stolen Valor Act was its failure to satisfy the other prong of the First Amendment strict scrutiny test—that a regulation be the "'least restrictive means among available, effective alternatives.'"[48]

In their merits briefs, the lawyers for respondent Alvarez contended that even if a compelling interest existed, the Stolen Valor Act could not survive strict judicial scrutiny because "the government has at its disposal *numerous* less-restrictive alternatives" for achieving the goal of protecting the integrity of the nation's military honors. The brief outlined five main possible alternatives for the federal government, alternatives that fell into two main categories: (1) "public accessibility" and (2) "legislative redrafting." The brief laid out three public accessibility options. First, the government could bring a greater degree of efficiency and speed to the awarding of such honors. Second, it could undertake publicly to "name and shame" individuals, such as Alvarez, who falsely claimed to be recipients. Third, it could engage in civic educational initiatives designed to emphasize the importance and value of the honors.[49] The government, in its merits brief, rejected these options. "Relying on the public to discover and refute false claims," the government contended, did not constitute an *effective* means of "address[ing] the aggregate harmful effects of false claims" because:

> There is no publicly accessible database of medal recipients nor, often, any reason to think that an individual's claim to have received a medal would be subject to skeptical scrutiny by the public. Moreover, public refutation is necessarily an inadequate solution because some military records have been lost, rendering some claims unverifiable.[50]

To support this argument, the government pointed to a series of investigations conducted in 2008 by Congress and the Department of Defense, which "concluded that such a database would be impracticable and insufficiently comprehensive." For reasons very similar to those laid out in the respondent's brief, Kennedy dismissed this argument out of hand, dispensing with it in one sentence: "Without more explanation, it is difficult to assess the Government's claim, especially when at least one database of Congressional Medal of Honor winners already exists."[51]

The two other possible alternatives—legislative drafting options—offered in the respondent's brief were: (1) the government could seek to strengthen the punishment of those for whom the false claims were bound up with fraudulent activities and (2) the law could be rewritten to target only those who made the false claims in an effort to secure items of "pecuniary value."[52] The Court's holding in *Alvarez* makes it very clear that this would have been a very different case had Alvarez benefited in this manner; and a majority of the Court agreed that a law rewritten to address those who received material gain in response to making these false claims represented a strong, less-speech-restrictive alternative. As Justice Stephen Breyer noted in his concurrence, it was "the statute *as written*" that posed "risks [of] significant First Amendment harm." Congress has since accepted this invitation to initiate legislative action.[53]

Kennedy's decision to subject the Stolen Valor Act to strict scrutiny review is a potentially significant element of the *Alvarez* legacy because of the justice's deep-seated hostility to the use of this test in First Amendment cases. He has a long-held belief that the test has only one legitimate home—the Court's equal protection jurisprudence.[54] The test, he argues, sanctions restrictions when they are accompanied by a "compelling interest." However, he has never achieved a majority of his colleagues' support for his desire to abandon strict scrutiny in content-based speech cases. Consequently, he has instead hewed to a position that he believes has far more support in the Court's precedents. Similarly, his use of the strict scrutiny test in *Alvarez* is not evidence of a change in his doctrinal position. Rather, as noted above, in *Alvarez* Kennedy did not write alone; he was instead composing an opinion *for the Court.* It is therefore striking that even with these opinion-writing constraints Kennedy opted for a strict scrutiny route that ultimately ensured a result of "extreme dissensus"—a plurality opinion. He seemed unconcerned with "guarding against . . . defecting justices" and sacrificing the votes of Justices Breyer and Elena Kagan—who did not join Kennedy's opinion, concurring only in the judgment.[55]

In a very succinct manner, Breyer distilled the entirety of his concurrence into the following four opening sentences:

> I agree with the plurality that the Stolen Valor Act of 2005 violates the First Amendment. *But I do not rest my conclusion upon a strict categorical analysis.* Rather, I base that conclusion upon the fact that the statute works First Amendment harm, *while the Government can achieve its legitimate objectives in less restrictive ways.*[56]

This "intermediate scrutiny" approach, he argued, found support in the Court's precedents, and involved administering a "proportionality" test. Kennedy has used separate opinions relentlessly to pursue his own crusade of ridding First Amendment law of the strict scrutiny test. By contrast, Breyer has repeatedly penned separate opinions calling for the adoption of a balancing approach, which in *Alvarez* he described as involving a judicial "determin[ation] whether the statute works speech-related harm that is out of proportion to its justifications." Breyer noted that while members of the Court have, over the years, given this approach many different names—"'intermediate scrutiny,'" "'proportionality' review," "an examination of 'fit'"—or sometimes no label at all, it has been *his* practice to describe the approach as "proportionality." On this occasion, however, he concluded that "the Court's term 'intermediate scrutiny' describes what I think we should do," which is to avoid knee-jerk reactionary use of either strict scrutiny review (resulting in "near-automatic condemnation") or rational basis evaluation (which generates "near-automatic approval") of the numerous laws that "adversely affect . . . constitutionally protected interests." When such laws do not merit review using either of these standards, concluded Breyer, and an alternate, intermediate standard is employed, the protection afforded by the First Amendment is accentuated rather than threatened.[57]

For reasons outlined in detail elsewhere, *Alvarez* was only the latest round in this battle between Kennedy and Breyer.[58] As Mark Tushnet demonstrates in Chapter 9 herein, this comes as no surprise because many of the elements of Breyer's pragmatic approach to the First Amendment are incompatible with the animating principles of libertarianism in Kennedy's free speech jurisprudence. However, it remains significant that in *Alvarez* Kennedy showed no desire to accommodate the differing perspective of his colleague. In not doing so, he also lost the vote of Justice Kagan. It is of course too early to tell whether Kagan's decision to join Breyer in *Alvarez* will eventually be viewed as a fact-driven anomaly or the beginning of a specific jurisprudential approach to the First Amendment. Nevertheless, reasons remain for viewing as significant her decision to align with Breyer, rather than Kennedy, in *Alvarez*.[59]

* * *

In order to review a recently ended Term of the Court, Chief Justice Rehnquist was fond of identifying a decision that had received insufficient media attention. Using the words from Thomas Gray's "Elegy Written in a Country Churchyard," Rehnquist called these cases "flowers which are born to blush unseen and waste their sweetness on the desert air."[60] If *Alvarez* is given the degree of scholarly attention it deserves, then it will blossom into what it arguably should be viewed as—the most doctrinally significant freedom of expression case decided during the first decade of the Roberts Court.

There are, however, at least two reasons why *Alvarez* is unlikely to command this level of scholarly attention—and both reasons come wrapped in the form of other Roberts Court decisions. First, the decision in *Alvarez* should have garnered a high amount of attention because it was announced on Thursday, June 28, 2012, the last day of the Court's October 2011 Term. However, it was not the *last* decision to be announced that morning, and on this particular occasion that fact was of considerable significance. The last decision came in *National Federation of Independent Business v. Sebelius* (upholding the Patient Protection and Affordable Care Act), a decision upon which the spotlight of the nation was focused.[61] The second reason why *Alvarez* might find it difficult to break into the spotlight is its potential to be overshadowed by *Citizens United*, another blockbuster decision.

Citizens United: "Putt[ing] the Brakes On" or Initiating "a Slide Down a Very Slippery and Very Dangerous Slope"?[62]

In November 2008, the Court granted certiorari in *Citizens United*, and it heard oral arguments four months later. A decision in the case was expected by the end of the Court's Term in June 2009. However, what the justices instead issued that month was an order that the case be reargued and that the parties submit briefs addressing whether it was necessary, in deciding the case, to overrule parts of *McConnell v. FEC* (2003) and/or the whole of *Austin v. Michigan Chamber of Commerce* (1990).[63] The final decision of the Court in *Citizens United* demonstrated that a five-justice majority did indeed believe that it was necessary to overrule those precedents. A part of *McConnell* and the entire decision in *Austin* fell as the Court held that it was unconstitutional for the 2002 Bipartisan Campaign Reform Act (BCRA) to place limits upon the use of corporate funds to finance independent "electioneering communications."

The decision to hear another round of oral arguments in *Citizens United* portended a sweeping ruling. As Adam Liptak observed in the *New York Times* the day after the order was issued, "[t]he court could have ruled in favor of Citizens United in relatively narrow ways. Its decision to set the case down for reargument suggests that it is considering a much broader ruling."[64] On Thursday, January 21, 2010, Chief Justice John Roberts announced that Kennedy would deliver the ruling in the case. Anyone familiar with Kennedy's jurisprudence could have had little doubt about the nature of the opinion that he had written for the Court. It is precisely the kind of far-reaching opinion that we have come to expect from Kennedy in such cases. Jan Crawford Greenburg observes that "[c]onservatives had long believed that landmark cases brought out the worst in Kennedy," and when their colleague "tries to write with sweep and scope, he reaches for grand phrases and philosophical musings—the . . . stuff that drives conservatives bananas."[65] But ideological bristling at the "musings" that flow from Kennedy's pen can just as easily come from his more moderate colleagues, as *Citizens United*—and, in particular, Stevens's long and bitter dissent in that case—demonstrated.

Austin v. Michigan Chamber of Commerce: "There Is No Such Thing as Too Much Speech"[66]

In order to understand the way in which Kennedy's *Citizens United* opinion fits into his free speech jurisprudence, it is necessary to revisit his strongly worded dissenting opinion in *Austin*. There does not appear ever to have been any doubt in his mind that Section 54(1) of the Michigan Campaign Finance Act—which prohibited corporations from spending their general treasury funds on campaign activities in support of, or in opposition to, candidates for state elections—was unconstitutional. What troubled Kennedy about the Michigan law (and the provision of the BCRA struck down in *Citizens United*) was its singling out of one form of political speech for restriction. In other words, the challenged provision of the Michigan law was susceptible to arguments that it was both overbroad and under-inclusive, and as such it represented an effort to express governmental preferences for certain types of speech. Yet that was not the worst of it for Kennedy (or for his fellow dissenters in *Austin*). In addition to being a content-based restriction, it regulated political speech, expression long considered deserving of the highest level of constitutional protection because it addresses "subjects central to the integrity of our democratic system."[67]

Kennedy's hostility to the Michigan law[68] was evident from the opening minutes of the oral argument on October 31, 1989. In his notes about that afternoon's proceedings, Justice Blackmun made no substantive comments about the arguments made in defense of the law by Louis J. Caruso, the Solicitor General of Michigan. But, as was customary for him to do, he used a green pencil to write down his own related impressions of the argument; on this occasion all Blackmun wrote was "ak" and "as."[69] There is little doubt that he was referring to the domination of the questioning of Caruso by Kennedy and Scalia. Every argument Caruso attempted to make was met with an extremely hostile reception from both justices.

Kennedy (and Scalia) concluded that the only "compelling interest" Solicitor General Caruso was identifying was the need to prevent "too much speech." This line of questioning began early on with an inquiry from an incredulous Scalia: "here the only evil, as I understand it, is that there will be too much speech on one side of the issue, funded by vast amounts of money. Is that right? We mistrust too much speech."[70] Caruso's responses focused on the threat that speech in the form of corporate campaign finance expenditures poses to the democratic process. But for Scalia and Kennedy these concerns fell on deaf ears. Kennedy relentlessly—in exchanges that lasted over five minutes—pushed the lawyer into a corner. He employed hypotheticals that suggested that upholding the Michigan law would have dire First Amendment consequences for corporate speech far beyond the realm of campaign finance. "We are talking about a matter of principle," he observed. "And we are asking you to tell us what evil is in the speech that nonprofit corporations present in election campaigns." This was really a rhetorical inquiry because Kennedy's default position was that there was no "evil that has to be corrected"—that there was no compelling interest underpinning the Michigan law. When the decision in *Austin* was announced on March 27, 1990, there was nothing surprising about the dissenting opinions issued by Scalia and Kennedy. They simply restated what they had said during oral argument—the Michigan law sought to prevent "too much speech." This was, Kennedy declared, a dark day for the First Amendment as the Court "sanctioned" its "most severe restriction on political speech ever."[71]

Six months later, at a Constitution Day dinner at the Waldorf-Astoria Hotel in New York City, Kennedy delivered the inaugural Gauer Distinguished Lecture in Law and Public Policy at an event organized by the conservative National Legal Center for the Public Interest (NLCPI). Much of the lecture was little more than a fluffy, albeit "heartfelt exegesis on the framers of the Constitution" in which Kennedy emphasized the importance of maintaining the boundaries between the private and public spheres of Americans' lives. However, one aspect of the speech does provide a valuable insight into Kennedy's jurisprudential views and remains an underappreciated part of his extra-judicial writings.[72] The "private sphere"—which Kennedy labeled "[t]he great sphere of freedom of action"—was not "marked off by the Framers" simply to secure "the right of the individual to be left alone, isolated. It necessarily implied that progress as a nation and our contribution to civilization as a whole must be measured in large part by the activities undertaken in the private realm." In facilitating that progress, he continued, "the Court acts as a referee when the powers of the government brush up against the private sphere in an impermissible manner." In that respect, he said, *Austin* was a clear example of the Court shirking from its constitutional duty. The decision struck at the freedom "to promote beliefs and ideas, beliefs and ideas that may be contrary to the government agenda, in support of it, or not on the government agenda at all"—this was "one of the most vital rights in the whole private realm." To view this freedom as individualized was "understandable," and what the First Amendment protected was of course, above all else, an individualized freedom. However, "it is naïve," Kennedy emphasized,

> to think that an individual alone and in sole reliance on his own resources can counterbalance the power of great modern states. If there is to be real opportunity for autonomy and individual expression, it often must be within the context of groups or institutions, not through individual actions, however courageous. Groups and institutions in the private realm must have a real part in shaping society or they will be seen as irrelevant, as indistinguishable from the allurements of the state, a state always ready to co-opt private initiatives and talents for its own perpetuation.[73]

The notes from the conference at which the justices discussed and voted on *Austin* in November 1989 demonstrate that this is entirely consistent with the view that Kennedy has long held. As he remarked to his colleagues gathered in the room with him, his thoughts about the case were shaped by the fact that "corporations are at the center of our national life."[74]

Kennedy's opinion for the Court in *Citizens United* is very simply a restating of this observation. And to Kennedy it is nothing more complex than a statement about reality. There is nothing to suggest that in this observation Kennedy was either lamenting or celebrating the prevalence of corporations in America. So it would be wrong to say that Kennedy's opinions in campaign finance cases evince a First Amendment "absolutist" and "uncompromising" attitude toward campaign finance restrictions. As Steven B. Lichtman demonstrates in the next chapter, those adjectives instead are better used to describe this aspect of Justice Clarence Thomas's free speech jurisprudence.

CONCLUSION

Justice Kennedy did not invoke *Marbury v. Madison* (1803) in *Alvarez*, but in his mind a powerful and expansive interpretation of that Court's statement about the "province and duty of the judicial department to say what the law is" was just as relevant as it had been on earlier occasions, as in *Texas v. Johnson*, *Simon & Schuster v. Crime Victims Board*, and *Citizens United*. All of these First Amendment cases involved governmental efforts to impose content-based restrictions upon expressive freedom. These are efforts that Kennedy has often argued should be subjected to something even stronger than strict judicial scrutiny—perhaps "super-duper" strict scrutiny?[75] Why? The answer is, to Kennedy, beautifully simple. The government should be given very little power to impose such Orwellian limits upon the speech of its citizens—"speech is the beginning of thought," and "governments *are* most dangerous when they try to tell people what to think."[76]

NOTES

1. Robert Reinhold, "Restrained Pragmatist Anthony M. Kennedy," *New York Times*, November 12, 1987, A1. This chapter incorporates a section of Helen J. Knowles, *The Tie Goes to Freedom: Justice Anthony M. Kennedy on Liberty* (Lanham, MD: Rowman & Littlefield, 2009), Chapter 2. Permission to reprint this material has been granted by Rowman & Littlefield. It also incorporates material from Helen J. Knowles, "What a Difference Five Years Haven't Made: Justice Kennedy and the First Amendment, 2007–2012," *University of Missouri-Kansas City Law Review* 82 (2013): 479. Permission to reprint that material has been granted by the UMKC Law Review.
2. Academy of Achievement. "Anthony Kennedy Biography—Academy of Achievement." September 23, 2010. http://www.achievement.org/autodoc/page/ken0int-1
3. Jeffrey Rosen, "Supreme Leader: The Arrogance of Justice Anthony Kennedy," *The New Republic* 236(18) (June 2007).
4. Reinhold, "Restrained Pragmatist."
5. Dahlia Lithwick, "Why Justice Kennedy Is Just Like America," June 13, 2012, http://www.slate.com/articles/news_and_politics/jurisprudence/2012/06/justice_anthony_kennedy_holds_the_deciding_vote_on_many_of_the_supreme_court_s_most_significant_cases_.html
6. Rosen, "Supreme Leader," 16; Lithwick, "Why Justice Kennedy Is Just Like America."
7. Jeffrey Toobin, *The Oath: The Obama White House and the Supreme Court* (New York: Doubleday, 2012), 183.
8. Knowles, *The Tie Goes to Freedom*, Chapter 2.
9. *Simon & Schuster v. Crime Victims Board*, 502 U.S. 105, 127 (1991) (Kennedy, J., concurring in the judgment).
10. *Texas v. Johnson*, 491 U.S. 397, 420 (1989) (Kennedy, J., concurring).
11. Texas Penal Code Ann. 42.09 (1989), quoted at 491 U.S. at 400, footnote no.1.

12. *Johnson* is, therefore, an excellent example of the characteristic, discussed by myself and Steven Lichtman in our joint introduction to this volume, of many First Amendment free speech decisions—namely the fact that they do not fit neatly into "conservative" or "liberal" boxes.
13. 491 U.S. at 404, quoting *Spence v. Washington*, 418 U.S. 405, 410–411 (1974).
14. *United States v. O'Brien*, 391 U.S. 367 (1968). Douglas Edlin discusses *O'Brien* in his exploration of Justice Harlan's jurisprudence in Chapter 4 herein.
15. Title 50, App. United States Code, Section 462(b), quoted at 391 U.S. at 370.
16. 391 U.S. at 377.
17. 491 U.S. at 410, 414.
18. 491 U.S. at 429 (Rehnquist, C.J., joined by White and O'Connor, JJ., dissenting).
19. 491 U.S. at 420 (Kennedy, J., concurring).
20. Jeffrey Rosen, "The Agonizer," *The New Yorker* 72 (1996): 82; 491 U.S. at 420–421 (Kennedy, J., concurring).
21. 491 U.S. at 421 (Kennedy, J., concurring).
22. *Texas v. Johnson*, Justice Kennedy concurrence, first and final drafts, Box 533, Harry A. Blackmun Papers [hereafter HAB-LOC] (first draft); Box 478, Thurgood Marshall Papers, (final draft); both at the Manuscript Division, Library of Congress, Washington, DC.
23. Richard C. Reuben, "Man in the Middle: Justice Anthony Kennedy," *California Lawyer* 12 (October 1992): 38.
24. 502 U.S. 105 (1991).
25. Ibid., 118.
26. Ibid., 121 (italics added).
27. 502 U.S. at 123 (Blackmun, J., concurring in the judgment).
28. 502 U.S. 105, 128 (Kennedy, J., concurring in the judgment).
29. Memo from Jeff Meyer to Justice Blackmun, December 1, 1991; First draft of Kennedy's concurrence in the judgment in *Simon & Schuster*, December 5, 1991; Box 589, HAB-LOC.
30. 502 U.S. at 124 (Kennedy, J., concurring in the judgment).
31. Ibid., 124–125 (italics added). On Kennedy's views on the origins of the test, see Knowles, *The Tie Goes to Freedom*, 69.
32. 502 U.S. at 127 (Kennedy, J., concurring in the judgment).
33. *Brandenburg v. Ohio*, 395 U.S. 444 (1969).
34. *Chaplinsky v. New Hampshire*, 315 U.S. 568 (1942).
35. *United States v. Alvarez*, 132 S. Ct. 2537, 2544 (2012).
36. 502 U.S. at 127 (Kennedy, J., concurring in the judgment).
37. 132 S. Ct. at 2544.
38. Ibid., 2542.
39. Beverly Blair Cook, "Justice Brennan and the Institutionalization of Dissent Assignment" (unpublished manuscript, 1995), 19, footnote no. 85.

40. *Stolen Valor Act of 2005.* Public Law 109-437, § 704(b), *United States Code* 18 (2005).
41. 132 S. Ct. at 2542; quoting from 617 F.3d 1198, 1201–1202 (CA9 2010).
42. 132 S. Ct. at 2545, 2547 (italics added).
43. Ibid., 2547; *Alvarez* oral argument transcript, 2012 U.S. Trans. LEXIS 13, 25–26 (comments of counsel Jonathan D. Libby); 132 S. Ct. at 2542.
44. 132 S. Ct. at 2550.
45. *Whitney v. California*, 274 U.S. 357, 377 (1927) (Brandeis, J., concurring); *Abrams v. United States*, 250 U.S. 616, 630 (1919) (Holmes, J., dissenting); both quoted at 132 S. Ct. at 2550.
46. 132 S. Ct. at 2551.
47. *United States v. Alvarez*, 2011 U.S. Briefs 210, 14 (2011) (United States *Alvarez* brief); *Alvarez* transcript, 1–2.
48. 132 S. Ct. at 2548–2549; 132 S. Ct. at 2555 (Breyer, J., joined by Kagan, J., concurring in the judgment); 132 S. Ct. at 2565 (Alito, J., joined by Scalia and Thomas, JJ., dissenting); 132 S. Ct. at 2551 (quoting from *Ashcroft v. American Civil Liberties Union*, 542 U.S. 656, 666 (2004)).
49. *United States v. Alvarez*, 2011 U.S. Briefs 210, 22–23 (2012) (Respondent brief; italics added).
50. Ibid., 50.
51. Ibid., 55; 132 S. Ct. at 2551.
52. Respondent *Alvarez* brief, 22–23.
53. 132 S. Ct. at 2555 (Breyer, J., joined by Kagan, J., concurring in the judgment); Associated Press, "House votes for revised Stolen Valor Act," September 14, 2012, http://www.firstamendmentcenter.org/house-votes-for-revised-stolen-valor-act
54. Knowles, *The Tie Goes to Freedom*, Chapter 2.
55. Pamela C. Corley, Udi Sommer, Amy Steigerwalt, and Artemus Ward, "Extreme Dissensus: Explaining Plurality Decisions on the United States Supreme Court," *Justice System Journal* 31(2) (2010): 6.
56. 132 S. Ct. at 2551 (Breyer, J., joined by Kagan, J., concurring in the judgment) (italics added).
57. Ibid., 2551–2552.
58. Knowles, "What a Difference Five Years Haven't Made," 479.
59. Additional observations about what scholars might expect from Justice Kagan's free speech jurisprudence are made in the conclusion to this volume.
60. Quoted in Richard W. Garnett, "William H. Rehnquist: A Life Lived Greatly, and Well," *Yale Law Journal* 115 (2006): 1849.
61. *National Federation of Independent Business v. Sebelius*, 132 S. Ct. 2566 (2012).
62. David N. Bossie, "'Congress shall make no law. . .': There's nothing hard to understand about that," *Washington Times*, January 22, 2010, B1.
63. *Citizens United v. Federal Election Commission*, 555 U.S. 1028 (2008); *Citizens United v. Federal Election Commission*, 557 U.S. 932 (2009).

The reargument of Supreme Court cases is quite a rare occurrence and, as scholars have shown, such decisions are most often prompted by the justices seeking to "use reargument in order to resolve uncertainty about how they should act in light of the actions of their colleagues." Valerie Hoekstra and Timothy Johnson, "Delaying Justice: The Supreme Court's Decision to Hear Rearguments," *Political Research Quarterly* 56 (September 2003): 357. However, it is widely acknowledged that in *Citizens United* the decision to set the case over for reargument was a deliberate move, by the more conservative members of the Court, to transform the case into a vehicle with which to reduce campaign finance restrictions significantly. Toobin, *The Oath*, 180–181.

64. Adam Liptak, "Case Could Overhaul Rules on Campaign Spending," *New York Times*, June 30, 2009, A12.
65. Jan Crawford Greenburg, *Supreme Conflict: The Inside Story of the Struggle for Control of the United States Supreme Court* (New York: Penguin, 2007), 82, 176.
66. *Austin v. Michigan Chamber of Commerce*, 494 U.S. 652, 695 (Scalia, J., dissenting).
67. 494 U.S. at 696 (Kennedy, J., joined by O'Connor and Scalia, JJ., dissenting).
68. This was one of the many enacted by the states on the heels of the Federal Election Campaign Act of 1971 (FECA), a federal law which, among other things, prompted the litigation that culminated in the Supreme Court's decision in *Buckley v. Valeo*, 424 U.S. 1 (1976) (FECA's relationship to subsequent campaign finance cases is discussed, in part, by Steven Lichtman in the next chapter).
69. Justice Blackmun's *Austin* oral argument notes, Box 549, Folder 6, HAB-LOC.
70. *Austin* oral argument transcript, 1989 U.S. Trans. LEXIS 109, 11.
71. Ibid., at 15, 6; 494 U.S. at 713 (Kennedy, J., joined by O'Connor and Scalia, JJ., dissenting).
72. David Margolick, "Law: At the Bar; When the Public Interest Becomes the Interest of the Corporate World," *New York Times*, September 21, 1990, B7.
73. Anthony M. Kennedy, *The Constitution and the Spirit of Freedom*, The Gauer Distinguished Lecture in Law and Public Policy, Vol. 1 (Washington, DC: National Legal Center for the Public Interest, 1990), 17–19.
74. *Austin* conference notes, November 3, 1989, Box 549, Folder 6, HAB-LOC. This is based upon my best efforts to decipher Justice Blackmun's notes. It is also possible, although less likely, that the notes read that, "corporations are at the center of our natural life."
75. *Marbury v. Madison*, 5 U.S. 137, 176 (1803); "super-duper" is a reference to Senator Arlen Specter's description of *Roe v. Wade* during the Supreme Court nomination hearings of John Roberts. Adam Liptak, "Roberts Drops Hints in 'Precedent' Remarks," *New York Times*, September 18, 2005, A30.
76. *Ashcroft v. Free Speech Coalition*, 535 U.S. 234, 253 (2002) (italics added).

CHAPTER 8

Black Like Me: The Free Speech Jurisprudence of Clarence Thomas

Steven B. Lichtman

Since his arrival on the Supreme Court in 1991, Clarence Thomas has emerged as a distinctive and interesting voice on free expression.[1] While his First Amendment principles often dovetail with those of his fellow conservative Antonin Scalia, Thomas's approach to freedom of speech is not an exact match with Scalia's, nor is it an exact match with any of his other colleagues on the Court. In the modern era, Thomas has advanced an uncommon, perhaps idiosyncratic, vision.

Indeed, we must go back in time to find a true analogue to Clarence Thomas on free expression. The singular characteristic of Thomas's free speech jurisprudence—at least until recently—has been a mostly uncompromising absolutism on the meaning of the First Amendment and how little leeway it affords government to finesse its protections, even at the margins. Where his contemporaries on the Court fashion compromises or tolerate corner-cutting on free speech, Thomas disposes of artificial distinctions that strike him as intellectually bankrupt ways to sneak governmental regulation of speech in through a side door.

In that respect, Clarence Thomas's analogue is Hugo Black. Both can be described as boisterous advocates of an absolutist vision of a First Amendment that proscribes any governmental attempt to place restrictions on speech, no matter how incremental or allegedly necessary those restrictions might be. As Black did a generation earlier, Thomas revels in his status as a stubborn and even iconoclastic free speech dogmatist. In addition, just as Black at the end of his career suddenly moved away from this posture in a manner that confounded his colleagues,[2] after fifteen years on the Court Thomas seemed to shift direction and has increasingly stood in favor of restrictions on speech rather than against them.

Nomination: Doubting Thomas

Like Hugo Black a half century earlier, Clarence Thomas had to navigate a controversial path to his seat on the Supreme Court. Born in rural Georgia in 1948, Thomas did his undergraduate work at the College of the Holy Cross and received his law degree from Yale Law School. The early part of his legal career was spent in Missouri, in both the public sector and private practice, where he caught the eye of Missouri Senator John Danforth, who brought him to Washington as a legislative aide in the late 1970s. Taking advantage of his new contacts in the national's capital, in 1982 Thomas was appointed by President Ronald Reagan to be chairman of the Equal Employment Opportunity Commission (EEOC). He held that position until 1990, when President George H. W. Bush nominated him to a vacancy on the US Court of Appeals for the District of Columbia Circuit.

The following year, one week after his forty-third birthday, Thomas was nominated to fill the US Supreme Court seat vacated by the retiring Thurgood Marshall. Although President Bush insisted Thomas was the most-qualified person for the job, detractors pointed out that Thomas had only just over a year of experience as a judge. An implacable critic of affirmative action, Thomas was also subjected to speculation that he was selected only because he was African American.

As his confirmation hearing seemingly wound toward its conclusion, University of Oklahoma law professor Anita Hill emerged with the explosive accusation that Thomas had sexually harassed her while she was working for him at the EEOC. The hearing degenerated into a morass of acrimony. Hill was aggressively—and, some felt, contemptuously—questioned by several male senators, which led to a tense national debate on sexual harassment. Thomas, in an angry closing statement, denounced his treatment as a "high-tech lynching." Ultimately, Thomas was confirmed by a narrow 52-48 margin, one of the smallest in history.

CLARENCE THOMAS'S FREE SPEECH PHILOSOPHY

In certain ways, Hugo Black and Clarence Thomas arrived at their absolutist destinations by traveling very different roads. Where Black's emphasis on the original understandings behind the First Amendment may have been "underdeveloped,"[3] Thomas's perspective on these understandings is the fulcrum of his free speech jurisprudence. Thomas has undertaken expansive efforts to explore the intentions of the Framers and to work his conclusions about their intentions into his jurisprudence. To the extent that Black did this, he did so in a casual and, at times, assumptive manner. For Thomas, divining the Framers' intentions is central to the interpretive enterprise.

Furthermore, while both men's legal philosophies can fairly be characterized as offshoots of their broader views on the role of government, they could hardly come from more divergent angles, especially in their worldview on the relationship between the state and the economy. Black, preternaturally suspicious of big business, was an ardent Senate champion of governmental efforts to spur economic recovery, to the point that, in the words of Roger Newman, one of his biographers, "Hugo Black was a New Dealer before there was a New Deal."[4] Thomas, by contrast, is preternaturally suspicious of governmental attempts to induce individuals to make sacrifices for the purported greater economic good. Indeed, Thomas's jurisprudence is representative of contemporary neoconservative hostility toward the regulatory state that Franklin Roosevelt established. As one scholar observes, Thomas's concurrence in *United States v. Lopez*[5] is a good example of "his true desire: launching a full-scale rebellion against the rulings of the New Deal era."[6] In this respect, Thomas is about as far removed from Hugo Black—the "New Dealer before the New Deal"—as someone could possibly be.

It is fair to describe Thomas as an acolyte of classic economic libertarianism.[7] As chair of the EEOC, Thomas convened regular showings of the 1949 film version of Ayn Rand's *The Fountainhead* for his staff,[8] a practice that he continues on the Court every year for his clerks.[9] F. A. Hayek is also a common inspiration. In a speech he gave several times in the mid- and late 1990s, Thomas followed up a reference to James Madison's *Federalist 10* declaration that government's main job is to protect "the diversity of faculties in men" with an immediate bow to Hayek for the idea that "the chief aim of freedom is to provide both the opportunity and the inducement to insure the maximum use of the knowledge that an individual can acquire."[10]

Linking Clarence Thomas's overall jurisprudence to Randian and Hayekian libertarian philosophy is a relatively easy matter, but it is much more difficult to situate Thomas's free speech jurisprudence along traditional theoretical continuums of First Amendment analysis. Thomas clearly shares little commonality with the view, most famously advanced by Thomas Emerson, that "the proper end of man is the realization of his character and potentialities as a human being," and thus, "freedom of expression is essential as a means of assuring individual self-fulfillment."[11] Emerson's perspective, which has been critiqued in some quarters as rationalizing self-indulgence with "an unseemly ring of hedonism,"[12] is far too disorderly and unencumbered by rules to resonate with Thomas.

Nor does Thomas appear to value the individual right to freedom of speech as a means of protecting nonmainstream ideas or individuals from being overrun by a stampeding majority. David Richards's "toleration model" depicts free speech as a control over not so much government, but rather over an inflamed democratic mob. Drawing heavily on John Hart Ely,[13] Richards argued that free speech safeguards "the democratic political process from the abusive censorship of political debate by the transient majority who has democratically achieved political power."[14] Thomas, however, does not speak much to the problem of tyranny of the majority.

If there is one traditional theory of free speech that can be detected in Thomas's jurisprudence, it is the work of Alexander Meiklejohn. This is an unsurprising observation considering that Meiklejohn titled a 1961 essay, "The First Amendment Is an Absolute."[15] But it is Meiklejohn's landmark 1948 work, *Free Speech and Its Relation to Self-Government*, which provides us with the clearest pathway into Clarence Thomas's thinking. Meiklejohn argued that free speech is necessary in a democracy because it is the people, and not the institutional elite, that retain the real decision-making power on public affairs. In order to make those decisions properly, the people need reliable information to guide their collective thought processes: "The welfare of the community requires that those who decide issues shall understand them, and this in turn requires that . . . all facts and interests relevant to the problem shall be fully and fairly presented."[16] Like Meiklejohn, Thomas sees free speech through a lens of purposiveness. It is not, as Emerson would posit, a good and an end in itself. Rather, free speech to Thomas and to Meiklejohn is designed to accomplish something: the facilitation of popular decision making.

The influence Meiklejohn's theory exerts on Thomas's free speech jurisprudence, however, has clear limits. Meiklejohn's instrumentalism was cabined by the boundaries of the democratic process. He saw free speech as merely a way for a democratic polity to acquire the information that it required in order to make its choices in political affairs.[17] Although Thomas similarly posits that free speech enables good decisions on public affairs, he does not limit his conception of public affairs to politics. As we shall see, Thomas considers individual decision making on private economic matters to be of equal import as individual decision making on public political issues. To Thomas, governmental interference with private economic decision making is unreservedly noxious—it pollutes the waters of freedom with unconscionable paternalism. At its core, Thomas's economic libertarianism is a proxy for general disdain of governmental regulation. Thomas may be a flaccid celebrant of markets, but he is an energetic critic of controls. To the extent that Thomas does embrace the free market, he does so only for its ability to nourish individual freedom and growth (as opposed to its ability to generate wealth and national progress). Private economic speech, to Thomas, clearly implicates the First Amendment; to Meiklejohn, this position would likely have been a nonstarter.

Perhaps it is best to say that where Meiklejohn's conception of free speech is yoked to participatory democracy, and where Emerson's conception is about self-actualization, and where Richards's conception is about safeguarded dissidence, Thomas's conception of free speech is simply a vindication of core libertarian principles: exalting individual autonomy, recognizing that human instincts for self-maximization can serve valid social ends, limiting governmental ability to interfere with self-maximization.[18] His free speech outlook has several influences, but no real model. By mixing this libertarian philosophy with an insistence on simplicity, Clarence Thomas is a true free speech original.

SELECTED CASES: MONEY AND SPEECH

In his first three-and-half-years on the Supreme Court, Clarence Thomas did not issue any kind of opinion on free speech. Then, on April 19, 1995, the Court published not one, but two Thomas-authored speech opinions: one an opinion of the Court and one a concurrence. Interestingly, the concurring opinion revealed more about Thomas's free speech philosophy than the main opinion did.[19]

The concurrence was attached to *McIntyre v. Ohio Elections Commission*,[20] in which the Court threw out a fine assessed to a protestor who was anonymously leafleting against a proposed school tax ballot initiative but doing so in violation of a state ban on leaflets that did not contain the name and address of the author or sponsoring organization.[21] Although he agreed with the result, Thomas refused to join the main opinion by Justice John Paul Stevens because he felt that Stevens had committed the cardinal sin of balancing in his First Amendment analysis. Stevens essentially weighed the public interest in knowing the identity of political speakers against the interest of a speaker in remaining anonymous if they so desired. For Thomas, the fact that Stevens had arrived at the correct result when balancing these interests was beside the point; the problem was Stevens had sought in the first place to make a finding "that anonymous speech has an expressive value both to the speaker and to society that outweighs public interest in disclosure,"[22] instead of recognizing that a speaker's right to be anonymous was absolute.

Thomas's critique of Stevens was subtle, but it pointed toward the stringent outlook that would come to dominate his future free speech work. That stringency, however, was curiously absent in the other Thomas speech opinion that was released that day: his opinion of the Court in a commercial speech case, ***Rubin v. Coors Brewing Company***.[23]

The Supreme Court's case law on commercial speech is notoriously erratic. In 1942 the Court had declared that advertising was not entitled to First Amendment protection.[24] Eventually the Court's hostility toward advertising receded, though it did not completely evaporate. Even as the Court haltingly afforded advertising some limited form of free speech protection in the 1970s and 1980s,[25] it continued to adhere to the view that advertising is not entitled to full constitutional shelter. In ***Rubin***, Thomas simply used this existing approach to invalidate a 1935 federal law prohibiting beer labels from disclosing alcohol content via a routine application of the existing approach.

The following year, however, Thomas dramatically shifted gears. In *44 Liquormart v. Rhode Island*,[26] the Court unanimously threw out a state law banning the advertisement of prices of alcoholic beverages. But as had been the case in *McIntyre*, Thomas refused to join Justice Stevens's main opinion and opted to submit a separate concurrence instead. Directly challenging the Court's longstanding assumption that commercial speech was not entitled to the full protections of the First Amendment, Thomas witheringly declared, "I do not see a philosophical or historical basis for asserting that 'commercial speech' is of 'lower value' than 'noncommercial' speech."[27] The Court had previously recognized that "'a particular consumer's interest in the free flow of commercial information' may be as keen, or keener than, his interest in 'the day's most urgent political debate.'"[28] In the intervening years, however, the Court had paid only lip service to that sentiment. Now Thomas urged that the Court should be more mindful of:

> the importance of free dissemination of information about commercial choices in a market economy; the antipaternalistic premises of the First Amendment; the impropriety of manipulating consumer choices or public opinion through the suppression of accurate "commercial" information; the near impossibility of severing "commercial" speech from speech necessary to democratic decisionmaking; and the dangers of permitting the government to do covertly what it might not have been able to muster the political support to do openly.[29]

In so doing, Thomas became the first (and to this point, still the only) justice explicitly to take the position that commercial advertising should receive the identical constitutional protections that political speech enjoys.

This position is a fusion of Meiklejohn and Hayek. Thomas believes advertising is constitutionally valuable in Meiklejohnian terms, as information that facilitates economic decision making by consumers. Concomitantly, he views governmental attempts to restrict advertising through a Hayekian lens, as invasions of individual decisional autonomy with potentially darker political overtones. Thomas's emphatic opinion in *44 Liquormart* marked the emergence of a truly libertarian perspective on not only commercial speech but on the First Amendment writ large. As one biographer observes, Thomas's concurrence "was one of the staunchest defenses of economic liberty in the Court's history, and an opinion that no doubt would have pleased Ayn Rand immensely."[30]

This libertarian perspective was also evident in a later commercial speech case. In *Lorillard Tobacco v. Reilly*,[31] the Court unanimously invalidated Massachusetts's regime of restrictions on the advertising of cigarettes. Although Thomas joined Justice Sandra Day O'Connor's main opinion, he also contributed a separate concurrence. In a stark contrast to O'Connor's technocratic approach, Thomas's concurrence reads like a clarion call reminding readers of the role free speech plays as a weapon against governmental overreaching:

> No legislature has ever sought to restrict speech about an activity it regarded as harmless and inoffensive. Calls for limits on expression always are made when the specter of some threatened harm is looming. The identity of the harm may vary. People will be inspired by totalitarian dogmas and subvert the Republic. They will be inflamed by racial demagoguery and

embrace hatred and bigotry. Or they will be enticed by cigarette advertisements and choose to smoke, risking disease. It is therefore no answer for the State to say that the makers of cigarettes are doing harm: perhaps they are. But in that respect they are no different from the purveyors of other harmful products, or the advocates of harmful ideas. When the State seeks to silence them, they are all entitled to the protection of the First Amendment.[32]

Advertising is not the only intersection of money and speech in which Clarence Thomas has blazed an uncompromising trail. Beginning with its 1976 decision in *Buckley v. Valeo*,[33] the Supreme Court has produced jurisprudence on the First Amendment dynamics of campaign finance reform that is marked by a struggle for coherence and internal comity. *Buckley* centered on the Court's distinction between candidates' expenditures and donors' financial contributions to candidates. Limits on candidates' spending were held to be constitutionally unacceptable, but since donors' contributions to candidates raised the specter of political corruption, the Court indicated that some limits on donations could be acceptable, even though those donations were a variant of political speech.

In his very first foray into campaign finance, the 1996 case *Colorado Republican Federal Campaign Committee v. Federal Election Commission* (also known as "*Colorado I*"), Thomas pronounced himself highly dissatisfied with the *Buckley* framework in general. Specifically, he argued that the distinction between contributions and expenditures was nonsensical and should be eliminated:

I believe that contribution limits infringe as directly and as seriously upon freedom of political expression and association as do expenditure limits. The protections of the First Amendment do not depend upon so fine a line as that between spending money to support a candidate or group and giving money to the candidate or group to spend for the same purpose. In principle, people and groups give money to candidates and other groups for the same reason that they spend money in support of those candidates and groups: because they share social, economic, and political beliefs and seek to have those beliefs affect governmental policy.[34]

Thomas also stated flatly that the entire premise of *Buckley*—that some regulations on political money were constitutionally acceptable—was deeply flawed: "Broad prophylactic bans on campaign expenditures and contributions are not designed with the precision required by the First Amendment because they sweep protected speech within their prohibitions."[35]

Similar to his path-breaking commercial speech gambit the previous year, Thomas now declared open war on the Court's campaign finance principles. *Buckley* had been beset by critics prior to Thomas, but those critics' objections were premised on the argument that the decision did not allow enough regulation. In *Colorado "1"* Thomas was the first justice to suggest that *Buckley* needed to go because it allowed *too much* regulation. Prior to this decision, even Scalia had been of the opinion that "*Buckley v. Valeo* should not be overruled, because it is entirely correct."[36] In *Colorado "1,"* however, Scalia signed onto Thomas's opinion.

Four years later, in *Nixon v. Shrink Missouri Government PAC*,[37] the Court upheld Missouri's low ceiling on campaign contributions, over the protest of candidates and donors who argued that the ceiling was so low that it impeded speech. Justice David Souter's 6-3 majority opinion was bookended by strident calls to overturn *Buckley* from both sides of the issue. In one concurrence, Justice Stevens disputed one of *Buckley*'s central premises by declaring that "money is property; it is not speech"; in another concurrence, Justice Stephen Breyer suggested that the time may have come to strike *Buckley* from the books and replace it with a structure that would tolerate more regulation of political money.[38]

The dissenters' fury at *Buckley* was wholly unrestrained. Justice Anthony Kennedy charged that, "*Buckley* has not worked," and declared, "I would overrule *Buckley* and then free Congress or state legislatures to attempt some new reform, if, based upon their own considered view of the First Amendment, it is possible to do so."[39] In his own dissent, Thomas was even more trenchant. He shared Kennedy's distaste for *Buckley* but did not see any need to give Congress or any state legislature a second bite at the apple:

> In the process of ratifying Missouri's sweeping repression of political speech, the Court today adopts the analytic fallacies of our flawed decision in *Buckley v. Valeo.* Unfortunately, the Court is not content to merely adhere to erroneous precedent. Under the guise of applying *Buckley*, the Court proceeds to weaken the already enfeebled constitutional protection that *Buckley* afforded campaign contributions. In the end, the Court employs a *sui generis* test to balance away First Amendment freedoms. Because the Court errs with each step it takes, I dissent. . . . *Buckley* was in error, and I would overrule it. I would subject campaign contribution limitations to strict scrutiny, under which Missouri's contribution limits are patently unconstitutional.[40]

Thomas's dissent was the broadest attack on the very notion of the constitutionality of campaign finance laws that had ever been produced by the Supreme Court. Unlike his opinion in *Colorado 1*, which was focused only on the fatuities of the contributions-expenditures distinction, Thomas's *Shrink Missouri* dissent was a thorough deconstruction of every major regulation-justifying principle that *Buckley* announced. And unlike Kennedy, whose critique left the door open for renewed attempts to constitutionally square the campaign finance circle, Thomas insisted that the entire enterprise was illegitimate and unsalvageable. Political money, to Thomas, should be constitutionally bulletproof.

Time did not moderate Thomas's blistering contempt for campaign finance regulation. In 2003, in *McConnell v. Federal Election Commission*, the Court upheld most of the new Bipartisan Campaign Reform Act of 2002 (BCRA).[41] Thomas stood alone in concluding that the BCRA rules requiring candidates to disclose the size and source of donations violated core free speech principles. Expanding on his *McIntyre* arguments, he saw forced disclosure as a threat to the right of individuals to express themselves anonymously, acidly declaring that "the Court today upholds what can only be described as the most significant abridgment of the freedoms of speech and association since the Civil War."[42]

Thomas reinforced that point in his separate concurrence in *Citizens United v. Federal Election Commission* in 2010.[43] Less than a decade after *McConnell*, a new iteration of the Court—now missing one of *McConnell*'s joint authors, the retired Sandra Day O'Connor—reduced that precedent, and BCRA, to ashes. One of the few provisions of BCRA that survived Kennedy's majority opinion was its disclosure requirements, but Thomas again objected to such rules. Seizing on anecdotal evidence that disclosure provisions had led to retaliation against donors, Thomas declared that "I cannot endorse a view of the First Amendment that subjects citizens of this Nation to death threats, ruined careers, damaged or defaced property, or preemptive and threatening warning letters as the price for engaging in core political speech."[44]

The intersection of money and speech makes application of the First Amendment significantly more complicated. This observation is not only borne out by simple logic but it is also manifested in the meandering Supreme Court case law on commercial speech and campaign finance. Yet amidst this jurisprudential incoherence, the work of Clarence Thomas stands out for its uncluttered lucidity.

Selected Cases: Obscenity and the Media

As disjointed as the Supreme Court's work on commercial speech and campaign finance has been, those lines of cases appear holistically consistent when compared to the Court's work on obscenity. Perhaps more than any other set of cases, the Court's obscenity jurisprudence has been pockmarked by confusion, false starts, and course corrections. If any set of cases would test a justice committed to consistency and simplicity, it would be this one.

It should be noted that Clarence Thomas took his seat on the Court well after the major internecine battles on obscenity had been fought (the end result of those battles, one could argue, is that all of the justices lost). By the early 1990s, the Court seemed to have retired the issue; unable to develop an enduring and persuasive definition of exactly what constituted obscenity, the justices simply quit the field. In the ensuing years, whenever the Court dared to take up the topic of obscenity, it did not confront obscenity on its face but rather as a component in a hybrid situation, such as the extent of the Federal Communications Commission's regulatory authority or the way obscene material can be disseminated using new communicative technologies.

Although Thomas approached these cases with his customary procedural preference for simplicity and consistency, it is here that we can see some minor substantive wobbles in his early and mid-career speech jurisprudence. While most of his output in obscenity cases is of a piece with his overall constitutional libertarianism, there are moments when Thomas's desire for simplicity induced him to accept at least the concept of paternalistic regulation.

Thomas's first obscenity opinion arrived in 1996's *Denver Area Education Television Consortium v. Federal Communications Commission*, in which the Court invalidated the Helms Amendment, a federal law that permitted cable operators to ban "indecent" material from public access channels and required that such material be scrambled if it was made available.[45] As Thomas framed the case in his separate opinion, the core question was not whether indecent material could be restricted, but rather "how and to what extent the First Amendment protects cable operators, programmers, and viewers from state and federal regulation."[46] The main threat to individual rights was not the Helms Amendment; instead, the main threat was the other laws that the government could promulgate in the absence of the Helms Amendment. Without this law, Thomas surmised, government could essentially force cable operators—private businesses—to offer speech to which they objected.

In the past, this possibility would have been accepted as unremarkable. Government has the ability to compel certain speech by television stations—it can require public affairs programming as a condition of a broadcast license. This power is rooted in the assumed need for governmental regulation of broadcast airwaves. Unlike the limitless universe of print, broadcast media exist within a finite spectrum of frequencies, making regulation unavoidable.

Ever the simplifier, Thomas questioned the validity of this assumption. Just as he refused to tolerate the false dichotomies of contributions and expenditures, or commercial and noncommercial speech, Thomas did not see any constitutional value in dividing media into print and broadcast spheres. Instead, he argued that all media should be treated identically and be heavily protected from governmental interference. Critical of the Court's approach, Thomas tersely observed that "[t]he text of the First Amendment makes no distinctions among print, broadcast, and cable media, but we have done so."[47] The unique features of cable television should not be a predicate for government meddling, and to Thomas, the Helms Amendment (even though it was, technically, government action itself) was designed to keep government out of the media's business.

Thomas remained attuned to how technological advances can be deployed as a predicate for alteration of the meaning and scope of the First Amendment, in 2002, in *Ashcroft v. American Civil Liberties Union*.[48] Involving another Congressional attempt to regulate the flow of indecent material over the Internet, the case questioned the constitutionality of an injunction on the enforcement of the Child Online Protection Act (COPA) of 1998. As in *Denver AETC*, Thomas took a nuanced approach to the subject, appearing to tolerate, at least in spirit, some form of regulation of objectionable material while simultaneously fitting this regulatory indulgence into his overall philosophy on speech.

The ACLU's primary objection to the law was its use of the customary "community standards" approach to determining obscenity.[49] That approach might work when the material is a magazine on a newsstand physically located in a town, but the Internet, the ACLU maintained, changes the calculus, because material available on the web is available to anyone with a connected computer. Adhering by rote to the "community standards" approach could mean that a community that is maniacally disturbed by any sexually explicit material (including material on safe sex) could claim that having that material available on any Internet-connected computer in its homes violated its standard. Because one community could effectively impose its standards on the entire country, the ACLU maintained that COPA's reliance on community standards rendered it facially invalid.

Writing for a plurality of the Court, Thomas saw the ACLU's argument as yet another attempt to invoke the allegedly unique vicissitudes of a communicative medium as a justification for changing the established rules of the game. Rejecting the ACLU's argument that new technology must mean new rules, Thomas held that the "community standards" approach to obscenity would stand. Once again opting for simplicity, Thomas declared that there was nothing so distinctive about the Internet that required treating it differently under the First Amendment than other communicative media.[50]

THOMAS AGONISTES: THE END OF ABSOLUTISM?

Their philosophical differences on economic matters notwithstanding, Hugo Black and Clarence Thomas share an absolutist vision of the First Amendment. Each of them insisted that the authors of the First Amendment intended for it to be a breathtakingly broad provision, based on their immediate history with a British crown eager to silence dissent from an ocean away. Each of them refused to tolerate internal tinkering with the rules of free speech, disdaining "'ifs,' 'buts,' or 'whereases,'"[51] or any artificial tests designed to legitimate governmental intrusion into matters of conscience, or any suggestion that the right to free speech could be bargained away in exigent times.

And each of them, late in their Supreme Court tenures, suddenly abandoned absolutism.

Hugo Black's reversal-of-field came in a pair of cases in 1969. In *Street v. New York*, Black dissented from the invalidation of a conviction of a protestor who had burned an American flag, insisting that flag burning was simply not protected by the First Amendment.[52] Two months earlier, Black had also dissented from the invalidation of a suspension of two students who had worn armbands to school in protest of the war in Vietnam, in *Tinker v. Des Moines Independent Community School District*. Writing for a 7-2 Court, Justice Abe Fortas underscored the decision in a famous remark, "it can hardly be argued that either students or teachers shed their constitutional rights to freedom of speech or expression at the schoolhouse gate."[53] Black voiced his displeasure in portentous terms:

> One does not need to be a prophet or the son of a prophet to know that after the Court's holding today some students in Iowa schools and indeed in all schools will be ready, able, and willing to defy their teachers on practically all orders. This is the more unfortunate for the schools since groups of students all over the land are already running loose, conducting break-ins, sit-ins, lie-ins, and smash-ins.[54]

Hugo Black, insistent champion of the notion that the Free Speech Clause brooked no exceptions, cantankerously announcing a categorical limit on students' ability to invoke the First Amendment? His colleagues, to put it mildly, were stunned.[55]

Fortas's "schoolhouse gate" dictum has endured as a classic constitutional sound bite, but its value as governing law has ebbed over time. In the decades after *Tinker*, the Court backtracked markedly and allowed school administrators to censor school newspapers[56] and suspend students for off-color remarks at a school assembly.[57] This retrenchment reached its apex in 2007, and Clarence Thomas played a key role.

In *Morse v. Frederick*,[58] the Court considered the First Amendment challenge case of Joe Frederick, a high school student who had hoisted a banner reading "BONG HiTS 4 JESUS" as the Olympic torch relay traveled through Juneau, Alaska, on its way to the 2002 Salt Lake City Olympics. Upon seeing the banner, Principal Deborah Morse had demanded that Frederick take it down and then suspended him when he refused to do so. Morse insisted that because classes had been dismissed early so that students could see the torch go through town, the relay was a school-sponsored activity and thus the school maintained disciplinary authority over students. Characterizing Frederick's banner as advocacy of illegal drug use,[59] the Court upheld his suspension. Chief Justice John Roberts's 6-3 majority opinion focused on a school's legitimate power to restrict speech contrary to the school's mission that is offered during school activities.[60]

By exploring the outer boundaries of a school's administrative discipline—presumably, speech that did not contradict a school's mission was entitled to more constitutional protection—Roberts at least paid lip service to Fortas's *Tinker* idea that students do enjoy some degree of guaranteed civil liberties while in school. In comparison, Clarence Thomas's solo concurrence took another line entirely and professed that, "the standard set forth in *Tinker* . . . is without basis in the Constitution."[61]

Thomas undertook a detailed examination of the history of public education in the United States and concluded that at no point prior to *Tinker* were schoolchildren's rights ever deemed to trump the notion of *in loco parentis*, which assigned a virtual parenting function to school officials during school hours. Invoking Black's *Tinker* dissent, Thomas branded student speech as nothing more than casual defiance: "Frederick asserts a constitutional right to utter at a school event what is either gibberish, or an open call to use illegal drugs. To elevate such impertinence to the status of constitutional protection would be farcical, and would indeed be to 'surrender control of the American public school system to public school students.'"[62]

Black and Thomas's shared willingness to temper their visions of the First Amendment by declaring it inapplicable in schools is a microcosm of a larger commonality. Over time, both of them lurched away dramatically from their impassioned absolutist stances on free speech. In the case of Black, the shift occurred only in the final two years of a Supreme Court tenure that lasted for over three decades and was only evident in two cases. But in the case of Thomas, the shift has been more longstanding and more variegated.[63]

Indeed, the first sign of Thomas's shift came well before *Morse*. When the Court's 2003 decision in *Virginia v. Black* was first announced, Thomas's position in that case seemed to be nothing more than an incongruity that could be explained away on a personal level.[64] But as more time has passed, Thomas's stance must be seen as part of a distinct and identifiable trend in his First Amendment thinking.

On August 27, 1998, a Ku Klux Klan rally was held at a farmhouse in rural southern Virginia. The Klansmen were there at the invitation of the owner of the farmhouse (who participated in the rally), which was located in a clearing some 350 yards away from the nearest road. At the end of the rally, a 25-foot-tall cross was set on fire. While the rally was visible to onlookers off in the distance, it had occurred on private property. No African Americans, Catholics, Jews, or other traditional focuses of KKK enmity were at the scene, and accounts of the rally indicated that the cross burning was purely ceremonial, the traditional ending to a Klan gathering.

Under Virginia law, however, it was still illegal:

> It shall be unlawful for any person or persons, with the intent of intimidating any person or group of persons, to burn, or cause to be burned, a cross on the property of another, a highway or other public place. Any person who shall violate any provision of this section shall be guilty of a Class 6 felony. Any such burning of a cross shall be prima facie evidence of an intent to intimidate a person or group of persons.[65]

As a result, after a brief investigation the leader of the rally, Barry Black, was arrested, ultimately convicted, and fined $2,500.

Six years earlier, in *R.A.V. v. City of St. Paul*,[66] the Court had invalidated a St. Paul municipal hate speech ordinance on the grounds that it was impermissible viewpoint discrimination. In that case—in which a band of allegedly intoxicated teenagers burned a cross in the front yard of a neighborhood black family—Scalia drew a distinction between criminalizing cross burning because of antipathy for the racism inherent in the message (which the Constitution forbids) and criminalizing it because it was an act of intimidation and harassment (which the government may do).

Attempting to avoid the constitutional infirmity that doomed the poorly written St. Paul ordinance, Virginia included a "prima facie" clause that defined any cross burning as intimidation. However, in her opinion of the Court Sandra Day O'Connor made it clear that while Virginia was clearly empowered to ban intimidating cross burnings, it could not assume that every cross burning is an act of intimidation. "As the history of cross burning indicates," O'Connor wrote, "a burning cross is not always intended to intimidate. Rather, sometimes the cross burning is a statement of ideology, a symbol of group solidarity. It is a ritual used at Klan gatherings, and it is used to represent the Klan itself."[67] The Virginia law failed (and Barry Black's conviction was invalid) because it defined even ceremonial cross burnings as intimidation, even when there was no target present. Unlike in *R.A.V.*, in which a black family was singled out for a message of hate and fear that was planted on their front lawn, in *Virginia v. Black* no blacks (or any potential objects of the Klan's pathologies) were exposed to the cross burning. This was clearly a mere ceremony, and it was clearly expressive conduct. And for eight of the nine justices, it was clearly protected by the Free Speech Clause.

The ninth justice, alone in dissent, was Clarence Thomas.

To those who attended the oral argument in *Black*, Thomas's solo dissent was not unanticipated. Although Thomas famously prefers to be silent during oral arguments,[68] during the presentation of Deputy Solicitor General Michael Dreeben, arguing in favor of the Virginia law's constitutionality, the normally mute Thomas startled the courtroom by interjecting:

> I indicated, I think, in the Ohio case that the cross was not a religious symbol and that it has—it was intended to have a virulent effect. And I—I think that what you're attempting to do is to fit this into our jurisprudence rather than stating more clearly what the cross was intended to accomplish and, indeed, that it is unlike any symbol in our society . . . there was no communication of a particular message; it was intended to cause fear, and to terrorize a population.[69]

For a free speech absolutist such as Clarence Thomas, the decision in this case should have been obvious. As distasteful as Barry Black's behavior was, it was expressive. The cross burning was part of the initiation ceremony for a group with a central belief system (as noxious as those beliefs may be to most people). And unlike in *R.A.V.*, there was no hated "target" in the vicinity, nobody at whom the burning cross was directed.

Yet just as Hugo Black had insisted back in 1969 that flag burning was simply an exception to the First Amendment and its partial protection of symbolic speech, Thomas here argued that the Court should disregard the communicative dimension of cross burnings. State and local governments should be empowered to call it as they see it—intimidation, and nothing more:

> This statute prohibits only conduct, not expression. And, just as one cannot burn down someone's house to make a political point and then seek refuge in the First Amendment, those who hate cannot terrorize and intimidate to make their point. In light of my conclusion that the statute here addresses only conduct, there is no need to analyze it under any of our First Amendment tests.[70]

In effect, Thomas was making a provocatively counterintuitive argument. The action that Barry Black and his fellow Klansmen intended to be expressive—and certainly thought was expressive—was not expressive at all. Thomas further bent reality by depicting the ceremony as an attempt to terrorize. However, there was nobody present at whom the terror was aimed. Why did Thomas play so fast-and-loose with the facts? This was the only way he could get the result he preferred without undermining his general First Amendment philosophy. As long as he could say that a ceremonial cross burning is not expressive conduct, then he could tolerate laws which proscribe it; were he to concede that there is an expressive dimension to a ceremonial cross burning, then he could not tolerate regulation of it while being consistent with his view of free speech.

Thomas's remarks during oral argument in *Black* were not the only unusual element of the case. The emotional tone of Thomas's written opinion was likewise a departure from his accepted habits. A large portion of his opinion, like O'Connor's majority opinion, was devoted to an historical analysis of cross burning. But unlike O'Connor, who confined herself stylistically to the dry rhetoric of the professional researcher, Thomas's dissent coursed with personal testimony on the horrors of the burning cross and what it portended. Coming from a man with a well-known zeal for privacy and equally well-known disdain for infusing professional work with personal unburdenings,

Thomas's written opinion in *Virginia v. Black* was just as out of character as was his outburst during the oral argument. One astonished analyst went so far as to describe Thomas as "the Justice in *Black* whose view most closely resembles that of the critical race theorists."[71]

Were *Morse* and *Black* the only speech-restrictive blips in an otherwise uniform history of speech-protective decisions authored by Thomas, they could be explained away as mere curiosities. The latter case, in particular, could be seen as an outgrowth of Thomas's life experiences as an African-American man, experiences which induced him to depart from his normal techniques and perspectives in free speech cases.[72] Indeed, at the time *Morse* was decided in 2007, that is certainly how things appeared.

Since *Morse*, however, evidence has emerged that it was not an anomaly but rather a line of demarcation. *Morse* stands as the beginning of a new phase in Clarence Thomas's free speech jurisprudence, a signal that for some as-yet-unknown reason Thomas has shed his absolutist skin and adopted a new viewpoint on freedom of speech that is difficult to explain.

The contempt for student speech rights that Thomas expressed in *Morse* is of a piece with his dissent in 2011's *Brown v. Entertainment Merchants Association*.[73] In that case, Antonin Scalia—Thomas's usual running-mate—wrote for a 7-2 majority and ruled that a California law that banned the sale of violent video games to minors ran afoul of the First Amendment on the grounds that it was a content-based restriction on protected speech. Applying originalist analysis, Thomas argued in his dissent that, "'freedom of speech,' as originally understood, does not include a right to speak to minors (or a right of minors to access speech) without going through the minors' parents or guardians."[74]

If we are trying to ascribe some analytical consistency to the new Thomas jurisprudence on speech, *Brown* can be twinned with *Morse*. Both cases can be described as embodying a general notion that minors simply do not enjoy the benefits of First Amendment shelter. Though this is a miserly version of the core American principle of freedom of speech, it at least has the virtue of enabling a narrative that explains Thomas's new position on free speech.

But there is little value to establishing this narrative—it in turn cannot be squared with another recent case in which Thomas has veered away from his old self. Although Thomas did not write an opinion in *United States v. Alvarez*, he did sign onto Samuel Alito's dissent from the majority's judgment that the "Stolen Valor Act"—which made it a federal crime to lie about having received military decorations—was unconstitutional.[75] It is hard to contemplate Thomas countenancing such a direct restriction on speech earlier in his career. But by 2012 something in Thomas had clearly shifted. The absolutist of old, who seemed to be a modern-day embodiment of no-law-means-no-law resolve, has now been replaced by a justice who indulges multiple exceptions to the First Amendment: cross burnings, speech by children, fabrications about military honors. The old Clarence Thomas was an identifiable heir to Hugo Black's absolutist tradition; the new Clarence Thomas seems to have sacrificed that principle to a vague sense of situational ethics.

CONCLUSION

As Clarence Thomas approached the end of his first decade on the Supreme Court, the famed civil libertarian Nat Hentoff—who ordinarily would not be expected to have a high opinion of either Thomas or his jurisprudence—nevertheless acknowledged that Thomas's record on the First Amendment was emphatically speech-protective. "To the incremental surprise and perhaps discomfiture of some of his critics, Justice Clarence Thomas is growing harder to stereotype," Hentoff commented. "He has written as boldly and uncompromisingly in celebration of the First Amendment as did Justices William O. Douglas and William Brennan Jr. in days of yore."[76] For most of the next several years, Thomas would continue to blaze this speech-embracing trail, and he would do so by fusing Meiklejohnian instrumentalism about free expression's role in a democracy with Hayekian and Randian libertarian disdain for governmental paternalism.

But by the time Thomas completed his second decade on the Court, the picture had changed. As Ronald Collins puts it, the Thomas record on free speech must now be described as "mixed": "[I]n a few select categories of cases, Justice Thomas votes like an absolutist, though in a good number of other free speech categories he moves in quite the opposite direction."[77] The Supreme Court of the late twentieth century had few figures that were as strong a defender of freedom of speech as Clarence Thomas. His free speech jurisprudence was uncompromising, lucid, and straightforward. For some reason—a reason that Thomas has not explained himself, and a reason that is difficult to divine through scholarly analysis—that Clarence Thomas seems to have left the scene. Time will tell if he returns.

Notes

1. This chapter is an updated adaptation of Steven B. Lichtman, "Black Like Me: The Free Speech Jurisprudence of Clarence Thomas," *Penn State Law Review* 114 (2009): 415–468. Permission to reprint that material has been granted by Penn State Law Review.
2. Although as Kevin McMahon and Michael Paris point out earlier in this volume in Chapter 3, Black's "shift" might be overstated.
3. David L. Lange and H. Jefferson Powell, *No Law: Intellectual Property in the Image of an Absolute First Amendment* (Stanford, CA: Stanford Law Books, 2009), 259.
4. Roger K. Newman, *Hugo Black: A Biography* (New York: Pantheon Books, 1994), 157.
5. *United States v. Lopez*, 514 U.S. 549, 584–602 (1995) (Thomas, J., concurring). In *Lopez*, a 5-4 majority led by Chief Justice William Rehnquist invalidated the Gun-Free School Zones Act of 1990. Congress's power to regulate crime exists under the authority of the Commerce Clause, but in *Lopez* Rehnquist held that having a gun within 1000 feet of a school did not sufficiently impact interstate commerce so as to justify the regulation. In so doing, the Supreme Court limited Congress's power under the Commerce Clause for the first time since 1937 and began the decade-long "Rehnquist Revolution" on federalism.
6. Andrew Peyton Thomas, *Clarence Thomas: A Biography* (San Francisco, CA: Encounter Books, 2001), 505. See also, generally, Chapter 2 herein, by Samuel Olken, about the free speech jurisprudence of George Sutherland.
7. A reference to him as a political libertarian, however, would suffer from a massive internal contradiction; as Thomas himself has wondered aloud, "if I were a true libertarian I wouldn't be here in government." See Bill Kauffman, "Clarence Thomas," *Reason* (November 1987), http://reason.com/archives/1987/11/01/clarence-thomas/
8. See Kevin Merida and Michael A. Fletcher, *Supreme Discomfort: The Divided Soul of Clarence Thomas* (New York: Doubleday, 2007), 163.
9. Thomas, *Clarence Thomas*, 470.
10. See Clarence Thomas, "The James McClure Memorial Lecture in Law Delivered by the Honorable Clarence Thomas, October 19, 1995," *Mississippi Law Journal* 65 (1996): 465; Clarence Thomas, "Victims and Heroes in the Benevolent State," *Harvard Journal of Law and Public Policy* 19 (1996): 671–683; Clarence Thomas, "Personal Responsibility," *Regent University Law Review* 12 (2000): 319, citing Friedrich A. Hayek, *The Constitution of Liberty* (Chicago, IL: University of Chicago Press, 1960).
11. Thomas I. Emerson, *The System of Freedom of Expression* (New York: Random House, 1970), 6.
12. Rodney A. Smolla, *Free Speech in an Open Society* (New York: Alfred A. Knopf, 1992), 9.

13. See generally John Hart Ely, *Democracy and Distrust: A Theory of Judicial Review* (Cambridge, MA: Harvard University Press, 1980).
14. David A. J. Richards, "Free Speech as Toleration," in W. J. Waluchow, ed., *Free Expression: Essays in Law and Philosophy* (Oxford: Clarendon Press, 1994), 34.
15. Alexander Meiklejohn, "The First Amendment is an Absolute," *Supreme Court Review* 1961 (1961): 245–266.
16. Alexander Meiklejohn, *Free Speech and Its Relation to Self-Government* (New York: Harper, 1948), 23.
17. Notably, Meiklejohn's original formulation of free speech did not account for artistic speech, which he deemed a purely private matter that did not merit First Amendment concern. Later, in an article he published shortly before his ninetieth birthday, Meiklejohn expanded his theory, and suggested that "[l]iterature and the arts must be protected by the First Amendment," because like "education in all its phases" and "the achievements of philosophy and the sciences," knowledge of these subjects improves voters' "intelligence [and] sensitivity to human values," which in turn leads to better political judgments. Meiklejohn, "The First Amendment is an Absolute," 256–257.
18. Mark Graber has similarly characterized Thomas's free speech work as "libertarian." See Mark A. Graber, "Clarence Thomas and the Perils of Amateur History," in Earl M. Maltz, ed., *Rehnquist Justice: Understanding the Court Dynamic* (Lawrence, KS: University Press of Kansas, 2003), 80. And, as Helen Knowles demonstrates in the previous chapter, Justice Kennedy's free speech jurisprudence is also infused with core elements of libertarian thought.
19. For a fine study on concurring opinions, see Pamela C. Corley, *Concurring Opinion Writing on the U.S. Supreme Court* (Albany, NY: SUNY Press, 2010).
20. *McIntyre v. Ohio Elections Commission*, 514 U.S. 334 (1995).
21. In an eerie coincidence, the Court's emphatic defense of the free speech rights of an anonymous antigovernment protestor was released on the same day that Timothy McVeigh and Terry Nichols blew up the Alfred Murrah Federal Building in Oklahoma City.
22. 514 U.S. at 370 (1995) (Thomas, J., concurring).
23. *Rubin v. Coors Brewing Co.*, 514 U.S. 476 (1995).
24. *Valentine v. Chrestensen*, 316 U.S. 52 (1942).
25. See *Virginia Pharmacy Board v. Virginia Consumer Council*, 425 U.S. 748 (1976); *Central Hudson Gas & Electric Company v. Public Service Commission of New York*, 447 U.S. 557 (1980).
26. *44 Liquormart Inc. v. Rhode Island*, 517 U.S. 484 (1996).
27. 517 U.S. at 522 (Thomas, J., concurring in part, and concurring in the judgment in part).
28. Ibid., 518–519, quoting 425 U.S. at 763.
29. Ibid., 520.

30. Thomas, *Clarence Thomas*, 524.
31. *Lorillard Tobacco Co. v. Reilly*, 533 U.S. 525 (2001).
32. Ibid., 590 (Thomas, J., concurring in part, and concurring in the judgment).
33. *Buckley v. Valeo*, 424 U.S. 1 (1976).
34. *Colorado Republican Federal Campaign Committee v. Federal Election Commission*, 518 U.S. 604, 640 (1996) (Thomas, J., joined in part by Rehnquist, CJ., and Scalia, J., concurring in the judgment and dissenting in part). The case later returned to the Supreme Court: *Federal Election Commission v. Colorado Republican Federal Campaign Committee* ("*Colorado 2*"), 533 U.S. 431 (2001).
35. 518 U.S. at 642 (Thomas, J., joined in part by Rehnquist, CJ., and Scalia, J., concurring in the judgment and dissenting in part).
36. *Austin v. Michigan Chamber of Commerce*, 494 U.S. 652, 683 (1990) (Scalia, J., dissenting). For a discussion of the opinions in *Austin* by Scalia and Kennedy, see Chapter 7 herein by Helen Knowles on Kennedy's jurisprudence.
37. *Nixon v. Shrink Missouri Government PAC*, 528 U.S. 377 (2000).
38. 528 U.S. at 398 (Stevens, J., concurring); 528 U.S. at 399 (Breyer, J., joined by Ginsburg, J., concurring).
39. 528 U.S. at 408, 409–410 (Kennedy, J., dissenting).
40. 528 U.S. at 410 (Thomas, J., joined by Scalia, J., dissenting).
41. *McConnell v. Federal Election Commission*, 540 U.S. 93 (2003).
42. 540 U.S. at 264 (Thomas, J., concurring in part, concurring in the judgment in part, and dissenting in part).
43. *Citizens United v. Federal Election Commission*, 558 U.S. 310 (2010).
44. 558 U.S. at 982 (Thomas, J., concurring in part and dissenting in part).
45. *Denver Area Educational Telecommunications Consortium, Inc. v. Federal Communications Commission*, 518 U.S. 727 (1996).
46. 518 U.S. at 812 (Thomas, J., joined by Rehnquist, CJ., and Scalia, J., concurring in the judgment in part and dissenting in part).
47. Ibid.
48. *Ashcroft v. American Civil Liberties Union*, 535 U.S. 564 (2002).
49. That standard was announced in *Miller v. California*, 413 U.S. 15 (1973).
50. At the same time, though, Thomas left the injunction against COPA in place, and remanded for a determination as to whether the injunction was defensible on overbreadth grounds. After the lower court found that the law probably was fatally overbroad, that decision was appealed back to the Supreme Court, which upheld that conclusion in 2004 in an opinion written by Anthony Kennedy . . . and joined by Clarence Thomas. See *Ashcroft v. American Civil Liberties Union*, 542 U.S. 656 (2004). Following that decision, the inevitable trial on the merits was held. COPA was indeed found to be overbroad . . . that decision was appealed . . . and the Court denied certiorari—and thus killed off COPA for good—in

early 2009, over a decade after the never-enforced law was first passed. See *American Civil Liberties Union v. Mukasey*, 555 U.S. 1137 (2009) (denying a writ of certiorari).

51. See *Beauharnais v. Illinois*, 343 U.S. 250, 275 (1952) (Black, J., joined by Douglas, J., dissenting).
52. *Street v. New York*, 394 U.S. 576 (1969).
53. *Tinker v. Des Moines Independent Community School District*, 393 U.S. 503, 506 (1969).
54. 393 U.S. at 525 (Black, J., dissenting).
55. As he read a draft of Black's dissent, an amazed Abe Fortas wrote in the margins, "Hugo Black!!" See Newman, *Hugo Black*, 592.
56. *Hazelwood School District v. Kuhlmeier*, 484 U.S. 260 (1988).
57. *Bethel School District No. 403 v. Fraser*, 478 U.S. 675 (1986).
58. *Morse v. Frederick*, 551 U.S. 393 (2007).
59. Frederick insisted it was nothing more than a nonsense phrase that was designed to get him and his friends on television. See James C. Foster, *Bong Hits 4 Jesus: A Perfect Constitutional Storm in Alaska's Capital* (Fairbanks, AK: University of Alaska Press, 2010), especially 30–31.
60. On the complexities of the lengthy and "messy" litigation in *Morse*, see ibid.
61. 551 U.S. at 410 (Thomas, J., concurring).
62. Ibid., 421, quoting 393 U.S. at 526 (Black, J., dissenting).
63. It has also been, arguably, much more stark. Thomas's opinion in *44 Liquormart* was a spirited condemnation of governmental paternalism; his opinion in *Morse* however, is an embrace of governmental paternalism. As one article put it, his *Morse* opinion "represents a unidirectional flow of communication, in which there is a transmission of speech from government authorities (school teachers) to students. The receipt of information is completely controlled by the government, with students having no input. . . . Thomas's pro-paternalism stance affects not just what students can say, but also the speech that they can receive. Students are not allowed to challenge the received information—to question it, to debate it—in any way because the government knows best what speech they should receive." Matthew D. Bunker and Clay Calvert, "Contrasting Concurrences of Clarence Thomas: Deploying Originalism and Paternalism in Commercial and Student Speech Cases," *Georgia State University Law Review* 26 (2010): 357–358.
64. *Virginia v. Black*, 538 U.S. 343 (2003).
65. Ibid., 348, quoting VA Code § 18.2-423.
66. *R.A.V. v. City of St. Paul*, 505 U.S. 377 (1992).
67. 538 U.S. at 365–366.
68. This posture is often unfairly characterized as a lack of curiosity, attentiveness, or intellect. As Thomas has explained, it is instead rooted in an elegantly simple philosophy of common courtesy: "If I invite you to argue your case, I should at least listen to you." See Adam Liptak,

"No Argument: Thomas Keeps Five-Year Silence," *New York Times*, February 12, 2011, A1.

69. See argument of Deputy Solicitor General Michael Dreeben, recording and transcript available online at Oyez.org, http://www.oyez.org/cases/2000-2009/2002/2002_01_1107/argument
70. 538 U.S. at 394–395 (Thomas, J., dissenting).
71. Guy-Uriel E. Charles, "Colored Speech: Cross-Burnings, Epistemics, and the Triumph of the Crits," *Georgetown Law Review* 93 (2005): 577.
72. It must be pointed out that Thomas signed onto Scalia's majority opinion in *R.A.V.* More importantly, Thomas had written his own concurrence in *Capitol Square Review and Advisory Board v. Pinette*, 515 U.S. 753 (1995), in which the Court upheld a lower court directive for the Board to issue a permit for the Klan to display a cross during the holiday season at Columbus's Statehouse Plaza, which was a designated public forum (this was the "Ohio case" that Thomas mentioned to Michael Dreeben). Even though *Pinette* hinged on the Board's determination that displaying of any cross—Klan-proffered or otherwise—might have violated the Establishment Clause, and had refused to issue the permit on those grounds, Thomas pointed out that "to the extent that the Klan had a message to communicate [via the cross] in Capitol Square, it was primarily a political one." 515 U.S. at 771 (Thomas, J., concurring).
73. *Brown v. Entertainment Merchants Association*, 131 S. Ct. 2729 (2011).
74. 131 S. Ct. at 2751 (Thomas, J., dissenting). The other dissenter was Stephen Breyer.
75. *United States v. Alvarez*, 132 S. Ct. 2537 (2012); see 132 S. Ct. at 2556 (Alito, J., joined by Scalia and Thomas, JJ., dissenting).
76. Nat Hentoff, "First Friend," *Legal Times*, July 3, 2000, 62.
77. Ronald Collins, "The Roberts Court and the First Amendment," *SCOTUSblog*, July 9, 2013, http://www.scotusblog.com/2013/07/the-roberts-court-and-the-first-amendment/

Chapter 9

Stephen Breyer and the First Amendment as Legal Doctrine

Mark Tushnet

Writing in 2005, Justice Stephen Breyer outlined the principles that animate his interpretation of "our democratic constitution."[1] He focused on several areas of constitutional doctrine, including two areas of free speech doctrine, namely the law dealing with campaign finance regulation and the law dealing with the regulation of commercial speech. In addition, he defended the broad outlines of the Court's categorization approach to free speech, which the justices employ to distinguish between political speech and commercial speech. As Breyer explained, the reason for this approach is that regulations of political speech pose a threat to active liberty while regulations of commercial speech do not. "[I]f strong First Amendment standards were to apply across the board, they would prevent a democratically elected government from creating necessary regulation," Breyer wrote, "[but] to apply across the board uniform First Amendment standards weak enough . . . [for commercial speech] would undermine the First Amendment so much that it would not offer sufficient protection for the free exchange of ideas necessary to the health of our democracy."[2]

Breyer described his approach as resting on the principle of "active liberty," which Breyer defined as "the people's right to 'an active and constant participation in collective power.'"[3] Active liberty "argues for judicial modesty in constitutional decision-making" but also is "a source of judicial authority" in assisting "a community of individuals democratically [to] find practical solutions to important contemporary problems."[4] So, for example, political campaigns are an important locus for participation in exercising collective power, and campaign finance regulation is in principle aimed at ensuring wide and active participation. It follows, for Breyer, that courts should be "modest" in assessing the constitutionality of campaign finance regulations. Modesty is even more appropriate in cases involving regulation of commercial speech because such speech (including ordinary commercial advertisements) has little to do with the exercise of collective power. In performing the task of modest judicial review to promote active liberty, judges should "consider[ ] practical consequences, that is, consequences valued in terms of constitutional purposes."[5]

Breyer's focus on practical consequences is rooted in his background as a legal academic and technocrat, heir to a Progressive tradition valuing expertise in developing policy and technical proficiency in making law, both in legislatures and in courts. Born in California, Breyer attended Stanford University and Harvard Law School. His performance at the law school led him to a clerkship with Justice Arthur Goldberg. After working in the Antitrust Division at the Department of Justice, Breyer joined the Harvard Law School faculty, where he specialized in administrative law. His scholarship emphasized the importance of leadership by technocratic experts in generating sound public policy. His service as counsel to the Senate Committee on the Judiciary, led by Edward Kennedy, gave him a deep respect for the seriousness with which Congress could approach its tasks. Nominated to the federal court of appeals by President Jimmy Carter after Carter had lost his reelection bid, Breyer was nonetheless confirmed by an overwhelming bipartisan vote, demonstrating the respect he had garnered on both sides of the aisle because of his work for the Judiciary Committee. President Bill Clinton appointed him to the Supreme Court in 1994.

This chapter examines some of Breyer's free speech opinions in the decade since the publication of *Active Liberty* in light of the account of constitutional interpretation he offered there. The theme is that Breyer's opinions reflect an increasing awareness that, although the distinction between political and commercial speech captures some important core ideas, the distinction is itself too crude to identify when strong (or weak) standards should be invoked.[6] His opinions generally do distinguish between political and commercial speech, but within each category the standards he invokes have become less crisp. "Strong" and "weak" are no longer good descriptions of the standards Breyer uses in his free speech opinions.[7] Yet, as the standards *within* each category come to resemble each other, the distinction *between* the categories becomes less important.

CLEARLY POLITICAL CASES

Breyer's dissenting opinion in *Garcetti v. Ceballos* in 2006 set out his general interpretive approach: "Because virtually all human interaction takes place through speech, the First Amendment cannot offer all speech the same degree of protection. Rather, judges must apply different protective presumptions in different contexts, scrutinizing government's speech-related justification differently depending on the general category of activity."[8] *Active Liberty* argued that a stronger "protective presumption" should be used in cases involving direct government regulation of political speech, a weaker one in connection with campaign finance regulation. His favored approach for campaign finance regulation was "proportionality": "Does the statute strike a reasonable balance between electoral speech-restricting and speech-enhancing consequences?"[9]

Campaign Finance

Breyer adhered to his balancing approach in the one campaign finance opinion he has written since 2005. He announced the Court's judgment in a highly fractured case, *Randall v. Sorrell*, which held unconstitutional Vermont's limitations on campaign expenditures and contributions. The contribution limits were quite low—for statewide offices, individuals could contribute $400, and for legislative positions $300 to a candidate for senator, $200 to a candidate for state representative. Breyer concluded that the contribution limits were unconstitutional "because in their specific details . . . they fail to satisfy the First Amendment's requirement of careful tailoring."[10] That requirement is part of standard First Amendment doctrine, but Breyer immediately reformulated it: "That is to say, they impose burdens upon First Amendment interests that . . . are disproportionately severe."[11]

Breyer observed that "ordinarily we have deferred to the legislature's determination" of "empirical judgments," but there had to be "some lower bound," because "contribution limits that are too low can . . . harm the electoral process by preventing challengers from mounting effective campaigns against incumbent officeholders."[12] The Court had to "exercise . . . independent . . . judgment as the statute reaches those outer limits." Breyer found "danger signs" in the Vermont statute.[13] The limits were low compared to the ones the Court had approved, low compared to those in other states, and they applied to an election cycle consisting of *two* elections, a primary and a general election. Breyer's opinion calculated inflation-adjusted values and per capita values to carry out these comparisons.

Where comparisons might seem to favor Vermont, Breyer discussed the fact that campaigning for state auditor "is likely to be less costly than a campaign for governor," and "campaign costs do not automatically increase or decrease in precise proportion to the size of an electoral district." These and similar considerations "offset any neutralizing force of population differences."[14]

These danger signs led to Breyer's examination of the state's justifications for its low limits, which he found inadequate. "We reach this conclusion based not merely on the low dollar amounts . . . but also on the statute's effect on political parties and on volunteer activity in Vermont elections."[15] He enumerated "five factors" that "together lead us to this decision": The likely restriction of funding due to contribution limits, especially from political parties to candidates; the anomaly of treating political parties exactly like individual contributors, which "threatens harm to a particularly important political right, the right to associate in a political party";[16] the apparent fact that incidental expenses of volunteers counted as contributions, which meant that a volunteer "who makes four or five round trips driving across the State . . . can find that he or she is near . . . the contribution limit";[17] that the limits were not adjusted for inflation; and the absence of anything special about Vermont to justify such low limits, only a reliance on the general anticorruption principles already accepted in campaign finance law.

An important feature of Breyer's approach to the problem of determining when some regulation is too much regulation is that it is strikingly legislative in character. Breyer's approach relies on hypothetical examples to illustrate the regulations' impact, copious facts, and evaluations of the importance of those facts, not different in kind from the sort of discussion one might find in a legislative report on a campaign finance proposal. For Breyer, a policy-oriented analysis flows from the combination of a proportionality test and the "danger signs" he found in a regulation of political expression.

Pure Political Speech

Breyer dissented when, in *Humanitarian Law Project v. Holder* (2010), the Court found it constitutionally permissible to prohibit, as "material support" for terrorism, purely political speech done in coordination with a terrorist group even when the speech's content had nothing to do with terrorism and indeed when the speech was aimed at achieving the group's political goals through nonviolent means.[18] The group challenging the ban planned to provide information to the

Tamil Tigers and a Kurdish resistance group about such matters as the use of "humanitarian and international law to peacefully resolve disputes," how to "petition various representative bodies such as the United Nations for relief," and how "to engage in political advocacy."[19] As Breyer put it, "All these activities are of a kind that the First Amendment ordinarily protects."[20] As a result, in Breyer's view, the government had to provide a strong showing that punishing those who engage in such activities was justified, and the government had failed to do so.

As detailed in previous chapters of this book, free expression doctrine with respect to political speech developed over the twentieth century as the Court dealt with prosecutions of speakers for making political statements of which the government disapproved. Disapproval alone, though, was never enough to justify regulation. Rather, the government had to show some causal connection between the speech and some harm of a type the government was entitled to attempt to minimize. At the outset, the Court's test asked only whether either a legislature or a jury could reasonably determine that the speech had a "bad tendency," that is, had some causal connection to harm.[21] Experience with these prosecutions led the Court to tighten up the causal connection between speech and harm, first to words whose utterance posed a "clear and present danger" of resulting harm,[22] and then to words whose utterance was "likely to produce" "imminent lawless action."[23]

What were the harms in *Humanitarian Law Project*, and how closely were the Project's words connected to those harms? Chief Justice Roberts's opinion for the Court identified several harms. First, the Chief Justice argued that money supplied or made available to a terrorist organization for nonterrorist activities freed up resources the organization could use for its terrorist activities (he called this the "fungibility" argument). So, for example, if one of the organizations used the Project's training to petition for humanitarian relief, such as food and medicine, from international organizations and obtained that relief, the organization could forgo spending its own money on food and medications and spend it on weapons instead. Second, Roberts argued that training terrorist organizations about international law might give the organizations legitimacy on the international plane, as they framed their appeals not in terms of terrorist objectives but rather in terms of objectives acknowledged to be legitimate under international law. And, finally, the organizations might use the training in negotiation and mediation they received as part of a strategy of delay, allowing them during a negotiating period to build up military resources they could use when they walked out of the negotiations. Roberts bolstered all of these arguments by referring to the deference the Court had to give Congressional and executive judgments in connection with antiterrorist activities. He also limited the Court's holding to speech activities undertaken in coordination with a terrorist organization, thereby apparently protecting speakers who, independently of such coordination, came to agree with the terrorist organization and advocated in its favor.

Breyer's dissent argued that none of the harms Roberts identified were connected closely enough to the Project's speech activities to satisfy late-twentieth century free speech requirements and—in effect—that deferring to legislative and executive judgments returned the law to the long-rejected "bad tendency" test. Invoking the modern test, Breyer wrote, "[n]o one contends that the plaintiffs' speech to these organizations can be prohibited as incitement under *Brandenburg*."[24]

Breyer used his standard methodological approach, asking "whether a statute worked speech-related harm 'out of proportion to the statute's salutary effects upon' other interests."[25] Or, "precisely how does application of the statute to the protected activities . . . *help achieve* [the government's] important security-related end?"[26] He examined the government's three justifications. All of them, he concluded, were "general and speculative."[27]

First, as to the possibility that one form of material support might free up the terrorist organization to use its other resources for terrorism. The argument might have some force were the material support to come in the form of cash contributions, but "[t]here is no *obvious* way in which undertaking advocacy" before international bodies "is fungible with other resources that might be put to more sinister ends."[28] Because the causal connection was not obvious, the government had to provide "evidence to support its claim," and it had failed to do so.[29] Everything the government produced to support the fungibility claim involved donations of cash and other material goods, such as computers, not speech. So, to Breyer, what the government showed was that the speech activities at issue *might* enable the terrorist organization to do more with its other resources—and Breyer himself emphasized the word "might." But that was simply the old "bad tendency" test.

On the next rationale, Breyer asked, "What is one to say about the[] argument[] . . . that an opponent's . . . willingness to negotiate might be faked . . .?"[30] He observed that "[n]either Congress nor the Government advanced these particular hypothetical claims,"[31] so there really was nothing the Court could defer to.[32] Once again, he alluded to the return to a "bad tendency" test: "the risk that those who are taught will put otherwise innocent speech . . . to bad use is omnipresent, at least where that risk rests on little more than (even informed) speculation."[33]

Finally, with respect to the legitimation flowing from training in using international law and the like, Breyer observed that such legitimation could occur equally from speech *un*coordinated with the terrorist organization, so the Court's limitation of its holding to coordinated speech was, with respect to this harm, arbitrary. "[W]ere the law to accept a 'legitimating' effect, in and of itself . . . , as providing sufficient grounds for imposing such a ban, the First Amendment battle would be lost in untold instances where it should be won. Once one accepts this argument, there is no natural stopping place."[34]

Breyer framed his argument with reference to proportionality, but that framing was almost certainly unnecessary. All he actually relied on was well-established doctrine requiring a close causal connection between political speech and resulting harm. One can describe such a requirement in the language of proportionality, of course, but one can also describe it as a categorical rule. Breyer's approach to core political speech does not seem that different from existing categorical approaches. Perhaps his aim was to push the Court toward a reformulation of standard doctrine—here, the requirement of a close causal connection between political speech and resulting harm—by offering the more general methodology of proportionality review that is more systematic but nonetheless yields results compatible with much existing doctrine.

Borderline Cases: Breyer's General Approach

In 2011 and 2012 the Supreme Court decided four cases that for many observers raised questions about the appropriateness of drawing a sharp line between the regulation of political speech and the regulation of other categories of speech, including commercial speech.[35] In all four cases, the Court found the regulations unconstitutional. Breyer concurred in two cases that he thought fit into the "political" category and dissented in one that he placed on the borderline between artistic and literary speech and commercial speech and one that he placed in the "commercial speech" category. Yet, despite the variations in outcome, an examination of his opinions shows that the doctrine he applied in all the cases is strikingly similar.

The comparison between his opinions in *United States v. Alvarez*[36] and *Brown v. Entertainment Merchants Association*[37] is instructive. Breyer treated *Alvarez*, which held unconstitutional the federal Stolen Valor Act prohibiting knowingly false statements by a person that he or she had been awarded military honors, as involving political speech. Breyer said that the approach he would take had sometimes been called "intermediate scrutiny," sometimes "'proportionality' review," sometimes "an examination of 'fit.'"[38] Here is how he described the approach. It involves "examin[ing] speech-related harms, justifications, and potential alternatives. In particular, it . . . take[s] account of the seriousness of the speech-related harm the provision will likely cause, the nature and importance of the provision's countervailing objectives, the extent to which the provision will tend to achieve those objectives, and whether there are other, less restrictive ways of doing so."[39]

Now consider *Brown v. Entertainment Merchants Association*, where Breyer dissented from the Court's conclusion that a California statute strictly regulating the distribution to young people of violent video games violated the First Amendment. There, Breyer wrote that he "would apply . . . a strict form of First Amendment scrutiny."[40] That "strict" form required that the statute "be 'narrowly tailored' to serve a 'compelling interest,' without there being a 'less restrictive' alternative that would be 'at least as effective.'"[41] Yet, Breyer continued, he would "not apply this strict standard 'mechanically.'" Rather, he "would evaluate the degree to which the statute injures speech-related interests, the nature of the potentially justifying 'compelling interests,' the degree to which the statute furthers that interest, the nature and possible effectiveness of possible alternatives, and, in light of this evaluation, whether, overall, 'the statute works speech-related harm . . . out of proportion to the benefits that the statute seeks to provide.'"[42] The doctrinal formulation of "strict" scrutiny here is barely distinguishable from the formulation of "intermediate" scrutiny in *Alvarez*, which demonstrates that Breyer does indeed have a unified approach to developing First Amendment doctrine.

Borderline Political Cases

Breyer's opinion in *Alvarez* disclaimed the use of "a strict categorical analysis."[43] He referred here not to the distinction between political speech and commercial speech but to a more finely grained set of categories drawn from *Chaplinsky v. New Hampshire*[44] and *United States v. Stevens*.[45] According to those cases, a limited set of categories of speech was largely outside the First Amendment's umbrella.[46] *Stevens* held that the Court would not expand the set of categories by identifying new ones—there, animal crush videos—that were similar to the exempt categories in their marginal contribution to the values promoted by the First Amendment. The majority in *Alvarez* relied on *Stevens* in refusing to hold that lies as such were outside the scope of the First Amendment. Rather, for the plurality in *Alvarez* false statements could be regulated only if they resulted in provable material harm, as in commercial fraud cases.

Breyer concurred in the result. After setting out his general approach, quoted earlier, he observed that, though there were dangers associated with "[l]aws restricting false statements about philosophy, religion, history, the social sciences, the arts, and the like," *Alvarez* did not involve such a statute.[47] Rather, the case involved "easily verifiable facts" about something quite different, and "[s]uch false factual statements are less likely than are true factual statements to make a valuable contribution to the marketplace of ideas."[48] Why then was the Stolen Valor Act unconstitutional? Because, apparently, "the pervasiveness of false statements, made for better or for worse reasons, made thoughtlessly or deliberately, made with or without accompanying harm, provides a weapon to a government broadly empowered to prosecute falsity without more."[49] He also noted the possibility not of broad but rather of selective prosecution: of "a pacifist who supports his cause by (falsely) claiming to have been a war hero, while ignoring members of other political groups [such as supporters of a war] who might make similar false claims."[50] Breyer acknowledged that some statutes did make "the utterance of certain kinds of false statements unlawful," but they "tend to be narrower" than the Stolen Valor Act, for example, by "requiring proof of specific harm to identifiable victims."[51]

The Stolen Valor Act, then, was too broad. Exactly why remains unclear. Breyer's argument gets rhetorical force by trading on intuitions about false statements made "for better motives" or "thoughtlessly." Yet even on his analysis the Stolen Valor Act had a *mens rea* requirement (i.e., a requirement that the liar have a specific mental attitude toward the truth) of knowledge that the statement was false. Somehow, though, the requirement of knowing falsity (and, as Breyer would have required, an intent that the statements be taken as true) does not limit the weapon's targets sufficiently. The statute "ranges very broadly," because "it applies in family, social or other private contexts . . . [and] in political contexts, where . . . the risk of censorious selectivity by prosecutors is also high."[52] The *mens rea* requirement was not enough, because "a speaker might still be worried about being *prosecuted* for a careless false statement, even if he does not have the intent required to render him liable."[53] Further, Breyer mentioned other statutes that impose liability for lies "in contexts in which a tangible harm to others is especially likely to occur."[54] Such contexts also narrow the potential for abusive uses of these statutes.

Agreeing that the Stolen Valor Act "has substantial justification" in "protect[ing] the interests of those who have sacrificed their health and life for their country," Breyer believed that the government could achieve its goals "in less burdensome ways," for example by distinguishing among military awards (and penalizing only lies about having won one of the more prestigious ones) or by "focus[ing] its coverage . . . on contexts where such lies are most likely to cause harm."[55] And, he thought, "it is likely that a more narrowly tailored statute combined with . . . information-disseminating devices will effectively serve Congress' end."[56]

Had the government known that Breyer would take this approach, it might well have defended the statute on grounds he laid out.[57] The reason is that Stolen Valor lies appear to be made quite often in such contexts. Had Breyer examined the contexts in which Stolen Valor lies are made, he would have discovered that they tend to be made in circumstances where there is a high likelihood that the liar will gain material advantage and that not infrequently the circumstances are such that it may be difficult to show that they were made with an intent to gain such advantage.[58] And, just as he interpreted the statute to have a *mens rea* requirement of knowledge of falsity, Breyer could have interpreted it to narrow the "contexts" by allowing the defendant to show that the lie was uttered under circumstances under which there was no realistic prospect of gaining material advantage.[59] The Stolen Valor Act, on this view, actually is a rather narrow statute, in which the omission of a requirement of proof of material gain is something like a presumption based on a realistic evaluation of the circumstances under which Stolen Valor lies are made. In the end, Breyer's opinion in *Alvarez* seems to rest on an almost legislative-like evaluation of what a good statute dealing with lies about military honors would look like.

The other "political" case testing the category's boundaries is *Snyder v. Phelps*,[60] known as the funeral protest case. Fred Phelps, a homophobic preacher, and his supporters regularly attended the funerals of soldiers killed in the line of duty. Fully complying with state laws regulating how close they could come to funeral ceremonies, a group accompanying Phelps held up signs near where Matthew

Snyder was to be buried. The signs were grossly offensive—"Thank God for Dead Soldiers," "Fags Doom Nations," "America is Doomed," "Priests Rape Boys," and "You're Going to Hell." When Snyder's father learned of the protest and the signs' content by seeing them on a television news broadcast, he sued Phelps for intentional infliction of emotional distress. A prior case, *Hustler Magazine, Inc. v. Falwell*,[61] drew upon Justice Brennan's opinion in *New York Times v. Sullivan*[62] (see Chapter 5 herein) to hold that the First Amendment allowed public figures—there, the prominent preacher Jerry Falwell—to recover damages for intentional infliction of emotional distress from the publication of statements only if they could show that the statements were either false or made with reckless disregard for their truth or falsity. In *Snyder v. Phelps*, the Court extended that holding to cover statements made on matters of public concern, even if about someone like Matthew Snyder, who was not a public figure.

That the statements in *Snyder v. Phelps* were on a matter of public concern meant for Breyer that they fell within the category of political speech. But, he said, for him it was not enough that the statements were on a matter of public concern. In addition, he argued, the precise facts of the case mattered. The protest occurred in a place where picketing was lawful, and it could not be seen from the funeral site itself. Breyer acknowledged that the state had an interest in protecting its citizens from serious emotional harms. But he concluded that "in these circumstances" imposing liability "would punish [Phelps] for seeking to communicate its views on matters of public concern without proportionately advancing the State's interest in protecting its citizens against severe emotional harms."[63] Exactly why liability was disproportionate is not entirely clear. A jury had found that the statements were grossly offensive and did in fact inflict serious emotional harm. Breyer's judgment of disproportionality probably can best be explained by his view that the jury was overly influenced by the offensiveness of Phelps's statements and mistakenly found that Snyder had indeed suffered substantial emotional harm. Here, too, one can discern how stated commitments to deference (in the Vermont campaign finance case to the legislature, here to the jury) can be silently overridden through the use of conclusory judgments of disproportionality.

In both *Alvarez* and *Snyder v. Phelps* Breyer agreed that statements fairly described as political were protected by the First Amendment. But, for him, it was not enough that they were political. Rather, they were protected because, under the circumstances, there were better ways to advance the government's interests. And "better" here means pretty much "better in the eyes of Justice Breyer."

Speech That Is Artistic, Political, and Commercial

As noted above, Breyer dissented in the violent video case. The seven-justice majority divided on the question of what rendered the statute unconstitutional.[64] Justice Samuel A. Alito and Roberts argued that the California statute was unconstitutionally vague because "violence" could not be given a sufficiently precise meaning to satisfy First Amendment standards. Justice Antonin Scalia, writing for himself and Justices Anthony M. Kennedy, Ruth Bader Ginsburg, Sonia Sotomayor, and Elena Kagan, found the statute unconstitutional because, first, depictions of violence were not categorically excluded from the First Amendment's coverage, and second, the California statute failed the stringent tests invoked in connection with the regulation of material under the First Amendment's umbrella.

California's statute barred sales of violent video games to persons under the age of eighteen (although they could obtain such games when purchased on their behalf by a parent or another older person). Against Alito, Breyer argued that the term "violent" was no less vague than the term "nudity," which was used in a statute barring the distribution to minors of material deemed obscene as to them because it contained nudity (and satisfied other criteria, which were included in California's violent-video statute). For the purposes of this chapter, Breyer's alternative to Scalia's majority opinion is of greater interest. He began with the observation that "[v]ideo games combine physical action with expression," which meant that he had to "apply[] a strict standard of review."[65]

After articulating the standard of "strict but not mechanical scrutiny" quoted earlier, Breyer applied it. First, the violent-video statute "imposes no more than a modest restriction on expression."[66] Anyone could *play* violent video games—older people by buying them, younger ones by finding someone who would purchase them. Upholding the regulation would not "create a precedent that would adversely affect other media, say films, or videos, or books" because video games, unlike those other media, "involve[] a significant amount of physical activity."[67] Nor was that activity—"pushing buttons"—"just like watching a typical movie."[68]

Next, Breyer examined the government's interest, which combined an interest in supporting parents' choices about how to raise their children, with the state's general interest in ensuring that children were socialized appropriately. As to the latter interest, Breyer emphasized—at length, citing numerous social scientific studies—that "video games are excellent teaching tools," which meant that the government had an interest in ensuring that what the tools taught was appropriate.[69] "California argues that when the teaching features of video games are put to . . . [un]desirable ends, harm can ensue. . . . [E]xtremely violent games can harm children by rewarding them for being violently aggressive in play, and thereby often teaching them to be violently aggressive in life."[70]

Note the use of "can" in those sentences. They describe risks of harm without asserting that there is a close causal connection between viewing violent video games and actually being aggressive in life. The contrast with Breyer's analysis in *Humanitarian Law Project* is obvious. There Breyer applied strict scrutiny and asked for proof of a close causal connection between speech and ensuing harm, whereas here he found strict (but not mechanical) scrutiny satisfied without strong proof of a close causal connection between speech and harm. Why the difference? First, because violent video games, while having an artistic component, are not at the core of political or similar speech. And second, because in *Brown* the government directed Breyer's attention to social-science material—evidence—supporting its empirical judgment, whereas in *Humanitarian Law Project* the government supplied no such evidence, and Breyer was unwilling to credit "even informed speculation" about the causal connection. Breyer did not defer to the studies, as sometimes is said, but rather to "an elected legislature's conclusion that the video games in question are particularly likely to harm children. This Court has always thought it owed an elected legislature some degree of deference in respect to legislative facts of this kind, particularly when they involve technical matters that are beyond our competence, and even in First Amendment cases."[71] To drive the point home, Breyer cited Roberts's opinion in *Humanitarian Law Project* to support that proposition.[72]

Breyer's opinion concluded with an uncharacteristically pithy and eloquent paragraph:

> This case is ultimately less about censorship than it is about education. Our Constitution cannot succeed in securing the liberties it seeks to protect unless we can raise future generations committed cooperatively to making our system of government work. Education, however, is about choices. Sometimes, children need to learn by making choices for themselves. Other times, choice are made for children—by their parents, by their teachers, and by the people acting democratically through their governments. In my view, the First Amendment does not disable government from helping parents make such a choice here—a choice not to have their children buy extremely violent, interactive, video games, which they more than reasonably fear pose only the risk of harm to those children.[73]

Here Breyer's methodological approach, which seeks to reduce the significance of rigid analytic categories distinguishing political from commercial speech and strict from intermediate scrutiny, converges with his insistence that the Constitution promote active liberty. Breyer the technocrat finds valuable studies produced by expert psychologists, and Breyer's respect for legislatures leads him to defer to the California legislatures. Active liberty too plays a role. Through their legislative representatives, parents exercise active liberty in guiding the choices their children make, so as to make the children capable of becoming active citizens.

Commercial Speech

After bringing commercial speech under the First Amendment's umbrella in 1976, the Supreme Court has moved slowly but almost uninterruptedly toward treating truthful commercial speech as constitutionally indistinguishable from political speech. The most potent argument the Court has deployed is that denying people (consumers) access to truthful information about products always rests on a legislature's paternalistic judgment that ordinary people are unable to deal with such information in a socially responsible manner, or in a way compatible with their own values, and that the First Amendment—or perhaps our entire constitutional tradition—rules such paternalism out of bounds.

In *Active Liberty*, Breyer argued that commercial speech differs from political speech because at most it contributes to the citizenry's ability to participate in its own self-government only weakly and indirectly.[74] In 2011, *Sorrell v. IMS Health Services, Inc.* gave him the opportunity to apply his approach in a case involving relatively new technologies of data mining.[75]

"Big Pharma" uses salespeople known as detailers to inform physicians about their employers' patented products. Detailers and their employers believe that they can be more effective in explaining why doctors should prescribe their products rather than prescribing generic versions of the products if the detailers know how many in-patent and generic drugs the doctors have prescribed. Pharmacies get that data in raw form from the prescriptions themselves, and state law requires that they retain that information. A collateral industry of data assembly has developed. Data assemblers purchase the information from pharmacies to create databases linking prescriptions to doctors. So, for example, the database allows someone to determine that a particular physician in Burlington prescribed generic drugs to treat depression five times more often than she prescribed in-patent drugs.[76] With that information in hand, the detailers can talk with the physician about why the in-patent drug the physician is rarely prescribing is actually better than the generic drugs. And when those conversations are effective from the detailer's point of view, the doctor will increase the number of in-patent prescriptions. But doing so increases overall expenditures on medications because in-patent drugs are more expensive than generic ones. State budgets include expenditures for prescription medications through health programs like Medicare, so the state has an interest in keeping the number of in-patent prescriptions down to what is truly necessary. Vermont enacted a statute barring pharmacies from selling the information they had for purposes of "marketing," which meant, in effect, selling the information to the data assembly (or data mining) companies.

Data mining companies challenged the statute as a violation of the First Amendment. They argued that the information was in private hands—the pharmacies—and that the statute prevented the pharmacies from communicating truthful information to the data assembly company without adequate justification. According to the companies, the state was preventing them from acquiring information that they would then sell to "Big Pharma," whose detailers would use it in framing their discussions with physicians about the relative benefits of using in-patent drugs rather than generic ones. Those discussions dealt with matters of obvious concern to both the prescribing physicians and their patients and fell within the First Amendment's coverage. And, the companies argued, the state's concern about cost-saving was too attenuated to satisfy stringent causal requirements. Costs would go up only if the conversations led doctors to change their prescription practices, which might not occur to a large enough extent to justify the restriction on the dissemination of information. And even if doctors did change their prescriptions practices, they would do so only because their conversations with the detailers persuaded them that the in-patent drugs were better. First Amendment standards for allowing regulation are especially stringent, almost to the point of an absolute ban, where the mechanism by which one person's statements cause harm is through persuasion of another person. Yet that was the mechanism Vermont targeted. In an opinion by Kennedy, a majority of the Court accepted the data assembly companies' argument.[77] For Kennedy, Vermont's statute unconstitutionally singled out a specific use of information (by detailers but not researchers) and a specific set of speakers (data mining companies), in violation of the libertarian principles—not necessarily confined to freedom of thought—to which he is inclined (see Chapter 7 herein).

Breyer dissented, using his standard approach: "I would ask whether Vermont's regulatory provisions work harm to First Amendment interests that is disproportionate to their furtherance of legitimate regulatory objectives. And in doing so, I would give significant weight to legitimate commercial regulatory objectives."[78] Restating his view that context matters, Breyer said that the Court had developed "test-related distinctions" between "'core' political speech" and commercial speech or "the regulation-related speech of a firm subject to a traditional regulatory program."[79] The distinctions reflected both the relative "constitutional importance" of the subject matter—in light of the values served by the First Amendment, a free marketplace of ideas with respect to politics was more important than a free marketplace for goods—and "the democratic importance of permitting an elected government to implement through effective programs policy choices for which the people's elected representatives have voted."[80] Stressing that "ordinary regulatory programs can affect speech," Breyer argued that "to apply a 'heightened' First Amendment standard of review whenever such a program burdens speech would transfer from legislatures to judges the primary power to weigh ends and to choose means."[81]

Breyer enumerated the reasons for reviewing the statute as an economic regulation. Although it restricted the sale of information, it did not prohibit anybody from saying anything; it was similar to regulations adopted by the Food and Drug Administration that, he implied, were unquestionably constitutional but threatened by the possibility of invoking a heightened First Amendment standard; its requirements "form part of a traditional, comprehensive regulatory scheme" dealing with prescription medications; and, the information existed in the first place only because Vermont required that pharmacists obtain it.[82] He referred to other regulatory schemes—for consumer credit data and medical records—that involved "tailored restrictions on the use of information subject to their jurisdiction."[83]

Breyer effectively used those other regulatory schemes to counter the majority's view that Vermont's regulation was both content-based and speaker-based. Each regulatory scheme was necessarily content-based, in the sense that the regulations affected only the content of speech within the regulator's jurisdiction. "Electricity regulators . . . oversee company statements, pronouncement, and proposals, but only about electricity."[84] And they were also speaker-based, applying only to the regulated firms—here, pharmacies. "[T]he FDA might control in detail just what a pharmaceutical firm can, and cannot, tell potential purchasers about its products" even though a third party such as a researcher could make statements to exactly the same audience that the regulated firm could not.[85]

Having set out his view that the proper evaluative standard was not a heightened one, Breyer found Vermont's statute constitutional. "The statute threatens only modest harm to commercial speech."[86] There was no evidence that anyone other than the data assembly companies was interested in obtaining the information pharmacies had, except perhaps for an occasional researcher. Had there been evidence that someone would buy the information for nonmarketing purposes, such as a "counterdetailing" program promoting the use of generic drugs, Breyer conceded, the statute's impact on commercial speech would have been more substantial, but, scouring the record, he could find nothing substantial to support the concern about any actual counterdetailing program affected by Vermont's statute.

For Breyer, the state's interests in public health and protecting against excessive spending on medications were sufficiently "substantial" to justify the regulatory ban on sales of information for marketing purposes. Detailers could engage doctors in conversations about the benefits of their drugs as against generics, for example, without needing to know exactly what the specific doctor's prescription practices were:

> Shaping a detailing message based on an individual doctor's prior prescription habits may help sell more of a particular manufacturer's particular drugs. But it does so by diverting attention from scientific research about a drug's safety and effectiveness, as well as its cost. This diversion comes at the expense of public health and the State's fiscal interests.[87]

Breyer then referred to the substantial factual record the Vermont legislature had compiled before enacting its statute. That record "required the legislature to make judgments about whether and how to ameliorate these problems. And it is the job of regulatory agencies and legislatures to make just these kinds of judgments."[88] Once again, deference has an important role in promoting active liberty—here, the liberty of the people and not judges to determine the regulatory policies they believe best.

Then, following his usual template of asking last whether there were adequate effective alternatives to the regulation, Breyer concluded that there were not. Doctors could refuse to see detailers, but "physicians are unlikely to turn detailers away at the door, for those detailers . . . are . . . providers of much useful information."[89]

Before becoming a judge, Breyer was a scholar of administrative law and the regulatory state. He saw the data mining case as implicating the following question. How can the First Amendment and the regulatory state coexist, with neither one trenching too substantially on the other? He thought that the majority's approach "[a]t best . . . opens a Pandora's Box of First Amendment challenges to many ordinary regulatory practices that may only incidentally affect a commercial message."[90] The Court's approach threatened to subordinate too much of the regulatory state to the First Amendment—or, more precisely, would authorize judges to use the First Amendment to displace legislative judgments about regulatory policy. The majority, that is, was using the First Amendment to accomplish the antiregulatory goals the Due Process Clause served in the early decades of the twentieth century, the "happily bygone era when judges scrutinized legislation for its interference with economic liberty."[91] Though the Due Process Clause did not entirely level the regulatory state, it did whittle away at it for many years. The First Amendment in the majority's hands, Breyer feared, could do the same.

CONCLUSION

To this point, this chapter has been focused on Breyer's approach to free speech doctrine. But doctrinal development occurs in a political context. Breyer has set his proportionality approach against what he describes as the more mechanical categorical tests employed by the Court's majority.

Why has the Court's majority settled on categorical tests in free speech cases? One reason links categorical tests to the conservative philosophy of adjudication developed over the past two generations. That philosophy in turn was a reaction to the Warren Court's liberalism. For judicial conservatives, the Warren Court was characterized by a free-wheeling decision-making style in which judges wrote into the Constitution their policy preferences. Conservatives developed a judicial philosophy aimed at ensuring that judges would find themselves under a methodological discipline that constrained them. The component of that philosophy that has garnered the greatest attention is of course originalism.[92] But a jurisprudence of rules is an independent component of the philosophy.[93] According to today's conservative judicial philosophy, the very terms of categorical rules impose significant constraints on what judges can do. They identify a small number of features of a problem—whether the speech involved deals with a matter of public concern, for example—and make outcomes turn on them and on nothing else.[94]

The cost of categorical rules is that they can become disconnected from social reality. "Active liberty" and its methodological counterpart, proportionality, are attractive ideas because they accommodate that reality. In their best form, categorical rules precipitate out of repeated confrontations with regulations and fact patterns. In those confrontations, judges more or less openly discuss the relevant issues of fact and value, in what an earlier generation called (case-focused) balancing. But, as experience with fact-patterns accumulates, judges first develop rules of thumb or presumptions that guide decision, and then, hard-edged rules that conceal the underlying questions of fact and value. Categorical rules, then, are opaque. In contrast, proportionality analysis inevitably requires judgments about fine-grained matters of fact and value and so can be more transparent than mechanical categorical rules. A judge discussing whether a regulation is a proportionate response to a problem will identify in some detail where the regulation falls along the many dimensions relevant to determining proportionality. Proportionality analysis, that is, is more realistic than categorical rules. Whereas conservative judicial philosophy tends to seek methods that constrain judges, liberal judicial philosophy seeks methods that allow judges to take social reality into account.

Yet, for that very reason, proportionality analysis is more suitable for upholding legislation than for striking it down. Proportionality analysis will often seem to the reader not readily distinguishable from the kind of analysis a legislator interested in developing good policy would offer. Untethered to deference to other decision makers, which is to say, when used to invalidate legislation, proportionality analysis does not seem distinctively judicial. Tethered to deference, which is to say, when used to uphold legislation, proportionality analysis does what Breyer claims it should do. That is why his opinions in *Brown* and *IMS Health* are more effective than his opinions in *Alvarez* and *Snyder*. And it is probably worth noting as well that Breyer's dissent in *Humanitarian Law Project*—where he would have held the material support statute unconstitutional—seems to deploy a method that is more categorical, less "proportionality" than Breyer's stated theory would suggest.

The transparency of proportionality analysis compared to categorical rules has another feature that locates Breyer's free speech jurisprudence in the broader controversy over conservative and liberal judicial philosophies. One theme in conservative judicial philosophy has been the deprecation of the judicial exercise of judgment, a deprecation captured in Roberts's notorious "balls and strikes" metaphor but also embedded in the jurisprudence of originalism, which locates judgment in the Framers and objectivity in contemporary judges.[95]

The liberal judicial philosophy, in contrast, contends—more accurately, in my view—that judges inevitably exercise judgment, sometimes in the framing of categorical rules, sometimes in applying a complex system of categorical rules to a specific problem, and sometimes openly through proportionality and similar forms of analysis. For Breyer, proportionality analysis does *two* things well. It exposes to public view the relevant considerations, and it provides a structured way of discussing those relevant considerations and thereby provides some constraint on the free-wheelingness that conservatives properly criticize. In that sense, Breyer's free speech jurisprudence is liberal.

Finally, it is worth speculating about why Breyer's ideas about proportionality and active liberty do not appear to have captured the imagination of liberals seeking to construct a modern liberal judicial philosophy. The language of a "living Constitution" still prevails among such liberals, not the language of proportionality and active liberty. One possibility is that Breyer's analysis cannot take hold of the imagination when it is, as it has been, essentially the language of dissent, as in *Brown* and *IMS Health*, or of disagreement on the margins, as in *Alvarez* and *Snyder*. Originalism and the jurisprudence of rules originated in dissents but flourished when conservatives came to control the Court's discourse. Perhaps the same would be true of proportionality and active liberty were liberals to become dominant. Another possibility, though, is that Breyer's literary style is that of a pedant—clear and meticulous but rarely rhetorically captivating. Perhaps it will take someone other than Breyer to embed his ideas in liberal judicial philosophy. Here, as throughout our history, we can see that ideas about freedom of expression and the doctrinal formulations used to implement it map only imperfectly on to conventional distinctions between liberals and conservatives.

NOTES

1. Stephen Breyer, *Active Liberty: Interpreting Our Democratic Constitution* (New York: Knopf, 2005), 5.
2. Ibid., 41–42.
3. Ibid., 5 (quoting Benjamin Constant).
4. Ibid., 37.
5. Ibid., 6.
6. The distinction's inadequacy arguably was in fact shown in *Nike, Inc. v. Kasky*, 539 U.S. 654 (2003), a case Breyer treated in *Active Liberty* as falling clearly in the domain of the political. See *Active Liberty*, 51–53. The case involved, among other things, letters Nike wrote to athletic directors at universities (and released to the public) defending its labor practices

outside the United States. As Breyer said, these letters clearly dealt with a matter of public importance and current political controversy. But the case was founded on a state law—commercial in character—aimed at preventing one competitor from gaining a business advantage over other competitors by making false factual statements. The case, therefore, was simultaneously political and commercial.

7. See Mark Tushnet, "Justice Breyer and the Partial De-Doctrinalization of Free Speech Law," *Harvard Law Review* 128 (2014): 508–516 (in which I call this a "partial de-doctrinalization" of First Amendment law).
8. *Garcetti v. Ceballos*, 547 U.S. 410, 444–445 (2006) (Breyer, J., dissenting). See also *Sorrell v. IMS Health Inc.*, 131 S. Ct. 2653, 2673 (2011) (Breyer, J., joined by Ginsburg and Kagan, JJ., dissenting) ("Because many, perhaps most, activities of human beings living together in communities take place through speech, and because speech-related risks and offsetting justifications differ depending upon context, this Court has distinguished for First Amendment purposes among different contexts in which speech takes place.")
9. Breyer, *Active Liberty*, 49.
10. *Randall v. Sorrell*, 548 U.S. 230, 237 (2006).
11. Ibid.
12. Ibid., 248–249.
13. Ibid., 249.
14. Ibid., 252.
15. Ibid., 253.
16. Ibid., 256.
17. Ibid., 260.
18. *Holder v. Humanitarian Law Project*, 561 U.S. 1 (2010).
19. 561 U.S. at 41–42 (Breyer, J., joined by Ginsburg and Sotomayor, JJ., dissenting).
20. Ibid., 42.
21. The form of the statute under which the government proceeded determined whether it was the jury's reasonable belief or the legislature's that mattered. If the statute proscribed words it itself identified, the legislature's reasonable belief mattered; if the statute proscribed the resulting harm, it was the jury's. Compare *Gitlow v. New York*, 268 U.S. 652 (1925) (involving a statute identifying words of "criminal anarchy" as the offense), with *Schenck v. United States*, 249 U.S. 47 (1919) (involving a statute criminalizing interference with the draft).
22. *Dennis v. United States*, 341 U.S. 494 (1951).
23. *Brandenburg v. Ohio*, 395 U.S. 444 (1969). Brandenburg also required that, at least in connection with speech critical of existing government policy, the words uttered must be words of incitement. That requirement does not travel well to other contexts, but the requirement of a close causal connection between speech and harm does.
24. 561 U.S. at 43–44 (Breyer, J., joined by Ginsburg and Sotomayor, JJ., dissenting).

25. Ibid., 46 (quoting *Nixon v. Shrink Missouri Government PAC*, 528 U.S. 377 (2000)).
26. 561 U.S. at 46 (Breyer, J., joined by Ginsburg and Sotomayor, JJ., dissenting).
27. Ibid., 55.
28. Ibid., 47.
29. Ibid.
30. Ibid., 52.
31. Ibid.
32. Ibid., 54. ("Throughout, the majority emphasizes that it would defer strongly to Congress' 'informed judgment.' But here there is no evidence that Congress has made such a judgment regarding the specific activities at issue.")
33. Ibid., 53.
34. Ibid., 49.
35. The Court had decided a similar case in 2010, *United States v. Stevens*, 559 U.S. 460 (2010). The Court held unconstitutional a statute aimed at prohibiting the dissemination of "animal crush" videos. It applied the political speech standard in finding the statute unconstitutional. Only Justice Alito dissented; Justice Breyer did not write separately.
36. *United States v. Alvarez*, 132 S. Ct. 2537 (2012).
37. *Brown v. Entertainment Merchants Association*, 131 S. Ct. 2729 (2011).
38. 132 S. Ct. at 2551–2552 (Breyer, J., joined by Kagan, J., concurring in the judgment).
39. Ibid., at 2551.
40. 131 S. Ct. at 2762 (Breyer, J., dissenting).
41. Ibid., 2766.
42. Ibid., 2765.
43. 132 S. Ct. at 2551 (Breyer, J., joined by Kagan, J., concurring in the judgment).
44. *Chaplinsky v. New Hampshire*, 315 U.S. 568 (1942).
45. 559 U.S. 460 (2010).
46. The categories include fighting words, obscenity, and libel.
47. 132 S. Ct. at 2552 (Breyer, J., joined by Kagan, J., concurring in the judgment).This seems banal, but it actually conceals some complex judgments if the statutes penalize making false statements about history, philosophy, and the like knowing them to be false. Such a statute would not cover a Holocaust denier who believes that the Holocaust did not occur, although it would cover someone who stated that Jefferson was a Roman Catholic, knowing that to be false. The difficulty is that decision makers may mistakenly conclude that a person did not believe the false statements although he or she actually did believe them.
48. Ibid.
49. Ibid., 2553.
50. Ibid.
51. Ibid., 2554.

52. Ibid., 2555.
53. Ibid.
54. Ibid., 2554.
55. Ibid., 2555.
56. Ibid., 2556.
57. For a description of alternative ways of giving the Stolen Valor Act a narrower construction, see Chapter 7 herein, discussing Justice Kennedy's opinion in *Alvarez.*
58. For an instructive compilation, which seems accurate and well-sourced despite its somewhat sensationalistic presentation, see Stolen Valor: Secured Targets, http://www.stolenvalor.com/target.cfm?source=link&sort=order, archived at http://perma.cc/VV6J-AQMR
59. On my reading of the facts in *Alvarez*, the defendant would not have been able to avail himself of such a defense; he made his statement while introducing himself to other members of a public board, presumably to enhance the weight that would be given his views in the board's deliberations.
60. *Snyder v. Phelps*, 131 S. Ct. 1207 (2011).
61. *Hustler Magazine v. Falwell*, 485 U.S. 46 (1988).
62. *New York Times v. Sullivan*, 376 U.S. 254 (1964).
63. 131 S. Ct. at 1221–1222 (Breyer, J., concurring).
64. Justice Thomas dissented in a separate opinion, arguing that the California statute was consistent with the original understanding of the First Amendment, according to which (on Justice Thomas's view) children had no rights to access information without their parents' permission.
65. 131 S. Ct. at 2765 (Breyer, J., dissenting).
66. Ibid., 2766.
67. Ibid.
68. Ibid., 2766–2767.
69. Ibid., 2767.
70. Ibid., 2767–2768.
71. Ibid., 2770.
72. Justice Breyer rejected alternative modes of attempting to deny children access to violent video games without an adult's intervention because they were unlikely to be as effective as California's ban on direct sales. Voluntary labeling and voluntary restrictions on sales were difficult to enforce, and children had ready access to information that would allow them to defeat the technology used by parents to block video consoles.
73. 131 S. Ct. at 2771 (Breyer, J., dissenting).
74. Breyer, *Active Liberty*, 53–54.
75. *Sorrell v. IMS Health Services, Inc.*, 131 S. Ct. 2653 (2011).
76. The database does not allow the person using it to identify which patients were prescribed which drugs.
77. 131 S. Ct. 2653.
78. 131 S. Ct. at 2673 (Breyer, J., joined by Ginsburg and Kagan, JJ., dissenting).
79. Ibid., 2674.

80. Ibid.
81. Ibid., 2675.
82. Ibid., 2676.
83. Ibid.
84. Ibid., 2677.
85. Ibid., 2678.
86. Ibid., 2680. Recall the reference to "modest restrictions" in the violent video games case.
87. Ibid., 2682.
88. Ibid., 2682.
89. Ibid., 2683.
90. Ibid., 2685.
91. Ibid., 2679.
92. For a political history of originalism, see Jonathan O'Neill, *Originalism in American Law and Politics: A Constitutional History* (Baltimore, MD: Johns Hopkins University Press, 2005).
93. The most prominent articulation of that component is Antonin Scalia, "The Rule of Law as a Law of Rules," *University of Chicago Law Review* 56 (1989): 1175–1188.
94. I note, though, that this may be true of a single rule but is not true of complex sets of rules, which is to say, not true of legal systems taken as a whole. Judges can operate within complex rule sets to reach the goals they prefer just as Warren Court liberals did more openly.
95. For a more general discussion, see Mark Tushnet, "*Heller* and the Critique of Judgment," *Supreme Court Review* 2009 (2008): 61–87.

Conclusion: It's Complicated . . .

Helen J. Knowles and Steven B. Lichtman

Imagine that you are a politics professor (whose area of study focuses on law and courts) working at a private, small liberal arts college. You receive an unsolicited email from a member of Congress; using offensive language, that politician bitterly criticizes your work, implying that you are contributing to the "vast gay conspiracy" by failing to expose the US Supreme Court's gay rights decisions for what they are, namely "moral abominations that are rapidly sending the country to hell in a hand basket." Viewing the email as a rather pathetic piece of ideological screed, you post the text of it on your personal, private Facebook page (which is only viewable by your friends—twenty-five in total). You also mention that the politician's words are proof that he is an "intolerant, homophobic nut-job who would benefit from doing what he did last weekend—namely to f*** his mother in a portable toilet."

Thinking that this is the end of your bizarre day, you drive home, only to find two items in your mailbox. Knowing that you are an animal lover, an organization has sent you an unsolicited package containing a DVD bearing the label "God's creatures" and featuring pictures of beautiful animals on the cover (computer hackers told the organization that you regularly purchase cat litter at the local pet store). You and your cat are distraught when you play the DVD and discover it contains multiple "animal crush" scenes—of scantily clad women wearing stilettos, taking sexual pleasure from stomping on kittens strapped to the floor (you subsequently realize that the women are locally elected officials). Frustrated, in the middle of the night you climb into your car, drive to the local town hall, walk up to the steps of the building, douse two flags—Old Glory and the local town flag—in lighter fuel and set fire to them. As you leave the scene, you notice that an elderly gentleman, who was sitting on a nearby bench and playing a guitar, has now begun to collect up the ashes of the flags while gently weeping.

To what extent can governments in the United States regulate and/or restrict these forms of expression? As the chapters in this book suggest, the answer to this question is: not much. However implausible the above hypothetical may seem, it incorporates some of the "colorful scenarios" that the Court has confronted in real free speech cases.[1] And as those cases demonstrate, while the nation's rich history of zealously preserving freedom of speech through Supreme Court rulings about the scope of the First Amendment might only date back to the second decade of the twentieth century, since then advocates of "freedom for the thought that we hate" have had much to be thankful for.[2]

Thankful for the Supreme Court's decision that "the First Amendment gives" Larry Flynt "a right to be offensive." For as the morally shameless publisher of the pornographic *Hustler* magazine said after the 1987 oral argument in *Hustler v. Falwell* (in which the Court held (unanimously) that public figures cannot receive damages for intentional infliction of emotional distress unless they can show that the "distressing" publication contains a false statement of fact made with "actual malice"):[3] "To live in a free society, you've got to pay a price, and the price is toleration."[4]

Thankful for the 1989 ruling overturning Gregory Lee "Joey" Johnson's conviction for violating a state flag desecration statute when he set fire to the American Flag to make a point of political protest. "If there is a bedrock principle underlying the First Amendment," wrote Justice William J. Brennan Jr. "it is that the government may not prohibit the expression of an idea simply because society finds the idea itself offensive or disagreeable."[5]

And even thankful for the 2010 decision in *United States v. Stevens*, in which the Roberts Court gave First Amendment protection to the sellers of so-called animal crush films, rejecting the government's effort to categorize that as impermissible speech because "[t]he First Amendment itself reflects a judgment by the American people that the benefits of its restrictions on the Government outweigh the costs." And the "Constitution forecloses any attempt to revise that judgment simply on the basis that some speech is not worth it."[6]

This brief march through First Amendment history demonstrates there is much truth to Justice John Marshall Harlan's response to Paul Robert Cohen's decision to protest the Vietnam War by wearing a jacket emblazoned with the words "Fuck the Draft": "[O]ne man's vulgarity is another's lyric."[7] As Justice Robert H. Jackson famously wrote in *West Virginia v. Barnette* (1943), "[i]f there is any fixed star in our constitutional constellation, it is that no official, high or petty, can prescribe what shall be orthodox in politics, nationalism, religion, or other matters of opinion, or force citizens to confess by word or act their faith therein."[8]

However, as the chapters in this volume also make clear, the First Amendment never has, nor ever will offer absolute expressive freedom protection to those who wish to speak their minds. As we saw in Chapter 3 herein, even Justice Hugo L. Black—the member of the Court who came closest to being a First Amendment absolutist and declared in 1959 that "'no law abridging' [can be read] to mean *no law abridging*"—was not above supporting governmental abridgement of expressive freedom.[9] As Rodney Smolla observes, "[a]bsolutism may have a place in a sensible theory of freedom of speech, but not as the comprehensive methodology."[10]

Indeed, as the contributors to this book have shown, on one level Anthony Lewis is right that "[t]he Holmes-Brandeis views of free speech . . . [especially] Brandeis' words in *Whitney* [*v. California*] . . . gradually wove their way into the Court's definition of 'the freedom of speech, and of the press' guaranteed by the First Amendment."[11] Yet history is also littered with examples of Supreme Court decisions wherein a majority of the justices has deferred to government regulation over individual freedom. As a recent study of the Court has observed, "[n]obody would nominate 'simplicity' as a defining virtue of the First Amendment."[12]

This trend of complication seems set to continue.

TO THE ROBERTS COURT (AND BEYOND) . . .

During the 1981 news conference when he announced his decision to retire from the US Supreme Court, Potter Stewart ruefully recalled the seven-word phrase that was destined to become his epitaph. "I know it when I see it" was Stewart's description, in *Jacobellis v. Ohio*, of "hard-core" pornography.[13] He was ribbed by his colleagues (and their clerks) for its usage,[14] and at the news conference he lamented the inevitability of the fact that "that's going to be on my tombstone. When I remember all of the other solid words I've written . . . I regret a little bit that if I'll be remembered at all I'll be remembered for that particular phrase."[15] Political scientists and legal scholars have not, of course, reduced to the Stewart maxim their efforts to discern historical free speech jurisprudence patterns (although, on occasion, one might forgive them for doing so). However, it is tempting to conclude that, thus far, that might be the best tool for analyzing the Roberts Court's free speech decisions.

The Roberts Court, which came into being in the fall of 2005 upon the appointment of John Roberts to become the institution's seventeenth chief justice, has confounded efforts to categorize its free speech decisions. Indeed, the only thing upon which scholars seem to agree is that there is little upon which to agree when analyzing expressive freedom opinions issued during the first decade of that Court's existence. "[I]f the First Amendment had a Facebook page," as Mark Tushnet observes elsewhere, "many people seem to think the Roberts Court would 'like' it."[16] Indeed some observers (primarily the Court's admirers) have gone so far as to label it "the most consistently and strongly protective free speech Court in history."[17] However, there are also plenty of critics ready to contend that the Roberts Court has engaged in a "deregulatory hijacking of the First Amendment" and to describe it as "[n]ot a free speech court."[18] In reality, the one certainty about "[t]he Roberts Court record on freedom of speech," thus far, is that it "presents an interesting puzzle."[19]

Continuing to Take Opinions Seriously

So how might we go about figuring out the pieces of that puzzle? How might we analyze the Roberts Court's decidedly mixed expressive freedom record, with an eye to the future of judging free speech? To reemphasize a point made in the introduction to this volume, we as editors join our contributors united in the belief that judicial opinions should be taken seriously. Quantitative data about judicial voting patterns can only get us so far. The data can tell us how many justices of one identified ideological persuasion (presuming, of course, that it is possible accurately to code such behavior) voted for a particular claimant in a case. Ultimately, however, "'[s]tatistics cannot tell the story of the willingness of a court to defend free expression. . . . Cases do," cases as understood through analysis of the actual written products of the justices.[20]

As we also noted from the outset, this is a particularly important methodological observation to be mindful of when studying free speech cases because the subject matter has always had a distinct tendency to generate strange ideological bedfellows. This is just as applicable to studying the Roberts Court as it has been for previous courts. Mark Tushnet has noted, "[w]ith the important exception of cases involving advertising and similar business activities that happen to fall under the First Amendment, politics doesn't explain much."[21] Any other ideology-driven conclusion simply could not explain why when the Roberts Court rules in favor of the free speech claimant the three justices most likely to form a coalition in the majority are Kennedy, Ruth Bader Ginsburg, and Sonia Sotomayor.[22] As Brandon Metroka has convincingly shown, "there is more to freedom of speech on the Roberts Court than partisanship and ideology."[23]

Beyond 2015 . . .

In *Uncertain Justice*, Laurence Tribe and Joshua Matz make the following observation about the first decade of the Roberts Court's free speech rulings: "If speech does make the cut, values such as self-development, education, and public accountability are all swept under the rug. If speech doesn't make the cut, nearly anything goes. There is little room to be found in these majority opinions for alternative views of free speech rights."[24] To the extent that it is possible to identify a consensus of opinion about the subject matter, this is a very useful summary and encapsulation of that consensus. As they also note, however, it is a summary that "may soon change." This is because "[e]ach in his own way and for his own reasons, Thomas, Breyer, and Alito have openly expressed deep unease with the Court's current approach to free speech issues."[25] Justices Thomas and Breyer have been systematically analyzed in this volume, but a few words about Samuel Alito are also warranted.

Since joining the Court in January 2006, the one constant element of Alito's free speech jurisprudence is its idiosyncratic nature. However, he has been a constant, visible, and unusual force arguing in defense of limitations on speech. On multiple occasions, he has stood alone in dissent, railing against a determination by all of his colleagues that a speech restriction was flagrantly unconstitutional. For example, in *Stevens* Chief Justice Roberts authored a majority opinion rejecting the government's contention that depictions of animal cruelty constituted a category of unprotected speech, akin to libel, obscenity, and fraud. To accept the government's argument would be to generate a definition of "bad speech" which would surely sweep up otherwise protected speech.[26] Alone in dissent, Alito not only rejected the majority's overbreadth analysis but also argued that the videos could be categorized as unprotected speech. He analogized them to child pornography, which the Court held to be outside of the First Amendment's shelter in *New York v. Ferber*.[27] Stressing the fact that both portrayed conduct that is illegal in every state, Alito argued that crush videos, like child pornography, produced harmful consequences which outweighed whatever dubious minimal value they might have.[28]

The following year, in *Snyder v. Phelps*, the Court held that the father of a US Marine killed in Iraq could not file a civil suit for intentional infliction of emotional distress against members of the Westboro Baptist Church who had descended upon the funeral in order to engage in a protest during which they fulminated that Corporal Matthew Snyder deserved to die because of the US military's toleration of homosexuality. Although clearly disgusted by the actions of the Church members, the majority of the Court noted that the protest took place 1,000 feet from the memorial service and concluded that it was public speech on a matter of public concern, thus shielding it from the chilling effect of Albert Snyder's lawsuit.[29] In dissent, however, Alito argued that Mr. Snyder had been "brutalize[d]" by the protestors and that the First Amendment should not immunize the Church for its intentionally hurtful action. Together, *Stevens* and *Snyder* demonstrate that Alito exhibits a tendency to be skeptical toward free speech claims.[30]

Alito's coolness toward the First Amendment certainly makes him interesting and distinctive, and arguably an outlier against long-standing trends—both institutional in nature, and ascribable to many individual justices—to expand the First Amendment's reach and scope. Yet it is hard to identify a workable set of principles that animate Alito's outlook on the First Amendment. If anything, his assessments of the constitutionality of speech regulations are evocative of Potter Stewart's unfortunate maxim: Alito cannot quite explain what constitutes an acceptable speech regulation, but he knows it when he sees it. Animal snuff films seem dodgy, so banning them must be constitutionally permissible. The Westboro Baptist Church's funeral protests are mean, so subjecting them to a lawsuit must be constitutionally permissible. Lying about getting the Congressional Medal of Honor demeans veterans, so making that a crime must be constitutionally permissible. There is no unifying precept here—and Alito comfortably disdains the need to identify one. The only common theme is the "ick factor." Perhaps this is a strength of Alito's free speech opinions; he speaks from the heart, offering a jurisprudence of empathy for people whose feelings are hurt by certain speech or speakers. Here, however, the emphasis needs to be on the word *perhaps*.[31]

"Perhaps" is also an apt tempering word for any observations made in 2015 about discernible patterns in the free speech jurisprudence of Justice Elena Kagan, ostensibly because she was only appointed to the Court in August 2010. And yet, notwithstanding her short time on the Court as of this writing, there are signs that Kagan is a jurist with the potential to make a major jurisprudential and doctrinal impact.[32]

The subject of freedom of expression consumed a considerable amount of the questioning during Kagan's 2010 Supreme Court nomination hearings, but this was primarily because of her involvement, as the nation's solicitor general, in *Citizens United v. FEC*. And while several of the most substantive law review articles she penned addressed free speech rights, experts were understandably hesitant to say what these pre-judicial writings might portend for Kagan's tenure as a justice.[33] Early into that tenure, however, Kagan is emerging as a dynamic leader of the Court's liberal wing who is taking her analytical cues on free speech from Breyer, specifically building upon Breyer's conception of "active liberty."

At the end of Chapter 9 herein, Mark Tushnet speculated that there were two possible reasons "why Breyer's ideas about proportionality and active liberty do not appear to have captured the imagination of liberals." First, wrote Tushnet, is the "possibility . . . that Breyer's analysis cannot take hold of the imagination when it is, as it has been, essentially the language of dissent . . . or of disagreement on the margins." Second, it may be the case "that Breyer's literary style is that of a pedant—clear and meticulous, but rarely rhetorically captivating. Perhaps it will take someone other than Breyer to embed his ideas in liberal judicial philosophy."[34] Although Kagan only wrote one free speech opinion during her first three terms as a member of the Roberts Court, that opinion—a biting dissent in 2010's *Arizona Free Enterprise Club v. Bennett*[35]—shows why it is entirely possible that she may be the "someone" to whom Tushnet alludes.

Decided at the end of Kagan's first term on the Court, *Arizona Free Enterprise Club* involved a challenge to a provision of an Arizona campaign finance law that provided matching funds to state office candidates who accepted public financing. The amount of matching funds a candidate was entitled to receive was, in part, determined by the amount of money raised by their privately financed opponent(s). Continuing to be hostile to regulations on political money, the five conservative justices held that the law's matching funds provision was a content-based restriction on political speech, and thus was unconstitutional because it was not supported by a compelling governmental interest. The law "plainly forces the privately financed candidate to 'shoulder a special and potentially significant burden' when choosing to exercise his First Amendment right to spend funds on behalf of his candidacy."[36]

In her dissent (which was joined by Ginsburg, Breyer, and Sotomayor), Kagan rejected the majority's contention that the law discriminated against "particular ideas" and was therefore a vehicle for the government to make unconstitutional content-based judgments. "The State throws open the doors of its public financing program to all candidates who meet minimal eligibility requirements and agree not to raise private funds. Republicans and Democrats, conservatives and liberals may participate . . . Arizona disburses funds based not on a candidate's (or supporter's) ideas, but on the candidate's decision to sign up for public funding."[37]

At this point, Kagan ratcheted up her rhetorical flair, in direct contrast to the rarely captivating style of Breyer. As Marcia Coyle has observed, "Kagan's years as a law teacher appear to influence her approach to writing opinions . . . [she] communicate[s] her arguments in a vivid way that is clear, simple, and likely to stick with her audience."[38] Kagan's next words were emblematic of the bravura that Coyle has noted:

> [t]his suit . . . may merit less attention than any challenge to a speech subsidy ever seen in this Court. In the usual First Amendment subsidy case, a person complains that the government declined to finance his speech, while bankrolling someone else's; we must then decide whether the government differentiated between these speakers on a prohibited basis—because it preferred one speaker's ideas to another's. But the candidates bringing this challenge do not make that claim—because they were never denied a subsidy. Arizona, remember, offers to support any person running for state office. Petitioners here *refused* that assistance. So they are making a novel argument: that Arizona violated *their* First Amendment rights by disbursing funds to *other* speakers even though they could have received (but chose to spurn) the same financial assistance. Some people might call that *chutzpah*.[39]

Such was the vehemence with which Kagan rejected the reasoning employed by the majority that she decided to read passages of her dissenting opinion from the bench, a practice accurately described as "the final and most severe expression of disagreement."[40]

She began by observing that "[t]he First Amendment's core purpose is to foster a vibrant political system of robust discussion and debate."[41] As the chapters in this book have shown, this is a nonideological precept that has played a central role in the Court's free speech jurisprudence for much of the twentieth century and into the twenty-first century. Kagan contended that the Arizona law was entirely consistent with that precept, a reality that the majority either misunderstood or disregarded. In her closing two paragraphs, Kagan powerfully emphasized that theme of "robust discussion" in a manner reminiscent of Breyer's concept of "active liberty":

> This case arose because Arizonans wanted their government to work on behalf of all the State's people. On the heels of a political scandal involving the near-routine purchase of legislators' votes, Arizonans passed a law designed to sever political candidates' dependence on large contributors. They wished, as many of their fellow Americans wish, to stop corrupt dealing—to ensure that their representatives serve the public, and not just the wealthy donors who helped put them in office. The legislation that Arizona's voters enacted was the product of deep thought and care. It put into effect a public financing system that attracted large numbers of candidates at a sustainable cost to the State's taxpayers. The system discriminated against no ideas and prevented no speech. . . . Less corruption, more speech . . .
>
> No fundamental principle of our Constitution backs the Court's ruling; to the contrary, it is the law struck down today that fostered both the vigorous competition of ideas and its ultimate object—a government responsive to the will of the people. *Arizonans deserve better. Like citizens across this country, Arizonans deserve a government that represents and serves them all. And no less, Arizonans deserve the chance to reform their electoral system so as to attain that most American of goals.* Truly, democracy is not a game.[42]

The year after *Arizona Free Enterprise Club*, Breyer produced a concurring opinion in *Alvarez* that was shown in Chapter 9 herein to be a classic statement of his free speech jurisprudence. Kagan joined that opinion (and she was the only member of the Court to do so), further evidence to suggest that she may take up the "active liberty" reins.

However, if Kagan is going to be "a new force to be reckoned with on the Court," (as Marcia Coyle has predicted),[43] she will have to overcome the existing freedom of speech force that is Chief Justice John G. Roberts.

As chief justice, Roberts has taken full advantage of his structural opportunities to shape the contemporary Court's free speech jurisprudence, most notably his prerogative to assign the opinion in any case in which he votes with the majority. As of the end of the October 2013 term, Roberts has been in the majority in free speech cases approximately 80 percent of the time, and in over one-third of the cases he has chosen to assign the opinion to himself.[44] Indeed, in his first nine years on the Court, Roberts authored the main opinion of the Court (either for a majority or a plurality) in free speech cases twice as often as the member of the Court with the second-most such opinions, Justice Kennedy.[45] As Ronald Collins has commented, "Chief Justice John Roberts is at the helm of this ship of the Court's First Amendment jurisprudence."[46]

Whether this ship is being sailed by a beloved Mister Roberts or a reviled Dread Pirate Roberts is a matter of taste, and perhaps politics. Whether this ship is being sailed in a consistent jurisprudential direction, however, is a much thornier question.

Roberts's record on free speech is both extensive and contradictory. At times, he has embraced restrictions on speech, with *Morse v. Frederick* being perhaps the most well-known example. But Roberts's opinion in *Holder v. Humanitarian Law Project*[47] may be more far-reaching. In that case, writing for a 6-3 majority, the Chief Justice rejected a free speech challenge to the USA PATRIOT Act's prohibition on providing material support to foreign terrorist organizations. HLP wished to advise separatist groups in Turkey and Sri Lanka on nonviolence, but since the State Department had designated the groups as terrorist organizations, HLP was barred from offering that counsel.

Although he conceded that "both plaintiffs and the Government take extreme positions on the question,"[48] Roberts felt that HLP's position was the untenable one. HLP's desire to teach Kurdish separatists in Turkey how to rely on international law to resolve disputes peacefully, for example, could play into a larger rope-a-dope strategy of temporarily suspending violence in order to regroup (and in order to lull their targets to sleep) before renewing bloodshed. The government, Roberts insisted, had the power to prevent such hypothetical terrorist dangers without the First Amendment interfering. "If only good can come from training our adversaries in international dispute resolution, presumably it would have been unconstitutional to prevent American citizens from training the Japanese Government on using international organizations and mechanisms to resolve disputes during World War II," Roberts gravely intoned. "That view is not one the First Amendment requires us to embrace."[49]

Prominent commentators suggested, however, that such a view might well have been required, and those suggestions came from diverse ideological camps. Noting that Roberts had acknowledged that applying the "material support" provision to HLP was a content-based restriction on speech, Eugene Volokh opined that this made the case "the only non-overruled majority opinion to uphold a content-based restriction under strict scrutiny."[50] Erwin Chemerinsky harshly criticized the speculative nature of Roberts's ruling, pointing out that there was no real evidence that "the speech would have the slightest effect on increasing the likelihood of terrorist activity. The deference that the Court gave to the government was tremendous and the restrictions it placed on speech were great."[51]

Yet the very same Roberts who can provide unprecedented constitutional approval to direct restrictions on speech can be equally doctrinaire in a speech-protective fashion. It was Roberts who authored the majority opinion in *Arizona Free Enterprise Club* that so angered Kagan. More tellingly, it was Roberts who authored the majority opinion in *Snyder*. While the 8-1 vote breakdown in *Snyder* indicates the consensus nature of the holding, one important (and often-neglected) aspect of that case must be stressed—as noted above, the legal proceeding was not a criminal prosecution but rather a civil lawsuit. It is one thing to decry governmental actions that restrict speech, but in *Snyder* Roberts fervently opposed the actions of a private individual who had unquestionably been victimized (and who had been targeted for that victimization).

Ironically, a generation earlier, in another famous case of targeted hate speech, the idea of a civil lawsuit for intentional infliction of emotional distress had been *embraced* by a federal court as an alternative to governmental regulation. In *Collin v. Smith*, the Seventh Circuit Court of Appeals rejected the attempt by the village of Skokie, Illinois, to bar a group of Nazis from marching through the center of the town (which had a majority of Jewish residents, many of whom were Holocaust survivors). In so doing, the Court not only confirmed that Illinois law recognized the "'new tort' of intentional infliction of severe emotional distress," it also assumed that "specific individuals could proceed in tort under this theory to recover damages provably occasioned by the proposed march, and that a First Amendment defense would not bar the action."[52]

What was seen as the solution to a free speech dilemma in the Skokie case was seen as the embodiment of a free speech problem by Roberts in *Snyder*. Insistently—and, in the eyes of Alito, insensitively—applying the *New York Times v. Sullivan* standard for robust debate on matters of public concern, Roberts interpreted Westboro Baptist Church's attack on Corporal Snyder as a political commentary on US military policy and ascribed to it a level of importance so elevated that not even a private lawsuit by an emotionally wounded target should be afforded the smallest chance of chilling it.[53] He closed his opinion as follows:

> Speech is powerful. It can stir people to action, move them to tears of both joy and sorrow, and—as it did here—inflict great pain. On the facts before us, we cannot react to that pain by punishing the speaker. As a Nation we have chosen a different course—to protect even hurtful speech on public issues to ensure that we do not stifle public debate. That choice requires that we shield Westboro from tort liability for its picketing in this case.[54]

Snyder demonstrates that Roberts has an impassioned preference for a rigorous version of freedom of speech. *Morse* and *Humanitarian Law Project*, however, demonstrate that this impassioned preference is wholly situational.

That conclusion is entirely consistent with what history tells us about the ways in which members of the US Supreme Court have interpreted the deceptively simple "fourteen little words"[55] of the First Amendment's Free Speech Clause. And from that history we know that the clause will continue to "beat . . . on, a sometimes skipperless boat drifting deeper into uncertain waters, ruddered only imperfectly by selected values and stories drawn from our murky past."[56] In other words, judging free speech, and judging the judges who judge free speech, always has been, and always will be *very* complicated.

NOTES

1. We are grateful to Brandon Metroka for providing us with this useful description.
2. *United States v. Schwimmer*, 279 U.S. 644, 655 (1929) (Holmes, J., dissenting).
3. *Hustler Magazine v. Falwell*, 485 U.S. 46 (1988).
4. Larry Flynt quoted in Stuart Taylor Jr., "Sharp Words in High Court on Hustler Parody of Falwell," *New York Times*, December 3, 1987.
5. *Texas v. Johnson*, 491 U.S. 397, 414 (1989).
6. *United States v. Stevens*, 559 U.S. 460, 470 (2010).
7. *Cohen v. California*, 403 U.S. 15, 25 (1971).
8. *West Virginia v. Barnette*, 319 U.S. 624, 642 (1943).
9. *Smith v. California*, 361 U.S. 147, 157 (1959) (Black, J., concurring).
10. Rodney A. Smolla, *Smolla and Nimmer on Freedom of Speech: A Treatise on the First Amendment*, Vol. 2 (New York: M. Bender, 1994), 57.
11. Anthony Lewis, *Make No Law: The Sullivan Case and the First Amendment* (New York: Random House, 1991), 89.
12. Laurence H. Tribe and Joshua Matz, *Uncertain Justice: The Roberts Court and the Constitution* (New York: Henry Holt, 2014), 152.
13. *Jacobellis v. Ohio*, 378 U.S. 184, 197 (1964) (Stewart, J., concurring).
14. Bob Woodward and Scott Armstrong, *The Brethren: Inside the Supreme Court* (New York: Simon & Schuster, 1979), 234.
15. Stewart speaking at his 1981 news conference, reprinted in Al Kamen, "Retired High Court Justice Potter Stewart Dies at 70," *Washington Post*, December 8, 1985.
16. Mark Tushnet, *In the Balance: Law and Politics on the Roberts Court* (New York: W. W. Norton, 2013), 215.

17. Michael McConnell quoted in Marcia Coyle, *The Roberts Court: The Struggle for the Constitution* (New York: Simon & Schuster, 2013), 324. Ken Starr has expressed similar sentiments. See Erwin Chemerinsky, "Isaac Marks Lecture: Not a Free Speech Court," *Arizona Law Review* 53 (2011): 724 (referencing an address that Starr gave at the Pepperdine Judicial Law Clerk Institute on March 18, 2011). There is more than a little bit of irony here, because Starr was the victorious counsel in *Morse v. Frederick*, which was a "messy" decision that undermined precedents that provided expansive protection for public school students (551 U.S. 393 (2007)). On the "messy" nature of the *Morse* decision, see James C. Foster, *Bong Hits 4 Jesus: A Perfect Constitutional Storm in Alaska's Capital* (Fairbanks, AK: University of Alaska Press, 2010).
18. Linda Greenhouse, "The Next Nine Years," *New York Times* (online), October 1, 2014, http://nyti.ms/1nNqeo0; Chemerinsky, "Not a Free Speech Court."
19. Brandon Thomas Metroka, "Speaking in Tongues? Understanding the Roberts Court Record on Freedom of Speech," unpublished paper presented at the Annual Meeting of the Northeastern Political Science Association (Boston, MA, November 12–15, 2014), 2.
20. Floyd Abrams, quoted in Adam Liptak, "Study Challenges Supreme Court's Image as Defender of Free Speech," *New York Times*, January 7, 2012, 15.
21. Tushnet, *In the Balance*, 215. One set of scholars has reached the conclusion that in free speech cases the justices' votes are to a large extent determined by the ideology of the speakers/speech in particular cases (especially on the Roberts Court). Conservative justices look more favorably upon the free speech claims of conservative speakers/speech and vice versa. There are a number of reasons—methodological and substantive—why this conclusion is controversial, and the findings have generated a robust debate about their veracity. See Lee Epstein, Christopher M. Parker, and Jeffrey A. Segal, "Do Justices Defend the Speech They Hate? In-Group Bias, Opportunism, and the First Amendment" (2014), unpublished paper, http://epstein.wustl.edu/research/InGroupBias.pdf. For a particularly pointed criticism of that working paper, see Todd E. Pettys, "Free Expression, In-Group Bias, and the Court's Conservatives: A Critique of the Epstein-Parker-Segal Study" (2014), working paper, http://ssrn.com/abstract=2499274. For the Epstein et al. response to that criticism, see Lee Epstein, Christopher M. Parker, and Jeffrey A. Segal, "A Response to a Critique of Our Study on In-Group Bias (September 30, 2014)" (2014), unpublished paper, http://epstein.wustl.edu/research/InGroupBiasResponse.pdf
22. Liptak, "Study Challenges." Admittedly, as Ronald Collins points out, through the end of the October 2012 term all of the Roberts Court free speech cases decided by a 5-4 vote found the justices split into what is generally considered to be two groups of ideologically distinct

("conservative" versus "liberal") justices. See Ronald K. L. Collins, "Exceptional Freedom: The Roberts Court, The First Amendment, and the New Absolutism," *Albany Law Review* 76 (2013): 456, footnote no. 319. However, in *Morse*, one of the five cases that Collins cites (the others are *Arizona Free Enterprise Club v. Bennett*, 131 S. Ct. 2806 (2011); *Citizens United v. FEC*, 558 U.S. 310 (2010); *Davis v. FEC*, 554 U.S. 724 (2008); and *Garcetti v. Ceballos*, 547 U.S. 410 (2006)), the Court was so fractured that it is difficult to reach the conclusion that it was a 5-4 decision.

23. Metroka, "Speaking in Tongues?" 25.
24. Tribe and Matz, *Uncertain Justice*, 153.
25. Ibid.
26. 559 U.S. 460 (2010).
27. *New York v. Ferber*, 458 U.S. 747 (1982).
28. 559 U.S. at 494–495 (Alito, J., dissenting).
29. *Snyder v. Phelps*, 131 S. Ct. 1207 (2011).
30. 131 S. Ct. at 1222 (Alito, J., dissenting). While not a solo dissent like his opinions in *Snyder* and *Stevens*, Alito's dissent in *United States v. Alvarez*, 132 S. Ct. 2537, 2556–2565 (2012) (Alito, J., joined by Scalia and Thomas, JJ., dissenting), in which he defended the constitutionality of the "Stolen Valor Act" (which made it a federal crime to make a false claim to have been awarded the Congressional Medal of Honor), is of a piece with those two cases. It is important to note that this tendency does not always manifest itself. For example, in *Entertainment Merchants Association* Alito declined to join Scalia's majority opinion. He instead chose to write a separate concurrence (joined by Roberts) in which he indicated that he thought that violent video games might have a deleterious effect on children and thus felt it would be unwise constitutionally to foreclose future regulatory efforts.
31. For a very instructive and incisive analysis of Justice Alito's dissenting opinions in free speech cases, see the following article by the late Richard E. Morgan, a beloved and much-missed colleague. Richard E. Morgan, "Justice Alito, Dissenting," *Claremont Review of Books*, XII, no. 4 (2012). http://www.claremont.org/article/justice-alito-dissenting/#.VXnHr6azCt-. Dick Morgan embodied everything that makes the New England Political Science Association – of which he was President in 1989 – home to such a great group of scholars and friends; and he had an infectious passion for the study of law and courts that will live on in those of us who were lucky enough to know him.
32. Generally, see Tushnet, *In the Balance*.
33. United States Senate, Committee on the Judiciary, *Hearings on the Nomination of Elena Kagan to be Associate Justice of the Supreme Court of the United States*, 111th Cong., 2nd sess., June 28–30, July 1, 2010; Eugene Volokh, "Elena Kagan as Scholar," May 10, 2010, *The Volokh Conspiracy*, http://www.volokh.com/2010/05/10/elena-kagan-as-scholar/; Tom Goldstein, "9750 Words on Elena Kagan," May 8, 2010, *SCOTUSblog*, http://www.scotusblog.com/2010/05/9750-words-on-elena-kagan/

34. *Judging Free Speech*, 234.
35. 131 S. Ct. 2806 (2011).
36. Ibid., 2818.
37. 131 S. Ct. at 2834 (Kagan, J., joined by Ginsburg, Breyer, and Sotomayor, JJ., dissenting).
38. Coyle, *The Roberts Court*, 329.
39. 131 S. Ct. at 2835 (Kagan, J., joined by Ginsburg, Breyer, and Sotomayor, JJ., dissenting). Chutzpah: "From the Hebrew word for 'audacity.' Nerve, gall. Gutsy, sometimes arrogant behavior that is outrageous but at the same time admirable." Joyce Eisenberg and Ellen Scolnic, *The JPS Dictionary of Jewish Words* (Philadelphia, PA: Jewish Publication Society, 2001), 28.
40. William D. Blake and Hans J. Hacker, "'The Brooding Spirit of the Law': Supreme Court Justices Reading Dissents from the Bench," *Justice System Journal* 31 (2010): 21.
41. The audio and transcript of Kagan's dissent from the bench are available at http://www.oyez.org/cases/2010-2019/2010/2010_10_238
42. 131 S. Ct. at 2845–2846 (Kagan, J., joined by Ginsburg, Breyer, and Sotomayor, JJ., dissenting). The added italics represent the portion of this passage that Kagan chose to include in her dissent from the bench.
43. Coyle, *The Roberts Court*, 329.
44. Notably, as of the end of the October 2013 term, Roberts had yet to assign a single free speech opinion to Kagan.
45. Collins, "Exceptional Freedom," 455–456. When one uses the Supreme Court Database, one gets slightly different results from those presented by Collins, but the Roberts-Kennedy opinion-writing data hold true across both sources. See Harold J. Spaeth, Lee Epstein, Andrew D. Martin, Jeffrey A. Segal, Theodore J. Ruger, and Sara C. Benesh. 2014 Supreme Court Database, Version 2014 Release 01, http://supremecourtdatabase.org
46. Collins, "Exceptional Freedom," 452.
47. *Holder v. Humanitarian Law Project*, 561 U.S. 1 (2010). Also see Mark Tushnet's discussion of this case, situated within analysis of Justice Breyer's jurisprudence, in Chapter 9 herein.
48. 561 U.S. at 25.
49. Ibid., 38.
50. Eugene Volokh, "*Humanitarian Law Project* and Strict Scrutiny," on *The Volokh Conspiracy*, June 21, 2010, http://volokh.com/2010/06/21/humanitarian-law-project-and-strict-scrutiny
51. Chemerinsky, "Not a Free Speech Court," 730.
52. 578 F.2d 1197, 1206 (7th Cir. 1978). For the authoritative account of the Skokie case, see Philippa Strum, *When the Nazis Came to Skokie* (Lawrence, KS: University of Kansas Press, 1999).
53. It is instructive to compare Roberts's approach in *Snyder* to the approach taken by the courts in two other former British colonies. In 1990, the Supreme Court of Canada upheld the criminal conviction of a high school social studies teacher who had not only peppered his lessons with anti-Semitic rants but also required students to parrot those views back to

him on their exams. See *R. v. Keegstra*, [1990] 3 S.C.R. 697. Similarly, in 2011 the Federal Court of Australia ruled against a pundit who had been sued over a series of newspaper columns in which he questioned the integrity of prominent Aborigines who he felt were exploiting their heritage in order to win governmental grants (the legal basis of the suit was in fact a criminal statute that could also be used in civil proceedings). See *Eatock v. Bolt* [2011] FCA 1103. Where courts in Canada and Australia will consider free speech questions against the backdrop of broader notions of community and a nation's desire to structure itself as inclusive, American courts steadfastly refuse to engage in this type of inquiry. Roberts's opinion in *Snyder* was emblematic of this refusal. In acknowledging that Albert Snyder had been injured and that Fred Phelps had caused those injuries, but nevertheless denying Snyder even the possibility of legal recourse against Phelps, the Chief Justice was essentially asking whose rights mattered more, Albert Snyder's or Fred Phelps's . . . and determining that the answer was Fred Phelps. It is not merely that Canadian and Australian courts would never have arrived at that answer; it is that Canadian and Australian courts never would have asked the question like this in the first place.

54. 131 S. Ct. at 1220.
55. *Judging Free Speech*, Chapter 5 herein, p. 123.
56. Tribe and Matz, *Uncertain Justice*, 153.

List of Contributors

Keith J. Bybee is Paul E. and the Hon. Joanne F. Alper '72 Judiciary Studies Professor at Syracuse University. He directs the Institute for the Study of the Judiciary, Politics, and the Media. His most recent book is *All Judges Are Political—Except When They Are Not: Acceptable Hypocrisies and the Rule of Law* (2010).

Douglas E. Edlin is Associate Professor of Political Science at Dickinson College. He is the author of *Judges and Unjust Laws* (2008) and the editor of *Common Law Theory* (2007). His articles have appeared in the *American Journal of Comparative Law*, the *Canadian Journal of Law and Jurisprudence*, *Polity*, and several other journals. He received his PhD from Oxford University and his JD from Cornell University.

James C. Foster is Professor of Political Science at Oregon State University—Cascades Campus. He has devoted his forty-year career to understanding the politics of American law, lawyers, and courts. Among his works are: *The Ideology Of Apolitical Politics: Elite Lawyers' Response To The Legitimation Crisis Of American Capitalism, 1870–1920* (1990); *Constitutional Law: Cases In Context* (1992); and *Bong Hits 4 Jesus: A Perfect Constitutional Storm In Alaska's Capital* (2010).

Helen J. Knowles is Assistant Professor of Political Science at the State University of New York at Oswego. She is the author of *The Tie Goes to Freedom: Justice Anthony M. Kennedy on Liberty* (2009) and numerous articles about constitutional law, civil liberties, and legal history. She received her PhD from Boston University.

Frederick P. Lewis is Professor Emeritus of Political Science at the University of Massachusetts Lowell and a former Department Chair. He writes on constitutional law and politics and is a past president of the New England Political Science Association. He received his JD from Harvard Law School and his PhD in Political Science from Tufts University.

Steven B. Lichtman is Associate Professor of Political Science at Shippensburg University. He has authored articles on constitutional law and jurisprudence, and his work has appeared in the *Maryland Law Review* and the *Penn State Law Review*. He received his PhD from Brandeis University and his JD from New York University School of Law.

Kevin J. McMahon is the John R. Reitemeyer Professor of Political Science at Trinity College in Hartford, Connecticut. His book, *Nixon's Court: His Challenge to Judicial Liberalism and Its Political Consequences* (2011), was selected as a 2012 CHOICE Outstanding Academic Title and won the Supreme Court Historical Society's Erwin N. Griswold Prize in 2014. His first book, *Reconsidering Roosevelt on Race: How the Presidency Paved the Road to Brown* (2004), won the American Political Science Association's Richard E. Neustadt Award for the best book published on the American presidency that year.

Samuel R. Olken is a professor at The John Marshall Law School in Chicago, Illinois. He is the author of several articles and essays about constitutional law and history, as well as constitutional theory and Supreme Court judicial biography. Olken holds a JD from Emory University and an AB from Harvard University.

Michael Paris is Associate Professor of Political Science at the College of Staten Island, City University of New York. He is the author of *Framing Equal Opportunity: Law and the Politics of School Finance Reform* (2010). He is currently working on a book on the history and possible futures of school desegregation.

Mark Tushnet is the William Cromwell Professor of Law at Harvard Law School. He is the author of *In the Balance: Law and Politics on the Roberts Court* (2013) and *A Court Divided: The Rehnquist Court and the Future of Constitutional Law* (2005).

List of Cases Cited

44 Liquormart v. Rhode Island, 517 U.S. 484 (1996)
A Book Named "John Cleland's Memoirs of a Woman of Pleasure" v. Att'y Gen. of Mass., 383 U.S. 413 (1966)
Abrams v. United States, 250 U.S. 616 (1919)
Adderley v. Florida, 385 U.S. 39 (1966)
Adkins v. Children's Hospital, 261 U.S. 525 (1923)
Adler v. Board of Education, 342 U.S. 485 (1952)
Allgeyer v. Louisiana, 165 U.S. 578 (1897)
American Booksellers v. Hudnut, 771 F.2d 323 (1985)
American Civil Liberties Union v. Mukasey, 555 U.S. 1137 (2009)
American Communications Association v. Douds, 339 U.S. 382 (1950)
Arizona Free Enterprise Club v. Bennett, 131 S. Ct. 2806 (2011)
Ashcroft v. American Civil Liberties Union, 535 U.S. 564 (2002)
Ashcroft v. American Civil Liberties Union, 542 U.S. 656 (2004)
Ashcroft v. Free Speech Coalition, 535 U.S. 234 (2002)
Ashwander v. Tennessee Valley Authority, 297 U.S. 288 (1936)
Associated Press v. NLRB, 301 U.S. 103 (1937)
Austin v. Michigan Chamber of Commerce, 494 U.S. 652 (1990)
Baltzer v. United States, 248 U.S. 593 (1918)
Barenblatt v. United States, 360 U.S. 109 (1959)
Barron v. Baltimore, 32 U.S. 243 (1833)
Barsky v. Board of Regents, 347 U.S. 442 (1954)
Bartels v. Iowa, 262 U.S. 404 (1923)
Baze v. Rees, 553 U.S. 35 (2008)
Beauharnais v. Illinois, 343 U.S. 250 (1952)
Bell v. Maryland, 378 U.S. 226 (1964)
Bethel School District No. 403 v. Fraser, 478 U.S. 675 (1986)
Bowers v. Hardwick, 478 U.S. 186 (1986)
Bountiful Brick Co. v. Giles, 276 U.S. 154 (1928)
Boy Scouts of America v. Dale, 530 U.S. 640 (2000)
Brandenburg v. Ohio, 395 U.S. 444 (1969)
Branzburg v. Hayes, 408 U.S. 665 (1972)
Bridges v. California, 314 U.S. 252 (1941)
Brown v. Board of Education, 347 U.S. 483 (1954)
Brown v. Board of Education (II), 349 U.S. 294 (1955)
Brown v. Entertainment Merchants Association, 131 S. Ct. 2729 (2011)

Buckley v. Valeo, 424 U.S. 1 (1976)
Cantwell v. Connecticut, 310 U.S. 296 (1940)
Capitol Square Review and Advisory Board v. Pinette, 515 U.S. 753 (1995)
Carpenters & Joiners Union v. Ritter's Café, 315 U.S. 722 (1942)
Carter v. Carter Coal Co., 298 U.S. 238 (1936)
CBS, Inc. v. Democratic National Committee, 412 U.S. 94 (1973)
Central Hudson Gas & Electric Corp. v. Public Service Commission, 447 U.S. 557 (1980)
Chaplinsky v. New Hampshire, 315 U.S. 568 (1942)
Charles Wolff Packing Co. v. Court of Industrial Relations, 262 U.S. 522 (1923)
Citizens United v. Federal Election Commission, 555 U.S. 1028 (2008)
Citizens United v. Federal Election Commission, 557 U.S. 932 (2009)
Citizens United v. Federal Election Commission, 558 U.S. 310 (2010)
Civil Rights Cases, 109 U.S. 3 (1883)
Clements v. Fashing, 457 U.S. 957 (1982)
Cohen v. California, 403 U.S. 15 (1971)
Colgate v. Harvey, 296 U.S. 404 (1935)
Collin v. Smith, 578 F.2d 1197 (1978)
Colorado Republican Federal Campaign Committee v. Federal Election Commission, 518 U.S. 604 (1996)
Columbia Broad. Sys., Inc. v. Democratic Nat'l Comm., 412 U.S. 94 (1973)
Commonwealth v. Blanding, 3 Pick. 304 (1825)
Connick v. Myers, 461 U.S. 138 (1983)
Constance v. Harvey, 215 F.2d 571 (1954)
Cox v. New Hampshire, 312 U.S. 569 (1941)
Curtis Publishing Co. v. Butts, 388 U.S. 130 (1967)
Davis v. FEC, 554 U.S. 724 (2008)
De Jonge v. Oregon, 299 U.S. 353 (1937)
Debs v. United States, 249 U.S. 211 (1919)
Dennis v. United States, 341 U.S. 494 (1951)
Denver Area Education Television Consortium v. FCC, 518 U.S. 727 (1996)
Desist v. United States, 394 U.S. 244 (1969)
Dun & Bradstreet, Inc. v. Greenmoss Builders, Inc., 472 U.S. 749 (1985)
Eatock v. Bolt [2011] FCA 1103
Edmondson v. Leesville Concrete Co., 500 U.S. 614 (1991)
Edwards v. South Carolina, 372 U.S. 229 (1963)
Elfbrandt v. Russell, 384 U.S. 11 (1966)
Elrod v. Burns, 427 U.S. 347 (1976)
Euclid v. Ambler Realty Co., 272 U.S. 365 (1926)
FCC v. Pacifica Foundation, 438 U.S. 726 (1978)
FEC v. Colorado Republican Federal Campaign Committee, 533 U.S. 431 (2001)
Feiner v. New York, 340 U.S. 315 (1951)
Fiske v. Kansas, 274 U.S. 380 (1927)

Fox v. Standard Oil Co. of NJ, 294 U.S.87 (1935)
Frohwerk v. United States, 249 U.S. 204 (1919)
Frontiero v. Richardson, 411 U.S. 677 (1973)
Garcetti v. Ceballos, 547 U.S. 410 (2006)
Garland v. Torre, 259 F.2d. 545 (1958)
Garrison v. Louisiana, 379 U.S. 64 (1964)
Gertz v. Robert Welch, Inc., 418 U.S. 323 (1974)
Giboney v. Empire Storage & Ice Co., 336 U.S. 490 (1949)
Gilbert v. Minnesota, 254 U.S. 325 (1920)
Ginsberg v. New York, 390 U.S. 629 (1968)
Ginzburg v. United States, 383 U.S. 463 (1966)
Girouard v. United States, 328 U.S. 61 (1946)
Gitlow v. New York, 268 U.S. 652 (1925)
Great Atlantic & Pacific Tea Co. v. Grosjean, 301 U.S. 412 (1937)
Griffin v. California, 380 U.S. 609 (1965)
Griffith v. Kentucky, 479 U.S. 314 (1987)
Grosjean v. American Press Co., 297 U.S. 233 (1936)
Hague v. C.I.O., 307 U.S. 496 (1939)
Hazelwood School District v. Kuhlmeier, 484 U.S. 260 (1988)
Herbert v. Lando, 441 U.S. 153 (1979)
Herndon v. Lowry, 301 U.S. 242 (1937)
Holder v. Humanitarian Law Project, 561 U.S. 1 (2010)
Home Building & Loan Ass'n v. Blaisdell, 290 U.S. 398 (1934)
Houchins v. KQED, Inc., 438 U.S. 1 (1978)
Hurley v. Irish-American Gay, Lesbian and Bisexual Group of Boston, 515 U.S. 557 (1995)
Hustler Magazine v. Falwell, 485 U.S. 46 (1988)
Jacobellis v. Ohio, 378 U.S. 184 (1964)
Joint Anti-Fascist Refugee Committee v. McGrath, 341 U.S. 123 (1951)
Joseph Burstyn, Inc. v. Wilson, 343 U.S. 495 (1952)
Keyishian v. Board of Regents, 385 U.S. 589 (1967)
Kime v. United States, 459 U.S. 949 (1982)
Kingsley Books, Inc. v. Brown, 354 U.S. 436 (1957)
Kingsley Pictures Corp. v. Regents, 360 U.S. 684 (1959)
Konigsberg v. State Bar of California, 366 U.S. 36 (1961)
Kovacs v. Cooper, 336 U.S. 77 (1949)
Lawrence v. Texas, 539 U.S. 558 (2003)
Lewis v. Manufacturers Nat'l Bank of Detroit, 364 U.S. 603 (1961)
Liggett Co. v. Lee, 288 U.S. 517 (1933)
Lochner v. New York, 198 U.S. 45 (1905)
Lorillard Tobacco v. Reilly, 533 U.S. 525 (2001)
Marbury v. Madison, 5 U.S. 137 (1803)
Martin v. City of Struthers, 319 U.S. 141 (1943)
Masses Publishing Co. v. Patten, 244 F. 535 (1917)
McConnell v. FEC, 540 U.S. 93 (2003)

McCutcheon v. FEC, 134 S. Ct. 1434 (2014)
McIntyre v. Ohio Elections Commission, 514 U.S. 334 (1995)
Meyer v. Nebraska, 262 U.S. 390 (1923)
Miami Herald Publishing Co. v. Tornillo, 418 U.S. 241 (1974)
Milk Wagon Drivers Union v. Meadowmoor Dairies, 312 U.S. 287 (1941)
Miller v. California, 413 U.S. 15 (1973)
Moore v. City of East Cleveland, 431 U.S. 494 (1977)
Morse v. Frederick, 551 U.S. 393 (2007)
Munn v. Illinois, 94 U.S. 113 (1877)
NAACP v. Alabama, 357 U.S. 449 (1958)
NAACP v. Button, 371 U.S. 415 (1963)
National Federation of Independent Business v. Sebelius, 132 S. Ct. 2566 (2012)
Near v. Minnesota, 283 U.S. 697 (1931)
Nebbia v. New York, 291 U.S. 502 (1934)
New State Ice Co. v. Liebmann, 285 U.S. 262 (1932)
New York v. Ferber, 458 U.S. 747 (1982)
New York Times v. Sullivan, 376 U.S. 254 (1964)
New York Times v. United States, 403 U.S. 713 (1971)
Nixon v. Shrink Missouri Government PAC, 528 U.S. 377 (2000)
NLRB v. Friedman-Marks Clothing Co., 301 U.S. 58 (1937)
NLRB v. Fruehauf Trailer Co., 301 U.S. 49 (1937)
NLRB v. Jones & Laughlin Steel Corp., 301 U.S. 1 (1937)
Noto v. United States, 367 U.S. 290 (1961)
Orozco v. Texas, 394 U.S. 324 (1969)
Paris Adult Theatre I v. Slaton, 413 U.S. 49 (1973)
Patterson v. Colorado, 205 U.S. 454 (1907)
Pell v. Procunier, 417 U.S. 817 (1974)
People v. Cohen, 1 Cal. App. 3d 94, 81 Cal. Rptr. 503 (1969)
Pierce v. Society of Sisters, 268 U.S. 510 (1925)
Pierce v. United States, 252 U.S. 239 (1920)
Pittsburgh Press Co. v. Pittsburgh Comm'n on Human Relations, 413 U.S. 376 (1973)
Planned Parenthood v. Casey, 505 U.S. 833 (1992)
Plessy v. Ferguson, 163 U.S. 537 (1896)
Pointer v. Texas, 380 U.S. 400 (1965)
R. v. Keegstra, [1990] 3 S.C.R. 697
R.A.V. v. City of St. Paul, 505 U.S. 377 (1992)
Radice v. New York, 264 U.S. 292 (1924)
Randall v. Sorrell, 548 U.S. 230 (2006)
Regents of University of California v. Bakke, 438 U.S. 265 (1978)
Respublica v. Oswald, 1 U.S. 319 (1788)
Roth v. United States, 354 U.S. 476 (1957)
Rubin v. Coors Brewing Company, 514 U.S. 476 (1995)
Saia v. New York, 334 U.S. 558 (1948)

Saxbe v. Washington Post Co., 417 U.S. 843 (1974)
Scales v. United States, 367 U.S. 203 (1961)
Schaefer v. United States, 251 U.S. 466 (1920)
Schenck v. United States, 249 U.S. 47 (1919)
Service v. Dulles, 354 U.S. 363 (1957)
Shaw v. Reno, 509 U.S. 630 (1993)
Simon & Schuster v. Crime Victims Bd., 502 U.S. 105 (1991)
Slaughter-House Cases, 83 U.S. 36 (1873)
Smith v. California, 361 U.S. 147 (1959)
Snyder v. Phelps, 131 S. Ct. 1207 (2011)
Sorrell v. IMS Health Services, Inc., 131 S.Ct. 2653 (2011)
Speiser v. Randall, 357 U.S. 513 (1958)
Spence v. Washington, 418 U.S. 405 (1974)
Stanley v. Georgia, 394 U.S. 557 (1969)
State Bd. of Tax Comm'rs v. Jackson, 283 U.S. 527 (1931)
Street v. New York, 394 U.S. 576 (1969)
Stromberg v. California, 283 U.S. 359 (1931)
Sweezy v. New Hampshire, 354 U.S. 234 (1957)
Teague v. Lane, 489 U.S. 288 (1989)
Terminiello v. Chicago, 337 U.S. 1 (1949)
Texas v. Johnson, 491 U.S. 397 (1989)
Thomas v. Collins, 323 U.S. 516 (1945)
Thornhill v. Alabama, 310 U.S. 88 (1940)
Tinker v. Des Moines Independent Community School District, 393 U.S. 503 (1969)
Toledo Newspaper Co. v. United States, 247 U.S. 402 (1918)
Tyson & Bro. v. Banton, 273 U.S. 418 (1927)
UJO of Williamsburgh v. Carey, 430 U.S. 144 (1977)
United Public Workers v. Mitchell, 330 U.S. 75 (1947)
United States v. Alvarez, 132 S. Ct. 2537 (2012)
United States v. Associated Press, 52 F.Supp. 362, 372 (D.C.S.D.N.Y.1943)
United States v. Carolene Products Co., 304 U.S. 144 (1938)
United States v. Curtiss-Wright Export Corp., 299 U.S. 304 (1936)
United States v. Dennis et al., 183 F.2d 201 (1950)
United States v. Eichman, 496 U.S. 310 (1990)
United States v. Lopez, 514 U.S. 549 (1995)
United States v. Macintosh, 283 U.S. 605 (1931)
United States v. O'Brien, 391 U.S. 367 (1968)
United States v. Schwimmer, 279 U.S. 644 (1929)
United States v. Stevens, 559 U.S. 460 (2010)
United States v. Tarek Mehanna, 735 F.3d 32 (2013)
United States v. Vuitch, 402 U.S. 62 (1971)
United States v. Windsor, 570 U.S. 12 (2013)
United States ex rel. Milwaukee Social Democratic Publishing Co. v. Burleson, Postmaster General, 255 U.S. 407 (1921)

Valentine v. Chrestensen, 316 U.S. 52 (1942)
Virginia v. Black, 538 U.S. 343 (2003)
Virginia State Pharmacy Bd. v. Virginia Citizens Consumers Council, 425 U.S. 748 (1976)
Washington, Va. & Md. Coach Co. v. NLRB, 301 U.S. 142 (1937)
Watkins v. United States, 354 U.S. 178 (1957)
West Coast Hotel Co. v. Parrish, 300 U.S. 379 (1937)
West Virginia State Board of Education v. Barnette, 319 U.S. 624 (1943)
Whitney v. California, 274 U.S. 357 (1927)
Williams v. North Carolina, 317 U.S. 287 (1942)
Williams v. Standard Oil, 278 U.S. 235 (1929)
Yates v. United States, 354 U.S. 298 (1957)
Zurcher v. Stanford Daily, 436 U.S. 547 (1978)

BIBLIOGRAPHY

"Academy of Achievement Interview, Anthony Kennedy, June 23, 2005." http://www.achievement.org/autodoc/printmembet/ken0int-1

"The Court's Blow to Democracy." *New York Times*, January 22, 2010.

"Franken Bill Seeks to Limit Corporations' Influence on Elections." *St. Cloud Times*, April 29, 2010.

"Judicial Activism Inc." *Washington Post*, January 22, 2010.

"Obituary: Lawrence Speiser, 68, a Civil Liberties Lawyer." *New York Times*, September 1, 1991.

Abrams, Floyd. *Friend of the Court: On the Front Lines with the First Amendment*. New Haven, CT: Yale University Press, 2013.

Alsop, Joseph, and Turner Catledge. *The 168 Days*. New York: Doubleday, Doran, 1938.

Amar, Vikram David. "From Watergate to Ken Starr: Potter Stewart's 'Or of the Press' A Quarter Century Later." *Hastings Law Journal*, 50 (1999): 711–715.

Anderson, David A. "Freedom of the Press." *Texas Law Review*, 80 (2002): 429–530.

Arendt, Hannah. *On Revolution*. New York: Viking Press, 1963.

———. "Thinking and Moral Considerations: A Lecture." *Social Research*, 38 (Autumn 1971): 417–446.

Aristotle, *Politics* (C. D. C. Reeve, trans.). Indianapolis, IN: Hackett Publishing Company, 1998.

Associated Press. "*House Votes for Revised Stolen Valor Act*." 2012. http://www.firstamendmentcenter.org/house-votes-for-revised-stolen-valor-act

Baehr, Peter, ed. *The Portable Hannah Arendt*. New York: Penguin Classics, 2003.

Baker-Jones, Dan. "Sitting by Designation." *Nota Bene* (blog), April 25, 2012. http://notabeneuh.blogspot.com/2012/04/sitting-by-designation.html

Ball, Howard. *Hugo L. Black: Cold Steel Warrior*. New York: Oxford University Press, 1996.

Barnes, Robert. "High Court Shows It Might Be Willing to Act Boldly." *Washington Post*, January 22, 2010, A4.

Bates, Anna. *Weeder in the Garden of the Lord: Anthony Comstock's Life and Career*. Lanham, MD: University Press of America, 1995.

Bickel, Alexander M. *The Least Dangerous Branch: The Supreme Court at the Bar of Politics*. Indianapolis, IN: Bobbs-Merrill Company, 1962.

Binion, Gayle, "Potter Stewart." In *Biographical Encyclopedia of the Supreme Court: The Lives and Legal Philosophies of the Justices*, ed. Melvin I. Urofsky. Washington, DC: CQ Press, 2006, 486–492.

Black, Hugo Lafayette. "The Bill of Rights." *New York University Law Review*, 35 (1960): 865–881.

———. *A Constitutional Faith*. New York: Alfred A. Knopf, 1968.

Blake, William D., and Hans J. Hacker, "'The Brooding Spirit of the Law': Supreme Court Justices Reading Dissents from the Bench." *Justice System Journal*, 31 (2010): 1–25.

Blanchard, Margaret A. "The Institutional Press and Its First Amendment Privileges." *Supreme Court Review*, 1978 (1978): 225–296.

Blasi, Vincent. "The First Amendment and the Ideal of Civic Courage: The Brandeis Opinion in *Whitney v. California*." *William & Mary Law Review*, 29 (1988): 653–697.

Boll, Carol L. "Newhouse III Dedication: A Day to Remember." *Newhouse Network*, Fall 2007, 3.

Bossie, David N. "'Congress Shall Make No Law . . .': There's Nothing Hard to Understand About That." *Washington Times*, January 22, 2010, B1.

Breyer, Stephen. *Active Liberty: Interpreting Our Democratic Constitution*. New York: Knopf, 2005.

Brock, George. *Out of Print: Newspapers, Journalism, and the Business of News in the Digital Age*. London: Kogan Page, 2013.

Bunker, Matthew D., and Clay Calvert, "Contrasting Concurrences of Clarence Thomas: Deploying Originalism and Paternalism in Commercial and Student Speech Cases." *Georgia State University Law Review*, 26 (2010): 321–359.

Bybee, Keith J. "Open Secret: Why the Supreme Court Has Nothing to Fear From the Internet." *Chicago-Kent Law Review*, 88 (2013): 309–323.

Caine, Burton. "The Trouble with 'Fighting Words': *Chaplinksy v. New Hampshire* Is a Threat to First Amendment Values and Should Be Overruled." *Marquette Law Review*, 88 (2004): 441–562.

Calvert, Clay. "Mixed Messages, Muddled Meanings, Drunk Dicks, and Boobies Bracelets: Sexually Suggestive Student Speech and the Need to Overrule or Radically Refashion *Fraser*." *Denver University Law Review*, 90 (2012): 131–173.

Carpenter, William S. *Judicial Tenure in the United States with Especial Reference to the Tenure of Federal Judges*. New Haven, CT: Yale University Press, 1918.

Chafee Jr., Zechariah. "Freedom of Speech in War Time." *Harvard Law Review*, 32 (1919): 932–973.

———. *Freedom of Speech*. New York: Harcourt, Brace and Howe, 1920.

Charles, Guy-Uriel E. "Colored Speech: Cross-Burnings, Epistemics, and the Triumph of the Crits." *Georgetown Law Review*, 93 (2005): 575–632.

Chemerinsky, Erwin. "Isaac Marks Lecture: Not a Free Speech Court." *Arizona Law Review*, 53 (2011): 723–734.

Clayton, Cornell W., and Howard Gillman, eds., *Supreme Court Decision-Making: New Institutionalist Approaches*. Chicago, IL: University of Chicago Press, 1999.

Cohen, William. "A Look Back at *Cohen v. California*." *UCLA Law Review*, 34 (1987): 1595–1614.

Collins, Ronald K. L. "The Roberts Court and the First Amendment." *SCOTUSblog*, July 9, 2013. http://www.scotusblog.com/2013/07/the-roberts-court-and-the-first-amendment/

———. "Exceptional Freedom: The Roberts Court, The First Amendment, and the New Absolutism." *Albany Law Review*, 76 (2013): 409–465.

Comegys, Rowena Scott. "Potter Stewart: An Analysis of His Views on the Press as Fourth Estate." *Chicago-Kent Law Review*, 59 (1982): 157–208.

Comiskey, Michael. *Seeking Justices: The Judging of Supreme Court Nominees*. Lawrence, KS: University Press of Kansas, 2004.

Cook, Beverly Blair. "Justice Brennan and the Institutionalization of Dissent Assignment." Unpublished manuscript, 1995.

Cooley, Thomas. *A Treatise on the Constitutional Limitations Which Rest upon the Legislative Power of the States of the American Union*. Boston, MA: Little, Brown, 1883.

Corley, Pamela C. *Concurring Opinion Writing on the U.S. Supreme Court*. Albany, NY: SUNY Press, 2010.

Corley, Pamela C., et al. "Extreme Dissensus: Explaining Plurality Decisions on the United States Supreme Court." *Justice System Journal*, 31, no. 2 (2010): 1–21.

Corley, Pamela C., Amy Steigerwalt, and Artemus Ward. *The Puzzle of Unanimity: Consensus on the United States Supreme Court*. Palo Alto, CA: Stanford University Press, 2013.

Cortner, Richard C. *The Kingfish and the Constitution: Huey Long, The First Amendment, and the Emergence of Modern Press Freedom in America*. Westport, CT: Praeger, 1996.

Coyle, Marcia. *The Roberts Court: The Struggle for the Constitution*. New York: Simon & Schuster, 2013.

Curtis, Michael Kent. *Free Speech, 'The People's Darling Privilege': Struggles for Freedom of Expression in American History*. Durham, NC: Duke University Press, 2000.

Davis, Richard. *Justices and Journalists: The U.S. Supreme Court and the Media*. New York: Cambridge University Press, 2011.

Dickson, Del. *The Supreme Court in Conference, 1940–1985: The Private Discussions Behind Nearly 300 Supreme Court Decisions*. New York: Oxford University Press, 2001.

Dorsen, Norman. "A Tribute to Justice William J. Brennan Jr." *Harvard Law Review*, 104 (1990): 15–22.

Eisenberg, Joyce, and Ellen Scolnic. *The JPS Dictionary of Jewish Words*. Philadelphia, PA: Jewish Publication Society, 2001.

Eisler, Kim Isaac. *A Justice for All: William J. Brennan, Jr., and the Decisions That Transformed America*. New York: Simon & Schuster, 1993.

Elshtain, Jean Bethke. *Public Man, Private Woman*, 2nd ed. Princeton, NJ: Princeton University Press, 1993.

Ely, John Hart. *Democracy and Distrust: A Theory of Judicial Review*. Cambridge, MA: Harvard University Press, 1980.

Emerson, Thomas I. *The System of Freedom of Expression*. New York: Random House, 1970.

Epps, Garrett. "The Civil Rights Heroes the Court Ignored in *New York Times v. Sullivan*." *New York Times*, March 20, 2014.

Epstein, Lee, and Jack Knight, *The Choices Justices Make*. Washington, DC: CQ Press, 1998.

Epstein, Lee, and William M. Landes. "Was There Ever Such a Thing as Judicial Self-Restraint?" *California Law Review*, 100 (2012): 557–577.

Epstein, Lee, Christopher M. Parker, and Jeffrey A. Segal. "Do Justices Defend the Speech They Hate? In-Group Bias, Opportunism, and the First Amendment." Unpublished paper, 2014. http://epstein.wustl.edu/research/InGroupBias.pdf

———. "A Response to a Critique of Our Study on In-Group Bias (Sept. 30, 2014)." Unpublished paper, 2014. http://epstein.wustl.edu/research/InGroupBiasResponse.pdf

Fein, Bruce. "A Court of Mediocrity: Supreme Court Commentary." *American Bar Association Journal*, 77 (October 1991): 74–76, 78–79.

Feldman, Stephen M. "Free Speech, World War I, and Republican Democracy: The Internal and External Holmes." *First Amendment Law Review*, 6 (2008): 192–251.

Field, Martha A. "Justice Harlan's Legal Process." *New York Law School Law Review*, 36 (1991): 155–177.

Filler, Louis. *Crusaders for American Liberalism*. Yellow Springs, OH: Antioch Press, 1961.

Flack, Horace. *The Adoption of the Fourteenth Amendment*. Baltimore, MD: Johns Hopkins University Press, 1908.

Foster, James C. *Bong Hits 4 Jesus: A Perfect Constitutional Storm in Alaska's Capital*. Fairbanks, AK: University of Alaska Press, 2010.

Frank, Jerome N. "Some Reflections on Judge Learned Hand." *University of Chicago Law Review*, 24 (1957): 666–705.

Frankfurter, Felix. "The Supreme Court in the Mirror of Justices." *University of Pennsylvania Law Review*, 105 (1957): 781–796.

Freyer, Tony A. *Hugo L. Black and the Dilemma of American Liberalism*, 2nd ed. New York: Pearson Longman, 2008.

Friedman, Leon, "Potter Stewart." In *The Justices of the United States Supreme Court: Their Lives and Major Opinions*, eds. Leon Friedman and Fred L. Israel. New York: Chelsea House Publishers, 1997, 1546–1573.

Garnett, Richard W. "William H. Rehnquist: A Life Lived Greatly, and Well." *Yale Law Journal*, 115 (2006): 1847–1855.

Garrow, David J. "Justice Brennan, a Liberal Lion Who Wouldn't Hire Women." *Washington Post*, October 17, 2010.

Gewirtz, Paul. "On 'I Know It When I See It.'" *Yale Law Journal*, 105 (1996): 1023–1047.

Gillman, Howard, Mark A. Graber, and Keith E. Whittington. *American Constitutionalism: Volume II—Rights and Liberties.* New York: Oxford University Press, 2013.

Goldstein, Robert Justin. *"Saving Old Glory": The History of the American Flag Desecration Controversy.* Boulder, CO: Westview Press, 1995.

Goldstein, Tom. "9750 Words on Elena Kagan." *SCOTUSblog*, May 8, 2010. http://www.scotusblog.com/2010/05/9750-words-on-elena-kagan/

Goudsouzian, Aram. *Down to the Crossroads: Civil Rights, Black Power, and the Meredith March Against Fear.* New York: Farrar, Straus & Giroux, 2014.

Graber, Mark A. *Transforming Free Speech: The Ambiguous Legacy of Civil Libertarianism.* Berkeley, CA: University of California Press, 1991.

———. "Clarence Thomas and the Perils of Amateur History." In *Rehnquist Justice: Understanding the Court Dynamic*, ed. Earl M. Maltz. Lawrence, KS: University Press of Kansas, 2003, 70–102.

———. "Constructing Judicial Review." *Annual Review of Political Science*, 8 (2005): 425–451.

Greenburg, Jan Crawford. *Supreme Conflict: The Inside Story of the Struggle for Control of the United States Supreme Court.* New York: Penguin, 2007.

Greenhouse, Linda. "The Next Nine Years." *New York Times (online)*, October 1, 2014. Available at http://nyti.ms/1nNqeo0

Gunther, Gerald. "In Search of Judicial Quality on a Changing Court: The Case of Justice Powell." *Stanford Law Review*, 24 (1972): 1001–1035.

———. *Learned Hand: The Man and the Judge.* New York: Oxford University Press, 2010.

Gunther, Gerald, and Kathleen M. Sullivan. *Constitutional Law, 13th Edition.* Westbury, NY: The Foundation Press, 1997.

Hamilton, Alexander, John Jay, and James Madison. *The Federalist.* Indianapolis, IN: Liberty Fund, 2001.

Harrison, Robert. "The Breakup of the Roosevelt Court: The Contribution of History and Biography." Ph.D. diss., Columbia University, 1987.

Hayek, Friedrich A. *The Constitution of Liberty.* Chicago, IL: University of Chicago Press, 1960.

Healy, Thomas. *The Great Dissent: How Oliver Wendell Holmes Changed His Mind—And Changed the History of Free Speech in America.* New York: Henry Holt, 2013.

Heck, Edward V. "Justice Brennan and the Heyday of Warren Court Liberalism." *Santa Clara Law Review*, 20 (1980): 841–887.

———. "Justice Brennan and Freedom of Expression Doctrine in the Burger Court." *San Diego Law Review*, 20 (1987): 1153–1183.

Hentoff, Nat. "First Friend." *Legal Times*, July 3, 2000, 62.

Herbst, Susan. *Rude Democracy: Civility and Incivility in American Politics.* Philadelphia, PA: Temple University Press, 2010.

Hoekstra, Valerie, and Timothy Johnson. "Delaying Justice: The Supreme Court's Decision to Hear Rearguments." *Political Research Quarterly*, 56 (September 2003): 351–360.

Holmes Jr., Oliver Wendell, *The Common Law*, 1881; reprint Mineola, NY: Dover Publications, 1991.

Horwitz, Morton J. "In Memoriam: William J. Brennan, Jr." *Harvard Law Review*, 111 (1997): 23–28.

Horwitz, Paul. *First Amendment Institutions*. Cambridge: Harvard University Press, 2013.

Howe, Mark DeWolfe, ed., *Holmes-Laski Letters: The Correspondence of Mr. Justice Holmes and Harold J. Laski 1916–1935*. Cambridge, MA: Harvard University Press, 1953.

Huetteman, Emmarie. "'I Am a Female,' Manning Announces, Asking Army for Hormone Therapy," *New York Times*, August 23, 2013.

Irons, Peter H. "'Fighting Fair': Zechariah Chafee, Jr., the Department of Justice, and the 'Trial at the Harvard Club.'" *Harvard Law Review*, 94 (1981): 1205–1236.

———. *The Courage of Their Convictions*. New York: Free Press, 1988.

Jacobsen, Joel. "Remembered Justice: The Background, Early Career, and Judicial Appointments of Justice Potter Stewart." *Akron Law Review*, 35 (2002): 227–250.

Johnson, Steven, and Paul Starr. "Are We on Track for a Golden Age of Serious Journalism?" *Prospect*, May 4, 2009. http://www.prospectmagazine.co.uk/magazine/areweontrackforagoldenageofseriousjournalism/

Jones, Alan. "Thomas M. Cooley and 'Laissez-Faire Constitutionalism': A Reconsideration." *Journal of American History*, 53 (1967): 751–771.

Jones, RonNell Andersen. "U.S. Supreme Court Justices and Press Access." *Brigham Young University Law Review*, 2012 (2012): 1791–1817.

Kalven Jr., Harry. "The *New York Times* Case: A Note on the Central Meaning of the First Amendment." *Supreme Court Review*, 1964 (1964): 191–221.

———. *A Worthy Tradition: Freedom of Speech in America*. New York: Harper & Row, 1989.

Kamen, Al. "Retired High Court Justice Potter Stewart Dies at 70." *Washington Post*, December 8, 1985.

Kaufman, Andrew L. *Cardozo*. Cambridge, MA: Harvard University Press, 1998.

Kauffman, Bill. "Clarence Thomas." *Reason*, November 1987. http://reason.com/archives/1987/11/01/clarence-thomas/

Keller, Bill. "Is Glenn Greenwald the Future of News?" *New York Times*, October 27, 2013.

Kennedy, Anthony M. *The Constitution and the Spirit of Freedom, The Gauer Distinguished Lecture in Law and Public Policy*—vol. 1. Washington, DC: National Legal Center for the Public Interest, 1990.

Kiesel, Meghan. "Supreme Court Health Care Ruling Inspires Creative Vitriol." *ABC News*, June 29, 2012. http://abcnews.go.com/Politics/OTUS/supreme-court-health-care-ruling-inspires-creative-vitriol/story?id=16678659

Knake, Renee Newman. "Why the Law Needs Music: Revisiting *NAACP v. Button* through the Songs of Bob Dylan." *Fordham Urban Law Journal*, 38 (2011): 1303–1321.

Knowles, Helen J. "The Constitution and Slavery: A Special Relationship." *Slavery and Abolition*, 28 (2007): 309–328.

———. *The Tie Goes to Freedom: Justice Anthony M. Kennedy on Liberty.* Lanham, MD: Rowman & Littlefield, 2009.

———. "What a Difference Five Years Haven't Made: Justice Kennedy and the First Amendment, 2007–2012." *University of Missouri-Kansas City Law Review*, 82 (2013): 79–132.

Kovach, Bill, and Tom Rosenstiel. *The Elements of Journalism: What Newspeople Should Know and the Public Should Expect.* New York: Crown Publishers, 2001.

Krauthammer, Charles. "Philosophy for a Judge." *Washington Post*, July 8, 2005, A23.

Lange, David L., and H. Jefferson Powell. *No Law: Intellectual Property in the Image of an Absolute First Amendment.* Stanford, CA: Stanford Law Books, 2009.

Leonard, Thomas C. *The Power of the Press: The Birth of American Political Reporting.* New York: Oxford University Press, 1986.

Leuchtenburg, William E. *The Supreme Court Reborn: The Constitutional Revolution in the Age of Roosevelt.* New York: Oxford University Press, 1995.

Levy, Leonard W. *Legacy of Suppression: Freedom of Speech and Press in Early American History.* Cambridge, MA: Harvard University Press, 1960.

Lewis, Anthony. "High Court Curbs Public Officials in Libel Actions." *New York Times*, March 10, 1964, 1.

———. *Make No Law: The Sullivan Case and the First Amendment.* New York: Random House, 1991.

Lichtman, Steven B. "Black Like Me: The Free Speech Jurisprudence of Clarence Thomas." *Penn State Law Review*, 114 (2009): 415–468.

———. "The Disappearing Jurisprudence of Louis Brandeis." *Brandeis University Law Journal*, 3 (2013): 9–28.

Liptak, Adam. "Roberts Drops Hints in 'Precedent' Remarks." *New York Times*, September 18, 2005, A30.

———. "Case Could Overhaul Rules on Campaign Spending." *New York Times*, June 30, 2009, A12.

———. "No Argument: Thomas Keeps Five-Year Silence." *New York Times*, February 12, 2011, A1.

———. "Study Challenges Supreme Court's Image as Defender of Free Speech." *New York Times*, January 7, 2012, 15.

———. "Supreme Court Rejects Appeal from Reporter over Identity of Source." *New York Times*, June 2, 2014.

Lithwick, Dahlia. "Why Justice Kennedy Is Just Like America." Slate.com, June 13, 2012. http://www.slate.com/articles/news_and_politics/jurisprudence/2012/06/justice_anthony_kennedy_holds_the_deciding_vote_on_many_of_the_supreme_court_s_most_significant_cases_.html

Locke, John. *An Essay Concerning Human Understanding*, ed. A. Woozley. London: Fontana (first published 1689), 1973.

March, Andrew F. "A Dangerous Mind?" *New York Times*, April 21, 2012, SR1.

Marcus, Maeva, ed. *The Documentary History of the Supreme Court of the United States, 1789–1800*, 8 vols. New York: Columbia University Press, 1986–2007.

Margolick, David. "Law: At the Bar; When the Public Interest Becomes the Interest of the Corporate World." *New York Times*, September 21, 1990, B7.

Marion, David E. *The Jurisprudence of Justice William J. Brennan, Jr.: The Law and Politics of "Libertarian Dignity."* Lanham, MD: Rowman & Littlefield, 1997.

Martin, Andrew, and Kevin Quinn. "Dynamic Ideal Point Estimation via Markov Chain Monte Carlo for the U.S. Supreme Court, 1953–1999." *Political Analysis*, 10 (2002): 134–153.

Maveety, Nancy L., ed. *The Pioneers of Judicial Behavior*. Ann Arbor, MI: University of Michigan Press, 2002.

McIntosh, Wayne V., et al. "Textualism v. Active Liberty: Testing the Doctrinal Approaches of Justice Scalia and Breyer." Unpublished paper presented at the UK American Politics Group Annual Conference, Institute for the Study of the Americas, University of London, January 3–5, 2008.

McMahon, Kevin J. *Reconsidering Roosevelt on Race: How the Presidency Paved the Road to Brown*. Chicago, IL: University of Chicago Press, 2004.

Meiklejohn, Alexander. *Free Speech and Its Relation to Self-Government*. New York: Harper, 1948.

———. "The First Amendment Is an Absolute." *Supreme Court Review*, 1961 (1961): 245–266.

Merida, Kevin, and Michael A. Fletcher. *Supreme Discomfort: The Divided Soul of Clarence Thomas*. New York: Doubleday, 2007.

Metroka, Brandon Thomas. "Speaking in Tongues? Understanding the Roberts Court Record on Freedom of Speech." Unpublished paper presented at the Annual Meeting of the Northeastern Political Science Association, Boston, MA, November 12–15, 2014.

Michelman, Frank I. "Super Liberal: Romance, Community, and Tradition in William J. Brennan, Jr.'s Constitutional Thought." *Virginia Law Review*, 77 (1991): 1261–1332.

Morgan, Richard E. "Justice Alito, Dissenting." *Claremont Review of Books*, XII, no. 4 (2012). http://www.claremont.org/article/justice-alito-dissenting/#.VXnHr6azCt-

Morone, James A. *Hellfire Nation: The Politics of Sin in American History*. New Haven, CT: Yale University Press, 2004.

Neuborne, Burt. "First Amendment." *Touro Law Review*, 6 (1989): 113–136.

Newman, Roger K. *Hugo Black: A Biography*. New York: Pantheon Books, 1994.

Novick, Sheldon M. "The Unrevised Holmes and Freedom of Expression." *Supreme Court Review*, 303 (1991): 303–390.

Obama, Barack. "Address Before a Joint Session of the Congress on the State of the Union." January 27, 2010. Online by Gerhard Peters and John T. Woolley, *The American Presidency Project*, http://www.presidency.ucsb.edu/ws/?pid=87433

O'Brien, David M. *Storm Center: The Supreme Court in American Politics*, 9th ed. New York: W. W. Norton, 2011.

O'Donnell, Michael. "Without Artifice: On William Brennan." *The Nation*, November 17, 2010.

O'Neill, Jonathan. *Originalism in American Law and Politics: A Constitutional History*. Baltimore, MD: Johns Hopkins University Press, 2005.

Okin, Susan Moller. *Women in Western Political Thought*. Princeton, NJ: Princeton University Press, 1979.

———. *Justice, Gender and the Family*. New York: Basic Books, 1989.

Olken, Samuel R. "Justice George Sutherland and Economic Liberty: Constitutional Conservatism and the Problem of Factions." *William and Mary Bill of Rights Journal*, 6 (1997): 1–88.

———. "The Business of Expression: Economic Liberty, Political Factions and the Forgotten First Amendment Jurisprudence of Justice George Sutherland." *William and Mary Bill of Rights Journal*, 10 (2002): 249–357.

———. "Justice Sutherland Reconsidered." *Vanderbilt Law Review*, 62 (2009): 639–693.

———. "The Decline of Legal Classicism and the Evolution of New Deal Constitutionalism." *Notre Dame Law Review*, 89 (2014): 2051–2092.

Paschal, Joel Francis. *Mr. Justice Sutherland: A Man Against the State*. Princeton, NJ: Princeton University Press, 1951.

Perlstein, Rick. *Nixonland: The Rise of a President and the Fracturing of America*. New York: Scribner, 2009.

Perry, Mark J. "Creative Destruction: Newspaper Ad Revenue Continued Its Precipitous Free Fall in 2013, and It's Probably Not Over Yet." *American Enterprise Institute: Carpe Diem* (blog), April 25, 2014. http://www.aei-ideas.org/2014/04/creative-destruction-2013-newspaper-ad-revenue-continued-its-precipitous-free-fall-and-its-probably-not-over-yet/

Pettys, Todd E. "Free Expression, In-Group Bias, and the Court's Conservatives: A Critique of the Epstein-Parker-Segal Study." Working paper, 2014. http://ssrn.com/abstract=2499274

Pole, J. R., ed. *Alexander Hamilton, James Madison, John Jay, The Federalist*. Indianapolis, IN: Hackett Publishing, 2005.

Posner, Richard A. *The Federal Courts: Challenge and Reform*. Cambridge, MA: Harvard University Press, 1985.

———. *The Essential Holmes*. Chicago, IL: University of Chicago Press, 1992.

Post, Robert C. "The Constitutional Concept of Public Discourse: Outrageous Opinion, Democratic Deliberation, and *Hustler Magazine v. Falwell*." *Harvard Law Review*, 104 (1990): 603–686.

Powe Jr., Lucas A., *The Warren Court and American Politics*. Cambridge, MA: Harvard University Press, 2000.

Powell Jr., Lewis F. "What Really Goes On at the Supreme Court?" In *Judges on Judging: Views from the Bench*, 4th ed., ed. David M. O'Brien. Washington, DC: CQ Press, 2013, 127–130.

Pritchett, C. Herman. "The Development of Judicial Research." In *Frontiers of Judicial Research*, eds. Joel B. Grossman and Joseph Tanenhaus. New York: Wiley, 1969, 27–42.

Puglisi, Ricardo, and James M. Snyder Jr. "Newspaper Coverage of Political Scandals." *Journal of Politics*, 73 (2011): 931–950.

Rabban, David M. *Free Speech in Its Forgotten Years, 1870–1920.* New York: Cambridge University Press, 1997.

Reinhold, Robert. "Restrained Pragmatist Anthony M. Kennedy." *New York Times*, November 12, 1987, A1.

Richards, David A. J. "Free Speech as Toleration." In *Free Expression: Essays in Law and Philosophy*, ed. W. J. Waluchow. Oxford: Clarendon Press, 1994, 31–57.

Rose, Carol. "It's Official. There Is a Muslim Exemption to the First Amendment." *Boston Globe*, April 12, 2012.

Rosen, Jeffrey. "The Agonizer." *The New Yorker*, 72 (1996): 82–90.

———. "Supreme Leader: The Arrogance of Justice Anthony Kennedy." *The New Republic*, 236, no. 18 (June 2007): 16–22.

Ross, William G. "The Ratings Game: Ranking Supreme Court Justices." *Marquette Law Review*, 79 (1996): 401–452.

Rugemer, Edward B. "Caribbean Slave Revolts and the Origins of the Gag Rule: A Contest between Abolitionism and Democracy, 1797–1835." In *Contesting Slavery: The Politics of Bondage and Freedom in the New American Nation*, eds. John Craig Hammond and Matthew Mason. Charlottesville, VA: University of Virginia Press, 2011, 94–113.

Scalia, Antonin. "The Rule of Law as a Law of Rules." *University of Chicago Law Review*, 56 (1989): 1175–1188.

Schudson, Michael. *Discovering the News: A Social History of American Newspapers.* New York: Basic Books, 1978.

Segal, Jeffrey A., and Harold J. Spaeth. *The Supreme Court and the Attitudinal Model Revisited.* Cambridge: Cambridge University Press, 2002.

Silverstein, Mark. *Constitutional Faiths: Felix Frankfurter, Hugo Black and the Process of Judicial Decision Making.* Ithaca, NY: Cornell University Press, 1984.

Smith, Bradley A. "Newsflash: First Amendment Upheld." *Wall Street Journal*, January 22, 2010.

Smolla, Rodney A. *Free Speech in an Open Society.* New York: Alfred A. Knopf, 1992.

———. *Smolla and Nimmer on Freedom of Speech: A Treatise on the First Amendment*, vol. 2. New York: M. Bender, 1994.

Snowiss, Sylvia. "The Legacy of Justice Black." *Supreme Court Review*, 1973 (1973): 187–252.

Stampp, Kenneth M. "The Irrepressible Conflict." In *The Imperiled Union: Essays on the Background of the Civil War*, ed. Kenneth M. Stampp. New York: Oxford University Press, 1980, 191–245.

Stern, Seth, and Stephen Wermiel, *Justice Brennan: Liberal Champion.* Lawrence, KS: University Press of Kansas, 2010.

Stewart, Potter. "Or of the Press." *Hastings Law Journal*, 26 (1974–1975): 631–637.

Stone, Geoffrey R. "Justice Brennan and the Freedom of Speech: A First Amendment Odyssey." *University of Pennsylvania Law Review*, 139 (1991): 1333–1355.

———. *Perilous Times: Free Speech in Wartime from the Sedition Act of 1798 to the War on Terrorism.* New York: W. W. Norton, 2004.

———. "What You Can't Say Will Hurt You." *New York Times*, August 15, 2005.

———. "Free Speech in the Age of McCarthy: A Cautionary Tale." *California Law Review*, 93 (2005): 1387–1412.

———. "Free Speech in the Twenty-First Century: Ten Lessons Learned from the Twentieth Century." *Pepperdine Law Review*, 36 (2009): 273–299.

Strum, Philippa. *When the Nazis Came to Skokie.* Lawrence, KS: University of Kansas Press, 1999.

Sullivan, Kathleen M. "The Supreme Court, 2009 Term: Comment: Two Concepts of Freedom of Speech." *Harvard Law Review*, 124 (2010): 143–177.

Sunstein, Cass R. *Democracy and the Problem of Free Speech.* New York: Free Press, 1993.

———. *One Case at a Time: Judicial Minimalism on the Supreme Court.* Cambridge, MA: Harvard University Press, 1999.

Taylor Jr., Stuart. "Sharp Words in High Court on Hustler Parody of Falwell." *New York Times*, December 3, 1987.

tenBroek, Jacobus. *The Anti-Slavery Origins of the Fourteenth Amendment*, Oakland, CA: University of California Press, 1951.

Thomas, Andrew Peyton. *Clarence Thomas: A Biography.* San Francisco, CA: Encounter Books, 2001.

Thomas, Clarence. "The James McClure Memorial Lecture in Law Delivered by the Honorable Clarence Thomas, October 19, 1995." *Mississippi Law Journal*, 65 (1996): 463–475.

———. "Victims and Heroes in the Benevolent State." *Harvard Journal of Law and Public Policy*, 19 (1996): 671–683.

———. "Personal Responsibility." *Regent University Law Review*, 12 (2000): 317–327.

Tischler, Nancy M. "Pious Pornography." In *The Christian Ministry in a World of Crisis*, ed. Christianity Today, Inc. Washington, DC: Christianity Today, 1972.

Toobin, Jeffrey. *The Nine: Inside the Secret World of the Supreme Court.* New York: Random House, 2007.

———. *The Oath: The Obama White House and the Supreme Court.* New York: Doubleday, 2012.

Tribe, Laurence H. "In Memoriam: William J. Brennan, Jr." *Harvard Law Review*, 111 (1997): 41–48.

Tribe, Laurence H., and Joshua Matz. *Uncertain Justice: The Roberts Court and the Constitution.* New York: Henry Holt, 2014.

Tushnet, Mark. "Members of the Warren Court in Judicial Biography: Themes in Warren Court Biographies." *New York University Law Review*, 79 (1995): 748–771.

———. "*Heller* and the Critique of Judgment." *Supreme Court Review*, 2008 (2008): 61–87.

———. *In the Balance: Law and Politics on the Roberts Court.* New York: W. W. Norton, 2013.

———. "Justice Breyer and the Partial De-Doctrinalization of Free Speech Law." *Harvard Law Review*, 128 (2014): 508–516.

United States Senate, Committee on the Judiciary. *Hearings on the nomination David H. Souter to be Associate Justice of the Supreme Court of the United States.* 101st Cong., 2nd sess., September 13, 14, 17–19, 1990.

———. *Hearings on the nomination of Ruth Bader Ginsburg to be Associate Justice of the Supreme Court of the United States.* 103rd Cong., 1st sess., July 20–23, 1993.

———. *Hearings on the nomination of Samuel A. Alito, Jr. to be Associate Justice of the Supreme Court of the United States.* 109th Cong., 2nd sess., January 9–13, 2006.

———. *Hearings on the nomination of Elena Kagan to be Associate Justice of the Supreme Court of the United States.* 111th Cong., 2nd sess., June 28–30, July 1, 2010.

Volokh, Eugene. "Elena Kagan as Scholar." *The Volokh Conspiracy*, May 10, 2010. http://www.volokh.com/2010/05/10/elena-kagan-as-scholar/

———. "*Humanitarian Law Project* and Strict Scrutiny." *The Volokh Conspiracy*, June 21, 2010. http://volokh.com/2010/06/21/humanitarian-law-project-and-strict-scrutiny

———. "Freedom for the Press as an Industry, or for the Press as a Technology? From the Framing to Today." *University of Pennsylvania Law Review*, 160 (2012): 459–540.

Weissmann, Jordan. "The Decline of Newspapers Hits a Stunning Milestone." *Slate: Moneybox* (blog), April 28, 2014. http://www.slate.com/blogs/moneybox/2014/04/28/decline_of_newspapers_hits_a_milestone_print_revenue_is_lowest_since_1950.html

Wermiel, Stephen J. "Law and Human Dignity: The Judicial Soul of Justice Brennan." *William & Mary Bill of Rights Journal*, 7 (1998): 223–239.

West, Sonja R. "The Stealth Press Clause." *Georgia Law Review*, 48 (2014): 729–756.

Wheeler, Leigh Ann. *Against Obscenity: Reform and the Politics of Womanhood in America, 1873–1935.* Baltimore, MD: Johns Hopkins University Press, 2004.

White, G. Edward. *Justice Oliver Wendell Holmes: Law and the Inner Self.* Oxford: Oxford University Press, 1993.

Wiecek, William M. *The Sources of Antislavery Constitutionalism in America, 1760–1848.* Ithaca, NY: Cornell University Press, 1977.

Wirenius, John F. "The Road Not Taken: The Curse of *Chaplinsky*." *Capital University Law Review*, 24 (1995): 331–383.

Woodward, Bob, and Scott Armstrong. *The Brethren: Inside the Supreme Court*. New York: Simon and Schuster, 1979.

Yarbrough, Tinsley E. *Mr. Justice Black and His Critics*. Durham, NC: Duke University Press, 1988.

———. *John Marshall Harlan: Great Dissenter of the Warren Court*. New York: Oxford University Press, 1992.

Index

CPSIA information can be obtained
at www.ICGtesting.com
Printed in the USA
FFOW02n1749300915
17347FF

9 781137 434906